BETWEEN RHYME AND REASON

Vladimir Nabokov, Translation, and Dialogue

STANISLAV SHVABRIN

Between Rhyme and Reason

Vladimir Nabokov, Translation, and Dialogue

UNIVERSITY OF TORONTO PRESS
Toronto Buffalo London

Toronto Buffalo London
utorontopress.com

ISBN 978-1-4875-0299-7

Library and Archives Canada Cataloguing in Publication

Title: Between rhyme and reason : Vladimir Nabokov, translation, and dialogue / Stanislav Shvabrin.
Names: Shvabrin, Stanislav, author.
Description: Includes bibliographical references and index.
Identifiers: Canadiana 20190049790 | ISBN 9781487502997 (hardcover)
Subjects: LCSH: Nabokov, Vladimir Vladimirovich, 1899–1977 – Criticism and interpretation. | LCSH: Nabokov, Vladimir Vladimirovich, 1899–1977 – Language. | LCSH: Translating and interpreting.
Classification: LCC PG3476.N3 Z865 2019 | DDC 813/.54—dc23

Publication of this book was made possible, in part, by a grant from the First Book Subvention Program of the Association for Slavic, East European, and Eurasian Studies, a grant from the University of North Carolina at Chapel Hill Office of Research Development Publication Internal Funding Program, and a grant from the French Vladimir Nabokov Society La Société Française Vladimir Nabokov.

University of Toronto Press acknowledges the financial assistance to its publishing program of the Canada Council for the Arts and the Ontario Arts Council, an agency of the Government of Ontario.

Canada Council for the Arts
Conseil des Arts du Canada

Funded by the Government of Canada
Financé par le gouvernement du Canada

Ирине и Софье

Contents

Acknowledgments

For their help with my work I am profoundly grateful to Gennady Barabtarlo, Janice and Philip Bardsley, Sophie Bernard-Léger, Stephen H. Blackwell, Dimitri and Zinaida Breschinsky, Dana Dragunoiu, Agnès and Pierre Edel-Roy, Elisa Giaccaglia, Donald Barton Johnson, Michaël Federspiel, Michael Henry Heim and Priscilla Smith Heim, Michael and Nancy Linsley, Julie Loison-Charles, Claude and Ivan Nabokov, Eric Naiman, and Barry P. Scherr.

I have benefitted from the generous assistance of curators and librarians Alice L. Birney (Library of Congress), Stephen G. Crook and Isaac Gewirtz (New York Public Library), Stephen Ferguson, Thomas Keenan (Princeton University), Liladhar Pendse (Princeton University and University of California, Berkeley), and Kirill Tolpygo (University of North Carolina at Chapel Hill).

I gratefully acknowledge the support I received from the Institute for the Arts and Humanities (University of North Carolina at Chapel Hill) as Edith Lewis Bernstein Faculty Fellow.

This study would not exist without the teaching, advice, and criticism of Brian Boyd.

I am grateful to the late Dmitri Nabokov (1934–2012) for coming to my aid on a number of crucial occasions to supply me with much-needed information and otherwise unavailable documents, and to grant access to the restricted sections of his family archive.

Throughout my work on this study, Michael Arthur Green (1937–2018) and Jerome H. Katsell have been helpful to me in more ways than I can enumerate.

For all their work on my behalf I am indebted to Richard Ratzlaff (formerly of University of Toronto Press and presently of McGill-Queen's

University Press), Stephen Shapiro, and Leah Connor (University of Toronto Press). For her sound editorial advice and guidance my thanks go to Maureen Epp. I appreciate the criticism and suggestions given by the three anonymous reviewers who evaluated my manuscript.

I remain the sole responsible party for all and any shortcomings of this study.

On Transliteration and Translation

I follow a simplified version of the Library of Congress system when transliterating Russian texts. The simplification concerns the use of diacritical signs, omitted in all but one case. While the majority of contemporary Russian texts seldom distinguish "ë" and "e" characters, in my transliterations a diereses (umlaut) separates an accented – stressed – "o" (found in the first syllable of such English words as "yore") from an unaccented – unstressed – "e" (as in the second syllable of "never"). Thus the Russian equivalent of the English noun "roar" is spelled "rëv" (and not "rev" or "ryov"), and the first syllable in the Christian name of the author of "Silentium" is spelled "Fëdor" (not "Fedor" or "Fyodor"). Depending on the source text, I differentiate between old and new orthography, as in the ending of "sumrachnyia" (fem.) and "sumrachnye" (masc.) in the nominative plural forms of the adjective "sumrachnyi" (gloomy). I follow the same transliteration system for surnames. Thus I have "Solov'ëv" and not "Soloviev" (or "Solov'yov" and "Solovyov"), barring those instances where doing so would go against unambiguously expressed individual preferences (I retain the spelling of "Nabokoff" or "Schakovskoy" whenever my sources dictate such choices).

My citations from Vladimir Nabokov's works follow his transliteration. Like his views on translation, his "idea of transliteration" continued to evolve after he announced his arrival at its "final" version on 27 August 1950 (see *NWL*, 280). He adhered to his "Method of Transliteration" throughout the *Eugene Onegin* opus (see *EO*, 1:xix–xxiii), whereas earlier materials may have such spellings as "moujik" for "muzhik" (English "peasant man"), or "Joukovski" for "Zhukovskii" (or "Zhukovski" in *EO*). His transliteration of Bulat Okudzhava's

"Sentimental'nyi romans" of 1966 – along with that of its author's surname – diverged from the "Method" ("dobryy" and not "dobrïy," "Okujava" and not "Okudzhava"). For the sake of authenticity I preserve such variants in my citations.

All unattributed translations are mine.

Abbreviations

GSP	Gleb Struve Papers, Hoover Institution Library and Archives. Stanford, CA.
NPFMAD	Brian Boyd. *Nabokov's "Pale Fire": The Magic of Artistic Discovery*. Princeton, NJ: Princeton University Press, 1999.
Pushkin 1937	*Sochineniia Aleksandra Pushkina.* Iubileinoe izdanie Pushkinskago komiteta pod redaktsiei prof. M.L. Gofmana. Berlin: Speer & Schmidt, 1937. Vladimir Nabokov's personal copy, Department of Rare Books and Special Collections, Princeton University, Princeton, NJ. Available as part of Princeton University Digital Library at http://arks.princeton.edu/ark:/88435/st74ct10s.
SS	Mikhail Bakhtin. *Sobranie sochinenii,* 7 vols. Moscow: Izdatel'stvo Russkie slovari/Iazyki slavianskoi kul'tury, 1996–2003.
Tiutchev 1921	F.I. Tiutchev. *Stikhotvoreniia.* Berlin: Slovo, 1921. Vladimir Nabokov's personal copy, Department of Rare Books and Special Collections, Princeton University, Princeton, NJ. Available as part of Princeton University Digital Library at http://arks.princeton.edu/ark:/88435/7d278w65f.
VNA	Vladimir Nabokov Papers, The Henry W. and Albert A. Berg Collection of English and American Literature. The New York Public Library, New York.

Works by Vladimir Nabokov

A	*Ada* (LA 3).
ASC	L. Karrol' [Lewis Carroll]. *Ania v Strane Chudes* [*Alice in Wonderland*]. Per[evod] s angl[iiskago]. V. Sirina. Berlin: Gamaiun, 1923.
BS	*Bend Sinister* (LA 1).
Des	*Despair*. New York: Vintage, 1989.
E	*The Eye*. Translated by Dmitri Nabokov in collaboration with the author. New York: Vintage, 1990.
EO	*Eugene Onegin: A Novel in Verse by Aleksandr Pushkin*. Translated from the Russian, with a commentary, by Vladimir Nabokov. Rev. ed. 4 vols. London: Routledge & Kegan Paul, 1975.
G	*The Gift*. New York: Vintage, 1991.
GP	*Gornii put'*. Berlin: Grani, 1923.
H	Mihail Lermontov. *A Hero of Our Time*. Translated by Vladimir Nabokov in collaboration with Dmitri Nabokov. New York: Doubleday Anchor Books, 1958.
HM	*Vladimir Nabokov Reads His Own Prose and Poetry and His Translations of Russian Poets in English and Russian*. Edited by Stratis Haviaras and Michael Milburn. 2 audiocassettes. Cambridge, MA: Harvard College Library, 1988.
L	*The Annotated Lolita*. Edited with preface, introduction, and notes by Alfred Appel Jr. New York: Vintage, 1991.
LA	*Novels and Memoirs 1941–1951; Novels 1955–1962; Novels 1969–1974*. Edited by Brian Boyd. 3 vols. New York: Library of America, 1996.
LL	*Lectures on Literature*. Edited by Fredson Bowers. Introduction by John Updike. San Diego: Harcourt Brace Jovanovich, 1980.
LM	"The Lermontov Mirage." *Russian Review* 1, no. 1 (1941): 31–9.
LRL	*Lectures on Russian Literature*. Edited, with an introduction by Fredson Bowers. San Diego: Harcourt Brace Jovanovich, 1981.
LV	*Letters to Véra*. Translated and edited by Brian Boyd and Olga Voronina. New York: Alfred A. Knopf, 2015.
MO	"Mademoiselle O." *Mesures* 2 (15 April 1936): 146–72.
NP	*Nikolka Persik*. Berlin: Slovo, 1922.

NWL	*Dear Bunny, Dear Volodya: The Nabokov-Wilson Letters, 1940–1971*. Edited by Simon Karlinsky. Berkeley: University of California Press, 2001.
P	*Podvig* (*SSRP* 3).
PF	*Pale Fire* (LA 2).
PLT	*Pushkin, Lermontov, Tyutchev*. London: Lindsey Drummond, 1947.
Pn	*Pnin* (LA 2).
PP	*Poems and Problems*. New York: McGraw-Hill, 1971.
PS	*Perepiska s sestroi*. Ann Arbor, MI: Ardis, 1984.
PT	"Problems of Translation: *Onegin* in English." *Partisan Review* 22, no. 4 (1955): 496–512.
PVV	"Pouchkine, ou le vrai et le vraisemblable." *La Nouvelle revue française* 287 (1 March 1937): 362–78.
RB	"Rupert Bruk." In *Literaturnyi Al'manakh Grani*, 213–31. Berlin: Russkaia tipografiia E.A. Gutnova, 1922.
SIC	*The Song of Igor's Campaign: An Epic of the Twelfth Century*. Translated from Old Russian by Vladimir Nabokov. New York: Vintage, 1960.
SL	*Selected Letters 1940–1977*. Edited by Dmitri Nabokov and Matthew J. Bruccoli. San Diego: Harcourt Brace Jovanovich, 1989.
SM	*Speak, Memory: An Autobiography Revisited* (LA 1).
SO	*Strong Opinions*. New York: Vintage, 1990.
SP	*Selected Poems*. Edited by Thomas Karshan. New York: Alfred A. Knopf, 2012.
SSRP	*Sobranie sochinenii russkogo perioda*. Edited by Natal'ia Artemenko-Tolstaia et al. 5 vols. St Petersburg: Symposium, 2000.
St	*Stikhotvoreniia*. Edited by M.E. Malikova. St Petersburg: Akademicheskii proekt, 2002.
SVN	*The Stories of Vladimir Nabokov*. New York: Vintage, 1997.
TAT	"The Art of Translation." *New Republic* 105, no. 5 (1941): 160–2.
TOoL	*The Original of Laura*. Edited by Dmitri Nabokov. New York: Alfred A. Knopf, 2008.
VV	*Verses and Versions: Three Centuries of Russian Poetry Selected and Translated by Vladimir Nabokov*. Edited and annotated by Brian Boyd and Stanislav Shvabrin. Introduction by Brian Boyd. Orlando: Harcourt Houghton Mifflin, 2008.

BETWEEN RHYME AND REASON

Vladimir Nabokov, Translation, and Dialogue

Introduction

The Art of Verbal Transmigration – and the Milk of Human Kindness

Did Vladimir Nabokov mean what he said when he declared in 1966, "I shall be remembered by *Lolita* and my work on *Eugene Onegin*"?[1] What an odd statement to make for a sixty-seven-year-old writer with more than a decade of productive work ahead of him. Those who encountered the man behind the bewildering persona of the pre-typed interviews discovered that many of his statements came with a wink and an invitation to disagree, to start a conversation.[2] "Vladimir" may rhyme with "redeemer,"[3] yet the strength of Nabokov's opinions should not be mistaken for an invitation to engage in sacerdotalism; communication, interaction, dialogue must remain the default setting of inquiry and comprehension if we are to give his art, thought, and science their due. All the more so since Nabokov the writer is in no danger of becoming "the *Lolita* man," a literary one-hit wonder, a latter-day Mary Shelley – or her Russian counterpart Aleksandr Griboedov – with one outstanding work to his name. But what about Nabokov the translator, the man behind *Eugene Onegin*?

In 2005 David Remnick put together an informative account of the vicissitudes visited upon Russian authors by their English translators. As he surveyed the history of English-language adaptation of Russian classics, from Constance Garnett to Larissa Volokhonsky and Richard Pevear, Remnick dwelled on Nabokov's defence of his theory and practice of "literal" translation:

> Not long before publishing his own *Onegin*, Nabokov ... picked the wings off a translation by Walter Arndt ... Nabokov could not bear Arndt's

"Germanisms," his freewheeling sacrifice of semantic accuracy for rhythmic "beauty." Of all the sins of a translator, he would later write, "The third, and worst, degree of turpitude is reached when a masterpiece is planished and patted into such a shape, vilely beautified in such a fashion as to conform to the notions and prejudices of a given public. This is a crime, to be punished by the stocks as plagiarists were in the shoebuckle days."[4]

Famous the world over for its intellectual calibre, attention to factual accuracy, and hilarious cartoons, the *New Yorker* depicted Nabokov as a portly gentleman wrestling a hapless Pushkin, all sideburns and shoebuckles, from a detractor (Edmund Wilson), as Remnick proceeded to demonstrate that for all its rhetorical strength, Nabokov's position on the issue was far from unassailable.

Nabokov may have been right to make his dissatisfaction with Arndt's insensitivity to Pushkinian imagery known, but the spectacle of a globally renowned writer descending on a scholar-translator engenders some sympathy for the latter, especially when one realizes that the former was seeking to destroy the work of a rival threatening to steal the thunder of his own long-cherished endeavour. Arndt may have been punching above his weight when he attempted to represent Pushkin's unconventional work by conventional means, yet this can hardly justify Nabokov's vehemence when he raised a "lone, hoarse voice" in defence of "both the helpless dead poet and the credulous college student" from Arndt, whom he repeatedly branded a "pitiless and irresponsible paraphrast."[5] True, at that time his was certainly a lone voice striking a sharply discordant note in the approving chorus that greeted Arndt's translation, yet no one would think that this voice was lacking in power. One has to be naive not to get the insulting hint contained in the punning epithet with which Nabokov belittled his contender. Jokingly or not, it would seem that to insult Nabokov was quick to add injury: according to Remnick, upon giving Arndt short shrift, Nabokov went on to envisage his "paraphrast" adversaries in the stocks in a verbal re-enactment of a medieval public humiliation.

Except that Nabokov did no such thing. Remnick confuses two distinctly different stages in the development of Nabokov's views on translation: his humorous litany of crimes against the original text – along with his evocation of the punishment fit to serve as their retribution – had been composed in 1941, more than two decades *earlier* than his assault on Arndt's 1964 rhyming translation of Pushkin's novel in verse. Such lack of awareness of the bends in the road that Nabokov took to his mature theory and practice of translation may seem insignificant only as long as one ignores the context. When Nabokov published his essay "The Art of Translation" (TAT, 1941), where Remnick found his example of Nabokovian vengefulness, he believed that "authentic poets" in possession of "genius, knowledge," and "the gift of mimicry" could attain "the utmost degree of verisimilitude" required for the creation of inspired works of imaginative, literary – and not "literal," or strictly lexical – translation. In 1941 and later, this belief was matched by a certitude that it was fine to follow in the footsteps of both Charles Baudelaire, whose translations of Edgar Allan Poe constituted a major event in the history of European culture, and Vasilii Zhukovskii, whose renditions of Friedrich Schiller, Walter Scott, and Robert Southey had a beneficial effect on Russian literature during its adolescence. Between 1941 and 1955 Nabokov produced a number of superbly euphonious and evocative rhyming English paraphrases of an entire constellation of Russian poetic gems. His early criticism of insensitivity in translation was predicated on a conviction that a rhyming paraphrase of a foreign masterpiece was not only permissible, but desirable and preferable. Had Nabokov encountered Arndt's translation some twenty years earlier, he would not have found anything fundamentally amiss with Arndt's methodology. Remnick's difficulties with the chronology of Nabokov's evolving views on translation demonstrate that not every blind spot in our understanding of his contribution to translation debates has been eliminated. Too little is known about the fluid point of view from which Nabokov's numerous forays into translation were launched at different stages of his development as both artist and thinker.

Accounting for Nabokov's mercurial, evolving views on translation is no easy task; following Nabokov's circuitous itinerary around the pitfalls and triumphs associated with this intellectual activity requires undivided attention. So tightly was translation integrated into his creative enterprise that often it is difficult to tell one activity from the other, and not only when one turns to the earliest stages of his career in letters. It is here, however, where our grasp of the actual state of affairs much too frequently appears to be tenuous.[6]

Lack of familiarity with the nuances in Nabokov's position, such as an insufficient awareness of the path he took to his theory and practice of "literalism," breeds misunderstanding. Those unfamiliar with Brian Boyd's analysis of the reasons behind Nabokov's about-face on the "literary" mode of translation interpret his refusal to translate poetry as poetry as a camouflage for his failure as a poet.[7] In 1994 Caryl Emerson postulated: "Nabokov ... was ... right to stick to literalism. He wasn't a good enough independent poet to carry any other method off."[8] Originating among Slavists, such and similar assumptions have percolated into the burgeoning field of translation studies, where a discussion of the essence of Nabokov's argumentation has often been substituted by speculations on his wounded artistic pride or his suffering from a particularly severe case of "the anxiety of influence." Emboldened by the example of their Russophone colleagues, scholars with little or no knowledge of the Russian language and Russian literary context crucial for understanding both Pushkin's novel in verse and Nabokov's attitude toward it offer their interpretations of Nabokovian psychology rather than engage him as a fellow contributor to the ongoing translation debates. Upbraiding Nabokov for colouring "many arguments in the translation-studies field with a peculiarly vituperative tone," David Bellos builds a case for Nabokov's defence of literalism being motivated not by his hunger for verisimilitude but by his defeat at a game that Pushkin played better.[9]

Bold interpretations distract from a discussion of the merits of Nabokov's work, a discussion that must concentrate on much drier matters, his evolution as a translator being one of them. As someone who not only *began* his literary career with translation but made it an essential part of his activity as a writer for every decade from his second to his eighth – from French, Italian, English, German, and Latin into Russian, and from Russian into French and English – Nabokov has earned the right to be taken seriously as an earnest labourer in the employ of his peers, not only as an artist indulging his whimsical genius. A study of the combined sum of his experience in this area of his artistic enterprise, an outline of his trajectory both in independent composition and in translation of others promises to yield much useful information not only on his progress as a writer and translator but about literary creativity as well. Why has no such study emerged in the almost forty years since Nabokov's death?

The tonality of Nabokov's disparagement of Walter Arndt's translation of Pushkin's novel (1964) – and of Robert Lowell's "adaptations" of Osip Mandel'shtam's poems (1969)[10] – has provoked symmetrical responses: Douglas Robinson said it all when he stated that Nabokov's "perfectionist programming" is "deplored by mainstream translation theorists."[11] It does not surprise, then, that it is difficult to find analyses of Nabokov's stance on the issue that are informed by an acquaintance with his evolution.[12] When not explicated along the lines of a Bloomian "anxiety of influence," Nabokov's defence of "literalism" is frequently interpreted as a manifestation of his "elitist intellectualism," "his aristocratic contempt for the bourgeois reading public," a sentiment not dissimilar to "Martin Heidegger's romantic fascism."[13] When Nabokov is compared to Heidegger, one may be excused for thinking that Ronald Hingley's charge that Nabokov's "works in general secrete about as much milk of human kindness as a cornered black mamba" may not have been the most extreme response.[14]

With regard to *Lolita*, Nabokov declared: "For me a work of fiction exists only insofar as it affords me what I shall bluntly call aesthetic bliss, that is a sense of being somehow, somewhere, connected with other states of being where art (curiosity, tenderness, kindness, ecstasy) is the norm."[15] Seeking to whet his students' aesthetic sensitivity while covertly inoculating them against the hyper-moralist criticism of the origins of creativity in Tolstoi's "What Is Art?" (1897), he stated: "Literature was born on the day when a boy came crying wolf, wolf and there was no wolf behind him … Literature is invention. Fiction is fiction. To call a story a true story is an insult to both art and truth."[16] Nabokov's insistence that "literalism" is "true" translation relegates it to a plane inferior to anything resembling artistic self-expression, of which he was a fervent champion. This is merely the first of the many implications that Nabokov's post-1955 translation doctrine has on our understanding of his epistemology and ethics. Douglas R. Hofstadter points out that "truth in literature is not uni- but multi-dimensional," drawing our attention to a peculiar paradox: our pluralistic notion of verity is better aligned with Nabokov's defence of art's autonomy from external encroachments than with his advocacy of his monopoly on the truth in translation.[17] This perhaps is the most unsettling implication stemming from Nabokov's defence of his literalist doctrine, and what makes it particularly disturbing is how much of it flies in the face of the latest advances in the field of Nabokov studies, namely our newly augmented appreciation of his anti-totalitarian stance in general and his contribution to our knowledge of evolution in particular.[18]

Creation liberates individuality; translators subjugate their creativity to that of others. Nabokov the avowed individualist certainly struggled with this inalienable attribute of translation's ontology. In the course of his life in translation, however, he did reconcile his urge to present his sovereign insight into the texts he translated with his inability to attain absolute certainty matching that of their authors. The single most important unifying principle of all his attempts to preserve the form and significance of literary phenomena in tongues alien to their authors was his desire to initiate and maintain a direct, unmediated contact with them. My survey of the ways Nabokov's translating endeavours interact among themselves while informing his compositions has convinced me that nothing could be further removed from the truth than the impression that he sought to turn translation and conversation about its risks into an echo chamber where his authoritative voice would drown out those of others. No other facet of Nabokov's creative and scientific enterprise reveals his receptivity to the other to the extent that does translation: as few translators and translation theorists match his dedication to textual and contextual veracity, few writers so depend on translation as a source of verbal imagery to sustain their allusiveness. For far too long, however, our investigations of this allusiveness – Nabokov's "intertextuality" – have constituted a wild goose chase where scholars have explicated his compositions with the aid of allusions unsubstantiated by hard evidence of their presence in Nabokov's mind. His voluminous translations provide us with an opportunity to observe the interplay of his compositions with the works of his actual interlocutors rather than rely on our speculative ideas regarding his putative sources.

If Nabokov's allusive oeuvre is open to his interlocutors, do we stand a chance of developing an overarching model capable of accounting for his need for the other as it manifests itself in his translations and refracts in his compositions? Nabokov's resistance to theorizing notwithstanding, it may be profitable to make another attempt to re-examine his poetics from the vantage point provided by his compatriot and contemporary Mikhail Bakhtin (1895–1975).

Nabokov, Dialogue – and Translation

> Dostoevskii ... creates ... not voiceless slaves,
> but *free* people ... capable of standing *next* to their creator,
> disagreeing with him, and even rebelling against him.
>
> Bakhtin, *Problems of Dostoevskii's Poetics* (1929, 1963)[19]

> My characters cringe as I come near with my whip.
> I have seen a whole avenue of imagined trees
> losing their leaves at the threat of my passage.
>
> Nabokov, "The Last Interview" (1977)[20]

Bakhtin and Nabokov, what an uneasy pairing – at least at first blush.[21]

What two individuals could be more different: one the most articulate advocate of literary "heterology" (*raznorechie*), who postulated that save for the mythical Adam no speaker, let alone writer, can pretend to be the sole proprietor of words received from others, who went to extraordinary lengths arguing that authors may discourse with their protagonists; and the other, a champion of artistic singularity, a connoisseur of the unique who insisted that the "creative artist" was "his own ideal reader" while proclaiming, *urbi et orbi*, that his characters were "galley slaves"?[22] As far as his writing technique was concerned, Nabokov put an immeasurably higher value on the solitary pursuit of portrayal and poured scorn on the unchecked dependence on dialogue, coming dangerously close to knocking down that pillar of Bakhtinian poetics and ethics. And who can miss that awkward elephant in the room, Dostoevskii, whose "exceptional, distinctive" (*iskliuchitel'nyi, svoebraznyi*) place in the history of world literature Bakhtin worked so hard to highlight, and whom Nabokov actively sought to "debunk"[23] so that no Western reader would have any doubt that he was little more than a derivative, melodramatic, and overrated ideologue of a belletrist. Anyone undertaking a Bakhtinian reading of so openly author-centric, adamantly anti-dialogic a writer as Nabokov must either be irresponsible, desperate for a convenient theoretical framework, or both. Such has been the consensus among some of the most authoritative students of Nabokov for a while now. Students of translation, for their part, will have little difficulty in producing yet another, possibly decisive, argument against all attempts to affiliate Nabokov with Bakhtin, and vice versa. It was not that Bakhtin was not particularly keen on polemics; it was "absolutely impossible for him," as Caryl Emerson puts it, "to take a firm or final stand on a question, to impose rigid constraints, or to endorse any form of violence."[24] Nabokov relished a good skirmish, and many recognize in his censure of those deviating from his mature translation dogma a distorted reflection of his conviction that he had attained the ultimate truth.

Since Nabokov has come to be considered a standard-bearer for the monologic, authoritarian mode of discourse, there must be a good reason for it. "The design of my novel," one well-known Nabokovian dictum goes, "is fixed in my imagination and every character follows the course I imagine for him. I am the perfect dictator in that private world insofar as I alone am responsible for its stability and truth,"[25] and scholars have been paying heed to the multitude of ways in which Nabokov's compositions validate this vision. Pekka Tammi, in his perceptive survey of Nabokov's poetics (1985), was pointedly guarded in what he called his "appropriation" of certain Bakhtinian principles in his holistic exploration of Nabokovian narratology. Accepting the Bakhtinian vision of poetics as "'the principle [of an author's] *artistic* vision of the world,'" Tammi maintained that Bakhtin's "master idea of polyphony" is a "counterpoint to V[ladimir] N[abokov]'s novelistic strategies." Tammi's verdict was unequivocal: the forces shaping Nabokovian poetics are essentially "anti-polyphonic," which is to say anti-Bakhtinian, insofar as they are hierarchically organized to uphold "the superiority of the [story-]teller over the fictive hero."[26]

From his reading of the segments of Nabokov's oeuvre available in English and French, Maurice Couturier has drawn a set of far-reaching conclusions in his *Nabokov, ou La tyrannie de l'auteur* (Nabokov, or The Author's Tyranny; 1993). Citing Nabokov's attempts to impose his vision of his novels on his reader (the writer's aversion to Freudian interpretations of his books is but one example of this preoccupation), Couturier portrays Nabokov as a "tyrannical" author who seeks to overcome physical death by preserving his metaphysical dominance over his inventions. Couturier's elucidation of Nabokov's authoritarianism may have profited from his adept use of an entire arsenal of strategies inspired by Gérard Genette's imaginative adaptation of Bakhtin's analytical vocabulary, yet he remains convinced that Nabokov would never have accepted the Bakhtin-inspired understanding of the literary text as a "mosaic of quotations," suspicious as he was of all attempts to diminish authorial individuality and creativity in favour of general principles.[27] One may be excused for thinking that whenever Bakhtin's and Nabokov's names appear next to each other, a comparison of their intellectual legacies produces the impression of mutual incompatibility. This same impression appears to be borne out by the recent history of Nabokov studies in Russia.

In a pamphlet entited *"Anti-Bakhtin": Luchshaia kniga o Vladimire Nabokove* ("Anti-Bakhtin," or The Best Book on Vladimir Nabokov; 1994), Vadim Linetskii took it upon himself to counter attempts to interpret Nabokov through Bakhtinian optics. Bypassing the majority of the latest developments in the Nabokov studies of his time, yet exhibiting a proficiency in the psychoanalytical and deconstructive approaches practised by Jacques Lacan, Jacques Derrida, and their followers, Linetskii singled out Sergej Davydov's presentation of Nabokov's texts as dialogic constructs in *"Teksty-matrëshki" Vladimira Nabokova* (Vladimir Nabokov's "Nesting-Doll Texts"; 1982).[28] Wary of a tide of scholastic *ouvrages* based on the assumption that Bakhtin's analysis of Dostoevskii could be effortlessly transposed onto Nabokov, Linetskii challenged the critical concept of Nabokov's "intertextuality," insisting that it essentially amounted to a "fundamental disavowal" of Bakhtin-inspired academic "phantasms." In Nabokovian intertextuality he discerned a deliberately subversive appropriation of language, code, and dialogue.

Linetskii's salvo serves as an introduction to a particular anxiety that haunts the studies of Nabokovian allusiveness, one frequently introduced under the loose heading of "intertextuality." For all its enticing convenience and wide circulation, this term proves to be one of the most contested critical notions current today, as testified by the dissatisfaction with it on the part of its inventor, Julia Kristeva. This hermeneutic conundrum is hardly resolved by Nabokov's own aversion to "solid abstractions" and excessive theorizing, which has been reiterated by Brian Boyd's eloquent – and refreshingly humorous – critique of the pursuit of opaque generalities over specific details in the study of Nabokov.[29]

The term "intertextuality" continues to permeate Nabokov studies, a branch of literary scholarship at pains to confront a writer whom Eric Naiman has pronounced "the most promiscuously allusive author of our time."[30] Tempting as it is to follow in the wake of those scholars who share Nabokov's disdain for inordinate theorizing and obscurantist generalizing, one must acknowledge that this umbrella term designating the relationship of one literary text to others has already proven useful to understanding Nabokov – when wielded judiciously by a sophisticated practitioner.[31] What, then, do we stand to gain by overcoming the initial impression of incompatibility and attempting to delve deeper into a growing sense of mutual relevance tacitly linking Mikhail Bakhtin and Vladimir Nabokov? And, closer to home, how does this notion help us make sense of the evolution of Nabokov's views on translation and his reliance on translation in his original writing?

In 2012 came the much-awaited, long-delayed publication of the annotated critical edition of Bakhtin's magisterial theoretical treatise, *Slovo v romane* (The Word in the Novel; 1934–5).[32] From the editors' painstaking study of the archival materials, it transpired that the work that had widely circulated in the form of a pared-down essay had been envisaged as a full-length monograph, the purpose of which was an examination of the latest developments in the novelistic genre. Its recently discovered prolegomena make it clear that the guiding principle behind Bakhtin's forays into the history of the novel was not his preoccupation with its past, but fascination with its present. Today the obligatory facade of Bakhtin's introductory references to "Soviet material" cannot fool anyone: whenever, in accordance with the requirements of totalitarian doublespeak, Bakhtin evoked "current Soviet material" (*aktual'nyi sovetskii material*), he clearly had in mind the current state of the Russian novel at large.[33] This adjustment in our notion of his objectives leaves little doubt as to the relevance of Bakhtin's analysis to Vladimir Nabokov. The most consequential of the "younger" generation of émigré novelists, Nabokov was tightly integrated into the polarized literary world of his time and was aware of much of the experimentation and achievements of his fellow novelists on both sides of the political fault line separating the Soviet metropolis from the Russian diaspora. Like Bakhtin, Nabokov was cognizant of the most recent history of Russian literature; like Bakhtin, Nabokov belonged to the generation of writers and thinkers who had to make sense of the heritage of the scintillating, if short-lived, era in the history of Russian culture known as its Silver Age. Most pertinently, however, the breadth of their intellectual horizons and intimate familiarity with literary sources in Russian, German, and French would certainly have rendered Bakhtin and Nabokov ideal interlocutors. The fact that their dialogue never took place during their lifetimes makes little difference on the higher plane of their cultural affinity: Bakhtin's focus on the modern Russian novel renders Nabokov an implied, if unrecognized, presence on the broader spectrum of his work's implications, while Bakhtin's insights into the evolution and inner life of the twentieth-century novel have a direct bearing on Nabokov's work in this genre.[34]

Serious objections may be and have been raised in response to Bakhtin's unwavering conviction that poetry – particularly lyric poetry – operates within a set of stylistic limitations that prose, when given enough time, finds a way to eschew, and that as such these limitations are inherently irrelevant to our understanding of novelistic discourse as exemplified by the highest achievements in the genre of the novel. Forced to countenance the requirements of Soviet ideological dictate, Bakhtin preambles the complete version of *Slovo v romane* with references to "Soviet novels" in a half-hearted attempt to assure his potential censors that his ideas align with what he awkwardly terms "the light of the idea of socialist realism." He resorts to this rhetorical ruse to be able to account not only for the stellar examples of the doctrinally sound, sanctioned Soviet novel, of which there would have been plenty by 1935, but also for those officially marginal, as it were "insignificant" developments in the world of Russian poetry that saw a number of the most prominent poets of the day turn to prose in general and to novelistic prose in particular. Not only was Bakhtin familiar with Andrei Belyi's experimentation in the genre of the novel that was to produce *Petersburg* (1912–13), a book that Nabokov famously put next to Joyce's *Ulysses* in his minuscule selection of modernist novelistic masterpieces, he was acutely aware that the same spirit of innovation that had compelled Belyi to conduct his audacious pre-revolutionary experiments in grafting manifestly poetic techniques onto the modernist novel was quickening the imagination of some of the most accomplished poets as they were trying their hands at writing novels.[35]

Bakhtin and Nabokov shared an enduring conviction that the development of literature was predicated on an ever-increasing refinement of its potential to rival nature in its ability to generate complexity of both matter and mind. Using Dostoevskii as an example, Bakhtin defines a phenomenon the originality, indeed exceptionality, of which is not merely in concert with the entire progress of the novel as a genre, beginning with Socratic dialogues and Menippean satire, but is rendered inevitable by it. Bakhtin's vision of the evolution of the literary form reveals itself to be congenial to the essence of an entire array of Nabokov's pronouncements on this same issue. Dispersed throughout his writings, Nabokov's statements upholding the evolutionary nature of verbal art are to be found in highest concentration in his lectures on literature. His lectures on *Don Quixote* provide vivid and eloquent parallels to the Bakhtinian hypotheses regarding the emergence of a shapely novel from the amorphous foam of poetic effusion. Bakhtinian insight into the ascent of novelistic discourse from a set of archaic, manifestly monologic poetic genres to a vessel encompassing and preserving a dynamic interplay of nuclear consciousnesses – coupled with his willingness to allow for the possibility that such a transmutation may be replicated in the course of an individual artistic career – amounts to a fascinating commentary on what surely is one of the enduring mysteries of modern literature: the transformation of the Russian lyric poet Vladimir Sirin into the globally renowned novelist Vladimir Nabokov.[36]

Scholars attempting to shed light on the processes hidden behind this transition stress the indispensability of Nabokov's early experimental translations for his transition from poetry to prose.[37] Regrettably, there has been little progress in our understanding of this process, of the consequences and implications of Nabokov's engagements with others in the field of literary translation for his subsequent artistic achievements, and it is at this point in our evolving understanding of the "Nabokov phenomenon" where Bakhtin proves to be singularly useful. In addition, Bakhtin helps us zero in on the least ambiguous, verifiably tangible manifestations of these general processes in the specific material of a given literary text.

Nabokov may have found his voice as a novelist, but his readers and scholars agree that his prose is deliberately – some would say ostentatiously – poetic. In the course of his career he came to regard and treat all "good" literature as poetry, while discrediting those modes of literary creativity that favoured immediacy of expression over a heightened awareness of the formal attributes of that expression's medium. It is with this thought in mind that he chose to exalt the poetic qualities of Nikolai Gogol's dramatic compositions, for instance, expressing his conviction that *such* poetic discourse is uniquely suited for connecting both authors and readers with frankly suprarational states of being.[38] The author of the novel/narrative poem *Pale Fire* espoused and practised a maximally inclusive notion of novelistic discourse that purposefully subverted all and any attempts to divorce prose from poetry and vice versa.

Maintaining in 1967 that "the dividing line between prose and poetry in some of the greatest English or American novels is not easy to draw"[39] – by then *Lolita* and *Pale Fire* would have qualified for inclusion in this category – Nabokov never elaborated on his recognition in this no man's land of a fertile feeding ground for his imagination. His shift from poetry to prose, together with his realization that in order to be inspired prose must be poetic, however, must not obscure another aspect of this transition: Nabokov's writing begins to sound distinctly Nabokovian not when he encrusts it with multifarious poetic effects, but when he finds a way for it to encompass his lyrical "I" and other speakers vying for the reader's attention.[40] The success of this momentous development had been prefigured and, one suspects, rendered inevitable by Nabokov's ability to discern and appreciate the purely artistic aspects of the dialogue he conducted with others already in the earliest of his translation experiments, no matter how self-serving or appropriative they may seem to an onlooker with little awareness of their teleology. Nabokov's writing got off the ground when his readers realized that in addition to a confident authorial voice it offered a carefully orchestrated interplay of other voices' echoes, such as the Pushkinian undertones that permeate his deceptively Turgenevian novelistic debut *Mary* (1926). No other theorist of literary language has put forward a more nuanced anatomy of this mechanism than Mikhail Bakhtin, and it is he who offers a particularly accommodating framework for our understanding of the lasting effects of such processes on Nabokov the writer and supreme master of the literary allusion, be it deliberately and carefully planted, artfully disguised – or involuntarily integrated.

Bakhtin proposes not only an innovative paradigm for understanding literature but a remarkably idiosyncratic concept of what novelistic discourse is: for him not all novels are novels, some poets are novelists, and there are monologues that are dialogical.[41] Unconcerned with all the formal attributes traditionally separating prose from poetry, he discerns the germs of novelistic creativity in the "dialogic imagery" of Heinrich Heine and admits Pushkin's verse narrative *Eugene Onegin* into his pantheon of exemplary novels. Bakhtin's notion of the novel rests on an understanding that its single most important qualifying attribute is its ability to encompass and retain a multiplicity of consciousnesses engaged in a commerce of ideas, opinions, or sentiments. Such is the Bakhtinian notion of what he calls "the dialogic," which is to say "novelistic," "word" (*romannoe slovo*). The tension that arises from the exposure of different and diverging consciousnesses to each other ensures the protean nature of the novel as Bakhtin understands it, in addition to guaranteeing its survival and supremacy in the evolutionary struggle of genres.

The way the word "dialogue" functions in Bakhtin, both within and without the bounds of his analyses of Dostoevskii's poetics, reveals that Bakhtin the philosopher of language instils it with a meaning at once more encompassing and more rigorous. The expansive Bakhtinian vision of dialogue as a defining attribute of refined literary creativity – or indeed any of kind of fruitful, meaningful communication – merits our attention as a promising, if not self-evident, perspective on Nabokov's persistent admission into his texts the echoes of multiple other literary works, his abiding interest in the potential of such an echoing as a means of endowing his fiction with a plethora of additional possibilities, connotations, and emotional modes, parody being only one of them. It is here where our notion of intertextuality calls for a closer examination of its origins in Bakhtin's impassioned, lifelong argument in favour of its existence as an elemental particle, an awareness of which revolutionizes our idea of both literary creativity and the artistic application of language. A short digression summarizing Bakhtin's ideas concerning *dialogizm* – the strictly "indigenous" (purely Bakhtinian, that is) denomination of the phenomenon universally known today as intertextuality – is necessary before any attempt is made to test its fitness for the purposes of advancing our understanding Nabokov as a *homo traductoris*, a writer who devoted a significant part of his efforts to the translation of others.

In "From the Prehistory of Novelistic Discourse" (1930–6, 1940–1), Bakhtin emphasized the reliance of sophisticated forms of literary creativity on what he calls an "alien language" (*chuzhoi iazyk*; his markedly different choice of a modifier prevents confusion with "foreign," *inostrannyi*), whose beguiling resistance to the probing mind occasions and vivifies creation.[42] Depending on the context, Bakhtin's repeated use of the Slavic epithet *chuzhoi* ("not one's own," "strange," "foreign" – or indeed *alien*) oscillates widely enough to encompass a range of meanings. Thus it may refer to the linguistic representation of social stratification within a given monoglot culture or the differentiation within a given specimen of novelistic discourse capable of preserving and transmitting the verbal manifestations of one discrete consciousness as it comes into mutually revelatory contact with another. "From the Prehistory of Novelistic Discourse" describes a cultural situation where literary creation is predicated on a heteroglossia, which shaped and determined Hellenistic culture in its entirety.

Bakhtin underscores that an awareness of a mode of expression perceived as alien by a creative imagination in search of a unique – that is, "one's own" (or *svoi*, the Russian antonym of *chuzhoi*) – idiom serves as a beacon, guiding individual creativity out of silence or imitation toward the bustling, well-lit harbour of dialogic exchange. Also noteworthy is Bakhtin's insistence on dialogism's role in the awakening – or "objectivizing" (*ob'ektivizatsiia*) – of one's world view as a creative potential, set into motion to generate an individual ("untranslatable") style in response to the challenge contained in an alien utterance as it comes pre-equipped with an opaqueness ("untranslatability") of its own.

Predicated on heteroglossia – for Bakhtin its arrival signals advanced stages in the evolution of a given cultural discourse – sophisticated literary creativity thrives on a language's ability to house individual consciousness in a multitude of utterances or "speech acts" (*rechevoi postupok*). Since, in Tsvetan Todorov's elucidation, Bakhtin postulates that "no utterance is devoid of intertextual dimension," his doctrine of dialogic literary creativity assigns importance to one particular entity that renders dialogism, intertextuality, a palpable fact.[43] It is what Bakhtin famously denotes the "alien word" (*chuzhoe slovo*).

Slovo v romane (The Word in the Novel) offers an aphoristic philosopheme delineating the nature of the "alien word" as an agent of dialogism. A delineation that may be alternatively referred to as "the birth of literary creativity from the spirit of dialogue," it reimagines the basic subject-object dichotomy in terms of the interaction between the observer (purposefully inclusive in this instance, Bakhtin's phraseology encourages us to recognize in that observer a creative imagination in the act of verbal self-expression) and the observed (the object, posited here as a precedent-setting, dialogue-eliciting speech act): "The word is born in a dialogue as a lively retort within it; it takes shape in dialogic interaction with an alien word within the object."[44] Expansive as the noun "object" may appear in the context of this phrase (as noted, ultimately for Bakhtin language itself represents such an object), it is deliberately employed to engird in its scope a literary work satisfying the Bakhtinian requirements of dialogism as enabled by the interaction of minds engaged in a mutually beneficial exchange of speech acts.

Bakhtin continued to refine his definition of the "alien word" from the 1930s well into his seventh decade – arrival at the fittest verbalization of his intimation of dialogism was evidently one of his most cherished ambitions. Convinced that dialogism, with varying degrees of refinement, encompasses all areas of verbal interaction, he invariably insisted that it is of pivotal value to our understanding of literary creativity. In his notebook sketches dating from the sixties and seventies, he seeks to conclude his lifelong quest for a nuanced enough, yet compact, presentation of his expansive model. Dating as it does from that twilight period of his life, the following formulation is noteworthy for its succinct incorporation of an already established definition of the "alien word" into a wider framework of dialogism:

> I conceive of the "alien word"... as any word of any other man uttered or written either in his own (i.e., "my own") or any other language, i.e., any word-that-is-not-my-own. In this sense all words (utterances, spoken or literary works), excluding my own words, amount to alien words ... For each human all words are differentiated as one's own and alien, yet the borderlines between them may shift, and it is on those borders a tense dialogic struggle takes place.[45]

Bakhtinian understanding of the "dialogic struggle" reveals itself to be removed from the conventional ideas concerning the struggle (class and otherwise), which was the fixation of his Soviet peers, or the neo-Freudian interpretation of the libidinal forces shaping literary progress, as advanced by Harold Bloom in *The Anxiety of Influence* (1973) and its companion, *A Map of Misreading* (1975).[46] Content with what is essentially a Darwinian interpretation of ameliorative competition that spurs on the development of literature genres throughout history, from his remarkably un-confrontational (by Bloomian standards, at least) vision of "influence" Bakhtin proceeds to focus not on the modes of replication, imitation, and the eventual transcendence of one's paragon, but rather on that which makes literary creativity a collaborative, participatory environment. This point is usefully illustrated by the following passage from *Slovo v romane*:

> Above all here are relevant all the instances where the alien word exerts powerful influence on a given author. Discovery of such influences specifically amounts to a disclosure of such half-concealed life of the alien word in the new context of a given author. When an influence is profound and productive, it precludes superficial imitation or simple reproduction, but presupposes further creative development of the alien (half-alien, more precisely) word in a new context and under new circumstances.[47]

If Bakhtin never ventured to create anything like a dedicated translation theory, it was because his understanding of the dialogic presupposed that translation is a mode of linguistic activity inalienable from communication, an intellectual endeavour unimaginable without its perennial concern for the reaction and response it seeks to occasion, its orientation toward the other, its multiplicity of intentions, its potential for misunderstanding and misrepresentation, along with all the other defining attributes of translation in the narrow sense of the term. Today it would not be an exaggeration to state that generations of translation theorists have profited from their engagement with Bakhtin's philosophy of language, one of the cornerstones of which is his substantiation of the dialogic principle as a prerequisite of communication and literary creativity alike.

In his survey of the implications Bakhtinian dialogism holds for translation studies, Douglas Robinson stresses that it amounts to an inclusive perspective on language, where translation is given the place of honour that the nascent discipline of translation studies has sought to emphasize. Bakhtin's understanding of the ontology of verbal communication is predicated on the notion of the ultimate fluidity of units, all the linguistic and social obstacles and boundaries notwithstanding: "Words do not really belong to anyone … [they] float freely in the dialogical public domain"; "artificial boundaries can be set and jealously maintained, but dialogized words flow back and forth across any such boundaries and render them thus politically and historically contingent."[48] For Amith Kumar and Milind Malshe, Bakhtin's substantiation of the dialogic principle also amounts to a discrete vantage point on the specificity of translation as a "speech act," one inviting an approach to the study of "target-texts" as vessels of their "translator's dialogic relations" with their sources.[49] Susanna Witt, a student of translation's institutionalization as an integral part of the Soviet totalitarian project, has suggested that Bakhtin's analysis of what constitutes an utterance "might be brought to bear … on translations," since "a translation may be regarded as a paradigmatic example of the play between 'one's own word' (*svoe slovo*) and the foreign word, or word of the other."[50] Bakhtin the proponent of dialogism, it transpires, is no stranger to translation studies, a subfield of the humanities over which the figure of Vladimir Nabokov looms large – if not necessarily for all the right reasons.

So potent, so categorical and antagonizing in its rhetoric, Nabokov's substantiation and defence of literalism as the sole mode of translation worthy of this appellation does indeed obscure an entire dimension of translation's personal significance to him as a writer, which, in its turn, most certainly had an effect on the articulation of his translation theory throughout all of its evolutionary permutations and polemical travails. As Nabokov relied on translation as a way of conducting and maintaining a conversation with his interlocutors in no fewer than six languages, in his fiction he revisited the texts he translated. Nabokov's original writing, therefore, cannot but be singularly rich in the tangible verbal traces of his engagement with other creative minds through the medium of translation, as his translations remain the bountiful troves of his responses to these writers' uniquely stimulating challenges. His intuitive aversion to abstract schematization does not prevent us from recognizing in this rough, preliminary outline of this procedure a close match to the scenario where the creative development of the potential unleashed by "alien words" in the texts against whose background they qualify as such forms the heart of the Bakhtinian notion of dynamic – "generative" – dialogism. Apart from becoming rather late in Nabokov's life a scholarly pursuit of sheer equivalence, for Nabokov the writer translation never ceased to be a major supply route via which "words," utterances and images of discernably "foreign/alien" origin, reached his readers in the form of allusions incorporated into his own works. Vast as it may seem, the amount of images in Nabokov's oeuvre that may qualify as strictly "alien" in Bakhtinian terms is far from inexhaustible: in the course of his career in letters Nabokov, after all, translated a finite number of texts from a finite number of languages. Remaining clearly visible or suffering a sea change either by design or by accident, "alien words" with roots in the texts he translated continue to live a life of their own in Nabokov's writing, compelling his readers to make note of his partiality toward allusiveness while forcing his interpreters to make sense of the phenomenon commonly referred to as his intertextuality, which is to say his own brand of dialogism. Bakhtin's call for a "disclosure" of "alien" forms of life in their new setting inspires me to narrate the story of the existence such "alien words" lead in Nabokov's writing.

Tempting as it is to go chasing after a particularly promising literary allusion, the fear of tumbling headfirst into the bottomless rabbit hole of unbridled intertextual euphoria prevents many experienced scholars from loosening their grip on themselves in the focus of Nabokov's sardonic eye. After all, it was Nabokov who in his short story "Signs and Symbols" (1948) invented "referential mania," a psychiatric disorder that sends the sufferer on a suicidal search of "veiled references" around themselves; it was he who brought to life the risible personification of scholarly ineptitude Charles Kinbote, the editor-annotator obsessed with finding references that legitimize his own ludicrous whims, while utterly ignoring the meaning communicated by the author of a literary work he comes to possess and control. Nabokov – especially Nabokov the mature writer – excels at finding ever-subtler ways of exerting and maintaining his authoritarian control over his compositions, and in *Nabokov, ou La tyrannie de l'auteur*, Couturier shows how, in addition to fortifying his texts against those seeking to wring his inventions from his control, Nabokov furnishes his earlier works with forewords, afterwords, and statements whose sole focus is to ensure that his authorial dictate outlasts him. Much like Walter Arndt, the translator of a competing version of *Eugene Onegin*, those who interpret Nabokov's allusiveness, intertextuality as the manifestation of some general law of literary creativity of which the writer is unaware and unable to channel to his satisfaction subject themselves to not only his pre-emptive censure but also his devastating mockery. The snake appears to have bitten its tail: Ronald Hingley's "cornered black mamba" – Nabokov the self-confessed author-tyrant – rears its ugly head again.

Being facetious about what one's predecessors perceive as their responsibility comes at little to no cost. Let us not, however, ignore the fact that the actual issue at stake here concerns the genuine scholarly anxiety over the limits of interpretation, a problem that is not easy to laugh off in a world where the exegetic axiom of "the death of the author" has opened the floodgates of willful extrapolations. This is especially relevant to the current state of affairs in the sizeable and vibrant *monde Nabokovien*, with its ongoing discussion of the writer's legacy, his aesthetics, and his ethics. Did Nabokov act as an intertextual somnambulist when he wrote his masterpiece *Lolita* after encountering and then forgetting, in a spectacular case of "literary cryptomnesia," an eponymous novella by an obscure German feuilletonist, as Michael Maar would have it?[51] Did the writer evolve his tyrannical narrative authoritarianism as an evasive technique to obfuscate the sexual preferences he nourished, as Maurice Couturier would like the readers of his *Nabokov's Eros and the Poetics of Desire* (2014) to believe? Do countless juxtapositions following the formula "Nabokov and X" amount to breakthroughs in our understanding of this writer and his works?

It has been observed that Kristeva's oft-cited substantiation of the term "intertextuality" – "any text is constructed as a mosaic of quotations; any text is the absorbtion of and transformation of another. The notion of *intertextuality* replaces that of intersubjectivity, and poetic language is read as at least *double*"[52] – all its convenient comprehensiveness notwithstanding, harbours a specific conundrum. Proclaiming intertextuality a law governing any text, Kristeva neither draws a line separating mere similarity from an actual manifestation of intertextuality, nor does she attempt to describe the processes responsible for the ascent and expansion of intertextual significance from a pretext to a post-text it engenders. This concern appears abstract only insofar as it is examined as part of a purely notional discourse involving abstract definitions and cerebral paradigms. The Russian student of intertextuality Igor' Pil'shchikov reminds us that this debate quickly acquires all the urgency and specificity it may be lacking in the eyes of those disinclined to afford much attention to pure literary theory when it is examined in the light of the challenges faced by such applied branches of literary criticism as textual studies. For scholars tasked with establishing the dependence of one specific literary work on another in the context of a given literary period, the concept of intertextuality continues to be relevant as a way of conceptualizing their efforts: it provides them with a set of principles that guide their methodologies of applied research. It is surely no accident that in the course of his examination of the roots of the term "intertextuality" in the writings of Russian formalists, Pil'shchikov finds it imperative to touch on the history of literary translation. He specifically singles out the relationship between the original and its interlingual variant as an unambiguous manifestation of intertextuality in action: "In the history of literary translation we find a multitude of examples where the translator is forced to interpret and clarify an incomprehensible original (as to the relationship between the original and its translation, there is no doubt that it must be qualified as intertextual)."[53]

Pil'shchikov goes on to demonstrate that textual scholarship concerned with the preservation, reproduction, and interpretation of literary texts deriving from a cultural context where "strong" national poets considered literary translation a paramount area of their artistic enterprise (the "Golden Age of Russian poetry" is one example) calls for a more nuanced, flexible definition of intertextuality than the one found in Kristeva's influential essay. He then proceeds to pose the problem of historical mutability of the forms and markers of literary intertextuality as "one of the most pressing problems faced by linguistic poetics," while underscoring the importance of differentiating Bakhtin's theory of dialogism as both a universal principle *and* deliberate authorial strategy from Kristeva's vision of intertextuality as an anonymous, disembodied citation, the latent linguistic potential of moulding, transmission, and dissemination of speech formulae as well as rhythmic stereotypes.[54] Consequential as Kristeva's presentation of intertextuality in "Bakhtine, le mot, le dialogue et le roman" has proven to be, in light of this criticism we cannot afford to follow in Couturier's wake in equating Kristeva and Bakhtin indiscriminately, as if Kristeva's essay were not the virtuoso variation on Bakhtinian motifs it actually is, but rather an earnest, selfless attempt of transmitting Bakhtin's ideas to a wider world as it is so often taken to be.[55] As we have seen, as an analytical framework Bakhtin's dialogism is at once less rigid and more focused in its scope than intertextuality as defined by Kristeva and developed by her colleagues and followers in the post-structuralist school.

After establishing the dialogic principle as a property inherent to the utterance as a vessel of incessant interaction between meanings, or "the relation of every utterance to other utterances," in Tsvetan Todorov's summation, Bakhtin called on philologists to devote their efforts to "disclosing" that "half-concealed life of the alien word in the new context of a given author," a life that "precludes superficial imitation or simple reproduction, but presupposes further creative development of the [half-alien] word in its new context and under new circumstances." It is this call that I answer below by narrating and interpreting the story of Vladimir Nabokov's lifelong dependence on translation as a vehicle uniquely suited to answer his need for creative interaction with his peers across temporal and spatial barriers. By drawing inspiration from the implications of Bakhtin's inclusive understanding of the language of literature that encompasses translation as one of its key functions, I seek to counter what I see as the critical flaw of those applications of the Bakhtinian principle to the interpretation of Nabokov's allusiveness that stop short of transcending the Kristevian presentation of dialogism as a universal law of literary language that requires little or no textual proof to justify exercises in superficial parallelism. Such an uncritical understanding, or rather misunderstanding, of Bakhtin has led to the deluge of conjectures connecting Nabokov's texts with any number of putative literary precedents, more often than not unsupported by any proof of the writer's engagement with this or that literary precedent. This is the reason why the ensuing interpretative account of Nabokov's life in translation eschews interpretation based on the notion of a subjectively perceived similarity in favour of the introduction and interpretation of tangible, incontrovertible textual evidence testifying to Nabokov's engagement with his peers as reflected in his translations of their original literary texts. Thus the indisputable presence of a specific piece of textual evidence connecting Nabokov to, say, Rémy Belleau (1528–77) will be given immediate precedence over any number of tantalizing connections I may wish to draw between a particular Nabokovian image and that found in a novel by Henry de Montherlant (1895–1972), to cite a reasonably plausible example of a contemporary whom Nabokov could certainly have read, but for which he left no evidence demonstrating his acquaintance. Arbitrary parallelisms of this nature will not be pursued in the pages that follow.

Between Rhyme and Reason: Methodology, Organization, and Objectives

Between Rhyme and Reason logs a journey toward the dialogic origins of Nabokov's inspiration and accomplishment. This study is predicated on my conviction that Bakhtinian insights into the mysteries of verbal artistry and literary creativity are applicable to the totality of Nabokov's achievement, including such a lesser-known aspect of his activity as translation. Archival research and editorial work constituted this journey's point of departure but also served as vantage points supplying fresh perspectives on the body of well-known literary works. It is only logical, then, that the analytical strategy employed throughout this study should be that of *explication de texte*, or close reading: an examination of familiar literary artefacts, guided and enlightened by our newly gained awareness of their integration into a network of dialogic relationships with the utterances of others. Singled out by Nabokov for translation, such precedent utterances may well have led to the inception of at least some of his original and most consequential compositions; it is likely that they affected the eventual appearance of many such texts. This hunt for the "alien words" (what Bakhtin calls "utterances, spoken or literary works") testifying to the existence of multiple channels of communication linking the universe of Nabokov's invention with those of others is, therefore, an exercise in interpreting his works not so much as literary equivalents of Kantian *noumena* largely closed to outside perception, but rather as phenomena whose inner lives are open to observation. Tall as this order may seem at the outset, its scope, much like its methodology, is determined and dictated by the unique nature of its subject.

Opening with the analysis of the least explored section of Nabokov's creative evolution, his juvenilia, *Between Rhyme and Reason* traces his subsequent development into a Russian poet and writer, American novelist, and international literary figure. The scope of this study is determined by the scale of Nabokov's trilingual literary achievement, its integration into no fewer than six global literary traditions – English, French, German, Italian, Latin, and Russian – via such tangible points of entry as specific translated texts. Another fundamental assumption that provides my study with much of its momentum is that Nabokov, a writer who half in jest professed to be an adherent of the cult of Mnemosyne, the muse of memory, an artist who insisted that there is no "unseeing" something "once it has been seen," not only affected the texts he transposed from one language to another but was himself affected by his interaction with the creative minds that brought the originals he translated into existence.

Since translation forms such a powerful and constant parallel to Nabokov's artistic development, this study follows and traces this parallel throughout the totality of the author's oeuvre. The structure of this study is shaped not by my perceptions and predilections as a researcher but by my understanding of the logic of Nabokov's evolution as a writer-translator, a true *homo traductoris*. From examining dialogic encounters in the medium of translation, I will turn to Nabokov's original compositions – and in some cases from original compositions to their translations, as warranted by the specificity of these texts' creative history. The outer boundaries of this study are set by the textual evidence at hand: specific data derived from a close examination of Nabokov's translations both well known and newly discovered.

The objectives of this study range from an attempt to solve specific problems relating to our understanding of the Nabokov phenomenon in general to his dialogism ("intertextuality") in particular. On a number of levels, the need for such or similar research efforts is dictated by the tasks that all students of Nabokov the writer have to confront in one way or another. The logic of Nabokov's development as translator, for example, has never been traced with a satisfying degree of comprehensiveness, and this omission has repercussions not only for our awareness of his investment in translation but also for our appreciation of Nabokov as a complex and sophisticated writer. The absence of what might be an even approximate chronology of the factual framework of the evolving interrelationship between his original compositions and his own works in translation creates a considerable obstacle to acquiring a holistic view of Nabokov's career in letters. By focusing on Nabokov's interlingual translations of others, I will lift the veil of mystery shrouding a strong interdependence of translation and original creativity unique to this writer.

This present study constitutes a reading against the grain of a near-complete scholarly consensus discernable on at least two fronts of our present-day appreciation of Nabokov the writer: the first being the conviction that Nabokov's resistance to theory renders futile all attempts to apply it to the interpretation of his original work; the second being the contention that what Bakhtin has to say about literature does not apply to Nabokov. *Between Rhyme and Reason* attempts to produce enough verifiable information by studying one lesser-known aspect of Nabokov's work – his translations – so that this knowledge can be subsequently applied to our interpretation of his familiar compositions.

Chapter One

Before Sirin: A Foretaste of Translation (1910–1919)

Nabokov's juvenilia remains the least studied segment of his literary legacy. With the exception of the self-published collections *Stikhi* (Poems; 1916) and *Dva puti* (Two Paths; 1918), this body of materials is a *terra incognita* on the extant maps of his evolution. Some scholars have chosen to follow the author's example in dismissing his juvenilia as an inconsequential dalliance with metre and rhyme, a requisite rite of passage for a youngster of his milieu at a time when Russia was enamoured of verse and lionized her poets.[1] According to this school of thought, if Nabokov's poetic production dating from the 1920s has limited value as evidence of his delayed development, his pre-revolutionary, pre-emigration – pre-"Vl. Sirin" – experimentation merits no attention.[2]

Below, I counter this approach with textual data in hand.

A Texan Mustanger in a Powdered Wig: Mayne Reid's *Headless Horseman* in French Alexandrines

In the original French version of "Mademoiselle O" – Nabokov's first published attempt at casting his childhood memories in the form of an autobiographical essay – the writer gives a detailed account of his Swiss governess's endeavour to introduce him to her beloved French classicists. A vivid picture of Nabokov's early exposure to French literature under the steadfast, if simple-hearted, guidance of Cécile Miauton, an ardent admirer of Racine and Corneille,[3] the piece asserts his independence from her predilections. This version of "Mademoiselle O," however, contains an admission of Nabokov's first-hand acquaintance with so distinct a form of artistic expression as the French alexandrine, and the aura of the heroic and the lofty associated with the high genres of classicism. This exposure conditioned Nabokov's first outpouring of creative energy, one that took the shape of an early foray into the field of adaptation – and appropriation – of a foreign literary work through the medium of translation.

Chapter 11 of Nabokov's *Speak, Memory* (the book that formed around "Mademoiselle O") shows the author as a "lank fifteen-year-old lad" overcome by the "numb fury of versemaking" for the first time in his life in the summer of 1914.[4] Omitted from the intermediate Russian version of the autobiography due to the "psychological difficulty of replaying a theme elaborated on" in *The Gift*,[5] chapter 11 contains a detailed, if idealized, account of Nabokov writing his first poem. Thematically, it links chapter 10, with its humorous evocation of Nabokov's half-childish, half-adolescent fascination with Mayne Reid's *The Headless Horseman: A Strange Tale of Texas* (1865), with chapter 12, in which reminiscences of the author's star-crossed love affair with "Tamara" (Valentina Shul'gina) are intertwined with the story of his debut collection of poetry, an endeavour as ill-fated as its inspiration.

It was Nabokov's enthrallment with the flamboyantly outlandish, chivalrous, and quaintly sensuous world of Thomas Mayne Reid (1818–83) that gave impetus to his earliest known outpouring of creative energy. It occurred not in the rainy summer of 1914, which provides so tangible a background to *Speak, Memory*'s chapter 11, but four years earlier, in the summer of 1910. It was then that he rendered *The Headless Horseman* from the English into French alexandrines.[6] Looking back on it some eleven years later, Nabokov himself characterized this early experiment as "implausible" (*neveroiatnyi*).[7]

Apart from affording eleven-year-old Vladimir the pleasure of personal interaction with a beloved book, the task of translating Mayne Reid's novel into French alexandrines gave him a foreglimpse of the paradoxical and elusive nature of so peculiar an intellectual pursuit as translation.[8] On the one hand, he had one obvious advantage over the army of Mayne Reid's Russian admirers: "knowing English, [he] could savor [Reid's] *Headless Horseman* in the unabridged original."[9] On the other, this same knowledge did him something of a disservice, veiling the fact that his appreciation of the coveted original was also limited, albeit in a manner different from that of the monoglot devotees of the Irish-American novelist. Nabokov's version of *The Headless Horseman* has not survived; it is possible to surmise, however, that the translator's knowledge of English, conditioned as it was by age and upbringing, was unlikely to have saved him from misunderstanding the original – a factor that should be taken into consideration whenever one attempts to envisage what his version of the novel might have been like. Here, for example, is the scene where *The Headless Horseman*'s villain Cassius Calhoun toasts "America for Americans, and confusion to all foreign interlopers – especially the d–d Irish!" Nabokov confesses that this "evasion ... puzzled me sorely when I first stumbled upon it: dead? detested?"[10] On another occasion, Mayne Reid introduces Louise Pointdexter, the aforementioned villain's fair cousin, as the daughter of a "sugar planter, the highest and haughtiest of his class." This matter-of-fact description of a character, executed in strict keeping with the narrative's local colour, confronted Vladimir with another riddle, as he found himself pondering the question of "why an old man who planted sugar should be high and haughty."[11] The contextual, culturally specific reference contained in the word "planter" was beyond the translator's ken at age eleven in much the same way as was Mayne Reid's elision sparing the reader the ignominy of being exposed to Calhoun's mild expletive, all of which contributed to the widening gap between the original and the excessively imaginative version it inspired.

The informed perspective of a reader familiar with most of Nabokov's mature works affords a vantage point from which many an aspect of the significance of Nabokov's first artistic experiment on record can be appreciated. The syncretic nature of this experiment – the amalgamation of mimesis and the desire to be freed from it – points toward some particular traits Nabokov the writer was to develop. Mimesis was not to become something that he would eventually outgrow and discard entirely; in the guise of parody and mimicry it was to gain a prominent place in his mature poetics. For Nabokov the translator, this early experiment in literary adaptation was more than a learning experience: it paved the way to his subsequent, more compelling forays into the same territory. It would have been an early lesson in the art of compromise that translation essentially is – a compromise between the riddles the original poses before the translator, and the latter's limited ability to find for them a satisfactory, if not ideal, solution. The quest for such a solution was to last for the rest of Nabokov's life. Most important of all, however, it was his first attempt to establish an unmediated contact with an interlocutor of his choice, earn his attention, and prove himself worthy of retelling another's story in his own words.

"Du temps qu'il était écolier": First Translation

The experimental rendering of Reid's *Headless Horseman* into French alexandrines marked the beginning of Nabokov's journey to original poetic output and eventually to his more mature works. In *Speak, Memory* he readily admits that his choice of medium for his first original literary compositions was arbitrary, as it simply "happened to be Russian but could have been just as well Ukrainian, or Basic English, or Volapük."[12] This was not the case with Nabokov's earliest surviving translation, the first of his two Russian versions of "La Nuit de décembre." "Dekabr'skaia noch' (Iz Alfreda de Miusse)" (December Night [from Alfred de Musset]) is dated December 1915, exactly eighty years after the poem's publication in *La Revue des deux mondes* on 1 December 1835.[13]

In her pioneering study of Nabokov's affinity with Musset, Jane Grayson has demonstrated that this early translation affords us a rare glimpse of an important point of departure for Nabokov's subsequent growth, one laying the foundation for many features that would later become signature characteristics of the writer's mature art. According to Grayson, Musset provided Nabokov with an early model for his "intellectual and artistic constructions of biography and memory" before this model was supplanted by more sophisticated ones.[14]

At the centre of Musset's "Nuit de décembre" is a rhetorical exchange between the protagonist and an enigmatic Vision that has haunted him since childhood. A brother-like double, this spectre appears before the protagonist at all major crossroads, wearing black and offering no word of scorn or consolation, whether amid a bout of adolescent debauchery, in the wake of the protagonist's father's death, or in the aftermath of a mistress's betrayal. In a series of apostrophes, the perplexed protagonist prompts his inseparable companion to reveal his identity. In the poem's ultimate line the spectre finally acquiesces: "Ami, je suis la Solitude." To the modern reader, "La Nuit de décembre" – a poem of 217 lines comprising thirty-one carefully structured stanzas – might seem too elaborate a concoction to communicate much of the emotional charge it aims to convey. The poem's combination of romantic pathos, vivid imagery, and tight authorial control won the admiration of at least one sixteen-year-old Prince Tenishev School student, who was so captivated by it that he decided to translate the poem into Russian.

This 1915 version of "La Nuit de décembre" attests to a developing translator's capacity to overcome the difficulties of a task that would have proven too daunting for a young person of lesser determination and ability. Nabokov meticulously reproduces the poem's rhyming and stanzaic arrangements, while compromising little of its sense. Just as Musset remains in control of his medium at every point in the poem, Nabokov never loses sight of the original, only occasionally seeking the help of a convenient turn of speech or a readily available image or rhyme.

It is nothing short of remarkable that Nabokov was to retranslate this same poem in its entirety for a 1928 publication. What is fascinating, however, is how the earlier translating endeavour foreshadows so many mature traits peculiar to Nabokov the writer we know now, while commencing his lifelong dialogue with Musset.

"L'adolescent aimé des miroirs": The Fatal Attraction of Doubles – Musset, Régnier, and Beyond

The handwritten album "Stikhotvoreniia," where Nabokov's next translating experiment is preserved, bears a dedication to "E.L." Appearing as it does in Latin characters, it points to Ewa Lubrzyńska, a Polish-Jewish woman five years his senior with whom he became close after falling out with Valentina Shul'gina. The works included in this album originate from September to November 1917, the last months Nabokov was to spend in his home city before escaping to the Crimea, where he was to add a few poems to this album before starting a new one. The third poem in the album is a rendition of Henri de Régnier's "L'Allusion à Narcisse" (An Allusion to Narcisse; from *Les Jeux rustiques et divins* [Games Rustic and Divine]; 1897).

If "La Nuit de décembre" is a verse narrative in the form of a dramatic dialogue, "L'Allusion à Narcisse" consists of a compact lyrical statement. A mere fourteen lines long, it encapsulates the sea change French poetry had suffered since Musset. All their dissimilarities notwithstanding, both poems feature similar subject matter, as they contain first-person narratives relating encounters with spectral doubles. In place of Musset's effusiveness, precision, and directness, however, Régnier elects brevity, understatement, and an enigmatic allusion. It is no accident that his poetry and prose was to catch the eye of such major Russian poets and thinkers of the post-symbolist persuasion as Maksimilian Voloshin and Mikhail Kuzmin as they searched for effective ways to overcome symbolism without breaking with the tradition established by its adherents.

Apart from its title, "L'Allusion à Narcisse" does not contain a reference to the myth but rather suggests that readers bear it in mind as they contemplate the poet's variation on its theme. After apostrophizing the Fount, whose ability to reflect beauty has cost a certain boy-child his life, the lyrical hero recounts his own brush with the irrational, set against a bucolic backdrop. Whereas Musset's spectral double was a transparent allegory of grief and solitude, Régnier's variation on a similar theme is far less straightforward. As depicted in "L'Allusion à Narcisse," the water reflection possesses a mysterious and unsettling ability to present the phenomenal world in a decidedly ghostly aspect. The poem invites its readers to consider the potentially deadly power of reflections and visions, a spectral dimension that only appears to be mimicking ours while remaining subject to its own laws. The allure of this parallel reality is as potent as it is deadly; its effect on the susceptible is amplified by the fact that it hides in plain view.

The fourteen lines of the Russian dactylic trimeter into which Nabokov transposes Régnier's poem do not simply preserve the original's rhyming couplets, they betray no desire on the part of the translator to instil the original with meaning reflective of his own predicament at the time of his resetting it into his language and idiom. More than anything else, Nabokov's translation of the poem appears to be an exercise in approaching a dramatic premise similar to that of "La Nuit de décembre" from a fluid, unstable perspective of a modernist poet who has internalized his Baudelaire and Mallarmé, his Verlaine and Rimbaud:

… наклонясь, я себѣ показался
въ свѣтлой водѣ привидѣньемъ своимъ.
Не потому-ль, что свои-же старался
губы лобзать, и въ тотъ часъ умиралъ
[14] отрокъ, – любимецъ прозрачныхъ зеркалъ?

[… having bent down, to myself I appeared / a ghost of my own self in the lucid water. / Was it because his own lips strove / to kiss, while dying at the same hour, / that adolescent, beloved by transparent mirrors?]

Nabokov's "Namëk na Nartsisa" (*sic*) recreates the original's contemplation of the ghostly aspects of the phenomenal and their power to enchant and destroy those unfortunate enough to let themselves slip into a trance-like fixation on the otherworld. The tragic component of this predicament, one could argue, is to be attributed to the fact that these reflections originate in the phenomenal world and are forever doomed to remain reflections, which is to say surrogates, of other realms of being. It was this aspect of Régnier's variation on the Narcissus motif that must have caught Nabokov's eye during this early stage of his development as an artist and thinker devoted to the exploration of our existence's permeability to forms of being imperceptible to the senses. Examined in the larger context of Nabokov's life in art, "Namëk na Nartsisa" itself constitutes a trace of its translator's search for verbal images fit to convey his transcendental intuitions. As such, along with Musset's "La Nuit de décembre," Régnier's "Allusion à Narcisse" deserves to be considered another early conduit of the themes and means of expression pertaining to Nabokov's lifelong interest in the transcendental.

Having acquired an early taste for the suitability of the "Narcissus motif" for his own work in the course of his encounter with Henri de Régnier, Nabokov would go on to employ it as an evocative verbal emblem distinguishing some of his most accomplished inventions. The Narcissus motif – along with its contextual attributes of illusion, self-deception, and peril – finds a particularly striking realization in *Despair* (1932). Revolving around the crafty narrator Hermann's attempt to perpetrate an insurance fraud (prompted by his stumbling upon his "double"), this novel marks Nabokov's maturing ability to harness the potential of an image reminiscent of the Narcissus motif and tap into its rich possibilities for eliciting nuanced ethical connotations. The presentation of Hermann's recognition in Felix of his double in chapter 1 evinces Nabokov's sensitivity to this motif's evocative power.[15]

Though not exactly the handsome youth of the myth, Hermann develops a morbid fascination with his reflection and begins an intense relationship with all the mirrors that come his way, alternately admiring, avoiding, courting, and abhorring them. Sergej Davydov has pointed out that as he comes under the spell of his scheme, Hermann loses his ability to tell the actual world around him, with its innumerable nuances and differences, from his own reflection, since "his gaze is directed inward, toward a solipsistic, Narcissus-like cosmos, in which the mirror becomes the highest aesthetic idol, and a mirror likeness is the guarantee of artistic success."[16] An important constituent of the Narcissus motif, the mirror reflection pattern becomes the fundamental principle of the Hermann's "confessional" narrative, as his intended ten-chapter structure encases a symmetrical plot movement from its inception and climax to projected "triumph."[17] This motif forms a major tributary to the plentiful allusive and parodic undercurrents nourishing the intricately planned landscape of *Despair*. It is also an integral part of the novel's master plan that Nabokov replicated and enhanced in its English version, published in 1965. Crucial as it is to *Despair*, paramount as it is for *Lolita*, this same motif bursts into a dizzying array of central themes and subordinate variations responsible for the enduring magnetism of *Pale Fire* (1961). In his most daring experiment with the novelistic genre, Nabokov's playful and resourceful use of the Narcissus motif and its attributes permits him to conduct an unprecedented artistic exploration of the theme of solipsism, his constant subject of scrutiny. Charles Kinbote's pathetic narcissism is integrated into an entire system of semantic refractions emitted by the novel's preeminent visual metaphor, that of a reflexive glass surface that proves deadly to those deceived by its false promise of boundless freedom.[18]

Between Ovid's *Metamorphoses* and Oscar Wilde's *Picture of Dorian Gray*, Henri de Régnier's "Allusion à Narcisse" could not have been and certainly was not the sole source of Nabokov's familiarity with this mythologeme. It is striking, however, that his "Namëk na Nartsisa" should have become the earliest known instance of his deliberate employment of this motif. As such, this translation does not merely demonstrate his early interest in the ancient mythological subject and its potential for his own art, something he could not have foreseen in 1917. Régnier's evocative treatment of the Narcissus myth became the meeting point for these creative minds engaged in the contemplation of the Narcissus motif and the possibilities contained therein. "Namëk na Nartsisa" captures and documents Nabokov's coming into possession of a motif that was to recur throughout his writing, providing him with numerous opportunities to articulate some of his richest themes.

"L'interno lume": The Long Afterglow of Petrarchan Illuminations

Nabokov staged one of the most audacious translation experiments of his early youth on 2 March 1918, when he made a Russian version of a sonnet by Francesco Petrarca (1304–74). This text remains his only known translation from Italian and as such constitutes a key piece of textual evidence directly linking Nabokov's writings with the exceptionally rich Petrarchan topos. Attempting to untangle an archaic literary text composed in a language he could not have known well must have seemed an exciting challenge. Closer examination of this artefact shows that Nabokov's encounter with Petrarch led to the creation of a poetic text exceptionally evocative of many significant themes in his later work.

The album "Tsvetnye kameshki" (Motley Pebbles; VNA) preserves a text entitled "Iz Petrarki (Sonet CCXXXVIII)."[19] The poem opening with the line "O, esli pen'e ptits il' bystrykh vod glukhoi" (Oh, if the singing of the birds or the dull [splashing] of the rapid waters) proves to be an imaginative, sophisticated, and determined Russian resetting of one of Petrarch's sonnets inspired by Laura's death.

An example of the Petrarchan sonneteering practice at its most moving and memorable, "Se lamentar augelli, o verdi fronde" (If the lamentation of the birds, or the green foliage) presents the steady movement of a lyrical theme from thesis to antithesis to synthesis. If in the opening quatrain the forlorn lyrical hero struggles to interpret the living and breathing world around him as anything but an additional source for sadness, the second quatrain prepares the ground for this mood's resolution. Upon retiring to a riverbank where he contemplates and composes in solitude, the hero discovers that the woman he pines for – or rather, her empathetic spirit – finds a way to counter his mournful sighs with words of gentle rebuke and consolation, as she addresses him from her elliptically described grave (she whom the sky admitted and the ground concealed; l. 6). Apart from a short authorial remark establishing that the beloved's rebuke is motivated by pity ("mi dice con pietate" [tells me with pity], l. 10), the entirety of the sestet consists of a mini-soliloquy delivered by the dearly departed. Why should the protagonist let himself be wasted by time spent crying a river of painful tears, she asks him (ll. 9–11). There is no reason to cry for her: once she closed her eyes on her earthly existence they opened to a boundless inner light (ll. 12–14).

"Se lamentar augelli, o verdi fronde" is a combination of the signature characteristics associated with the continental strain in the grand Renaissance sonneteering tradition. In addition to its formulaic composition and idiosyncratic rhyming scheme, it evokes and encodes its heroine's sonorous name by means of the wordplay for which Petrarch's *Canzoniere* (Song Book) is famous. Laura is not addressed in the sonnet directly, so the poet ensures that it carries her name's onomatopoetic vestige ("l'aura"). Taken as a whole, this sonnet is a representative specimen of the individual imprint Petrarch has left on this form's compositional and formal characteristics as he demonstrated its potential, its ability not only to accommodate his signature wordplay but also to serve as an enduring vessel for his amorous and transcendental visions.

To become an adequate rendition of the Italian original, "O, esli pen'e ptits il' bystrykh vod glukhoi" had to go to the limits of the Russian sonnet canon. The imagery enclosed in the compact syllabic verse of the Italian model stretches the capacity of this foreign-language replica: instead of the iambic pentameter traditionally used in the Russian sonneteering practice, the translator chooses hexameters, as he seeks to accommodate as many of the original images as possible – and tease out the significance he finds worthy of retention and amplification. Examined in its entirety, the formal constitution of the resulting Russian sonnet can be said to conventionalize the original to some extent, as Nabokov sacrifices the alternating rhymes of the original octet in favour of the more traditional enclosing rhyming – in doing so, however, he stays within the general limits of the Petrarchan scheme.[20] This and other adjustments are on display in the comparison of the octet's second quatrain. It is here where the sonnet's lyrical hero acquires the characteristics of the thinker and writer Petrarch's sonnets are known for; it is here where he experiences the epiphany that puts him in touch with the spirit of his beloved.

Nabokov's version dispenses with the unambiguous reference to the hero's writing or composing while dwelling on his emotional state. The pensive hero sits "spellbound" (*zavorozhënnyi*) as he strains to hear the voice of his beloved, described rather loftily here as "the one chosen by the heavens" (*izbrannitsa nebes*) – an epithet not licensed by the original:

> любовныхъ полонъ думъ, сижу, заворожённый, –
> – прислушиваюсь я, и вижу предъ собой
> избранницу небесъ, что изъ страны иной
> [8] ответствуетъ на вздохъ моей тоски влюблённой.

[full of enamoured thoughts, I sit, spellbound – / – paying close heed, and see before me / the one chosen by the heavens, who from another country / answers the sigh of my amorous longing.]

Such and similar liberties notwithstanding, throughout the length of his sonnet Nabokov demonstrates his sensitivity to Petrarch's idiom. The original's Italian vulgate he substitutes with a markedly bookish and quaint Russian. Consistently deployed throughout the sonnet's length, inversions (*strana inaia*, l. 7; *toska vliublënnaia*, l. 8) and dated and poetic lexis (*il'* for "o," l. 1; *otvetstvovat'* for "rispondere," l. 8; *vezhdy* for "occhi," l. 14) create and sustain the mood of antiquated solemnity. It is the Russian sonnet's closing tercet that contains a surprising, if clearly deliberate, departure from the original.

As she urges the poet to defy despondency, Petrarch's Laura cites her newly acquired knowledge of the transcendental to allude to death as liberation from the torments and fetters of the transitory existence. In Nabokov's version, the concluding tercet presents the most forceful reiteration of a theme merely implied by the original. The last tercet's first line erupts with a categorical command delivering a startling revelation:

> "Не плачь-же обо мнѣ … Узнай, что смерти нѣтъ.
> Неугасающій я увидала свѣтъ
> [14] въ тотъ часъ, какъ на землѣ я вѣжды призакрыла."

["Don't cry for me, then … Know that there's no death. / I saw an unceasing light / at that hour when on earth I closed my eyelids."]

Where does Nabokov choose to veer off the path suggested by Petrarch's footsteps, which he is clearly capable of following as a translator? Where do his words cease to overlap with verbal vestiges of those left by Petrarch? Intriguingly enough, this happens in those instances where our awareness of Nabokov the future writer and thinker appears to be most useful for understanding his version of "Se lamentar augelli, o verdi fronde."

It is clear that "O, esli pen'e ptits il' bystrykh vod glukhoi" is crafted to augment and amplify the transcendental implications of the original. Both poems offer an effective account of the transformative power communication with the dead may have on the living, yet the Russian variant is more explicit in asserting the original message. The Russian poem is more specific in its description of the other world, presented here quite tangibly as "a land divergent" (*strana inaia*, l. 7). Even more to the point, the imperative mood of the verb "to learn, find out" (*uznat'*) along with the starkly unambiguous assertion (*smerti net*) are Nabokovian, not Petrarchan.

"O, esli pen'e ptits il' bystrykh vod glukhoi" proves that Nabokov's dialogue with Petrarch began in his early youth. Even if Dmitri Nabokov insisted that Petrarch's Laura had nothing to do with his father's inspiration for *The Original of Laura*, the emergence of this translation adds a crucial piece of hard evidence pertaining to what will forever remain Nabokov's most mysterious text.[21] Our awareness of this sonnet's presence within the gravitational pull of Nabokov's tenacious memory expands our incomplete knowledge of the unrealized design at the crux of his last work. The transformation undergone by Laura in "Se lamentar augelli, o verdi fronde," to take one specific example, forces us to re-examine some of the most tantalizing fragments of *The Original of Laura*.

As she is portrayed by her numerous lovers – or rather by the men vying for her attention – the initial and most vivid incarnation of the title character of *The Original of Laura* is a reckless and cruel seductress who is obsessed with sex but has no regard for the feelings of those she attracts and ruins. This is "Flora," the character that greets the reader in chapter 1, which revolves around her steamy fling with a young Russian writer (who may or may not be the Ivan Vaughn of the subsequent fragments). It is all the more surprising that in what most certainly is a fragment intended to appear toward the unfinished novel's end, this same "Flora" – or "Flaura," or "Laura," as she is alternately referred to throughout Nabokov's index cards – appears to undergo an unexpected transformation. The male narrator, whom readers have every reason to equate with the narrative voice in chapter 1 where he and "Flora" have sex, relates his guarded astonishment at something that can only be qualified as "Flora's" spiritual transfiguration.[22]

Another fragment clearly slated for the novel's finale[23] shows Flora contemplating a fictional depiction of her own demise. Winny Carr, the character at whose place Flora is shown to be beginning her affair with the Russian writer in chapter 1, has chanced upon the heroine holding a "soft cover copy of *Laura* issued virtually at the same time as its much stouter and comelier hardback edition. She had just bought it at the station bookstall, and in answer to Winny's jocular remark ('hope you'll enjoy the story of your life') said she doubted if she could force herself to start reading it. 'Oh you must! said Winnie, it is, of course, fictionalized and all that but you'll come face to face with yourself at every other corner. And there's your wonderful death. Let me show you your wonderful death.'"[24]

At first blush, "Se lamentar augelli, o verdi fronde" – or the entire Petrarchan topos, for that matter – does not appear to be connected with the tantalizingly incomplete fragments entitled *The Original of Laura*. Nabokov's choice of the heroine's name, along with that of the novel (as well as the novel embedded in it) was not accidental and was meant to be redolent of a plethora of literary and visual precedents. Petrarch's Laura, however, remains the most specific and purposeful of them all, even though *The Original of Laura* turns the world of Petrarchan chivalric piety upside down, becoming its grotesque reflection. Those seeking to make sense of Nabokov's vanishing design cannot afford to ignore the further textual links connecting *The Original of Laura* with *Il Canzoniere* via the intermediary of "O, esli pen'e ptits il' bystrykh vod glukhoi."

As a straightforward translation of the Italian original, Nabokov's 1918 version of "Se lamentar augelli, o verdi fronde" must be found wanting in one specific respect: it utterly fails to convey Petrarch's wordplay by means of which the poet encodes his beloved's name into the aural texture of his sonnet. This same translation quandary is revisited in *The Original of Laura,* where it is turned into a major compositional attribute. In the novel's surviving fragments the heroine's name shatters into an array of deceptive and misleading puns that prevent the reader from positively identifying the heroine with one woman. She figures in the text as "Flora," "Flaura," "Aurora," and "Laura," thus quite literally making it difficult to determine which one of them is the *original* suggested by the title. The manner in which this occurs is reminiscent not only of the Petrarchan wordplay, but also of the compromise with the integrity of "Se lamentar augelli, o verdi fronde" Nabokov had to make to create his version of the *original* that displayed this wordplay so prominently. The fact that one of the central strands of the unfinished novel's plot focuses on the heroine's death and spiritual transformation forces us to re-examine the ways in which *The Original of Laura* echoes similar features of Petrarch's *Canzoniere.* These correspondences notwithstanding, one is justified in casting doubt on the possibility of Nabokov's recalling a translation he had made in 1918 as he worked on his last novel in 1975 until his death on 2 July 1977.

Examination of Nabokov's manuscripts dispells such doubts.

Concurrently with *The Original of Laura,* Nabokov laboured to prepare his last, definitive collection of his Russian poetry, *Stikhi,* published posthumously with his widow's foreword in 1979. In 1975–7 he examined and evaluated his archive, going over each and every poem, both published and unpublished. It was then that he went over the "Tsvetnye kameshki" album and reacquainted himself with "O, esli pen'e ptits il' bystrykh vod glukhoi," his own translation of "Se lamentar augelli, o verdi fronde." His early transpositions of foreign poetry invariably rhymed and attempted to match the formal features of their models; as such they were far too frivolous in their treatment of the originals to meet the requirements he had come to place on works of translation before he pronounced them worthy of the name.

The writer's pencil hovered above each one of his poems in "Tsvetnye kameshki," more often than not crossing them out or leaving an emphatic "No!" in the margin. After he re-read his 1918 version of "Se lamentar augelli, o verdi fronde," Nabokov paused and enclosed "O, esli pen'e ptits il' bystrykh vod glukhoi" in a circle, making it the only poem selected for such a treatment in the entire album. Then he had second thoughts. A decisive strike-through cutting across the encircled poem makes it clear that after pondering this poem's significance for a short while, he decided against reviving it. There is no doubt whatsoever that even if he had forgotten all about expending considerable energy on transposing that Italian sonnet into Russian in what was an one-off case in his entire literary career, as he went over his manuscripts he recalled this episode of his Crimean youth with utmost lucidity.

The septuagenarian writer had every reason to linger over his sixty-year-old version of Petrarch's "Se lamentar augelli, o verdi fronde," as he would not have had any trouble appreciating the significance of "O, esli pen'e ptits il' bystrykh vod glukhoi" for his life and art. The sonnet represents the first articulation of one of his paramount themes: it explores and depicts communication with the dead. This was a subject Nabokov was to focus on for the rest of his career in letters, as he found increasingly sophisticated ways of expressing his metaphysical intuitions while exploring the possibility for human consciousness to survive death. Scholars have traced the development of this theme from a relatively artless short story, "Christmas" ("Rozhdestvo"; 1924),[25] to such mature works as the novella *The Eye* (*Sogliadatai*, 1927–30), the novelistic frament "Ultima Thule" (1939–40),[26] as well as such cornerstones of the Nabokov novelistic canon as *Pale Fire* (1961), *Ada, or Ardor* (1968), and *Transparent Things* (1972), to mention only a few representative works whose portent cannot be grasped without affording due attention to the transcendental peripeteias enlightening every aspect of their design and execution.

"Un banal instrument": The Strange Case of Vladimir Nabokov and Louis Bouilhet

Nabokov's account of the composition of his first poem in *Speak, Memory*'s chapter 11 features a reference to some embarrassingly facile influences that left a mark on his poetic debut. Straightforward as it is, this reference is compounded by the introduction of a rather obscure French poem of little apparent relevance to the topic at hand:

> Worst of all were the shameful gleanings from Apuhtin's and Grand Duke Konstantin's lyrics of the *tsïganski* type. They used to be persistently pressed upon me by a youngish and rather attractive aunt, who could also spout Louis Bouilhet's famous piece (*À Une Femme*), in which a metaphorical violin bow is incongruously used to play on a metaphorical guitar.[27]

For all its popularity with composers like Chaikovskii and Rakhmaninov, the salon poetry of Aleksei Apukhtin (1840–93) and K.R. (Konstantin Konstantinovich Romanov, 1858–1915) may not have been a worthy model for a writer and poet of Nabokov's ambition.[28] But the same is true of Louis-Hyacinthe Bouilhet (1822–69), the author of "À une femme" and Gustave Flaubert's confidant, whom Flaubert honoured in an introduction to Bouilhet's *Dernières chansons: Poésies posthumes* (Last Songs: Posthumous Poems; Paris, 1872). "Tsevetnye kameshki" documents a much closer encounter between the two than the fleeting reference in *Speak, Memory* suggests. It may well be that the very nature of this passing reference hints at a more substantial level of significance lying dormant under its innocuous surface in a validation of Eric Naiman's observation that "'the good reader' of Nabokov must be alert to the hidden meanings suggested by all sorts of seemingly chance or inconsequential details in the text."[29]

Nabokov's partial translation of "À une femme" (To a woman) is dated 7 June 1918. The later marginal notes accompanying the translation, however, are hardly flattering: in one of them Nabokov struggles to recall the author's name; in another he appears to be so dissatisfied with his translation that he writes "Out!" next to it.

Bouilhet's "À une femme" may appear to be a rather conventional, if impassioned, versified reproach to an unfaithful mistress: it is precisely this aspect of the original that Nabokov's incomplete and unpolished Russian resetting seems to be amplifying more than anything else. Bouilhet's nineteen-year-old Russian translator obliges the author by communicating rather well the wrath of the broken-hearted protagonist, who denigrates the object of his passion in a cascade of insults aimed at salvaging his bruised ego:

> [Въ дни счастья] Ты только вѣдь была послушливой струною
> Дрожащей подъ моей побѣдною рукой.

Какъ въ полости гитаръ трепещетъ звукъ порою,
[16] Такъ пѣли сны мои въ душѣ твоей пустой.[30]

[(In the days of happiness) You merely were an obedient string / Trembling under my victorious hand. / As a sound resonates in the guitar cavity sometimes / Thus my dreams sang in your empty soul.]

In the context of *Speak, Memory*'s chapter 11, a reference to "À une femme" remains somewhat unexpected. Our awareness of Nabokov's aborted struggle with this poem's Russian incarnation – together with his private dismissal of it – may well permit us to get to the significance of its appearance at so specific a moment in his autobiographical narrative.

The remaining fragments of Nabokov's version of Bouilhet's original leave no question as to Nabokov's ability to understand Bouilhet's French. A comparison of the two texts, however, reveals something unexpected: Nabokov's version of the same stanza that inspired his retrospective reference to its "incongruity" falls short of conveying the implications of Bouilhet's accusatory rhetoric. As the protagonist vents his anger at his unfaithful mistress, he saturates this stanza with thinly veiled sexual references. In the stanza's opening lines, Bouilhet's protagonist dismisses his former lover as hardly more than "a banal instrument" that only on rare occasions produced sounds under his "vanquishing bow." Lest the drift of this image get lost on the reader, in the ensuing lines it is amplified by his comparison of the fickle one to "the hollow wood of the guitars." The "obedient string" with which the nineteen-year-old translator equipped his version of this key stanza, the "dreams that occasionally sang in [the mistress's] empty soul" testify to his unwillingness or – perhaps still closer to the truth of the matter – inability to parallel Bouilhet's coital imagery with fitting Russian equivalents.

The fictionalized presentation of the newly discovered thrills of literary creativity the reader finds in chapter 11 of *Speak, Memory* is not a mere exercise in artistic invention. Instead of being a true-to-life recreation of the author's falling prey to the "numb fury of versemaking" for the first time, with the aid of this reference it reveals itself as a wry homage to literary innocence. As Nabokov backdates his encounter with Bouilhet's "À une femme," anchoring it in the lost Arcadia of his pre-revolutionary childhood and describing the incongruity of the poem's key images, he echoes the effect Mayne Reid's reference to the haughtiness of American planters had on him at that distant point in his life. His failure to find a fitting parallel to the imagery of Bouilhet's original due to its "incongruity" sheds light on the true implication of this poem's surfacing in the memoir of a sophisticated writer famous for his mastery of sexual innuendo: here he recalls and celebrates that tender age when poetry seemed to him free of such connotations. In stark contrast with Musset's "La Nuit de décembre," whose amorous invectives Nabokov had transmitted so effectively in his translation, Bouilhet's much shorter piece represented a different brand of Gallic literary eroticism in a distant prefiguration of Nabokov's own masterful play on secondary meanings and double entendres.

In yet another proof of the truthfulness of Nabokov's statement on the pertinacity of impressions acquired in the process of riddle solving, the fourth stanza of Bouilhet's "À une femme" figures prominently in Nabokov's short story "The Admiralty Spire" ("Admiralteiskaia Igla," 1933).[31] A powerful evocation of nostalgia-induced loneliness and heartbreak, this story is a masterwork of Nabokov's storytelling technique that subverts an array of narrative conventions, from confessional epistolary prose to unreliable narration. As the story parades the middlebrow literary tastes endemic to its protagonists' milieu, it focuses on the poem Nabokov had once struggled to put into Russian.[32] Nabokov's protagonist attempts to assert his intellectual superiority not merely by pointing out the same "incongruity" that was to make its way into *Speak, Memory*, but also by implying that he, unlike his addressee and love interest Katya (whom he suspects of hiding behind the masculine literary pseudonym "Serge Solntsev"), was aware of the sexual connotations of Bouilhet's forceful imagery.

Nabokov's struggle with an adequate Russian version of "À une femme" did not merely earn the poem a place in the depository of literary references at his disposal. In both "The Admiralty Spire" and *Speak, Memory*, the superficially dismissive context of Nabokov's references to the poem conceals their close integration into the core of his designs. In "The Admiralty Spire," the poem furnishes the story's theme of amorous longing and heartbreak with a tangible literary precedent that points out the theme's banality on the one hand and underscores its enduring quality as an inescapable attribute of life on the other. Revisiting "À une femme" in *Speak, Memory*, the writer pays homage to the days of his literary apprenticeship, when he had yet to develop the means of matching Bouilhet's innuendos. His attempt at translating this poem emerges as a milestone on his way toward acquiring a rich and flexible multilingual vocabulary to address such subjects.

"The enthralling mysteries of otherworldly plains": Émile Verhaeren and the Earliest Intimation of Nabokov's "Main Theme"

When Véra Nabokov drew the attention of her late husband's readers to the concept of *potustoronnost'* – the hereafter, the otherworldly, the beyond, or the otherworld – it opened a distinct perspective not merely on the entirety of the writer's art but also on his ethics and aesthetics. This 1979 disclosure lent additional credence to the earliest analyses of a problem that had long been considered marginal in the studies of a writer renowned for his metafictional hermeticism. Such pioneering treatises of Nabokov's metaphysics as W.W. Rowe's *Nabokov's Spectral Dimension* (1981) and Brian Boyd's *Nabokov's "Ada": The Place of Consciousness* (1985) paved the way for Vladimir E. Alexandrov's speculation on the origins and specificity of the writer's mystical intuition in *Nabokov's Otherworld* (1991). Yet for all its urgency and fecundity, the research into the philosophical significance of the concept of *potustoronnost'* has frequently neglected to approach it as a problem of language.

In his seminal article "Vladimir Nabokov and Rupert Brooke," D. Barton Johnson has pointed out that "Nabokov's first use of the term *potustoronnost'*... occurs as a preliminary to his discussion of Brooke's poem 'The Life Beyond.'"[33] While Johnson's finding of Nabokov's earliest known employment of the term in the 1922 essay retains its value, his conclusions regarding its presence in Nabokov's oeuvre stand in need of a reassessment. It may well be that once the familiar scope of Nabokov's juvenilia has been expanded to include such a long-neglected component as his translations, we might be closer to solving one of his most enduring, closely guarded mysteries, that of his personal spiritual convictions. It is here where the archival materials dating from the writer's Crimean days prove themselves a treasure trove.

Among Nabokov's earliest translation experiments, Émile Verhaeren's "Les Voyagers" must be assigned a place of distinction. It is clear that Nabokov laboured diligently to produce his Russian version this poem: the earliest extant version of his translation has "October 1917" under it, indicating that contrary to his usual translation practices, work on this poem lasted more than one day. Notable as this detail is, the most remarkable fact about Nabokov's encounter with the Flemish Belgian poet is that "Les Voyageurs" was one the few foreign-language texts he deemed worthy of not only translation but retranslation. "Stranniki (iz Émile Verhaeren)" (Wanderers [from Émile Verhaeren]), the initial version of "Les Voyageurs," appears in Album B, which preserves compositions immediately preceding the author's departure from his native city in early November 1917; "Tsvetnye kameshki" documents a reworking of this poem dated 7 June 1918, the same date as the aborted translation of Bouilhet's "À une femme." This subsequent version of "Les Voyageurs" bears the title of "Puteshestvenniki (iz Émile Verhaeren)" (Travellers [from Émile Verhaeren]). The heightened attention allotted by Nabokov to his work on this poem is underscored by the marginal note added at the end of the later version: "I made this translation last October. Now I have definitively reworked it. V.N." A closer examination of this textual artefact proves it to have been deserving of the effort that went into its creation.

Summoned by a strange echo of the "dreamy horizons" and the "ancient call of distant sibyls" (ll. 1–2), Verhaeren's anonymous voyagers set forth to visit equally indeterminate yet irresistibly beguiling locations, using a lavishly decorated vessel manned by dark-skinned ship boys (stanza 2). Throughout the ensuing journey the intentional dearth of such particular appellations as toponyms and other habitual bearings is compensated and complemented by Verhaeren's grippingly visual, if enigmatic, descriptions of the voyagers' faraway destinations (ll. 13–16). A degree of certainty arrives with the appearance of some Christian emblems, yet the imagery that follows once again plunges the poem's plot into the dream-like state of varicoloured indeterminacy. A location that may be taken for Byzantium, with its Christian emperors and temples, is superseded by another evocation of the sea and its ability to render all human endeavours futile (ll. 21–8).

A poetic narrative based on a principle of cyclical composition, "Les Voyageurs" concludes with a return to its point of departure, the world of quotidian concerns, which asserts itself through the sound of a chiming clock. The poem's protagonists may be returning to the place they come from, but its last quatrain contains a strong suggestion of a synthesis or a resolution that transcends the full circle made by the protagonists' itinerary (ll. 33–40).

Having visited a number of ancient, enigmatic lands, the poem's protagonists, the voyagers – much like the anthropomorphized "drunken boat" of Arthur Rimbaud's eponymous poem ("Le Bateau ivre," 1871) – must return home, yet they will never be the same, as every fibre of their being has now been irreversibly altered by their encounter with "other firmaments."[34]

In concert with the principles of Verhaeren's brand of symbolism, "Les Voyageurs" is an allegorical verse narrative. The crepuscular journey described in the poem takes place not in reality, but in a dream, hence the vagueness of much of its imagery. Verhaeren the symbolist, however, confronts his readers with a situation in which the realm of nighttime reveries spills over into the protagonists' quotidian existence, affecting and altering it forever. The poet depicts dreamers and visionaries partaking in a mystical ritual of an extrasensory communion in their sleep. The poem's finale makes it clear that people capable of experiencing such sensations are doomed to spend their lives straddling two planes of being, one belonging to the phenomenal world and the other existing elsewhere.

Recognizing the author of *Les Villes tentaculaires* (Many-Tentacled Cities; 1895) as Baudelaire's heir apparent, Verhaeren's Russian admirers and younger contemporaries did not fail to take notice of the preoccupations shaping his world view. In the unambiguously titled essay "Modern-Day Dante" (1913), Valerii Briusov (1873–1924), doyen of the symbolist school and Russia's principal champion of Verhaeren, highlighted the mystical orientation of "an entire period of [Verhaeren's] work ... devoted to his attempts with the force of intuition, with epiphany artistic rather than religious, to peer beyond the border of the accessible to cerebral knowledge."[35] A centrepiece of *Les Soirs* (Evenings; 1887), "Les Voyageurs" certainly is a manifestation of this "intuitive" approach to literary creativity: it is a poem about a longing for another world that colours every waking hour of the few sensitive people capable of experiencing private transcendental epiphanies.

Nabokov's treatment of "Les Voyageurs" proves beyond the shadow of a doubt that by the time he reached his late teens he had developed much more than a passive appreciation of this aspect of Verhaeren's outlook. In addition to demonstrating a nuanced understanding of the transcendental intuitions shaping the fluid, dream-like world of "Les Voyageurs," he proved himself prepared to find a fitting foreign-language representation for it. As he revised "Stranniki," his October 1917 resetting of the poem, into the subsequent and final "Puteshestvenniki" of June 1918, Nabokov did not merely reset the syllabic verse of Verhaeren's poem by means of the syllabotonic prosody at his disposal and transplant the original's rhyme scheme, attempting to preserve its anaphoras and enjambments. As he refined his version of the poem, he elevated the solemnity of its atmosphere.

Whereas the initial Russian incarnation of the French poem's first stanza contains a rather matter-of-fact designation of its plot's temporal bearings (*v tot vecher* for "un soir," l. 4) –

И дали грезящей, и странныхъ голосовъ
сибиллъ загадочныхъ, извѣчно-отдалённыхъ,
и тайнъ плѣнительныхъ равнинъ потустороннихъ
[4] въ тотъ вечеръ странники почувствовали зовъ.

("Stranniki," 1917)

[And of dreamy distances, and of the strange voices / of mysterious sibyls, ever-distant, / and of the enthralling mysteries of otherworldly plains / that night the wanderers sensed the summons.]

– the subsequent and finalized version of the same fragment leaves intact the succession of conjunctions echoing the effect of Verhaeren's orderly anaphoras, but opts for a more poetic and less specific "in the crepuscular hour" (*v vechernii chas*) –

И дали грезящей, и странныхъ голосовъ
сибиллъ загадочныхъ, извѣчно-отдалённыхъ,
и тайнъ плѣнительныхъ равнинъ потустороннихъ
[4] они – въ вечерній часъ – почувствовали зовъ.

("Puteshestvenniki," 1918)[36]

[And of dreamy distances, and of the strange voices / of mysterious sibyls, ever-distant, / and of the enthralling mysteries of otherworldly plains / they – at the crepuscular hour – sensed the summons.]

As he confronted Verhaeren's "les au-delà mystérieux des plaines," already in the initial version of 1917, Nabokov arrived at an opulent and expansive rendition of the original image that has stood the test of time. Inspired by Verhaeren's image, Nabokov conveys it in his Russian with the aid of "the enthralling mysteries of otherworldly plains" (l. 3). Since the substantive *l'au-delà* means "hereafter," Nabokov decisively orients his version of the poem's opening quatrain toward an allegorical meaning that amplifies the suprarational implication of the journey undertaken by its protagonist. More than anything else, Nabokov's reading of Verhaeren's original interprets the poem as a depiction of an exploration of those realms of being that are inaccessible to reason.

Whether such a determined interpretation does justice to the subdued tonality of Verhaeren's original, which invariably prioritizes implication over declaration, is largely beside the point when we consider the significance of this alteration for the eventual crystallization of Nabokov's individual language of transcendental inquiry. The 1917 translation of Verhaeren's "Les Voyageurs" marks the first known occasion of his employment of a derivative of the word *potustronnost'* as a denominator for so consequential a concept in his world view that his widow and closest confidante declared it his "main theme." More than any original composition dating from this same period, Nabokov's translations from Petrarch and Verhaeren make it clear that the notion of *potustoronnost'* had taken shape prior to his departure from Russia, prior to his experiencing exile and losses of those dear to him. Whereas his version of Petrarch's "Se lamentar augelli, o verdi fronde" testifies to Nabokov's early interest in the idea of communication with the dead and the related notion of the indestructability of human consciousness, his rendition of Verhaeren's "Les Voyageurs" documents the formation and formulation of an individual idiom with which to broach the subject of the multiplicity of realms of existence.

"Trois Chansons de Bilitis": Gallic Panpipes in Crimean Beech Groves

Sung poetry can be said to be the frontier at which music and verbal art, Nabokov's medium of choice, meet; not unlike the Texas of Mayne Reid's *Headless Horseman*, this area is far from tranquil. Does Robert Schumann's setting of a Heinrich Heine *lied* violate the integrity of the original poem? How much of Pushkin remains in Pëtr Chaikovskii and Konstantin Shilovskii's liberal adaptation of *Eugene Onegin*'s text, prepared with the aim of accommodating the composer's instinctive mode of artistic expression? When Nabokov articulated his position in the argument, he spoke from knowledge of the problem that was more extensive than many may be ready to acknowledge.[37]

Les Chansons de Bilitis (The Songs of Bilitis), a literary hoax perpetrated by Pierre Louÿs in 1894, left a discernible mark on Nabokov's writings, meriting distinct evocations in novels as different as *Glory* (1930) and *Ada* (1968).[38] Examined in conjunction with Nabokov's earlier experiments in translation, the versions of the three *chansons* put together in August 1918 in the Crimea represent another stage of his evolution as a translator.

Album 19, in which Elena Ivanovna Nabokova preserved many of her son's early experiments in translation, contains his versions of "La Flûte de Pan" (The Pan Flute), "La Chevelure" (The Hair), and "Le Tombeau des Naïades" (The Naiads' Grave), numbered respectively 30, 31, and 46 in the first part of *Les Chansons de Bilitis*, "Bucoliques en Pamphylie" (Bucolics in Pamphylia). The order of Nabokov's versions of the poems in Album 19 is slightly different from that of Louÿs's *roman lyrique*: the Russian version of "La Chevelure" is followed by "La Flûte de Pan" and then by "Le Tombeau des Naïades" (31, 30, and 46 in the original numeration).

At least on the surface, Nabokov's versions of the three poems seem to register a growing interest in experimentation: most visibly, the unrhymed French poems become rhymed in Russian, stripping Louÿs's hoax of an essential detail of its imitative facade. The absence of rhyme in the French original was an important part of Louÿs's ruse: as this French "compiler" and "translator" of Bilitis's poems obligingly assured his readers in the introduction to his volume, the poetess lived at the beginning of the sixth century BCE, which means that as a follower and personal acquaintance of Sappho, Bilitis simply could not have expressed herself in rhymed verse – it would have been ahistoric, an innovation unknown to that period in the history of classical verse. When it comes to rhyme, Nabokov's Russian versions of the poems refuse to follow their "authentic" – unrhymed – source.

The Russian poems that are brought to life by the translator's resolute reconsideration of the original differ from their foreign source in many other significant respects. On Louÿs's flowing, melodic free verse Nabokov imposes a regular metre and a fairly strict stanzaic structure – an experiment that results in textual entities characterized by a number of peculiar features. Thus, "La Chevelure" emerges as a rhymed poem in five-foot iambs with a regular alternation of feminine and masculine rhymes ("Kudri"); "La Flûte de Pan," a rhymed poem of six-foot iambs with a single curtailment of this scheme in the second stanza, which includes a couplet of five-foot iambs ("Svirel' Pana"); and "Le Tombeau des Naïades," a rhymed poem of five-foot iambs that displays the most elaborate rhyming scheme to be found in the entire cycle ("Mogila Naiad").

Although Nabokov's translations of the three poems from Louÿs's *roman lyrique* have a unity of their own, linked as they are by the same lyrical persona, the "I" of the narrative, this trio is not furnished with a specific umbrella title (instead, the translated title of each poem is followed by a uniform subtitle, "Pesni Bilitis. P. Luis."). The very choice of these poems (out of the 158 available from Louÿs) is, however, intriguing in itself: the nineteen-year-old translator foregoes many poems collected in a book that to this very day continues to be famous for its frank depiction of many aspects of feminine sexuality (by no means limited to Bilitis's homosexual affair with Mnasidika, famously depicted in "Élégies à Metilène" [Elegies at Mytilene], the book's second part). Nabokov's choice was clearly not dictated by an interest in the more popular aspects of Louÿs's work (he singled out the texts that can be said to be the least titillating – even though this was a notorious characteristic of *Les Chansons*, and one that he was to use in *Glory* and later in *Ada*). According to the hypothesis outlined here, it was music that provided Nabokov with the impulse to create Russian versions of Louÿs's poems.

There is a distinct possibility that Nabokov had discovered *Les Chansons de Bilitis* long before he made Alla Chernosvitova offer an edition of Louÿs's book to Martin Edelweiss in *Glory*: a copy of the *Chansons* is registered in the surviving catalogue of the Nabokovs' St Petersburg library.[39] The search for an explanation of why Nabokov specifically chose to translate the texts he did leads to what was in 1918 and remains to this day the most conspicuous joint appearance ever made by these three poems – their musical adaptation by Claude Debussy ("Trois Chansons de Bilitis," song cycle for voice and piano, L. 90, 1897–8). While the order in which the translated texts are transcribed in Album 19 differs from the original one in both Louÿs's and Debussy's *Chansons*, the date that is clearly marked at the end of each translation ("15-VII-18") places them in close proximity to Nabokov's work on German *lieder* by Heinrich Heine in the musical settings of Franz Schubert and Robert Schumann, translations undertaken at the request of a family friend, the singer Anna Ian-Ruban, about two months later. It may well be that in translating the three *chansons* into Russian, Nabokov was likewise satisfying a request from a performer or a music lover, as he was to do later with the Heine poems.

The title image of one of the three *chansons* translated by Nabokov in the Crimea finds its way into "Krym" (The Crimea; "Na zlo neistovym nevzgodam" [To spite the raging tribulations]; 30 June 1920), Nabokov's ode to his last abode on his native soil:

О, рощи буковыя, гдѣ я
подслушалъ, Панъ, свирѣль твою![40]

[Oh, the beech groves, where I / eavesdropped on your reed-pipe, Pan!]

The full significance of this invocation of a conventional allegory of animate wildlife can be grasped only in conjunction with Nabokov's translation of Pierre Louÿs's "Flûte de Pan," turning a generic literary image into not only a concrete autobiographical reference but also a rich verbal vestige of his dialogic encounter with Louÿs.[41]

Byronic Wild Cypresses, Nabokovian Tender Gloom

Nabokov's appraisal of Byron, much like that of Musset, was subject to change, and, much like Musset, Byron became one of the literary beacons of whose presence – however distant – Nabokov never ceased to be aware. A fascination with the English poet of Nabokov's erudite childhood and early youth gave way to the more sober evaluation of both the man and his myth.[42] And yet he never parted with Byron completely. Byron's grip on "Continental minds" would have made him an indispensable point of reference for Nabokov the Pushkinist, even if Nabokov the poet had not professed to have had a strong interest in Byron long before becoming a translator and interpreter of Pushkin for the English-speaking reader. In stanza 10 of his Pushkinesque *University Poem* (*Universitetskaia poema*, 1926), Nabokov makes a point of declaring that he is through with the brand of Romanticism traditionally associated with his fellow graduate of Trinity College, Cambridge: "But I have cooled toward his creations ... / so do forgive my unromantic side – / to me the marble roses of a Keats / have more charm than all those stagey storms."[43]

While Nabokov may have "cooled off" toward Byron's "stagey" ("theatrical," perhaps even "histrionic" – *butaforskii*) "tempests" by 1926, Byronic echoes and images in his writings are sufficiently persistent to be found in such different works as the early verse drama *Smert'* (1923) and the autumnal *Ada* (1968), to mention only two representative examples. It is not surprising, then, that having found himself in the Crimea, against the backdrop that once inspired Pushkin's and Mickiewicz's famous creations in a Byronic vein, Nabokov should have turned to Byron with a keen desire to partake of a noble tradition. Naturally enough, translation provided Nabokov with an opportunity to assimilate – some might say internalize – his freshly acquired Byronic experience, for it was in the Crimea that he suddenly "felt the pangs of exile" for the first time upon receiving a delayed letter from "Tamara" in a corner of the world that "seemed completely foreign," where "the smells were not Russian, the sounds were not Russian, the donkey braying every evening just as the muezzin started to chant from the village minaret ... was positively Bagdadian."[44]

Album 19 preserves versions of no fewer than four different poems by Byron, all of them translated into Russian within forty-eight hours. The earliest is the version of "The Dream" ("Our life is twofold; Sleep hath its own world," July 1816), dated "6-IX-18." The next day, according to the date written beneath them ("7-IX-18"), the remaining three poems were translated: "Oh! Snatched Away in Beauty's Bloom," "'All Is Vanity,' Saith the Preacher," and "Sun of the Sleepless."

Apart from providing Nabokov with yet another opportunity to revisit the theme of unhappy love, "The Dream" – Byron's contemplation of his unreciprocated passion for his distant cousin Mary Chaworth and the aftermath of her unhappy marriage with the man she chose instead of the future poet – gave the translator a chance to try his hand at a short narrative poem different from Musset's "La Nuit de décembre." With its 206 lines of blank verse, "The Dream" contains many a Shakespearean echo, chief among them being Byron's soliloquy-like reflection on the nature of dreams with which the poem opens and closes. To a Russian reader, "The Dream" is immediately recognizable as part of a nineteenth-century aristocratic discourse, complete with its depiction of a hereditary estate as well as the sense of a strong emotional attachment to ancestral land, a sentiment that becomes all the more important upon a sudden and painful severance of this connection. It is fitting that Nabokov, who was destined to write the closing page of Russian aristocratic narrative in *Ada*, should in his youth have translated Byron's "Dream."[45] Some descriptive passages in "The Dream" contain a direct precursor of Nabokov's later evocations of gentry country seats (both remembered and invented), thus providing an important piece of additional information on the genesis of this theme in his writings.

Byron's reflection upon the nature of dreams in their relation to waking reality is also of particular interest in connection with Nabokov's intuition of the transcendental, which not infrequently expressed itself in the depiction of visions and dreams (identified by Byron as "heralds of eternity," "spirits of the past;" "The Dream," 1:11, 12). Byron's poem not only draws a parallel between recollections and dreams, it also questions the very notion of reality in its relation – or opposition – to the supposedly illusory, insubstantial, world of visions and figments of the imagination that intrude on recollections of the past.

In "Son. Iz Bairona" (Dream. From Byron), Nabokov demonstrates that by the age of nineteen he had acquired the resourcefulness and skill needed to meet the challenge of recreating Byron's contemplative idiom in Russian. His translation is particularly successful in capturing the elevated, ruminative style of the English poem that dominates fragments 1 and 9 (opening and closing of "The Dream"), while continuing to be present in the poem's core (parts 2–8). To echo in Russian the tonality of Byron's blank verse, Nabokov makes the commendable choice of turning to Pushkin's works in the same medium, producing a confident stylization of Pushkinian blank verse, evocative of the diction of passages from the soliloquies in Pushkin's "little tragedies" (especially *Skupoi rytsar'* [*The Covetous Knight*], *Motsart i Sal'eri* [*Mozart and Salieri*], 1830, and "… Vnov' ia posetil…" ["… I have visited again…"], 1835, the Pushkin poems he was to translate into English).[46]

Of Nabokov's three translations of poems from Byron's *Hebrew Melodies* (late 1814 to early 1815), two are grouped under the title "Evreiskiie Melodii (iz Bairona)" in a mini-cycle of their own: these translations are "O skoro smert' prervët rastsvet chudesnyi tvoi!" ("Oh! Snatched Away in Beauty's Bloom") and "Vsë imel ia: liubov', slavu, mudrost' i vlast'" ("'All Is Vanity,' Saith the Preacher"). As will become clear from the analysis offered below, Byron's melancholic variations on the theme of bereavement and sorrow undergo certain changes in these Russian versions that may be indicative of the translator's desire to modify their elegiac intent.

The very opening line of Nabokov's translation of the first poem contains an alteration of the original, endowing it with an air of dark prophesy:

> О скоро смерть прервёт расцвѣтъ чудесный твой!
> Но камня тяжкого не будетъ надъ тобой …
>
> Нѣтъ! Розы раннія надъ ровною травой
> скрывающей тебя, распустятся весной
> и кипарисовъ дрожь обвѣетъ нѣжной мглой.[47]

[Oh, soon death will interrupt your marvellous flowering! / But no hefty stone will be above you … / No! Early roses above the smooth grass / that covers you, will bloom in spring / and the trembling of cypresses will waft [you] with tender gloom.]

The corresponding line of Byron's original, which also serves as the title of the poem, employs a past participle, as befits an evocation of a deceased (as Byron himself admitted to in "she is no more."[48]) Nabokov's future tense, however, appears to be based on its prevalence throughout the rest of Byron's poem, which focuses on the aftermath of the sad event alluded to in the opening line:

Oh! snatched away in beauty's bloom,
On thee shall press no ponderous tomb;
But on thy turf shall roses rear
Their leaves, the earliest of the year;
And the wild cypress wave in tender gloom ...[49]

Nabokov's lyrical hero seems to be declining all attempts to console him on the part of an interlocutor whose gender is revealed by the feminine form of the pronoun and the endings of the short-form adjectives (*sama, dolzhna, bledna,* ll. 14, 15). In the already established presence of a *ty* at the beginning of the poem, the ending of the Russian version suggests that the woman being addressed is trying to console the poem's lyrical hero in view of her own death, in a show of courage that is absent from Byron's original.[50]

"'All Is Vanity,' Saith the Preacher" provided the model for the second poem in Nabokov's "Evreiskiie Melodii (iz Bairona)." In another instance of a radical departure from the original, the Russian version of the poem omits its English title, effectively severing all connection with Ecclesiastes, which in the case of the English elegy prompted the reader to regard the Bible as the poem's ostensible source of inspiration.

Considered in conjunction with "O skoro smert' prervët rastsvet chudesnyi tvoi!" (Nabokov's translation of "Oh! Snatched Away in Beauty's Bloom"), the second poem complements the theme announced in the first by implying that the tragic event foreseen in the first instalment has occurred prior to the commencement of the second. The two poems united here under a single title assume positions on either side of an event implied in both poems without being named directly – the interrupted blossoming of the heroine's beauty – in an illustration of the formalist dichotomy of *siuzhet* and *fabula*. In the case of the two poems united under the title "Evreiskiie Melodii (Iz Bairona)," Nabokov the translator appears to have supplied Nabokov the poet and budding storyteller with the building blocks to construct a miniature narrative poem, complete with its set of characters and a tragic collision around which the two poems' common plot revolves, quite independently of the original English poetic cycle.

"Solntse bessonnykh," the Russian version of "Sun of the Sleepless," is a rare example of an early work in translation finding its way into Nabokov's collection of original verse (the other example being the 1921 version of Keats's "La Belle Dame Sans Merci," also included in *Gornii put'*, 1923). The entourage in which "Solntse bessonnykh" appears in *Gornii put'* (The Empyrean Path) reveals the place allotted to translation in Nabokov's early oeuvre, revealing a strong thematic affinity with the poems surrounding it. "Zabudesh' ty menya, kak etu noch' zabudesh'" (You will forget me as you will forget this night; 10.VIII.18), "O chëm ia dumaiu? O padaiushchikh zvëzdakh …" (What am I thinking about? About falling stars; 26.VIII.18), "I videl ia: stemneli neba svody …" (And I saw how the heavenly arches turned dark; 30.VIII.18), "Lunnaia noch'" (Lunar Night ["Poliany okropil kholodnyi svet luny…," The cold light of the moon sprinkled a forest clearing]; 18.IX.18), "Bol'shaia medveditsa" (Ursus Major ["Byl grozen voln polnochnyi rëv…," The midnight roar of the waves was threatening]; 23.IX.18), "Vdali ot berega, v mertsanii morskom" (Far from the shore, in the sea glimmer; 10.X.18) all share with "Solntse bessonnykh" a concentration on astral, and more specifically lunar, imagery.[51]

> Sun of the sleepless! – melancholy star!
> Whose tearful beam glows tremulously far,
> That show'st the darkness thou canst not dispel,
> How like art thou to Joy remembered well![52]

> Печальная звѣзда, безсонныхъ солнце! Ты
> указываешь мракъ, но этой темноты
> твой лучъ трепещущій, далёкій – не разсѣетъ.
> Съ тобою я сравню воспоминаній свѣтъ …[53]

[Doleful star, sun of the sleepless! You / point at the gloom, but that darkness / your trembling, distant ray – will not dispel. To you I will compare the light of recollections …]

In more than one way this octave-like piece attests to the growing confidence of Nabokov the translator. In what already emerges as a specific device that Nabokov may tend to employ when he wishes to preserve much of the original's meaning and imagery while retaining its representative technical characteristics, this version of an English poem features an augmentation of the original's metre, as the iambic pentameter of Byron's poem becomes hexameter in Russian.[54] The rhyming structure of the original is also subject to change, as Nabokov deviates from Byron's simple succession of rhyming couplets by introducing into his translation an enclosing rhyme. On the level of syntax and composition, bound as he is by the exigencies of verse translation, Nabokov allows for a certain degree of freedom in the transposition of the English original into Russian: thus, for example, the image of a "tearful beam" – one that presides over the poem's opening three lines – is moved from the second line to the third (equally characteristic is the compromise solution behind the choice of *trepeshchushchii* for "tearful"). In his version's fourth line Nabokov resolutely introduces the lyrical "I" that is absent from the original, which appears to be more impersonal in its portrayal of nocturnal recollection of "joy remembered well." The ultimate result, however, fully justifies the cautious subtitle that followed the original English title of the poem when it was first published in *Gornii put'*: this is a poem *iz Bairona* (lit. "from Byron"), and not "by Byron" by any means. Byron's pessimistic comparison of memory and recollection to a "light … which shines, but warms not with its rays," one that is "distinct, but distant – clear – but, oh how cold" has been conveyed in Nabokov's version as *bezsil'nyi ogonëk*, one that is "radiant, yet cold; distinct, yet distant" (*luchist, no kholoden, otchëtliv, no dalëk*) – an effective paraphrase of Byron's concise, epigrammatic wording.

Nabokov's subsequent cult of memory as one of inspiration's most fecund sources, as well as a natural medium uniquely suited to discerning latent patterns in a seemingly desultory progression of human existence from cradle to grave, could hardly be more antithetic to the pessimism expressed by Byron in his "Sun of the Sleepless." The known trajectory of the mature writer's development away from this pessimistic, narrowly Byronic notion (succinctly identified as "Byronic gloom" in Nabokov's notes to *Eugene Onegin*) helps to explain the true nature of Nabokov's disenchantment with the brand of Romanticism traditionally associated with Byron. Even at this early stage in the evolution of his world view, Nabokov turns to Byron in search of a formula that can be studied, echoed, and possibly discarded, providing a stepping stone for Nabokov's thought on its way toward independence. And yet even upon becoming fully aware of the metaphysical limitations of Byron's Romantic pessimism, Nabokov continues to pay homage to Byron by evoking Byronic imagery in his poetry and prose.

Byron's spectre is summoned in a passage of Nabokov's blank-verse drama *Smert'* (Death; 1923). His fleeting appearance in the background lends this drama, supposedly set in 1806 Cambridge, an air of credibility, as young student Edmund, hoaxed by his evil genius Gonville into believing that he has died, recalls some recent events of his "interrupted" life:

я что-то вспоминаю …
вошёлъ мой третiй гость, – красавецъ
хромой, – ведя ручнаго медвѣжонка
московскаго, – и цѣпью звѣрь ни разу
не громыхнулъ, пока его хозяинъ,
на столъ поставивъ локти и къ прозрачнымъ
вискамъ прижавъ манжеты кружевныя,
выплакивалъ стихи о кипарисахъ.[55]

[I recall something … My third guest entered – a lame handsome youth – / leading a Muscovian tame bear cub / and not a single time did the beast / rattle its chain, while its master, / put his elbows on the table and to his translucent / temples pressed laced cuffs, / sobbed out poems about cypresses.]

In the context of a drama centred on two deaths (real or merely imaginary; Nabokov does not give the reader a definite answer) – that of Stella, Gonville's wife of whom Edmund was secretly enamoured, and that of Edmund himself – the mention of cypresses acquires a special significance in view of a conventional association of the cypress with death. Of several evocations of cypresses in Byron's *Hours of Idleness* (the publication of which would have followed the fictitious events taking place in *Smert'*),[56] the closing stanza of "Love's Last Adieu!" is particularly relevant. This poem's protagonist (a "yon misanthrope shunning mankind" – an early incarnation of a Byronic hero, one who will never be able to recover fully from the effect of the "poison of love's last adieu"),

Who kneels to the God, on his altar of light,
Must myrtle and cypress, alternately, strew;
His myrtle, an emblem of purest delight,
His cypress, the garland of Love's last adieu.[57]

Thus the cypress – a symbol of the sorrow inflicted upon the poet by separation from the beloved, which can be metaphorically interpreted as a form of banishment, exile – enters Nabokov's early writing through Byron's mediation. While reference to a Byronic allusion in a 1923 verse drama may appear premature in the context of a conversation concerning the earliest stage in Nabokov's development as a translator, it is important to register that the image of a cypress with its Byronic associations makes an early appearance in Nabokov's version of Byron's "Oh! Snatched Away in Beauty's Bloom," where the last line of the opening stanza promises that a "wild cypress" will be waving in "tender gloom" over the tomb of a recently deceased beloved. An awareness of the presence of a Byronic subtext in many of Nabokov's Crimean poems collected in *Gornii put'* and elsewhere (composed either concurrently, or upon the completion of translation of the Byron poems) should encourage their reader to look further into an image that at first may appear to be a mere detail of an exotic landscape.[58] The iconic value of the cypress in Nabokov's writings may be demonstrated by the Crimean chapter of *Speak, Memory*, where Pushkin's banishment is associated with "naturalized cypresses and laurels."[59] The strong presence of a Byronic subtext in both Pushkinian and – as it becomes evident – Nabokovian exilic discourse, however, significantly enhances the appreciation of one of the writer's most cherished themes, while translation once again emerges not only as a medium crucial to formation of this theme, but also as a source of vital inspiration for an artist who from the very early stages of his creative career strove to occupy a place at the crossroads of literary traditions.

"Ein Lied von der Liebsten Mein": A Study in Fullness of Sound

Answering a question posed to him by Bayerischer Rundfunk journalists in 1971, Nabokov lamented his poor knowledge of the German language and lack of interest in German culture, but confessed that in his youth he translated "the Heine songs for a Russian contralto – who, incidentally, wanted the musically significant vowels to coincide in fullness of sound, and therefore I turned *Ich grolle nicht* into *Net, zloby net*, instead of the unsingable old version *Ya ne serzhus.'* "[60] The cumulative effect from Nabokov's work on the six *lieder* by Heinrich Heine in September 1918 amounted to much more than a mere success at providing Anna Ian-Ruban with a satisfactory rendition of Robert Schumann's famous setting of "Ich grolle nicht." By transposing those Heine lyrics into Russian, the young translator and poet joined a long and rich tradition of Heine reception in his homeland and made his own contribution to the peculiar phenomenon known as Russian Heineana. No less important, he came into direct contact with a writer who was the first to turn his position at the crossroads of cultures and languages into a source of inspiration.

No other foreign poet – including Goethe and Byron – exerted an influence on Russian poetry that would match that of the author of *Buch der Lieder* (Song Book). No other foreign poet inspired a comparable number of Russian adaptations, imitations, and parodies, compelling his countless Russian admirers to creativity, whatever the quality of those productions may have been. No other foreign poet got any closer to eclipsing an entire generation of native practitioners in the 1850s and beyond by becoming, in D.S. Mirsky's words, "more popular with the wide mass of the intelligentsia than any Russian poet."[61] No other foreign poet precipitated a tectonic shift in Russian prosody that revolutionized the way Russians conceive of literary poetry, in addition to enriching Russian literature with a set of distinct ("Heinean") themes and sensibilities. Apart from inspiring a veritable army of Russian imitators, Heinean lyricism and rhythms had a profound effect on such outstanding figures as Fëdor Tiutchev, Mikhail Lermontov, and Afanasii Fet. Last but not least, no other poet played a more significant role in the symbolist imagination of that idol of Nabokov's early youth, Aleksandr Blok.[62] The initial impression that the effect of Nabokov's encounter with Heine could not be restricted to his being able to oblige a *lieder* singer is confirmed by analysis of the archival documents pertaining to that event and its context.[63]

"Net, zloby net" (No, there is no anger), the version of "Ich grolle nicht" (I chide [you] not) Nabokov was to evoke in 1971, did not survive in any one of his Crimean albums. In a clear indication that the young poet-translator who painstakingly documented his experiments in verse and rhyme did not take much interest in that particular work, he never bothered to write it down, and the only reason we can talk about it today is that it produced a lasting impression on his younger cousin Sergei Nabokov (1902–98), who memorized it. Such an exceptional occurrence deserves an attentive treatment, promising to supply us with valuable information about Nabokov's tastes and preferences regarding translation, poetry, and music.

An early inkling of what may have triggered Nabokov's decision not to treat his work on "Ich grolle nicht" as a translation entitled to a place among his other literary experiments may be derived from a comparison of Heine's original and Schumann's adaptation of it. The eighteenth poem in the cycle "Lyrisches Intermezzo" (1822–3) of Heine's runaway bestseller *Buch der Lieder* (1827), "Ich grolle nicht, und wenn das Herz auch bricht" (I chide [you] not, and even though [my] heart breaks) occupies a carefully considered place in the cycle's lyrical plot.[64]

While iambic pentameters dominate this poem's prosodic constitution, on one significant occasion Heine chooses to deviate from this overarching pattern. In the poem's second line, "Ewig verlor'nes Lieb! ich grolle nicht" (Forever is lost love! I chide [you] not), the opening metrical foot is actually trochaic, which is to say choriambic (given that it is a feature of an otherwise resolutely iambic line, which in turn is a part of the larger unity of a poem composed in iambic pentameters).[65] While it may not be possible to reproduce the semantic and rhetorical emphasis put on the adverb *ewig* in the German by virtue of its strong position at the beginning of a line and its outstanding prosodic variance from the rest of the poem, to be faithful to the original, a poetic translation of "Ich grolle nicht, und wenn das Herz auch bricht" – especially one serving as its substitute in a musical setting – must attempt to reproduce at least one of its signature characteristics.

In Schumann's setting, the two quatrains of Heine's iambs grow into an impassioned poetic diatribe measuring almost double the original. The composer's liberal and insistent use of emphatic reiteration and inversion radically alters the original's appearance and emotional impact.[66] Schumann's adaptation of "Ich grolle nicht, und wenn das Herz auch bricht" is a classic example of a conflict that pits the integrity of a poetic text against a willful musical setting. Does the composer unleash the melodic potential concealed within the original, or does he use the original text as an excuse to voice his own emotions? For Eric Sams, Heine speaks "of sympathy, forgiveness, even a measure of reconciliation," whereas Schumann's adaptation tells a different story. "The vehement accents, the hammered chords, the declamatory style, all suggest the Old Testament rather than the New; the brooding tread of the bass minims sound menacing and retributive … Tension between music and words is heightened by Schumann's insistence on the phrase 'ich grolle nicht,' which he has six times to Heine's twice, thus protesting too much. The repetition of 'ewig verlornes Lieb' and 'wenn das Herz auch bricht' are also his."[67] Following in his colleague's wake, Stephen Walsh calls Schumann "an unscrupulous word-setter" who "misquoted" his literary sources, "sometimes inexplicably."[68] The musicologists concur that as much as a musical adaptation of Heine's lyrics, Schumann's *Dichterliebe* was a deeply personal expression of the composer's troubled passionate feelings for his future wife Clara.[69] Whether Nabokov wanted it or not, instead of supplying a superior version of Heine's original poem to Fëdor Berg's "Ia ne serzhus', pust' bol'no noet grud'" (I am not angry, let [my] breast ache painfully; 1863), it was Schumann's willful, resolutely appropriative vision of Heine's original that Nabokov had to accommodate first to fulfil Ian-Ruban's request to produce a new Russian version of this *lied*.

All things considered, Nabokov had every reason to be proud of his work on "Net, zloby net. Vsë glubzhe bol', ostrei" (No, there is no anger. All the deeper, sharper is pain).[70] In terms of respect for the integrity of the original text, it certainly was an improvement on the version by Berg rejected by Ian-Ruban. Composed with the aim of providing an aural match to Schumann's adaptation of Heine's poem, Berg's "Ia ne serzhus', pust' bol'no noet grud'" did exactly that but completely ignored various nuances distinguishing the original. A number of glaring semantic incongruities notwithstanding, this shallow denunciation of feminine frailty has persisted in remaining a staple in the repertoire of Russian male performers from Fëdor Shaliapin to this day.

Judging by the text memorized by Sergei Nabokov, his cousin's version of the poem succeeded where Berg's glossed over many of the original's nuances. Nabokov's version preserved the choriambic opening of the poem's second line (cf. "ewig verlor'nes Lieb, ich grolle nicht" and *schast'e navek ushlo, no zloby net*), while the richly expressive alliteration in the closing phrase of the first line, "wenn das Herz auch bricht," was echoed in *vsë glubzhe bol', ostrei* (cf. "bricht" and *ostrei*). And yet Nabokov never bothered to preserve "Net, zloby net" – probably because more than anything else it was meant to be a translation of Schubert's appropriative rendition of Heine's poem. This omission would also seem to suggest that Nabokov was primarily interested in coming into contact with his interlocutors without intermediaries. Those translations from Heine that he chose to preserve validate this hypothesis.[71]

Under the heading of "Perevody iz Geine" (Translations from Heine) Nabokov united his versions of five poems from *Buch der Lieder*, all of which had been set to music by Franz Schubert (*Schwanengesang*, D. 957, 1828) or Robert Schumann (*Dichterliebe*, op. 48, 1840). The date "IX-18" that appears under the two surviving copies of this cycle indicates that unlike the majority of Nabokov's early poetic translations, these were the result of a concerted effort that occupied him for a good few days, if not a considerable part of September 1918.[72]

The cycle begins with two poems from the "Lyrisches Intermezzo" in *Buch der Lieder*: "Ia dushu svoiu, lileia," a version of "Ich will meine Seele tauchen," followed by "O esli tsvetochki by znali," a translation of "Und wüsstens die Blumen, die kleinen" (And had [only] the flowers, the little ones, known). "Dvoinik" (The Double ["Tikhaia noch' i ulitsy dremliut," Quiet is the night and the streets are a-slumber]) is a translation of "Still ist die Nacht, es ruhen die Gassen" (Still is the night, and quiet are the alleyways) from "Die Heimkehr" (The Homecoming) is the third instalment. The fourth poem is entitled "Gorod" (City ["Na dal'nem nebosklone," On a distant skyline]); it is a translation of "Am fernen Horizonte" (On a distant horizon) from "Die Heimkehr." Nabokov's cycle closes with "Kogda zaslyshu ia pesniu," a rendition of "Hör ich das Liedchen klingen" ([As] I hear that little song resound) from "Lyrisches Intermezzo." The musical source that provided a middle ground for this particular encounter between Nabokov and Heine is revealed in the titles of the third and fourth poems of the cycle: "Dvoinik" (no. 3) comes from Schubert's *Schwanengesang*, "Der Doppelgänger" (D. 957, 13, which in its turn is a setting of Heine's "Still ist die Nacht, es ruhen die Gassen," from "Die Heimkehr"); "Gorod" (no. 4) owes its title to the same *Schwanengesang*, where it is named "Die Stadt" (Schubert's setting of "Am fernen Horizonte" [D. 957, 11], also borrowed from "Die Heimkehr"). The cycle, which opened with two pieces adapted by Schumann in his *Dichterliebe*, closes with yet another well-known setting of a Heine poem by Schumann.

Nabokov's translations of Heine differ radically from all of his other translations and the overwhelming majority of his original compositions from this period in one notable respect. Their prosody is nothing like that of the rest of his translations transposed into the steady, confident prosodic idiom of the Russian syllabotonic poetry. Be it Byron's eighteenth-century-influenced iambs, Petrarch's early Renaissance syllabic verse, or Verhaeren's French alexandrines, Nabokov's translations, in full accordance with the Russian tradition, render this variety of prosodic expression through the metrical devices sanctioned by the five-metre syllabotonic system of versification. The choriambic variation on the predominantly iambic metre found in the second line of "Ich grolle nicht, und wenn das Herz auch bricht" serves as an early warning that the prosodic medium for which Heine is deservedly well known is far less regular than the strictures of Russian versification would permit. Each and every one of the five poems selected for "Perevody iz Geine" departs from these strictures in a still more spectacular fashion: as far as the standards of nineteenth-century Russian literary poetry were concerned, these German poems were composed in a resolutely alien idiom. The freshness of the rhythmic cadence dominating these translations may have worn out considerably by now, yet in the autumn of 1918 these de-regularized rhythms had only recently become a standard medium of Russian literary poetry.

One of the secrets of *Buch der Lieder*'s success and lasting popularity was in Heine's genius at affecting the unfettered rhythmicity of the artless German folk song and putting it to the services of his sophisticated literary imitations. Any attempt to find a close – let alone exact – aural match for this medium in Russian would entail breaking free of the strictures of the classic syllabotonic versification, which depended on the repeated alternation of stressed and unstressed syllables per verse line occurring in positions determining any given poem's metre (iambic, trochaic, amphibrachic, dactylic, or anapestic). While the metre of the five poems Nabokov selected for this cycle may be interpreted as a variation on the binary (iambic, trochaic) cadence, to view it in those terms would be to ignore the fact that they exist according to a different set of rules. These poems are composed on the principles of the tonic system of versification, which depends on the regularity in the number of accented syllables per verse line, and not on the notion of a metric foot crucial to the syallabotonic system. Would a nineteen-year-old poet-translator raised on the classics of syllabotonic verse have been able to rise to such a challenge? Would he have been able to see past the limitations of the syllabotonic system, his chief medium of expression, to get closer to the heart of Heinean musicality? To answer these questions is to answer the question about the degree of young Nabokov's integration into the innovative culture of the Silver Age of Russian poetry and his ability to appreciate the formal innovation of its chief representative and his favourite poet, Aleksandr Blok.

Apart from recognizing in Heine his mystical double, Blok constructed an idiosyncratic notion of the German poet's place in European culture, a notion integrated into his symbolist historiosophy. Challenging an entire reception tradition of Heine as a poet consonant with the aspirations of the liberal intelligentsia, Blok advanced his own vision of Heine as a poet who had captured in his verse an "unfathomable accumulation of irreconcilable contradictions." This accumulation manifested itself through the "music of the future" that persisted in his poetry despite all the attempts on the part of "European civilization" to mute it.[73] As far as Blok was concerned, that "music of the future" was heard through the unconventional and asymmetric – by the prevalent standards of contemporaneous Russian versification – rhythms of Heine's lyrics. Upon realizing that the vast body of Russian translations had either ignored or misrepresented this aspect of the poet's legacy, Blok championed the creation of a new, exemplary set of equimetric translations of Heine's lyrics, leading by example: his *Nochnye chasy* (Nocturnal Hours; 1911) featured a special section consisting of his translations of twelve poems by Heine.[74]

Blok was exceptionally well qualified to spearhead a renewal in the Russian appreciation of the German poet. With his immensely influential poems of the early 1900s, he had succeeded in legitimizing tonic versification as an accepted medium of Russian poetry, broadening its formal arsenal together with readers' appreciation of it. According to the chief explicator of the complexities of Russian versification, Mikhail Gasparov, this realization of a long-suppressed potential of tonic prosody amounted to a "modernist poetic revolution."[75]

Nabokov's fledgling poetic diction in his renditions of these poems may not rival that of his predecessors, whose ranks included the likes of Blok and Innokentii Annenskii; his solutions to the problems posed by the imagery of these poems may not have been as ingenious. What is remarkable about these versions is the degree of prosodic fidelity he was able to attain in his attempt to replicate the aural effect of Heine's verse. Thus "Ia dushu svoiu, lileia" ("Ich will meine Seele tauchen") maintains the ratio of thirteen binary (iamb-like) units to nine ternary (anapest-like) ones, a close match to Heine's fourteen binaries to eight ternaries. "O esli tsvetochki by znali" ("Und wüssten's die Blumen, die kleinen") has thirty-four binaries to ten ternaries, while the original has thirty-six binaries to eight ternaries. "Na dal'nem nebosklone" ("Am fernen Horizonte") has twenty-four binaries and nine ternaries compared to Heine's twenty-six binaries and seven ternaries; "Kogda zaslyshu ia pesniu" ("Hör' ich das Liedchen klingen"), eighteen binaries and four ternaries to the German original's twenty binaries and three ternaries. It is "Tikhaia noch' i ulitsy dremliut" ("Still ist die Nacht, es ruhen die Gassen") that represents a true feat of translingual ingenuity: it is an exact metrical replica of Heine's original.

It would be a simplification, however, to reduce the ambition that guided Nabokov's crafting an entire poetic cycle out of the disparate Heine *lieder* he had encountered while fulfilling Ian-Ruban's request to formal achievement alone. In a move that recalls Heine's renowned mastery at uniting short lyrical poems with the aid of emotional plotlines forming the narrative core of his poetic cycles, the five poems in Nabokov's cycle are made to recount a story of their own. "Ia dushu svoiu, lilea," with its evocation of happiness the protagonist experienced upon becoming intimate with his mistress, provides its point of departure. This story's second instalment, "O esli tsvetochki by znali," complicates this idyll with an account of amorous torment and heartbreak (*ved' serdtse mne razbila, razbila mne ona*). "Dvoinik" ("Tikhaia noch' i ulitsy dremliut") develops and deepens this dramatic premise considerably. The simple love story at the heart of the cycle acquires tangible spatial and temporal perspectives: now its action is depicted against an urban backdrop and shifted into the distant past. The heartbreak causes an unmistakably tragic personality split in the protagonist, who is reduced to reasoning with his own self, as he is unable to break the vicious cycle of constant return to the pitiful ghost of his lost happiness. "Gorod" ("Na dal'nem nebosklone") complicates the story still further by augmenting the cycle's leitmotifs of heartbreak and longing with that of nostalgia for the city that provided his happiness with unforgettable scenery. The city where the protagonist claims to have lost his love appears to be no longer accessible to him, since he travels there in a dark, hazy dream (*mrachnyi, tumannyi son*). "Kogda zaslyshu ia pesniu," the fifth and last poem in the cycle, solidifies the overall lachrymose tonality with an evocation of solitary tears as the only outlet for the protagonist's "limitless sorrow" (*bezmernaia skorb'*) and "tempestuous suffering" (*burnoe stradan'e*).

Using another poet's works to piece together a cycle of his own cannot but point to Nabokov's pursuing an individual agenda that runs parallel to the ostensible pretext of providing Ian-Ruban with more precise Russian versions of the German *lieder*. It would hardly be an exaggeration to infer that the lovelorn nostalgia that permeates "Perevody iz Geine" owes a good deal of its inspiration to the translator's frame of mind at the time of this cycle's composition. When it comes to detailing its subject's past, Nabokov's autobiography may be at turns reticent or revealing, but on this particular occasion it provides a clue as to the emotional stimulus behind his desire to use Heine's words and images to narrate the story of his attachment to a distant lover. In chapter 12 of

Speak, Memory, Nabokov recalls that during the months that preceded his departure from the Crimea, he "did nothing but write to and think of" his Petersburg love "Tamara."[76] By employing a subtler appropriative technique than Schumann followed in using Heine's poems to express his amorous frustrations, Nabokov managed to encode references to his plight into his most exact replication of someone else's words, images, and rhythms. This process, however, was not as one-sided as it might seem at first. As he laboured to saturate a cycle of Heine poems with subtle echoes of his own plight, Heine's images found a way to make a lasting impression on him as well. Although this is true of all the poems in the cycle, the remarkable afterlife of "Still ist die Nacht, es ruhen die Gassen" ("Der Doppelgänger") in Nabokov's work supplies this thesis with a particularly persuasive proof.

A comparison of "Tikhaia noch' i ulitsy dremliut" ("Dvoinik"), the equimetrical translation of "Still ist die Nacht, es ruhen die Gassen" ("Der Doppelgänger"), with its model shows that to create the prosodic replica of the original – its interlingual double – Nabokov made a number of deliberate formal and semantic adjustments.

Each one of the translation's three quatrains paraphrases the original liberally enough. Among the examples of this technique we may consider the elaborate "ray of love" that "shone brightly" (*luch liubvi siial*), a replacement for the simple phrase "mein Schatz" (l. 2), a stylistic shift that comes with the conversion of the elevated term "Antlitz" (l. 7) to the rather matter-of-fact "face" (*litso*, l. 5), or the loss of the expressive, vivid, and ironic verb "äffen" ("Was äffst du nach mein Liebesleid" – "Why do you ape my lovesickness," l. 10) that fell victim to the tension between prosodic purity and semantic fidelity. All things considered, even if we take into account the fact that to navigate his way between the Scylla and Charibdis of literary translation Nabokov had to sacrifice the original's rhyming scheme and retain rhymes on only the odd lines, his translation is an impressive achievement capable of holding its own in competition with Blok and Annenskii.[77]

Compared with Musset's and Régnier's treatment of the "doppelgänger" motif, the Heinean interpretation appears to be its most articulate, indeed consummate, formulation. Nabokov's encounter with it, his painstaking work on finding his own words to verbalize it, amounts to the point of departure for his lifelong use of this motif in his own writing.

Along with the remaining four poems in the cycle, Nabokov's "Dvoinik" is a reminder that literary translation is an art of compromise, a never-ending vacillation between poetic licence and fidelity with good taste for a pivot. It should not escape our attention that when a major writer appears at the shifting centre of this vacillation, the effect of such struggles may not be limited to the obvious result alone. Behind the curtain of the complex negotiation regarding what may or may not be retained in a translation, a no less intriguing process is taking place. Preoccupied as he was with the competing tasks of providing a faithful reproduction of the original while imbuing it with personal significance, as translator Nabokov was forced to pay close attention to the particulars of Heine's execution of the doppelgänger theme. We cannot afford to forget that while Nabokov the young poet had yet to make any use of this theme in his original compositions, Nabokov the translator had already accumulated considerable experience in tackling it. His version of Alfred de Musset's "La Nuit de décembre" had been his first statement to that effect, his interaction with Régnier's "Allusion à Narcisse" a second, while his Heinean doppelgänger could only have been a major step toward internalizing this theme still further. It is also a piece of hard evidence proving once and for all that Nabokov had a keen interest in this theme. Contrary to his protestations of indifference to the doppelgänger theme ("a frightful bore"),[78] before he turned his virtuoso variations on it into a plotline critical for the integrity of such accomplished works as *The Eye* (1930), *Despair* (1934), *Invitation to a Beheading* (1936), *Lolita* (1955), *Pnin* (1957), and *Pale Fire* (1962), Nabokov had clearly paid close attention to its manifestations in the works of his interlocutors. Notwithstanding all the relevance of such writers as Gogol and Dostoevskii for Nabokov's ownership of this theme, it was his close active interaction with the doubles conjured up by Musset, Régnier, and Heine that marked this theme's entrance into the world of Nabokovian artifice. To say that Musset's, Régnier's, or Heine's treatments of this theme were more important than those by others would be an oversimplification, yet to argue that Nabokov's active work on recasting their visions in his words led to their acquiring a special status within the pool of the allusions at his disposal is not an exaggeration. His last, unfinished, and most mysterious work offers strong evidence in support of this observation.

Eager to orient *The Original of Laura* within the published corpus of Nabokov's work, scholars have commented on the vividness with which the doppelgänger motif manifests itself even within the limited space of the novel's surviving fragments.[79] *The Original of Laura* abounds in replications and doubles; some of them echo his earlier creations, some seem to become reversed mirror reflections of the phenomena endemic to the novel, only to reveal themselves as the likenesses of other characters from Nabokov's vast field of literary references. Finding himself on the last threshold and having a considerable array of possibilities to choose from, Nabokov ensured that Heine would not be omitted from the last round of his game of literary references.

The novel's wayward, promiscuous, and cruel heroine becomes a source of inspiration for a number of writers and lovers, proving herself a rather unconventional incarnation of a literary convention: "her exquisite bone structure immediately slipped into a novel – became in fact the secret structure of that novel, besides supporting a number of poems."[80] Further on Nabokov parades an entire gallery of jilted lovers: the narrator, who sees the heroine off after the tryst with which the novel opens, another lover whom she humiliates during a telephone conversation held in the narrator's presence, and her husband.[81] The mackintosh hastily thrown on top of the wretch's pyjamas may or may not be signalling the presence of an "intertextual echo" constituting a Joycean parallel, as Yannicke Chupin and René Alladaye have suggested.[82] Amid an array of ambiguous markers, the description of Flora getting out of her taxi "at the corner of Heine street," however, does set into motion the mechanism of a precise literary reference. It links the image of a spurned lover "wringing his hands" outside his former mistress's house with its source in the second quatrain of Heine's "Still ist die Nacht, es ruhen die Gassen," the protagonist of which recognizes in a man wringing his hands under his beloved's windows his own former self.

"For this Kingdom and this Glory and this Power and this Pride": Nabokov, Jean Richepin, and the Vicissitudes of History

Today the poet, dramatist, short-story writer, and novelist Jean Richepin (1849–1926) is hardly a celebrity, yet he was no stranger to the stupendously well-read Nabokov household. The systematic catalogue of Vladimir Dmitrievich Nabokov's personal library lists no fewer than three titles by Richepin: two books of poems – *Les Blasphèmes* (Blasphemous [Poems]; 1884) and *La Chanson de gueux* (The Song of the Ragged Ones; 1895); and a five-act drama in verse – *La Martyre* (1898), depicting Rome in second century CE.[83] To his contemporaries Richepin was known as a force to be reckoned with. Once a distinguished student at

L'École normale superiéure, he went on to garner first-hand life experience as a vagabond, sailor, soldier, stevedore, mercenary, journalist, and actor before gaining hard-won popularity as a poet, dramatist, and writer whose accomplishements became a model for many.[84] He might have become a member of the establishment upon turning fifty-nine, an occupant of the second chair at L'Académie française where Alfred de Musset had once sat, but, as Harry E. Wedeck put it, to his death this "immortal" remained "the most forceful, the most prolific and most articulate" of the French Bohemian poets, a bearer of the torch lit by François Villon.[85]

Richepin's "Bohémien" ("Gypsy") is a first-person narrative written from the point of view of a Gypsy traveller possessing the longevity of Agasfer the Wandering Jew. In keeping with his rebellious temper, Richepin turns the legend of that damned eternal upside down: instead of being a cursed wretch, his nameless Gypsy wanderer is something of a superman. An ironic observer of human hubris, thanks to his immortality he is able to see through not mere individual delusions of grandeur but also through those nourished and cherished by entire nations (ll. 1–20).[86]

In a sign of his eagerness to refocus the thrust of the sarcasm that permeates the poem, Nabokov called his version of "Le Bohémien" "Strannik" (Wanderer; 18 October 1918), replacing Richepin's "Gypsy" with a less specific, more comprehensive epithet. Having made this adjustment, he employed in his translation an unusual poetic measure. By choosing to convey Richepin's alexandrines by iambic heptameters, he aimed at being as attentive to and accommodating of the original imagery as possible in a rhyming translation. Richepin's precise, straightforward imagery fares exceedingly well in Nabokov's equilinear version, which only occasionally trades its model's enclosing rhymes for alternate ones. A comparison of the translated text with its original demonstrates that it amounts to a perceptive close reading.

As he traverses countries as well as millennia retracing the steps of Richepin's protagonist, Nabokov's wanderer repeatedly becomes the subject of his interlocutors' scorn as they, being unaware of his supernatural longevity, expose themselves as petty creatures with a minuscule attention span, quite incapable of appreciating their evanescence. As befits mere mortals, they mistake their limited notion of time for eternity and parade their ignorance to a stranger who appreciates the extent of their folly (ll. 1–20).[87]

It is difficult not to get the impression that Nabokov's journey to the heart of Richepin's sarcasm was driven by his desire to delve deeper into the essence of his protagonist's "I," to find a way to identify with his sense of superiority. His supernatural longevity notwithstanding, Richepin's Bohemian is a not-so-thinly veiled autobiographical hero, a projection of the author's self-image onto the world of philistines of whom he was so openly disdainful. A Gallic counterweight to Matthew Arnold's scholar-Gypsy, this Bohemian is clearly a poet, and his longevity is a metaphor for the immortal gift of creativity, allowing his thought to pierce the millennia and afford him a supernatural perspective on the human race. The mental procedure associated with the assumption of this poem's "I" by its translator was significant: by borrowing, adjusting, and trying on the persona of Richepin's all-knowing, world-weary, and sardonic protagonist, Nabokov continued to work toward the goal of acquiring a novel way of conceiving of himself as a poet for whom deracination, all premonitions to the opposite notwithstanding, might become a source of strength, not weakness. This aspect of Nabokov's encounter with Richepin, however, was far from the only interest he would have been pursuing as he was lending his voice to the thoughts of the French vagabond-rhetorician.

Nabokov's "Strannik" is a contemplation of historical ironies and vicissitudes quite literally crafted on the ruins of a once-mighty empire engulfed by an internecine civil strife. It is a big "if" whether Rudyard Kipling's "Russia to the Pacifists" (1918) with its famous lines –

> God rest you, peaceful gentlemen, but give us leave to pass.
> We go to dig a nation's grave as Great as England was.
> For this Kingdom and this Glory and this Power and this Pride,
> Three hundred years it flourished – in three hundred days it died.[88]

– had reached the Nabokovs in the Crimea the year it was published. The sarcastic pathos of "Le Bohémien," akin to the solemnity of Kipling's lines, however, attracted Nabokov to this particular poem at that particular moment in Russia's history. In the course of his conversation with Richepin – a poet whom he had known from his childhood, a good deal of which had been spent in his father's library – Nabokov found the words to express his reasoning behind his decision to stay above the fray at a time when the outcome of the Russian civil war was being determined.

In crafting his "Strannik" out of Richepin's "Bohémien," Nabokov was pursuing a particular goal. His attentive retelling of it became an early stepping stone on the path toward his self-realization as a poet-nomad whose one and only true homeland was his art, his own personal gateway to detached perspectives on the deeds of men. As will become clear from the following narrative, in 1918 Nabokov was far from being ready to synthesize his own experience of an uprooted, nomadic life reflected in his own early poetry with similar experiences and reflections associated with Pushkin, Byron, Heine, Musset, and Richepin. In 1918 he was only setting out on that personal spiritual journey, only beginning to evolve an understanding of the historical calamities that had forced him and his family from their idyllic Petersburg abode. As the hitherto untold aspect of Nabokov's evolution will tell, "Strannik" was certainly an important step in that direction, destined as it was to contribute to some of the most significant statements of his self-determination as a poet of exile.

Chapter Two

Before Nabokov: Sirin Translates (1919–1939)

Nowhere else do the interactive, dialogic origins of Nabokov's art manifest themselves more prominently than in his early translations. Before it became subject to playful transfiguration in some of his most famous works, the doppelgänger motif acquired for him the tangible personal connotations linked with Alfred de Musset, Henri de Régnier, and Heinrich Heine; with the aid of Émile Verhaeren and Francesco Petrarca, he had developed an individual idiom for his transcendental intuitions. Mayne Reid, Pierre Louÿs, and Louis Bouilhet provided him with opportunities to try his hand at broaching erotic subjects; Byron and Jean Richepin gave him a chance to begin laying the foundation of a distinct artistic identity. For all its outward incongruity, this rich and strange amalgamation of sources, this motley, quadrilingual crew of interlocutors so vastly dissimilar in stature gives us a better idea of the Nabokov to come than any other piece of biographical intelligence or sociocultural characterization. This improbable assembly of poets and thinkers was to be firmly ensconced in the writer's allusive imagination and tenacious memory, as he continued to welcome new entrants who joined an ongoing conversation that had begun in Russia.

"Out of the Strong, Sweetness": Expatriation, Transition, Translation

"Epitaph" by Walter Savage Landor (1775–1864) is the earliest surviving translation from what may be termed Nabokov's British period. Although it remained unpublished in his lifetime, its date of "13-VII-19" places it among the texts that yielded some of the earliest publications signed "V. Sirin."

Landor's absence is conspicuous in the catalogue of Vladimir Dmitrievich Nabokov's library. It is reasonable to suspect that he became a discovery for the future writer: it is likely that Nabokov found Landor in an anthology during his stay at 6 Elm Park Gardens, Chelsea, in anticipation of his first year at Trinity College, Cambridge. The quatrain that piqued Nabokov's interest may well be Landor's best-remembered work:

> I strove with none, for none was worth my strife.
> Nature I loved, and, next to nature, Art;
> I warm'd both hands before the fire of Life;
> It sinks, and I am ready to depart.[1]

Known to Nabokov as "Epitaph," in different anthologies it bears the title of "Dying Speech of an Old Philosopher" or "Finis." Written in 1849, it marked Landor's seventy-fourth birthday, and at first glance it may not immediately betray the secret of its appeal to a twenty-year-old Russian Anglophile. Closer inspection, however, reveals the congeniality of this terse statement to the Nabokov the world would get to know decades later. As is often the case with Nabokov's early translations, the appearance of Landor's "Epitaph" on the horizon of our familiarity with his mature subjects and themes demonstrates a close integration with some of Nabokov's deeply held convictions.

"Epitaph" asserts a true artist's independence from the dictates of public opinion and critical judgment. What is remarkable about Landor's variation on this theme is how it amplifies his statement of artistic autonomy with a testimony to his passionate involvement with nature. It presages Nabokov's numerous declarations to the same effect, from his protestations of freedom from literary influences to his self-professed indifference to criticism and his elevation of his mirror reflection to the status of his ideal reader. "Epitaph" puts contemplation of nature on the same pedestal where the admiration of art is to be found traditionally, in an uncanny prefiguration of such a programmatic Nabokovian statement as "A Discovery" (1943).[2]

The "dying speech of an old philosopher" contains words Nabokov was to make his own in the course of his subsequent career in letters, not least in his most consequential – and divisive – work in translation. Looking back at his labour on Pushkin's masterpiece in 1954, Nabokov recognized in it an amalgamation of natural science and artistic intuition, a blend of "a poet's patience" with "scholastic passion" ("On Translating *Eugene Onegin*"). Examining Nabokov's rendition of

Landor's "Epitaph" in light of the translator's subsequent work and pronouncements, we recognize in it one of the earliest formulations of one of his most cherished ambitions, his attempt to build a bridge between the natural sciences and verbal art. This makes it difficult to overlook a significant discrepancy distinguishing Nabokov's version of Landor's "Epitaph" from its model:

> Ни съ кѣмъ не дѣлилъ я борьбы:
> Ктó цѣли моей былъ достоинъ?
> Природу любилъ я,
> и рядомъ с природой – искусство.
> Я обѣ руки согрѣвалъ
> предъ огнёмъ бытія.
> Онъ гаснетъ. Готовъ я уйти.[3]

> [With no one did I share a fight: / *Who* was worthy of my goal? Nature I loved, / and next to nature – art. Both hands did I warm / before the fire of existence. / It is dying. I am ready to leave.]

Nabokov's resetting of Landor's original does not attempt to match its model's terseness: to Landor's four lines Nabokov has seven. This extension amounts to a refusal to honour the original's chief formal feature, its epigrammatic quality. In a further departure from the original, Nabokov substitutes Landor's "strife" with "goal" (*tsel'*, l. 2).

While Nabokov is far from doing away with the moribund tonality of the original, his version of the poem presents a more forward-looking variation on Landor's theme. The past tense that dominates all but the last line of this miniature cannot hide the fact that the translator chooses to interpret Landor's strife as something that may well continue in the future – odd as it may sound in a poem bearing so unequivocal a title as "Epitaph." As far as this translator was concerned, the strife associated with finding a fitting expression for his individual love of nature and art was ahead of him. At this point in his development it was a goal and not an accomplishment, and with the aid of Landor's prompting this goal found its articulation.

After tackling Landor on 13 July, on 14 and 15 July 1919 Nabokov turned to "The Sheep" and "Out of the Strong, Sweetness," by Seamus O'Sullivan (James Sullivan Starkey, 1879–1958). Almost two years later, these two versions were published in the 5 June 1921 issue of the Berlin-based Russian émigré daily, *Rul'* (The Rudder).

Nabokov's unexpected interest in O'Sullivan, a rather obscure representative of the Irish Literary Revival, may puzzle even more than his interest in Landor. As Nabokov's transcription of the poet's manifestly Goidelic pseudonym suggests, he did not know how to pronounce it – having come across the poems in an anthology, he did not feel like learning more about their author, clearly finding the poems themselves congenial.[4]

The unrhymed, mostly ternary dimeter of "The Sheep" (unorthodox as it may seem against the background of other works in Nabokov's early translating repertoire) is not the most striking formal feature of the poem. What makes this thirty-two-liner noteworthy is its lexical sparseness and effective use of repetition and inversion. A slow procession of sheep (or pale shapes moving against the darker background of the twilight) wending their way down a winding road in an unnamed town, the lulling incantatory intonation in which this picture is described by the poet all suggest an almost somnambulistic setting. This impression is tacitly reinforced in Nabokov's version, where the sheep make a slightly incongruous appearance on the street of a city (*gorod*; cf. "town" in the original) – the poem clearly captures the plight of an insomniac engaged in the act of counting sheep.

Both manuscript versions of the poem corroborate the absence of a subject-verb agreement in the first sentence (*stado ovets … prokhodiat*, not *stado … prokhodit*, ll. 1, 4), a textual feature Nabokov's modern Russian editors interpret as a typo.[5] The a-grammatical nature of this turn of speech is so self-evident, however, that the fact that it has persisted in spite of having gone through the hands of a number of sophisticated native speakers of Russian gives rise to a suspicion that it is intentional.[6] Although nothing of the kind can be observed in the original, this lack of grammatical agreement can be taken as a sign of the translator's desire to portray a transitional state of consciousness. As they pass before the poet's eyes, the sheep set into motion the mysterious machinery of recollection. The "memories" of the original, which correspond to "bygone days" (*proshlye dni*) of the translation, take the form of a slow procession of pale shapes across the viewer's field of vision.[7]

Both in the manuscripts and in the *Rul'* publication of 1921, "The Sheep" ("Ovtsy") is followed by another O'Sullivan poem, the title of which appears in its intact English variant. The title phrase "Out of the Strong, Sweetness" comes from chapter 14 of the Old Testament's Book of Judges, where Samson asks a group of Philistines to "expound" a riddle: "Out of the eater came forth meat, and out of the strong came forth sweetness." Before he divulged it to his cunning Philistine wife, Samson alone knew the solution of the riddle: en route to the Philistines he had encountered a lion that he – assisted by the Spirit of God – tore apart; upon revisiting the scene he discovered that "there was a swarm of bees in the mouth of the lion, and a honey-comb." Helpful as it is, this biblical reference does not quite expound the riddle posed by the English title of a poem translated into Russian. Why did Nabokov leave it as it was, why did he not provide his Russian audience with an equally sonorous and meaningful Russian title (*iz sil'nogo, sladkoe*), missing his chance to evoke the iconic representation of the same Old Testament episode in a famous Russian landmark, the Samson and the Lion fountain in Peterhoff?

It is likely that for Nabokov the English title of O'Sullivan's poem was one of its most valuable emblematic attributes, since it contained an echo of a precious recollection of home, an echo that Nabokov simply had to preserve intact. In his memoir Nabokov painstakingly recreates the idyllic atmosphere of his prosperous, cosmopolitan childhood. Chapter 4 of *Speak, Memory* opens with a catalogue of the material tokens of Anglo-Saxon civilization that surrounded the author at home. One entry in this catalogue is particularly sumptuous:

> At breakfast, Golden Syrup imported from London would entwist with its golden coils the revolving spoon from which enough of it had slithered onto a piece of Russian bread and butter.[8]

The first time the phrase "Out of the strong came forth sweetness" appeared on the label of Lyle's Golden Syrup was at the end of the nineteenth century, when the pious Scotsman Abram Lyle came from Greenock to London. Lyle founded a prosperous sugar-refining business, which was later to provide early twentieth-century England with one of its most recognizable commercial logos, that of Tate and Lyle's Golden Syrup. There is little doubt that the title of O'Sullivan's poem captured Nabokov's attention by reminding him of the English idyll of his St Petersburg childhood, one he was unable to relive in the real England of the early months of his British exile. As far as this translator was concerned, the appropriate Russian biblical reference, for all its aural richness and evocative potency, was no match for the English phrase with its host of personal associations, something that rendered the title of the O'Sullivan poem untranslatable.

All this is not to say that the poem itself would have been of little interest to the translator. At the centre of "Out of the Strong, Sweetness" is yet another astral image, presented against the background of an unorthodox cosmogony, by no means completely at ease with the poem's Old Testament title. "The dawn of the world," "chaos half-dispelled ... nebulous sea and land" – these images paint a picture of freshly created life by combining the elements of the Old Testament ("tremulous watery plains") with ancient Greek and Oriental cosmogonies ("chaos ... the eyes of gods"). While this newborn world is uninhabited by man, the first signs of terrestrial life are already present: "And there alone in the grey, / Slender and gentle and shy, / Large-eyed with wonder, and trembling, / A herd of deer."[9]

The wonder in the eyes of the animals is understandable: they have just come to life and have yet to become accustomed to their existence. In the poem's last stanza the deer are awakened from their state of bewilderment and gently prodded into discovering what from now on will be their natural domain. The poem portrays the omnipotent gods – "the strong" of the poem's title – as a formidable yet benevolent force. Their mirth ("the laughter of gods," l. 8) is but an expression of the heaven-dwellers' delight ("sweetness") with creatures that have no need to puzzle out the mystery behind their existence. This universal harmony would be irreparably upset were a querying human mind to enter it – thus the ideal state of "sweetness" becomes a metaphor for an idyll brought to life by the poet's and the reader's mutual awareness of the prelapsarian nature of this fragile vision. O'Sullivan's poetic challenge to the Old Testament notion of a monotheistic wrathful deity must have appealed to Nabokov: it is the harmony, the "sweetness" of this poem that is amplified in his Russian version.

Indifferent to O'Sullivan's patriotism, unappreciative of his penname's nationalistic connotations, Nabokov was touched by the mystically inclined Irishman's poetic insights. Whereas "The Sheep" was a study in an insomniac's lovelorn nostalgia, "Out of the Strong, Sweetness" amalgamated the Old Testament hermeticism with theosophic pantheism. It asserted an unorthodox world view enlivened by the benevolent laughter of the gods shown in the act of communion with the meekest of their creatures. A minor episode of his early career in letters, Nabokov's discourse with O'Sullivan was full of significance for his future articulations of his intuition of a similarly munificent universal order. Motivated by his ambition to establish an individual poetics of metaphysical insight, he initiated a dialogue with the author of a successful poetic representation of comparable principles. As such, this vestige of Nabokov's conversation with O'Sullivan lifts the veil concealing the evolution of his ability to communicate his individual world view. As he absorbed and retold his interlocutor's vision, Nabokov found a way to encrypt a cherished childhood memory into his response to O'Sullivan's utterance.

On 1 August 1919, Nabokov wrote another chapter in his lifelong association with Alfred de Musset. Unlike Landor or O'Sullivan, the author of "La Nuit de décembre" was no stranger to his young translator; returning to Musset after discovering new poets must have been akin to revisiting a school friend. It is no surprise, then, that Nabokov should have turned to Musset for help in articulating a notion of paramount importance. "Rappelle-toi (*vergiss mein nicht*). Paroles faites sur la musique de Mozart" (Remember [*forget me not*]; 1843) is an appeal for remembrance encased in three nine-line stanzas. One of the better-known short lyrics by the author of the "nuits," "Rappelle-toi" could not have remained unknown for Nabokov. It seems that the implications of his separation from Russia compelled him to reassess this poem's significance and relevance to his predicament.

Musset's poem is a thoroughly competent exercise in creating a short lyric centred on the motif of lovesick despondency, expressed in a tightly controlled, almost formulaic, poetic utterance. Its three stanzas comprise lines of varying length united by a single rhyme scheme (ababccddd). Each of the stanzas begins and ends in a passionate appeal to the poem's anonymous addressee: "Rappelle-toi." The author of the German *lied* that inspired Musset is unknown, and, contrary to the subtitle of the French poem, its musical setting is not by Mozart.[10] In Nabokov's version, however, Musset's poem is brought to life by the translator's desire to instil it with a meaning that is intensely personal – a feature that may be obscured by Nabokov's careful replication of the many characteristics of the poem's compositional facade, such as the anaphoric beginning and the epistrophic conclusion of each of the three stanzas and the overall rhyming scheme. The wording of the original poem's second stanza contains a clue as to why it might have appealed to Nabokov at a specific moment in his life, at a particular stop in his exilic itinerary.

In Musset's poem, grief ("chagrin") and the eternal separation inflicted on two suffering people by the fates ("les destinées / M'auront de toi pour jamais séparé") are aggravated by exile ("l'exil"). It is hard to dismiss the impression that Nabokov's version of the same stanza focuses on the circumstances of his personal predicament, placing the suffering protagonist at the centre of the fragment's composition:

> О вспомяни, когда насъ рокъ мятежный
> разъединитъ; когда въ чужомъ краю
> устану я, бездомный, безнадежный,
> [13] отъ непогодъ, – о вспомяни мою
> печальную любовь, послѣднее прощанье.
> Кто любитъ – для того, что время, что изгнанье!
> Пока не смолкнетъ сердца звонъ,
> [17] тебѣ твердить всё будетъ онъ:
> о вспомяни ...[11]

[O remember, when rebellious fate / separates us; when in an alien land / I will grow weary, homeless, hopeless, / of adverse weather – O remember my / sad love, last farewell. / To him who loves – both time and exile are the same! / As long as [my] heart keeps ringing, / it will be repeating to you: / O remember.]

Through Musset's mediation, one of the key concepts of Nabokov's oeuvre – "l'exil" / *izgnanie* / exile – makes its first appearance in this translation as a conscious reference to Nabokov's own predicament in recognition of the fact that his separation from his homeland may be lasting, if not eternal. The translator's awareness of his English banishment called for a name that would be expansive enough, capable of encompassing the enormity of the transition he was undergoing. It is no accident that the word "exile" (*izgnanie*) acquires the status of one of the most frequent token attributes of Nabokov's writings in 1919 and after, yet Musset's assistance in finding a fitting poetic term for defining this exiled poet's plight proves to have been crucial.

François Rabelais's "Barbarian Spirit": Nikolka Persik as Colas Breugnon

What undertaking marks the point at which Nabokov's literary career can be said to have begun in earnest? Many young people of his generation and background dabbled in poetry and translation, kept literary albums, and produced self-published verse collections, only to abandon these activities in favour of more practical pursuits. Completed in March 1921 and published in November 1922, *Nikolka Persik,*

Nabokov's adaptation of Romain Rolland's novel *Colas Breugnon* (1919) marked the beginning of his career as a professional writer. The outline of a voluptuous naked woman on this book's cover must not mislead anyone: Russianizing this frivolous stylization of a sixteenth-century Burgundian tale became an exacting rite of passage. Beginning as a wager with his father, work on this full-length novel did not merely put to the test Nabokov's dedication to writing, it taught him a number of lessons about the composition of artistic prose and the limits of the permissible in literature. More important, however, was that this close encounter with Rolland, an internationally recognized novelist and activist, forced him to countenance a committed and articulate proponent of ideas diametrically opposed to many convictions that Nabokov the mature writer and thinker was to formulate and espouse.

Scholars have focused on the formal challenges Nabokov faced in crafting *Nikolka Persik*, an aspect of his work the writer himself was eager to emphasize above all else. To Andrew Field he described Rolland's novel "a Vesuvius of words, an eruption of old French lexicon ... an uninterrupted game of rhythmic figures, assonances and internal rhymes, chains of alliterations, rows of synonyms ... puns, proverbs and jokes, flourishes and refrains, sayings and charms."[12] Brian Boyd underscores that while Nabokov relished a chance to prove himself worthy of his father's dare by demonstrating his readiness to apply his mastery of modern and medieval French and Russian (his newly chosen specialization), he had no respect for Rolland the writer. Critical and scholarly reception of this work has largely been limited by this view: thus Elizabeth Klosty Beaujour has relegated *Nikolka Persik* to one of the many of young Nabokov's "bravura performances, chosen and executed for their difficulty."[13] Yet what if restricting our understanding of the Nabokov-Rolland encounter to the formal aspects of this undertaking does not do justice to this complex work? Can we be certain that *Nikolka Persik*, a text with no precedent among Nabokov's juvenilia, has no secrets to divulge?

Iurii Ofrosimov greeted *Nikolka Persik* on the pages of *Rul'*, where excerpts from the novel were serialized prior to its publication. "Joyous is the book about Nikolka Persik and joyous, fresh is its translation," Ofrosimov proclaimed before stating that "[Nabokov] has preserved this book's juicy spirit well ... The style and spirit of the book have been transmitted very successfully, at times superbly."[14] Evaluating Nabokov's work some fifty years later, Soviet translation scholar Vladimir Shor came to the opposite conclusion, denying this émigré artefact any success at preserving the original's *Volksgeist*.[15] Harsh and partial as it may seem today, Shor's censure was not dictated by political considerations alone. In 1932 Nabokov's willful adaptation was superseded by Mikhail Lozinskii's translation of Rolland's novel, a hallmark achievement of the Soviet school of literary translation. Unlike twenty-two-year-old Nabokov's first substantial foray into literary prose, Lozinskii's *Kola Briun'on* is a tasteful, lively, and self-effacing rendition executed by a master in control of his craft. Useful as Shor's critical comparison of Nabokov's and Lozinskii's translations is, however, it will be of limited value for those seeking to re-evaluate *Nikolka Persik*'s significance for Nabokov. It was not until 1999 that Aleksandr Liuksemburg attempted to situate *Nikolka Persik* against the background of Nabokov's development as a translator and translation theorist, singling it out as a milestone in his evolution. According to Liuksemburg, all of *Nikolka Persik*'s weaknesses notwithstanding, it amounts to a "virtuoso" replication of an outstandingly difficult original.[16]

A conversation concerning *Nikolka Persik*'s success at preserving the "spirit" of the original requires revisiting a familiar statement from the 1936 version of "Mademoiselle O." A comparison of this text's different iterations shows that its earliest version differed considerably from its subsequent Russian and English variants, familiar to the vast majority of Nabokov's readers as chapter 5 in his biography. Instead of focusing on the aspects of the author's past, on his encounter with the pathetic creature that was his Swiss governess, the original French essay sought to introduce its author, "Vladimir Nabokoff-Sirine," as a figure worthy of the reader's fascination. A foreigner with deep roots in his native culture, he demonstrates an individual appreciation of French literature, the seeds of which were planted during his childhood. Contrary to Mademoiselle's efforts, he remained an unrepentant "barbarian," a self-professed "friend" of Shakespeare and Ronsard whose adolescence was spent under the tutelage of Stéphane Mallarmé and Paul Verlaine. As it is presented in the 1936 variant, however, the cornerstone of this "barbarianism" was Nabokov's preference for and knowledge of François Rabelais. As we have seen, a close examination of Nabokov's early translation experiments suggests that his association with all these authors was at least complicated by a strong partiality toward Alfred de Musset – a poet curtly dismissed in the initial version of "Mademoiselle O" – whereas no trace of his early acquaintance with Rabelais can be gleaned from his early literary productions.[17]

Was Nabokov's childhood "friendship" with that key representative of the French Renaissance an affectation? Was it a figure of speech uttered by an unreliable narrator in search of a better way of ingratiating himself with his French readers at a time when Nabokov was looking for a new audience in anticipation of the Russian émigré community's demise? And, more to the point, what exactly constituted that Rabelaisian "barbarity" to which Nabokov was so eager to draw the attention of his French readers? Answering this question involves enlisting outside help, and who can be a better guide to the world of Rabelais than Mikhail Bakhtin, the scholar who revolutionized our appreciation of *Gargantua and Pantagruel* with *Fransua Rablé i narodnaia kul'tura Srednevekov'ia i Renessansa* (François Rabelais and Popular Medieval and Renaissance Culture; 1965)?[18]

Few works of literary scholarship have enriched our appreciation of any literary monument to a degree comparable to Bakhtin's doctoral thesis on Rabelais; few works of literary scholarship have approximated the effect Bakhtin's foray into historical poetics has had on our understanding of the nature of the "barbaric" spirit embodied in *Gargantua and Pantagruel* (1534). Bakhtinian insight into the nature of Rabelaisian barbarism – his coarseness, ribaldry, and perceived crassness that for centuries prevented readers from grasping the true meaning of his celebration of sensuality and carnality – aids our understanding of Nabokov's desire to be associated with that strand in the Gallic literary tradition.

Bakhtin explicates a contextually determined "philosophy of laughter" that to Rabelais and his sixteenth-century readers embodied "a triumph over fear ... fear not only mystical ... but above all else a triumph over the fear of everything sanctified and forbidden ... over powers both divine and human, over authoritarian commandments and proscriptions."[19] Bakhtin demonstrates how a cheerful celebration of the "lower body" (*telesnyi niz*) and its functions enabled an all-pervasive and anti-hierarchical popular world view that considered "laughter ... a form of defense both internal and external."[20] Prior to Bakhtin's scholarly delineation of this world view, in his *Colas Breugnon* Romain Rolland had succeeded in creating an artistic celebration of that life-affirming "barbarity" which for centuries has defined Gallic joie de vivre. A latter-day stylization of the Rabelaisian idiom set in Rabelais's France, *Colas Breugnon* distils that spirit into a compact novelistic narrative. Rolland's critics and interpreters promptly grasped this aspect of his achievement: in 1923 Stefan Zweig lauded *Colas Breugnon* for capturing the "ancient French idiom in the spirit of Rabelais."[21] Whether he was aware of it at the time, it was that elusive Rabelaisian spirit that Nabokov needed to capture if he wished to emulate the effect of Rolland's uncharacteristically radiant stylization.

The title that Nabokov chose for *Colas Breugnon* in Russian immediately signals the translator's determination to find an original solution to some of the text's most difficult problems. The determined conversion of "Colas" into "Nikolka" and "Breugnon" into "Persik" is fraught with implications for the fate of Rolland's novel in this version, if not for an entire stage of Nabokov's translating career. Choosing to Russianize the protagonist's name by employing a deliberately rustic-sounding diminutive ("Nikolka" for Nikolai, cf. "Colas" for Nicolas), Nabokov at once reveals an intimate acquaintance with the subtleties of the original text but refuses to be bound by the constraints he would have encountered had he chosen to adhere to the cultural context of the French novel. This impression is reinforced by the protagonist's newly acquired surname: faced with the absence of a native term for *breugnon* (the word "nectarine" did not enter the Russian language until the end of the twentieth century), Nabokov settled on a compromise and translated Breugnon's *nomen omen* as Persik, "peach."

The *Nikolka Persik* onomasticon provides insight into Nabokov's strategy of adapting the French semantics of Rolland's names to a linguistic and cultural context familiar to its Russian readers. In the original, Breugnon's beloved granddaughter is called "Glodie"; in his version Nabokov uses the close euphonic approximation "Glasha" (diminutive of the quaint, rural and/or bourgeois first name Glafira). Glodie's mother, the only one of Breugnon's brood in whom he recognizes a kindred soul, is called Martine. Martine becomes "Marfa," a choice encapsulating many aspects of his translating method, including some of its strengths and many of its weaknesses. While it does provide a reasonably close approximation to the original name in terms of sound and appearance, in Russian this name has many associations of its own, suggesting a most prim and proper character – an image that could scarcely be more inappropriate for Breugnon's only daughter, whom he calls *la mâtine* (minx, hussy), confessing that it took him considerable effort to marry Martine off before her independent temper got her into trouble. Apart from having to deal with this minor imperfection in Nabokov's rendition of a character's name, the reader of *Nikolka Persik* will not be able to appreciate the fact that in naming his daughter Martine, Breugnon was paying homage to his favourite saint – the patron of Rolland's and Breugnon's native Clamecy St Martin des Gaules – to whom the novel is dedicated. As if to compensate for this loss, Nabokov provides a close rendition of Breugnon's mocking nautical metaphor when it comes to a discussion of the protagonist's paternal difficulties with Martine: "m'a-t-elle donné du mal à passer sans naufrage jusqu'au port du mariage!" In Nabokov's version, Persik sighs: "Skol'ko mne ponadobilos' terpen'ia, chtob do berega braka dovesti eë bez krushen'ia."[22]

The method that Nabokov adhered to in his version of *Colas Breugnon*, however, emerges as more complex than may appear at first, especially when instances of the retention of the original's signal features are viewed in juxtaposition with occasions when they are omitted. Nabokov amplifies the deliberate Russianness of *Nikolka Persik* not only by means of addition, but also by subtraction. Throughout the novel he often replaces French proper names with generic Russian terms: on a number of occasions the Yvonne becomes *reka*; Bethléem, *predmest'e*; and France, *otchizna*. While the overall effect may be likened to Shakespeare's "Bohemian sea," the Franco-Russian locale of *Nikolka Persik* represents Nabokov's first attempt at placing the action of his work in an imaginary universe. The unconvincing juxtaposition of Breugnon's Burgundy with the Russian provinces represented in the *Tolkovyi slovar'* (Reasoned Dictionary of Living Great-Russian Language) of Vladimir Dal' presages such imagined settings as Zoorland in *Glory*, Zembla in *Pale Fire*, and Antitrera in *Ada*. In one instance the overall tendency toward weakening the novel's late-medieval/Renaissance French context allowed the translator to avoid dealing with a multilayered reference to a cultural phenomenon of whose significance Nabokov was not aware.

Some thirty-five years after the moment when he and his buddy Quiriace Pinon lost their beloved to the fat miller, Jean Gifflard, Breugnon decides to pay a visit to the woman who left so indelible a mark on his life. Belette is not expecting to see Breugnon, yet recognizes him instantly:

> Et voilà que je vis qu'elle aussi, brusquement, elle m'avait reconnu … Oh! elle n'en montra rien, elle était bien trop fière; mais le seau qu'elle tenait coula de ses mains dans l'auge. Et elle dit:
> – Jean de Lagny, qui n'a point de hâte … Ne te presse donc pas.[23]

> [And then I realized that she too suddenly recognized me … Oh! she didn't show it; she was too haughty; yet the bucket she held tumbled from her

hands into the trough. And she said: "Jean de Lagny who has no reason to hurry … Don't rush."]

Belette has so much to say to Breugnon that she is lost for words; she strikes up a conversation by uttering an ancient proverb familiar to Rolland from his study of Pierre-Marie Quitard's *Dictionnaire étymologique, historique and anecdotique des proverbes* (Etymological, Historical, and Anecdotal Dictionary of Proverbs; 1842). The phrase "Jean de Lagny, qui n'a point de hâte" recalls the indecisiveness of Jean-sans-Peur (1371–1419), Duke of Burgundy, at a crucial point in the Armagnac-Burgundian civil war of 1407–35.[24] In its turn, this invocation of Jean de Lagny echoes a popular contemporary "licentious" chanson, "Jehan de Lagny" by Jacques Berchem, which would have been understandable to both Breugnon and Bellette and most certainly had a special significance for their creator Romain Rolland, who had studied the origins of opera and knew of Berchem's significance for Rabelais.[25] Sung by a soprano, "Jehan de Lagny" is the reproach of an abandoned woman to a man who has taken advantage of her; in the context of the novel the song's frivolous words – never stated, but present in the atmosphere of this encounter – acquire a new connotation, resounding with the sad irony with which Belette contemplates the ghost of their happiness thwarted by her, as well as Breugnon's, failure to realize the promise of their mutual attraction.[26]

Nabokov's translation of this episode is noteworthy:

И я замѣтил, что вдругъ, и она меня вспомнила … Не подала она виду, слишкомъ много было в ней гордости, но ведро изъ рукъ ея вылилось обратно въ колодецъ. И сказала она:

– Бродяга безпечный, куда же ты вдруг поспѣшилъ? Постой …[27]

[And I noticed that suddenly she recognized me too … She didn't show it, she had too much pride in her, but the bucket fell out of her hands back into the well. And she said: "Carefree vagrant, why such haste all of a sudden? Wait … "]

Not grasping the significance of the reference to Jean de Lagny, Nabokov turns to the context and conjectures a solution to the problem posed by the original. The phrase "carefree vagrant" is a tactical move, a compromise he resorted to in a few instances where Rolland's text proved impenetrable for him.

The reader of "Mademoiselle O" will recall that in 1936, long after *Nikolka Persik* was published in Berlin, Nabokov was describing his staunch resistance to all attempts on the part of his French governess to impose on him her cult of Corneille and Racine on the grounds that already, even as a child, he was "a barbarian, a friend of Rabelais and of Shakespeare."[28] Young Nabokov's allegiance to the respective creators of Frère Jean and Falstaff was put to the test by his exposure to the work of another Rabelais worshipper, the author of *Colas Breugnon*. Colas's humour is not restricted to the occasional use of a clever double entendre, as in the fragment cited below, which describes the disappointing outcome of his and Pinon's courtship of Belette, who marries neither of them but instead Gifflard:

> Sans le charivari qui fit au lit, au nid, trouver maître coucou (Ah! Pinon le braillard!) jamais l'écornifleur ne se fût laissé pincer à mettre son gros doigt en anneau trop étroit … Io, Hymen Hyménée![29]
>
> [Without the hullabaloo that discovered Mr. Cuckoo in the bed, in the nest (ah, Pinon the bigmouth!) that scrounger would not have found himself putting his fat finger into too narrow a ring. Oh, Hymen Hymenaeus!]
>
> Если-бъ не кавардакъ ночной, если-бъ кукушка в гнѣздѣ не попалась (и оралъ же Пинокъ!), блюдолизъ никогда бы не сунулъ толстаго пальца въ колечко узкое … Ахъ, Гименей, Гименей![30]
>
> [Had it not been for that nighttime hullabaloo, had the cuckoo not been caught (did Pinon howl!), the parasite would never have been able to stick his fat finger in the narrow ring. Oh, Hymen Hymen!]

Having successfully conveyed one Rabelaisian ambiguity ("gros doigt en anneau trop étroit"), on this particular occasion Nabokov can hardly be blamed for refraining from an attempt to convey the other (Hymen as the Greek god and symbol of matrimony, and hymen as an anatomical term). Certain of this novel's episodes, however, clearly made Nabokov weigh the consequences of maintaining his loyalty to some manifestations of its Rabelaisian spirit in view of a potentially negative response from his audience. A similar conflict between the translator's desire to be faithful to the original's spirit and his sense of propriety proved to be one of the most difficult tests of his acumen throughout the novel.

Standing before a group of sneering nobles, Breugnon the old master craftsman plays the fool, exposing his condescending interlocutors as idiots at every turn. Count de Maillebois tries to pin him down: "Je te demande, bonhomme, ce qu'on pense, ce qu'on croit. Est-on bon catholique? Est-on dévoué au roi?" ("Tell me, [my] good fellow, what do people think, what do they believe? Are they good Catholics? Are they devoted to the king?"). All in vain: Breugnon refuses to be caught off guard; the count will not get an incriminating answer from this dim-witted rustic: "Il ne faut pas, monsieur, péter plus haut que son cul" ("One mustn't, milord, fart higher than one's ass").[31] In the original this piece of conventional wisdom is conveyed with maximal transparency, and yet in translating it Nabokov elected to tone it down: "Skazano, sudar': ne plui vyshe nosa" ("It is said, Sir: don't spit higher than your nose").[32] In this tug-of-war between Nabokov's inner "barbarian" and the young member of polite society, the latter gained upper hand.

Nikolka Persik is an experiment in literary adaptation. While superficial acquaintance with this endeavour may produce the impression that it is a frivolous, indeed fanciful, Russianized variation on a French theme provided by Rolland, in reality *Nikolka Persik* is a deliberate exercise in the retention and transmission of the semantics of the original work, as well as certain representative features of its style and prosody. As demonstrated by this inquiry into the reasoning behind many of the choices made in this translation, Nabokov's adaptation is based on a profound comprehension of the French original. This conclusion is not undermined either by the fact that Lozinskii's practice of employing *raёshnyi stikh* as a parallel to the rhythmicity of Rolland's prose proved to be a superior solution to the problem of the recreation of *Colas Breugnon*'s idiosyncratic style in Russian, or that Nabokov's translation is not completely devoid of omissions and that it tends to tone down some of the more risqué descriptions and turns of speech.[33]

Nabokov's antagonism toward Rolland's politics and aesthetics is well known. And yet echoes of *Colas Breugnon* (and *Nikolka Persik*) continue to reverberate throughout Nabokov's mature prose, finding their way into *The Gift*, with its rhymed coda that puts one in mind of *Colas Breugnon*'s finale, its punning collation of the names of German philosophers recalling Breugnon's playful, punning juxtaposition of "Héraclite le pleurard et Démocrite hilare."[34] Could Nabokov have thought of Rolland when midway through *The Gift* he paused to write *Invitation to a Beheading*, replicating the circumstances of Colas Breugnon's unexpected appearance amid Rolland's work on *Jean-Christophe*? The name of Marfin'ka, the naively promiscuous wife of Cincinnatus C. in *Priglasheniie na kazn'* (*Invitation to a Beheading*; 1936), suggests that Nabokov may have revisited the name he had chosen for Breugnon's daughter Martine, endowing it this time around with a sound that is decidedly more playful than in *Nikolka Persik*.[35]

Was then *Nikolka Persik* a mere "bravura performance," a chance encounter with a stranger whose ideas had nothing in common with Nabokov the young man, challenged as he was by the difficulties associated with the task of matching Rolland's worldplay in a different language? The scholarly consensus regarding the limited usefulness of Nabokov's work on *Colas Breugnon* and Rolland's insignificance for Nabokov appears to be supported by the disdain he expressed for Rolland on a number of memorable occasions.[36]

Nabokov had every reason to despise the journey of Rolland's "enchanted soul." This translator of the sunniest of Rolland's works witnessed a well-publicized transformation of that pacifist into a prominent apologist of Soviet tyranny on par with H.G. Wells and G.B. Shaw. Rolland the "fellow traveller" did not merely defend Soviet Russia in the West and meet Stalin during his trip to Moscow in 1935. When in 1927 Konstantin Bal'mont and Ivan Bunin, luminaries of the Russian anti-Bolshevik diaspora, publicly challenged Rolland to use his international stature to condemn Soviet crimes against humanity and artistic expression, the Nobel laureate of 1915, who had nominated Bal'mont, Bunin, and Maksim Gor'kii for the same prize in 1923, refused to do so.[37] While acknowledging Soviet "errors," "excesses," and even "crimes," he vowed to continue to assist and encourage the Soviet experiment as "an inspiration for humankind."[38]

According to David James Fisher, Rolland "failed to probe deeply into the nature of the massacres that were being perpetrated" in Soviet Russia, and his failure raised "serious questions about his moral and intellectual principles and his commitment to speaking the truth at that moment of crisis."[39] This often overlooked aspect of Nabokov's disdain for Rolland's practice of subjugating art to ideological utilitarianism permits us to delve deeper into his mockery of *littérature engagée* as practised by Rolland, Thomas Mann, and Maksim Gor'kii. This larger context of Nabokov's rejection of Rolland, however, does little to explain the significance of his long-term engagement with that writer and thinker in the course of his work on *Nikolka Persik*.

At the time of Nabokov's work on *Nikolka Persik*, Rolland had yet to become Lenin's eulogist and Stalinist "fellow traveller." It is not difficult to imagine how *that* Romain Rolland would have appealed to Nabokov's contempt for the mob mentality that drove him into exile. Nabokov's civic poetry of that period chastises marauding mobs and upholds individual honour and integrity threatened by aggressive crowds. Rolland's individualism – before it was contaminated and devalued by his Sovietophilia – would certainly have attracted Nabokov. This is not to suggest that Nabokov's engagement with Rolland's aesthetics was devoid of confrontation.

The episode where Colas Breugnon outwits the haughty Count de Maillebois by exposing his aristocratic stupidity is a showdown between Breugnon's certainty in his calling of a master craftsman and Maillebois's conceited disdain for a commoner. A virtuoso woodcutter, Breugnon lets it slip that he considers his craft an art. He is convinced that the usefulness of the beautiful objects he produces is what constitutes their artistic value. An expression of his deeply held belief, Breugnon's remark catches the attention of the sneering count, who holds the opposite point of view. Describing the workings of a simple man's mind, Breugnon explains:

> D'esprit borné par pauvreté, il ne fait rien, ne conçoit rien qui ne soit d'usage quotidien. L'art utile, voilà son lot.
>
> – L'art utile! Les deux mots jurent ensemble, dit mon sot. Il n'est de beau que l'inutile.
>
> – Grande parole! Acquiesçai-je. Il est bien vrai. Partout dans l'art et dans la vie. Rien n'est plus beau qu'un diamant, un prince, un roi, un grand seigneur ou une fleur.[40]

> [Sordid due to indigence, [a simple man's mind] creates and invents nothing but things fit for everyday use. Useful art, that's its lot.
>
> – Useful art! These two words clash together," says my fool. "Only that which is useless is beautiful."
>
> – Well said, I agreed. This is too true. Everywhere, in art and in life. Nothing's more beautiful than a diamond, a prince, a king, a grandee, or a flower.]

Maillebois the aristocrat cannot conceive of the idea that something useful can be considered art. Siding with Breugnon the hardworking man, Rolland shows that the aesthetic judgment of a parasitic nobleman is determined by his social standing: for someone who takes the value of menial labour for granted, beauty cannot be useful. An apparent confirmation of the superiority of Maillebois's aesthetic sophistication, Breugnon's respectful answer actually undercuts the count's position by aligning him and people of his standing with beautiful yet ultimately useless objects, a diamond and a flower. Devoid of utilitarian value, such objects are as useless as princes and kings, implies the socially engaged author who towers over his clever protagonist.

Unable to bring himself to translate Breugnon's reference to flatulence in the earlier section of the same episode, Nabokov conveyed the crucial finale of the Breugnon-Maillebois exchange with utmost efficacy:

> Бѣдностью умъ нашъ придавленъ, ничего онъ не можетъ, ничего не смыслитъ, кромѣ заботъ обиходныхъ. Искусство полезное – вотъ нашъ удѣлъ.
>
> – Искусство полезное? Эти два слова не вяжутся, – воскликнулъ мой дурень. – Прекрасно только ненужное.
>
> Я въ отвѣтъ:
>
> – Великая мысль! Какъ это вѣрно! Такъ вездѣ и въ искусствѣ и въ жизни. Нѣтъ ничего прекраснѣй алмаза, вельможи иль розы.[41]
>
> [Poverty oppresses our mind, it can produce nothing, think of nothing apart from our everyday cares. Useful art – that's our lot.
>
> – Useful art? These two words don't go together, exclaimed my idiot. – Only that which is useless is beautiful.
>
> I respond:
>
> – Great thought! How true! That is the case everywhere, both in art and in life. There's nothing more beautiful than a diamond, a grandee, or a rose.]

Nabokov's rendition shows clear traces of his attention to the wording of Breugnon's rhetorical coup de grâce. Whereas Breugnon emphasizes the social provenance of the members of the beautiful but useless class ("un prince, un roi, grand seigneur"), Nabokov collapses this triad into one designator *vel'mozha* (grandee). When it comes to the generic term "une fleur," however, he opts for the specific term "rose."

Breugnon's position in his rhetorical duel with Maillebois epitomizes a stance diametrically opposed to the paramount tenet of Nabokov's mature aesthetics. Long after his encounter with Rolland, in his lecture "The Art of Literature and Commonsense," Nabokov would employ multiple parables to express his preference for suprarational attributes that define and distinguish true art – art that overcomes the utilitarian arithmetic of goal-driven common sense: "I take my hat off to the hero who dashes into a burning house and saves the neighbor's child; but I shake his hand if he has risked squandering a precious five seconds to find and, together with the child, its favorite toy."[42] In her refreshing analysis of the Kantian underpinnings of Nabokovian aesthetics, Dana Dragunoiu qualifies this lecture as "Nabokov's celebration of art's non-utilitarian impulse."[43]

Paradoxical, witty, and persuasive, this and similar mature formulations of Nabokov's non-utilitarianism are a product of focused contemplation of the philosophical problem at their root. Search for a fitting expression of his stance on the issue of art's autonomy from utilitarian concerns commenced long before he switched from Russian to English to become an American writer, yet its point of departure has never been properly identified. Nabokov's attention to this key episode of *Colas Breugnon* bespeaks his awareness that Rolland's defence of utilitarian art was dictated by a program of subjugation of literature to the task of improving the human condition. By searching for a better, more succinct way of formulating Rolland's stance, Nabokov entered a dialogue with a proponent of the idea that art should be subjugated to extra-aesthetic considerations. Doing so compelled him to begin a search for a formula that would encapsulate his conviction that for all the ridiculousness of the character expressing it, Maillebois's position on the inutility of beauty and art is worth defending.

It is far from accidental that in addition to collapsing Rolland's tripartite list of "useless" people into a single noun, Nabokov chose to replace the generic term "la fleur" with a specific descriptor, "rose." This adjustment amounts to a tacit expression of his disagreement with the logic behind Breugnon's commonsensical denigration of an object on the basis of its perceived lack of functionality. As it develops the capacity to appreciate the beauty of a "useless" rose, the human mind gains a degree of freedom from immediate – often frankly mundane – concerns. This is what Nabokov means when he states that the "capacity to wonder at trifles – no matter the imminent peril – these asides of the spirit, these footnotes in the volume of life are the highest form of consciousness, and it is in this childishly speculative state of mind, so different from commonsense and its logic, that we know the world to be good."[44] The earliest manifestation of Nabokov's urge to defend this considered opinion is noticeable in his dialogic tussle with Rolland, the thinker, activist, and writer whom Nabokov would continue to engage both implicitly and explicitly in his pronouncements on the problem of the indispensability of aesthetic appreciation for the human mind.

"La Belle Dame Sans Merci": Unreliable Narrative's Dialogic Origins

Nabokov's compositions form a veritable pageant of "unreliable narrators." Invited to form individual perspectives on Nabokov's fictional universes, his readers must never cede this responsibility to the storytellers they encounter – or mistake them for authorial stand-ins. Unreliable narrative is a time-tested literary ruse, to be sure, and as such it has been a tool for engaging and retaining readers' attention. Far from intimidated by this device's pedigree, Nabokov wrote a new chapter in its history – according to Wayne C. Booth, whose *Rhetoric of Fiction* (1961) has rendered "unreliable narrator" one of the most current scholarly terms today.

After acquiring a taste for its potential early in his career, in his mature works Nabokov reimagines unreliable narrative as a way of enlisting our ethical judgment. Are we to sympathize with the eloquent testimony of a certain "bewitched traveller" who builds his case for being persecuted by "maidens" whose nature is "not human" but "nymphic," which is to say "demoniac"?[45] What is the author's stance regarding some of his narrators' blatant egotism? Why are they allowed to vie for our attention and sympathy at the expense of other characters, as is the case with *Pnin* and *Ada*? Our ability to account for the admission of this major device into Nabokov's literary arsenal may not provide the answer to these and similar questions (we may well be the sole party responsible for answering them in the first place), but knowing the circumstances under which it occurred would certainly bring us closer to evolving a deeper appreciation of this technique and its evolution. The least studied of his literary adaptations, the 1 June 1921 Russian retelling of John Keats's "La Belle Dame Sans Merci," grants such an opportunity.[46]

We recall that Nabokov's "La Belle Dame Sans Merci" appeared in conjunction with his version of Byron's "Sun of the Sleepless" in *Gornii put'* (1923). This expression of his admiration for the two magnetic poles of English Romantic poetry, however, had another, technical aspect to it: the Cambridge "domestication" of Keats's ballad had followed an earnest translation of a poem by Byron made in the Crimea. Nothing like the scrupulous replica of "Sun of the Sleepless," "La Belle Dame

Sans Merci" (Iz John Keats [from John Keats], "Akh, chto muchit tebia, goremyka" [Ah, what is tormenting you, wretch]) is another experiment in literary adaptation, one on par with *Nikolka Persik* and *Ania v Strane Chudes*.

Russian in every aspect barring its title, "Akh, chto muchit tebia, goremyka" aspires to mimic the effect one poetic utterance has in its native context with the aid of comparable devices peculiar to another literary tradition. Having sacrificed so much local colour in his resetting of *Colas Breugnon* to accomplish so little, Nabokov became aware of the limitations of this approach. Hardly recognizable as an echo of a text written in any other language but Russian, this imprint of one of the most iconic poetic texts in the history of English literature demonstrates that Nabokov was not ready to capitulate to the difficulties associated with this task. Like *Nikolka Persik*, "Akh, chto muchit tebia, goremyka" rests on the assumption that translation is a realm of infinite possibilities. An amalgam of allusions to an array of precedents that in addition to Shakespeare encompasses Edmund Spencer's *Faery Queene*, Robert Burton's *Anatomy of Melancholy*, Wordsworth and Coleridge's *Lyrical Ballads*, and Henry Francis Cary's retelling of Dante's *Divine Comedy*, Keats's ballad would tantalize and tease an adherent of the "domesticating" approach by appearing an open invitation to recreate its effects by similar means. Notwithstanding the utopianism of such a vision, twenty-two-year-old Nabokov gave this mirage a good chase.

In the three opening quatrains of "Akh, chto muchit tebia, goremyka," the unnamed possessor of the querying voice asking the question that the narrator will be answering in the remaining nine stanzas refers to the inevitable arrival of the autumn in the language of rural husbandry. In conjunction with a strong colloquial term associated with the depiction of peasant life (*goremyka*), this places the action of Nabokov's ballad within the bounds of a Russian rural commune. Nabokov's *goremyka* is made to recount his story to a fellow member of his commune, to someone who has every right – if not an obligation – to be concerned with his well-being. Such concern for one's neighbour is but a part of a traditional mindset that pervaded every aspect of life in peasant Russia, another important facet of this mindset comprising a syncretic mythological outlook teeming with its own demonology. The intrusion of an adversarial demonic force into the life of a peasant is an alarming occurrence fraught with loss and ruin. Predicated on the shared lore of a peasant commune, it becomes deeply rooted in its beliefs and poetry.

In Nabokov's version, *goremyka*'s account of his star-crossed amorous encounter – more than once throughout its length it takes on the features of a morbidly introverted soliloquy – opens with an immediately recognizable borrowing of a signature image from Aleksandr Blok's symbolist poetic mythology, namely that of the Beautiful Lady ("Prekrasnaia Dama"). *Goremyka*'s plight is suggestive of this mystic and erotic commonplace of Blokian poetry, which frequently presents its lyrical "I" as a willing victim of a demonic seductress. Thus in "Ona prishla s zakata" ("She came from the sunset," 1907), the lyrical persona of Blok's poetry intimates the terms of his devotion to a mysterious woman whose black, serpentine locks have ensnared his reason and spirit.[47] This presages the transformation of the "long hair" of the Keatsean "lady in the meads" in "Akh, chto muchit tebia goremyka," where it is rendered by a compound epithet, *zmei-lokony* (serpents-locks). Jane Grayson has pointed out that by incorporating these images into the texture of his translation, Nabokov seeks to hint at the existence of a kinship connecting Keats and Blok, two Romantic poets separated from each other by space and time. In the context of "Akh, chto muchit tebia, goremyka," however, the appearance of the Beautiful Lady amid the token attributes of a rural way of life widens the gap between the matter-of-fact world of the ballad's protagonist and the fairytale realm of his elfin mistress.[48] Even prior to Nabokov's introduction of the adjective "fairytale" into the poem, under his hand it acquires the features of a fairy narrative reminiscent of a Russian folktale and its literary imitation. Nabokov's Beautiful Lady is the daughter of a mysterious enchantress (cf. *charodeiki nevedomoi doch'* and "a faery's child"), and in his ominous dream *goremyka* hears the warnings of *korolevichi* (princes) and *vitiazi* (knights, warriors), these two markedly poetic nouns being common attributes of Russian tales of heroic deeds and knight-errantry.

In 1942 – "almost a quarter of a century" after making it – Nabokov admitted in a letter to Edmund Wilson that his Russian rendering of Keats's ballad was "a very poor translation."[49] Notwithstanding all the ingenuity of this attempt to echo the effect the original has in its native context, numerous references to Russian poetry lead astray rather than recreate the allusiveness of his model. As is the case with the rest of Nabokov's translating juvenilia, however, the most significant part of such and similar engagements is not in the immediate result but rather in their consequences for the translator himself.

Nabokov's profession of allegiance to Keats over Byron in the *University Poem* was no affectation: his English was to bear an imprint of his assiduous reading of Keats in general and "La Belle Dame Sans Merci" in particular. *The Real Life of Sebastian Knight* features a futurist poet, Alexis Pan, whose translation of the ballad amounts to "a very miracle of verbal transfusion" whose aesthetic value surpasses that of his attempts at quasi-modernist poetry. Appearing in Nabokov's first English-language novel, this cryptic meta-description of the author's own struggles with the poem inaugurates a series of Keatsean verbal vestiges in his subsequent compositions. When in a 1964 interview Nabokov made a jocular reference to his weight gain, he spoke of becoming "stout like Cortez,"[50] borrowing a simile from "On First Looking into Chapman's Homer," the sonnet that figures so prominently in *Pale Fire*, his most recent publication at the time. When in the eponymous poem John Shade describes his breakdown after learning of his daughter's suicide, the unique lexeme "gloam," a Keatsean backformation from "gloaming," from "La Belle Dame Sans Merci," enhances the colouration of that emotional scene's backdrop.[51] Nabokov's fluency in the Keatsean idiom did not result from mere familiarity with it but was born out of a strong dialogic engagement with the mind behind it.

As transformative adaptation infuses a given literary text with significance that is manifestly personal, the act of adapting that text to novel demands and circumstances inevitably amounts to what might be termed artistic appropriation. As has been the case historically, the consequences of such an act brim with implications not only for the text in question and its reception in a fresh environment, but also for the party executing the adaptation, especially so whenever it involves a young artist of promise. Having come into contact with the dramatic premise of "La Belle Dame Sans Merci," having made it part of his storytelling repertoire through the medium of appropriative adaptation, Nabokov internalized and assimilated a narrative stratagem that was to lend a singularly productive device to his original fiction. The ambiguity of the wight's story, its dubious veracity and openness to different, even mutually exclusive, interpretations, as well as its lack of precedent in Nabokov's juvenilia, offset by the writer's subsequent predisposition toward placing similarly equivocal agents at the forefront of his mature works – all these factors point to the "wretched wight's" being Nabokov's earliest "unreliable narrator."

Did Nabokov need to come into contact with Keats's "wretched wight" to evolve into the virtuoso of unreliable narrative? Would he have discerned this device's potential without re-staging the Keatsean mini-drama of a mortal's encounter with an elfin child? To some extent this question is irrelevant. History, the Russian saying goes, tolerates no conditional mood. Even before discovering "La Belle Dame Sans Merci," Nabokov would have come across experiments in the same vein conducted by Aleksandr Pushkin or Edgar Allan Poe, to mention only two relevant examples. Keats's ballad and no other text, however, compelled him to create his first, admittedly imperfect, variation on a theme that would continue to resonate with him for the rest of his career in letters. The *goremyka*'s ambiguous tale is the earliest Nabokovian unreliable narrative that presents his reader with a dilemma whose implications have a discernibly ethical dimension: the *goremyka*'s account of the violent act that has been perpetrated against him by his demonic lover may be biased and incomplete. Could this be the case of a violator blaming his victim for the crime he committed against her? Is he deranged as a result of his demonic possession, or is he attempting to sway his audience's reaction in his favour? Each reader of the ballad has to find their own answer to this question, much like each reader of *Lolita* or *Pale Fire* must formulate their own response to the challenge presented by the tantalizing conclusions of these ambiguous tales.[52]

"Otherworldly Twilight": Tackling Rupert Brooke

In Album 19, Elena Nabokova's transcripts of her son's translations from Rupert Brooke are dated September 1921 ("1921-IX"). Together with the exegesis of Brooke's poetry drafted in Nabokov's 28 April 1921 letter from Cambridge to his Berlin-based parents, these translations formed the kernel of a major early essay, "Rupert Bruk," published in the first issue of the "literary almanac" *Grani* (Facets; 1922).[53] While the essay's ostensible goal was to introduce Russian readers to an unknown English poet, its true scope proved to be more expansive: "Rupert Bruk" bore a statement of some of the most important principles of its author's world view and aesthetic stance, and provided impetus for an advanced expression of his evolving poetics. Although the significance of his word choice would not be grasped until 1979, it was in the course of his discussion of Brooke that Nabokov for the first time *in print* used the word *potustoronnost'* as prime denominator of his individual metaphysical outlook.[54] Brian Boyd reckons that the essay's "exuberant metaphors" anticipated many of the hallmarks of Nabokov's mature style; Jonathan Sisson, D. Barton Johnson, and Aleksandr Dolinin second this opinion.[55]

While Nabokov scholars agree that the exuberance of "Rupert Bruk" was a sure sign of the Nabokov to come, their assessments of the translations at the heart of the essay differ. In his pioneering study "Nabokov and Rupert Brooke" (1983), Robin Kemball conducted a comparative statistical analysis of the verse translations, which convinced him of their "astounding accuracy."[56] Galya Diment's valuation is more reserved: "the translations are … smooth and competent if not always totally accurate. Nabokov tries to preserve the rhyming pattern and, wherever possible, even the meter of the original, yet he also feels free to paraphrase the poet as long as the general sense of the poem remains largely intact."[57]

A closer examination of Nabokov's translations alongside their models, aided by Kemball's statistics, demonstrates that already on the formal level he does not consider himself bound by the structural characteristics of the English poems. When it comes to metrics, Nabokov does indeed "follow the original meters" (all the original poems being, as Kemball observes, "basically iambic"). Two translated poems, however, are strikingly dissimilar from their models: "The Jolly Company" (no. 10) and "The Vision of the Archangels" (no. 12). And as Kemball has demonstrated, "considerable differences" come to light in a comparison of the overall number of feet per line, as only four (nos. 1, 2, 6, and 10) of the thirteen translations ("Menelaus and Helen" being a mini-sonnet sequence comprising two poems) follow the originals in this respect.

"Heaven," the first poem of Nabokov's selection, exhibits a marked tension between the translator's desire to retain the form of the original while communicating as much of its meaning as possible. Building his poem around a humorous paraphrase of the proverbial Old Testament injunction ("for dust thou art, and unto dust thou shalt return," Genesis 3:19), and possibly parodying the dexterity of his favourite, John Donne, in combining colloquial idiom with the register of a learned metaphysical discourse, in this late poem (1913) Brooke likens the lot of the humans – expelled from Eden, tormented by profound doubt regarding the hereafter – to that of thinking fish, which like humans dream of a better world, albeit in terms characteristic of their perspective on the universe.

Surprising as it may be, Nabokov's translation of the poem – which exceeds the length the original by no fewer than ten lines – opens with a paraphrase of Mikhail Lermontov's "Son" (Dream ["V poldnevnyi zhar v doline Dagestana," In midday heat in a vale of Daghestan]; 1841):[58]

Въ полдневный часъ, лѣнивымъ лѣтомъ,
овѣянная влажнымъ свѣтомъ,

въ струяхъ, съ изгиба на изгибъ,
[4] блуждаетъ сонно-сытыхъ рыбъ
глубокомысленная стая,
надежды рыбьи обсуждая,
и вотъ значенье ихъ рѣчей:[59]

[In midday hour, during a lazy summer, / suffused by moist light, / across the currents, from one bend to another, / roams of drowsily sated fish / a thoughtful school / as they discuss fish hopes, / and here's the significance of their speeches:]

While preserving the iambic tetrameter and the couplet-patterned rhyming of the original, here and elsewhere the translator extends the length of the Russian fragment to retain the imagery of the corresponding English unit. Likewise, the final couplet of Brooke's poem gains an additional line in the Russian, resulting in a closing that may not appear as maxim-like as the English couplet it represents (ll. 42–4):

И тамъ, куда всѣ рыбьи грёзы
устремлены сквозь влажный свѣтъ,
тамъ, вѣрятъ рыбы, суши нѣтъ ...[60]

[And there where all the fish dreams / are directed through the moist light, / there, the fish believe, there's no dry land ...]

The extension (as well as the diminution) of the original in translation has direct precedent in Nabokov's earlier experiments – in his versions of Byron's "'All Is Vanity,' Saith the Preacher" and "The Dream," as well as in his translations from Pierre Louÿs. In his translations such extensions point toward a greater degree of emotional engagement with the original text (such, for example, was the case of "The Dream" by Byron).

Just as Nabokov's seemingly spontaneous solutions to the problems posed by Rolland's *Colas Breugnon* and Keats's "La Belle Dame Sans Merci" frequently prove to be based on a thorough understanding of the inner workings of the original, the surface asymmetry of some of Nabokov's alterations in his versions of Brooke often turns out to be calculated rather than random. In his version of Brooke's sonnet "The Vision of the Archangels," Nabokov evades the obvious path the original seems to suggest and translates Brooke's six-foot iambs in a manner that cannot be said to be the most logical way of rendering a sonnet in a foreign language.[61]

On the surface, the poem's sonnet-like graphic appearance – Nabokov also separates octet from sestet by an interval – seems a futile attempt to be wise after the event. In his translation, Nabokov not only abandons the intricate rhyming scheme of the original (ababcdcd effegg) but also its metre – a clear departure from his model, which, after all, was an exercise in conventional sonneteering (Nabokov's version is written in rhyming couplets and amphibrachic pentameter). In the asymmetry of Nabokov's unconventional solution, however, lies the calculated effect of his Russian version. The subject matter of "Po krucham nemym, k belosnezhnoi vershine zemli" (Along the mute peaks, toward the snow-white pinnacle of the earth) – the image of the archangels carrying the body of a child that later in the poem is revealed to be a representation of the Christian sacrifice – along with its metre and rhyme scheme make the reader aware of the presence of the "strong" Russian subtext in this translation, considerably enhancing the reader's appreciation of Brooke.

This Russian version of "The Vision of the Archangels" resounds with echoes of Lermontov's "Angel" ("Po nebu polunochi angel letel" [An angel flew across the midnight sky]; 1831), with its haunting alternations of four- and three-foot amphibrachs encased in eight rhyming couplets. Nabokov's imagery projects Brooke's evocation of the evangelical sacrifice onto the majestic celestial landscape of the Lermontov poem. The sentimental tonality of the three poems – the original, the translation, and the chief Russian subtext of the latter – suggests their trilateral kinship while at the same time providing a uniquely Nabokovian justification for the prosodic departure from the English original.[62]

In order to appreciate how imaginative Nabokov's *prose* paraphrases of Brooke can be, consider Nabokov's fleeting reference to "Sonnet" ("Oh! Death will find me long before I tire") occurring halfway through "Rupert Bruk." The passage cited below exemplifies in the essay some of Brooke's "more tranquil" images (as opposed to those to be found in "Dust"):

> Вотъ на берегахъ Леты, среди миѳологическихъ кипарисовъ, поэтъ встрѣчаетъ свою умершую любовницу и она, безпечная Лаура эта, «вскидываетъ тёмнорусой очаровательной головой», такъ потѣшает её видъ древнихъ мёртвыхъ – Сократъ курносый, щуплый Цезарь, завистливый Петрарка.[63]

> [There on the banks of the Lethe, among mythological cypresses, the poet encounters his dead mistress and she, that careless Laura, "shakes her charming dark-russet head," amused as she is by the spectacle of the dead ancients – snub-nosed Socrates, skinny Caesar, envious Petrarch.]

One seeks in vain for Socrates, Caesar, and Petrarch in the text of the poem that served as the source of this reference. In his depiction of Hades, Brooke is far less explicit than Nabokov. It turns out that Nabokov peoples Brooke's "last land" with illustrious shades of his choice as he freely enlivens the Hadean landscape with Byronic cypresses and transfers the action of the entire scene to the banks of Lethe, and not the Styx as Brooke would have it.[64]

The ambiguity in the proprietary status of Nabokov's references to Brooke becomes clear when one examines Nabokov's paraphrase of "The Great Lover," where the absence of a clear borderline between Brooke's and Nabokov's texts is especially striking. While a quotation mark has been supplied to denote the end of the paraphrase of "The Great Lover," its beginning is not marked. The moment where Nabokov ends and Brooke begins is not as easy to pinpoint, but that may be this paraphrase's purpose in the first place. For all his skill in mirroring the formal features of the originals, this translator is not interested in self-effacement; he is determined to remain as visible to the reader as the author whose poems he is introducing to his Russian reader.

Nabokov's essay closes with the following assertion: "It is not difficult to discern the fundamental feature of [Brooke's] oeuvre: passionate devotion to pure beauty" ("netrudno razlichit' osnovnuiu chertu ego tvorchestva: strastnoe sluzhenie chistoi krasote").[65] Attempts to verify this conclusion have shown that Nabokov overstated the ease with which Brooke can be interpreted as a champion of "pure beauty." The same is true of his attempt to present the British poet as a mystically inclined visionary focused on the otherworldly.

Nabokov's perspective on Brooke is subjective. In Brooke's poetry Nabokov underscores the traits that correlate to his own intuitions of the otherworld, his own immediate apprehension of his estranged homeland, his own cult of "pure beauty"; he contends that "no other poet has so often, with such tormented and creative vigilance, looked into the dusk of the beyond." Citing examples of divergences between the actual meaning of Brooke's statements concerning the hereafter (to be found in his verse as well as in his correspondence) and Nabokov's interpretation of them, D. Barton Johnson deduces that Nabokov's presentation of the English poet as a "bard of eternal life" ("pevets vechnoi zhizni")[66] is in fact a "mistaken" one, not only in view of Brooke's "great suspicion" of psychic phenomena, as exemplified by the ironic sonnet "suggested by some of the proceedings of the Society for Psychical Research," but also with regard to his self-professed atheism. Johnson aptly identifies the nature of this experiment in translation: "Nabokov's Brooke translations are much freer and more personalized than in his later practice," and indeed his versions of Brooke's poems, and especially his presentation of Brooke's legacy as a whole, amount to an individual vision of the English poet.[67]

Would it be prudent to endorse unreservedly Johnson's appraisal of instances where Nabokov invested his paraphrases of Brooke with his own metaphysical intuitions as "misreadings" of the originals, prompted by Nabokov's "disproportionate and inaccurate" focusing on Brooke's theme of death and the otherworld? Nabokov's preoccupation with these themes, Johnson argues, rendered him "ill at ease" with Brooke's "tentativeness about the hereafter." Although it may be clear that he felt free to alter the originals according to his own vision, Nabokov provided his readers with some accurate equivalents of the originals both in terms of their prosody and meaning. In his 1921 interpretations of Rupert Brooke, Nabokov was first and foremost intent on discerning in the English poet a like-minded ally. Impatient to leave his individual imprint on every literary endeavour he undertook at the time, Nabokov proceeded to cast Brooke's metaphysical tentativeness in a mould of his own making, one that reflected what were then his largely untested philosophical convictions. Just as Nabokov was not aware of such aspects of Rupert Brooke's personality as his casual anti-Semitism and Russophobia, Nabokov's intensely poetic vision of Brooke may not have been attuned to the task of accessing the conflicted personality of the individual behind the "almost sacred, supreme poet-figure of his generation."[68]

The best way to appreciate the Rupert Brooke translations is to view them in the context of the stage in Nabokov's evolution as translator to which they belong. Together with *Nikolka Persik* and "Akh, chto muchit tebia, goremyka," they continue the line of experimentation that started in the Crimea with the liberal adaptations of Pierre Louÿs's *chansons* while paving the way for *Ania v Strane Chudes*. If one were to use Nabokov's essay to form an accurate idea of Brooke's poetry, it would be the least reliable source on this poet and thinker imaginable. The essay, however, will remain an invaluable source on Nabokov's evolution, unique as it is as an early snapshot of some of his most deeply held convictions, intuitions, and ambitions. Naive as it sounds, the phrase "passionate devotion to pure beauty" will never cease to be a useful formula for summarizing Nabokov's aesthetics.

"So the spirit bows before thee": A Star-Crossed Affair in Translation

In the intensely poetic world of twenty-three-year-old Vladimir Nabokov, translation and original creation went hand in hand, as can be seen from his version of Byron's "Stanzas for Music" ("There be none of Beauty's daughters," 1816).[69] In this trochaic, two-octave-long piece, the rhythms and images of the English poem have refracted to acquire a new aspect, giving rise to a text with perceptibly autobiographic overtones.

Grozd' (Cluster; 1922), Nabokov's first collection of poems to be published under the pseudonym "Vladimir Sirin," contains a section dedicated to his fiancée Svetlana Siewert ("II. Ty" [You]). It precedes a section of poems in memory of Vladimir Dmitrievich Nabokov ("III. Ushedshee" [The Bygone]). Nabokov first met Svetlana in June 1921; a year later they were engaged to be married, and *Grozd'* reflects its author's elation at that prospect. One of the attributes of the beloved's image in *Grozd'* is music, which is directly evoked in such poems as "O, svetlyi golos, chut' pechal'nyi" (O bright voice, with a touch of melancholy), "V polnolun'e, v gostinoi pyl'noi i pyshnoi" (On a full-moon night, in dusty and luxurious a parlour), and especially in "Vse okna otkryv, opustiv zanaveski" (Having opened all the windows and lowered all the curtains).[70] These poems are a direct echo of the summer of 1921 in Berlin, when Nabokov spent his evenings listening to Svetlana's piano.[71] The same source of inspiration most certainly gave impetus to "Stansy dlia muzyki" ("Uviadaiut vse viden'ia" [Pale/Wilt all visions]), Nabokov's version of Byron's "Stanzas for Music." The poem opens with an evocation of singing:[72]

Увядаютъ всѣ видѣнья
красоты – передъ тобой.
Какъ на вóдахъ звонъ и пѣнье
[4] проплываетъ голосъ твой.[73]

[Wilt all visions / of beauty – before you. / As ringing and singing above the water / your voice sails.]

In Nabokov's version the beloved's voice "floats by" the poet (*proplyvaet*); this dynamic representation of the same aural sensation replaces the original characterization of the addressee's voice as "sweet."[74] The second octave of the poem contains a departure from the original that is particularly revelatory of the translator's personal involvement with his work. Where Byron invokes a "spirit" that adoringly listens to the beloved ("So the spirit bows before thee, / To listen and adore thee," ll. 13–14), the lyrical "I" of Nabokov's version assumes the role of that spirit, entering the poem in person. The implication contained in the original (the "spirit" of Byron's poem is clearly that of the speaker) is made explicit in Nabokov's version:[75]

я склоняюсь предъ тобою,
внемлю полною душою,
жарко, медленно вздыхая,
[16] какъ живая гладь морская.[76]

[I bow before you, / Harking with a full soul / hotly, slowly breathing, / as if living expanse of the sea.]

Nabokov's version is no mere adaptation of Byron's model. The subtlety of this tribute is in its replication of some of the most conspicuous features of the original. The trochaic tetrameter of Nabokov's version is more regular than the metre of "Stanzas for Music," a poem that, according to Bernard Blackstone, "abounds" in metrical subtleties and ambiguities,[77] but the rhyming scheme of the English original is recreated in Russian with utmost accuracy.[78]

One of the poems from the Svetlana Siewert cycle in *Grozd'* mentions "a page from Glinka."[79] This evocation of the name of the one of the masters of the *romans* genre suggests that "Stansy dlia muzyki" might have been transposed into Russian with the intent of becoming an offering to someone capable of appreciating it not only as a poem per se, but also as a song. This particular poem by Byron has been set to music on a number of occasions, but the most popular setting of these two stanzas has long been the one by Fanny Mendelssohn (1836). Svetlana was not the most appreciative of Nabokov's readers, and it is quite likely that the import of his translating effort eluded her, even if one allowed for the possibility of her being acquainted with it in the first place. Nabokov's love for Svetlana, followed by the abrupt, if not altogether unforeseeable dissolution of their engagement left a discernable mark on his writings of the period. As will become clear later in this study, Nabokov's version of Byron's "Stanzas for Music" inaugurated an entire cycle of translations inspired by the affair.

"Quand vous serez bien vieille": First Translation Duel

Nabokov's name is synonymous with a combative approach to translation. An inquiry into the evolution of the dialogic underpinnings of Nabokov's engagement with translation would do well to make an attempt to travel to the origins of his bellicose stance. His early critical take on Sergei Krechetov's version of W.B. Yeats's "When you are old and grey and full of sleep" provides us with such an opportunity.

The transformative approach to the subject that is responsible for so much of the originality of "Rupert Bruk" is by no means characteristic of Nabokov's legacy as a critic. In his review of Krechetov's collection *Zheleznyi persten'* (The Iron Signet Ring), published in the 17 December 1922, issue of *Rul'*, Nabokov complimented the author for the "simplicity and accessibility" of his verse but chided him for the "pallidness of adjectives." In preparation for more substantial criticism to come, Nabokov voiced his disapproval of Krechetov's use of poetic licence in handling a piece of London realia, noting that Krechetov transferred Regent Street from the West End to the City, where the poet needed it to be.[80] The review offered a competing version of a fragment from Yeats's famous poem.

The method Nabokov implicitly advocates in the sample translation of the concluding stanza of Yeats's "When you are old and grey and full of sleep" allows for a substantial degree of freedom in transposing words and phrases within the larger unity of the quatrain. Nabokov's practice presupposes an appreciation of the fact that in translating verse into verse, far from all the traits of the original poem can be conveyed ("the glowing bars" of the original have been replaced by "fire"; the gender of "Love," modified by "his" in the original, is naturally lost in Russian, as is Yeats's allegorical personification; "a little sadly" in English is translated by *unylo*, which is far less nuanced than the original phrase it represents). The stylistic register of Nabokov's version is more elevated than that of the original (cf. *vozneslas'* and "fled"; *sonm* and "crowd"; *sokryla* and "hid"). Nabokov insists on the necessity of retaining not only the original rhyme scheme (something that Krechetov had done) but on the need to create a close metrical replica of the English poem. In his translation, the iambic pentameter of

"When you are old" is carefully preserved, although here too, Nabokov is ready to compromise, as the absence of hypermetrical stress on the opening syllable of line two – a common attribute of the English, rather than Russian, iamb – indicates (cf. "[m]urmur, a little sadly, how Love fled," and "o tom, kak vozneslas' liubov' i tam"). Nabokov's variant, based on a superior grasp of the distinct features of the English original, aspires to strike a balance between retaining a representative minimum of the meaning of the foreign text while adhering as closely as possible to its prosodic makeup. During the "*Nikolka Persik* period," in his own translations of verse Nabokov would permit himself greater freedom, occasionally altering the original's metre quite radically (cf. his versions of "La Belle Dame Sans Merci" by Keats; "The Jolly Company" ["Bylo pozdno, bylo skuchno," It was late, I was bored]; and "The Vision of the Archangels" ["Po krucham nemym, k belosnezhnoi vershine zemli"] by Rupert Brooke). Whenever Nabokov introduced such alterations, however, he did so with a specific goal in mind, which does not seem to be the case with Krechetov's alteration of the metre of Yeats's poem.

In his critique of Krechetov's translations, Nabokov once again reveals his first-hand knowledge of Anglophone poetry and that of W.B. Yeats. Nabokov's reference to the original text of "When you are old" should be especially relevant here, since Nabokov's translation (translations?) of Yeats have never been found, despite the writer's own recollection of having once translated and even published his translations of Yeats some time during his Berlin years.[81] Nabokov's reference to "When you are old" may shed light on the genesis of yet another, earlier translated text belonging to the same period, namely, his version of the famous sonnet 43 from *Le Second Livre des Sonnets pour Helene* (The Second Book of Sonnets for Helen) by Pierre de Ronsard, "Quand vous serez bien vieille, au soir, à la chandelle" (When you [will be] old, on an evening, [next] to a candle). Album 19 also preserves the original French text used by Nabokov for his translation. Its orthography makes it clear that for his translation Nabokov used an authoritative printed source, one that respected Ronsard's archaic spelling.[82]

When on 16 May 1922 Nabokov transposed this signature utterance of one of his favourite poets into Russian ("Quand vous serez bien vieille" would certainly have been one of the Ronsard poems that Nabokov knew by heart), he may well have been mindful of "When you are old," Yeats's version of the same text in English.[83]

In a move that identifies this translation as a work belonging to the "*Nikolka Persik* period," Nabokov concludes his version with an implicit reference to the circumstances surrounding its creation. The closing line of Ronsard's sonnet contains no reference to "May," as line 14 of Nabokov's version does, but with "speshite rozy vziat' u zhiznennogo maia," the alliterative accumulation of z's (*roZy, vZiat', zhiZnennago*) not only echoes the orchestration of this line in the original but also compensates for the internal rhyme lost in Russian: "[c]ueillez dés aujourd'huy / les roses de la vie".[84] Earlier in the text of his translation, Nabokov abandons the negative construction employed by Ronsard in the first and third lines of the second quatrain:

> Lors, vous n'aurez servante oyant telle nouvelle,
> Desja sous le labeur à demy sommeillant,
> Qui au bruit de mon nom ne s'aille resveillant,
> [8] Benissant vostre nom de louange immortelle.[85]

[Then, there will be no servant of yours hearing the news / Already under her work half-asleep, / Who at the sound of my name will wake up, / blessing your name immortalized by [my] praise.]

> – при имени моёмъ, служанка въ домѣ старомъ,
> – уже дремотою работу замѣня,
> очнётся, услыхавъ что знали вы меня,
> [8] вы, – озарённая моимъ безсмертнымъ даромъ.[86]

[at [the sound of] my name, a maid in an old house, / having already traded work for drowsiness, / will come to [her] senses, having heard that you have known me, / you, lit up by my immortal gift.]

Here Nabokov's translation considerably alters the original: Ronsard's second quatrain employs a different grammatical construction in order to introduce a drowsy serving-maid (in her dotage, Helene, the presently youthful addressee of Ronsard's sonnet, will not have a serving-maid who would be woken up by the sound of his name), and in the French there is no "old house" (*staryi dom*) as found in the Russian. The original interplay between the two names – that of the poet and his addressee – is cancelled in favour of a novel image that has all but lost the connection with the French one that engendered it: Ronsard's "immortal praise" ("louange immortelle," l. 8) has been superseded by an evocation of the poet's "immortal gift" (i.e., his genius) – "vy, – ozarënnaia moim bezsmertnym darom" (l. 8).

Nabokov's translation – in spite of his departures from the original – remains close to the meaning and the form of its French model. Ronsard's appeal to his beloved "to gather today the roses of life" is conveyed by Nabokov's line "make haste to take roses from lively May" ("speshite rozy vziat' u zhiznennogo maia," l. 14). Not only do Nabokov's six-foot iambs stay close to the metre of the original, the rhyme scheme of the Russian sonnet reproduces that of the French one. In his version of Ronsard's "Quand vous serez bien vieille," Nabokov struck a delicate balance between instilling his work with a personal purport and preserving the representative features of the original. Nabokov's "Kogda na sklone let i v chas vechernii, charam" can be enjoyed on either of these two levels – as a sonnet by Ronsard, with its strongly expressed *carpe diem*, and as a poem by Nabokov, with its eloquent extolment of the everlasting nature of art. The allusion to the date of the poem's composition/translation, woven into the closing line of Nabokov's version, does just that: the distant May day on which this Russian poem was created has been preserved for posterity in this version of Ronsard's sonnet.

When Nabokov wrote his critique of Sergei Krechetov's version of W.B. Yeats's "When you are old," he could hardly have missed the connection between the English poem by Yeats and the French poem by Ronsard that had inspired it. Yeats's appeal to to Maud Gonne used Ronsard's "Quand vous serez bien vieille" as a model and imparted its author's own feelings of a rejected lover. "When you are old" compresses the octet of Ronsard's sonnet into a single – opening – quatrain (echoes of "Quand vous serez bien vieille" will also resurge in the opening line of the poem's third and concluding stanza). Yeats then proceeds to create his own, personal view of his subject, embodying in verse his unique vision of the beloved's "pilgrim soul" and her "changing face." If Nabokov recognized this English poem's source, he recognized in "When you are old" a reflection of his own adaptations of French and English writers and poets in Russian, and this reflection must have presented him with a somewhat distorted image of his efforts. Nabokov's version of the same sonnet bears within itself a seed of polemic: it demonstrates how one can fill an ostensibly foreign – resistant – form with a native meaning without shattering the vessel that carries it.

Viewed in conjunction with Yeats's "When you are old," Nabokov's version of "Quand vous serez bien vieille" reveals the transitional nature of this experiment. Behind Nabokov's effort to revive the original encapsulated in the text of the English poem lies his attempt to evolve an alternative model for his own experiments in translation. As in his versions of Brooke's poems (most notably in Brooke's wartime sonnets, such as "The Soldier"), in his translation of this Ronsard sonnet Nabokov moves away from an excessively liberal mode of transposing foreign texts into Russian with the aid of native parallels. Yet another work that refuses to comply completely with the standards of literary adaptation exemplified in such versions of foreign texts as "La Belle Dame Sans Merci" and "Po krucham nemym, k belosnezhnoi vershine zemli," "Kogda na sklone let i v chas vechernii, charam" is indicative of Nabokov's growing dissatisfaction with free literary adaptation, and can be said to demonstrate a mounting effort on his part to separate the creation of a new, original text from one based on an ingenious amalgamation of the traits of various models.

A virtuoso performance in its own right, Yeats's "When you are old and grey and full of sleep" takes the technique of literary adaptation to its outer limits: this variation on a theme from Ronsard amounts to a new poem, since the French poet's name is not even mentioned by Yeats (it is notable that the editors of Yeats's poetry still waver as to whether this poem should be classified as an original piece or as an adaptation/translation).[87] Nabokov, who most certainly had come into contact with "When you are old" prior to his encounter with this poem in Sergei Krechetov's version, would have taken account of Yeats's experiment when he created his own translation of "Quand vous serez bien vieille."

As the image of Maud Gonne is imprinted on the text of Yeats's "When you are old," that of Svetlana Siewert, Nabokov's fiancée and dedicatee of his love lyrics written at the time, will likely be linked to this particular Russian translation of Ronsard's sonnet by any reader familiar with the circumstances of Nabokov's biography. Unlike Yeats's "When you are old," however, Nabokov's version of "Quand vous serez bien vieille," all its alterations notwithstanding, *is* a translation of the French poem. It presages many aspects of Nabokov's subsequent evolution, namely his progress past his experiments in adaptation and toward his later, more faithful versions of foreign originals.

Ronsard's "old woman" likewise left a permanent imprint on Nabokov's imagination, once this image secured a place for itself in his individual pool of literary allusions via translation and the polemic associated with it. Contemplating the afterlife of his verse while composing his programmatic poetic statement, Fyodor Godunov-Cherdyntsev cannot help but recall the certitude with which the French sonneteer regarded the durability of his craft.[88] Nabokov's association of "Quand vous serez bien vieille" with the theme of art's immortality in *The Gift* permits us to advance in our search for literary models implied in Humbert Humbert's cryptic reference to "prophetic sonnets" in the concluding passage of *Lolita*: "I am thinking aurochs and angels, the secret of durable pigments, prophetic sonnets, the refuge of art. And this is the only immortality you and I may share, my Lolita."[89] Being able to account for this reference's origin in Ronsard's sonnet and the circumstances under which it enters Nabokov's associative pool refocuses our attention from Humbert Humbert's dubious claims to yet another level in our appreciation of that tragic novel where "art (curiosity, tenderness, kindness, ecstasy) is the norm," as Nabokov asserts in his afterword to the novel.[90]

Escape from the Treacle Well: Ania in the Land of Wonders

Ania v Strane Chudes (Berlin, 1923) occupies a prominent place among Nabokov's juvenilia: this paraphrase of Lewis Carroll's *Alice's Adventures in Wonderland* is the most studied text of Nabokov's early years. In his *Alice in Many Tongues: The Translations of Alice in Wonderland*, Warren Weaver singles *Ania* out as an "especially clever and sensitive" foreign reincarnation of the novel. Prior to the appearance of the versions by Nina Demurova (1967, 1978) and Boris Zakhoder (1971) – whose successes were aided by their familiarity with Nabokov's work – *Ania v Strane Chudes* had certainly been the most accomplished imaginative adaptation of Carroll's classic in Russian.[91] While no match for Demurova's and Zakhoder's renditions, *Ania* has lost little of its ebullience to this day.

Prompted to revisit one of his earliest Russian works by Simon Karlinsky's article "Anya in Wonderland: Nabokov's Russified Lewis Carroll" (which seconded Weaver's assessment), the seventy-year-old author himself was far from enthusiastic about the quality of his adaptation.[92] Unlike *Nikolka Persik*, which was taken up by Nabokov on a wager with his late father, the Carroll translation was commissioned by the émigré publishing venture Gamaiun in the summer of 1922, on the strength of Nabokov's previous accomplishment. By the end of that summer Nabokov had finished the job. Having struggled with Rolland's *Breugnon*, he did not find the task of transposing Carroll into Russian to be demanding.[93] As the work of a White émigré, *Ania* waited sixty-six years to reach the majority of Russian readers in 1989. Even before its belated rediscovery in the metropole, however, it enjoyed unabated success throughout the diaspora, becoming a favourite book of many émigré children scattered across the globe.

Ania's scholarly reception has been twofold. On the one hand, a comparative analysis of Nabokov's version with those of his predecessors has demonstrated the extent of its originality, situated it within the history of Russian translations of Carroll, and raised the problem of Nabokov's hypothetical indebtedness to his forerunners.[94] On the other, scholars who have examined *Ania* in the context of the translator's evolution have commented on the kinship between Nabokov's and Lewis Carroll's poetics.[95] It is unfortunate, however, that to so many observers and interpreters *Ania* has remained the sole representative of "Nabokov's beginnings."[96] It is telling that in her valuable article on *Nikolka Persik*, Elizabeth Klosty Beaujour assumes that *Persik* came on *Ania*'s heels, and not the other way around.[97] In terms of the size and sheer magnitude of the translator's task, it may be difficult to internalize the notion that the much shorter work followed the longer and seemingly more demanding one; in reality, however, it was the diminutive *Ania* that benefitted from the expansive *Nikolka*. Unlike *Nikolka* – a work that cannot be fully appreciated unless aided by the dictionary of Vladimir Dal' – *Ania* is accessible to children and adults alike, giving an impression of spontaneity not commonly registered by *Nikolka*'s readers. *Ania v Strane Chudes* nevertheless owes much of its animacy to its predecessor *Nikolka Persik*. Far from being the study of a beginner, it marks the end of Nabokov's experimentation with literary adaptation that had begun with his Crimean resetting of Pierre Louÿs's prose poems (if not with his daring attempt to turn Mayne Reid's *Headless Horseman* into a latter-day *Henriade*).

Julian W. Connolly's informed and informative survey of the strengths of Nabokov's adaptation remains the single most useful study of the tale. Connolly demonstrates how despite the "lack of polish characteristic of a young writer" and "occasional lapses and omissions," *Ania* amounts to "a sterling piece of literary creation."[98] Along with Demurova's examinations of *Ania* as part and parcel of the Russian tradition of adapting Carroll's tales to the needs of Russian children, Connolly's study guides us toward those "good bits" that Nabokov himself considered to be *Ania*'s merits – its verse parodies and resourceful punning.[99] The strategy of adaptation employed by Nabokov in *Ania v Strane Chudes* goes a step beyond *Nikolka Persik*: it is possible to read *Ania* without suspecting that this story of a Russian girl's adventures in a wondrous land is spawned by a foreign model.[100]

Not only have the characters' names become Russian in this version; the majority of turns of speech and dialogues have been transformed to sound unmistakably native, as have many other minute details of Carroll's narrative. Seeking a parallel to British orange marmalade, Nabokov replaces it with Russian *klubnichnoe varen'e*; he proceeds to replace tarts with *pirozhki* (while translating cherry tart as *vishnëvyi tort*) and "brandy" with "water" (as a more culturally appropriate Russian means of resuscitation of Bill the Lizard after he is kicked up the chimney). Nabokov frequently lowers the stylistic register of the story's lexicon, using *durochka* for "ignorant little girl," *bratninoi* for "brother's," *skazano-sdelano* for "and in she went," *gliadelki* for "eyes," *udrat'* for "to escape," *porot' chush'* for "to talk nonsense," and *goremychnyi* (the epithet he had already tested in his translation of Keats's "La Belle Dame Sans Merci") for "miserable."[101]

The spatial dimensions of the world depicted in *Alice's Adventures in Wonderland* undergo similar transformations. With the exception of the inch (Carroll: "she was now only ten inches high"; Nabokov: "ona teper' byla ne vyshe desiati diuimov rostu," etc.), the Imperial measures of length, height, as well as currency have either been traded for their approximate Russian equivalents or omitted altogether. As was the case with *Nikolka Persik*, omissions from *Alice's Adventures in Wonderland* do not always receive adequate compensation in *Ania v Strane Chudes*. The often-cited example of the French Mouse, who, as Alice supposes, "came over with William the Conqueror" (Nabokov associates it with Napoleon's invasion of Russia in 1812), might be considered in conjunction with another episode of the tale in which Carroll's humorous reference to English literature becomes irrevocably lost in Nabokov's Russian. When in chapter 3 ("A Caucus Race and a Long Tale"; "Igra v kurolesy i povest' v vide khvosta") the Dodo assumes the position "in which you usually see Shakespeare, in pictures of him," in the Russian this tangible image is traded for a gallery of unspecific "great writers."

As earlier in *Nikolka Persik*, in *Ania v Strane Chudes* Nabokov may omit a word, phrase, or passage. Thus, judging Carroll's explanation of Alice's puzzlement with the "Do cats eat bats? Do bats eat cats?" conundrum to be superfluous within the framework of his version, Nabokov eliminates it:

> And here Alice began to get rather sleepy, and went on saying to herself, in a dreamy sort of way, "Do cats eat bats? Do cats eat bats?" and sometimes

"Do bats eat cats?" *for, you see, as she couldn't answer either question, it didn't much matter which way she put it.*[102]

Аня стала впадать въ дремоту и продолжала повторять сонно и смутно: "Кошки на крышѣ, летучія мыши" ... А потомъ слова путались и выходило что-то несуразное: летучія кошки, мыши на крышѣ ...[103]

[Ania began falling into drowsiness and continued to repeat sleepily and confusedly: "Cats on the roof, bats [lit., 'flying mice']..." And then words got confused and something disorderly came out: flying cats, mice on the roof ...]

In this passage the translator concentrates on providing a sonorous alternative to the key phrase at the centre of the English fragment. The rhyming couplet found here is demonstrative of the tendency toward conveying not so much the model's meaning as of finding a Russian approximation of its aural imprint. Unlike Alice, who is seen by the reader attempting to answer the question she poses to herself, Ania is lulled to sleep by the rocking intonation of Nabokov's equivalent. This is the effect that his adaptation emulates and amplifies.

Students of Nabokov's version of *Alice* have observed that *Ania v Strane Chudes* abounds in diminutive forms. For Fan Parker this particular trait of *Ania*'s style bespeaks Nabokov's desire to elicit a sympathetic response from his child readers: "the caressing color of love and tenderness, to which the Russian child can respond with emotional reciprocity is evoked through the extensive use of diminutives."[104] A few examples of such usage are *maliusen'kii* (for "very small" [cake] and "tiny little thing"); *chisten'kii domik* (for "neat little house"); *butylochka* (for "little bottle"); *bednen'kii* (for "poor little"); *uzen'kii* (for "little" [passage]); *ostren'kii* (for "sharp" [chin]). In one isolated instance – in the description of the Rabbit's room – Nabokov even embellishes Carroll's description by adding an especially endearing detail: cf. "she found her way into a tidy little room with a table in the window"[105] with "ona probralas' v pustuiu komnatu, svetluiu, *s goluben'kimi oboiami*" (she sneaked into an empty room, bright, with sweet-little-blue wallpaper).[106]

In another episode, Nabokov's use of a diminutive form is compounded by his modification of the original that endows it with a feature indicative of his emotional involvement with his translation. The passage in question presents one of Alice's faux pas with the Mouse, who cannot endure the girl's excited chatter about her favourite pets, cats and dogs (chapter 2, "The Pool of Tears"):

> "There is such a nice little dog, near our house, I should like to show you! A little bright-eyed terrier, you know, with oh, such long curly brown hair! And it'll fetch things when you throw them, and it'll sit up and beg for its dinner, and all sorts of things – I can't remember half of them – and it belongs to a farmer, you know, and he says it's so useful, it's worth a hundred pounds! He says it kills all the rats and – oh dear!" cried Alice in a sorrowful tone. "I'm afraid I've offended you again!"[107]

A comparison with the original provides a good idea of the asymmetric adjustments characteristic of Nabokov's adaptive technique as a whole. The proliferation of diminutivized nouns and adjectives (a means of conveying the speech of an excited child), the replacement of "farmer" with "miller" (who has every reason to be grateful to a dog for warding off rats), the hyperbolic inflation of the original one hundred pounds to one thousand rubles, as well as the replacement of Alice's pious ellipsis "oh dear!" with the decisively indiscreet by Victorian standards "Oh, God!" ("Akh, Gospodi!") – the presence of all these adjustments should not obscure another important meaningful shift, namely Nabokov's substitution of Carroll's rather nonspecific "terrier" for one very concrete dog:

> Въ соседнемъ домикѣ такой есть очаровательный пёсикъ, такъ мнѣ хотѣлось бы Вамъ показать его! Представьте себѣ: маленькій яркоглазый фоксикъ, в шеколадныхъ крапинкахъ, съ розовымъ брюшкомъ, съ острыми ушами! И если кинешь что-нибудь, онъ непремѣнно принесётъ. Онъ служитъ и лапку подаётъ и много всякихъ другихъ штукъ знаетъ – всего не вспомнишь. И принадлежитъ онъ, знаете, мельнику, и мельникъ говоритъ, что онъ его за тысячу рублей не отдастъ, потому что онъ такъ ловко крысъ убиваетъ и … ахъ, Господи! я, кажется, опять Васъ обидела![108]

> [In the neighbouring house there's such a charming doggy, I would so very much like to show him to you! Imagine: a small bright-eyed fox terrier with chocolate freckles, with rosy belly, with pointy ears! And if you throw anything, he is sure to carry it back. He sits upright and lets you shake his paw and does sundry other tricks as well – I can't remember everything. And he belongs, you know, to the miller, and the miller says he won't sell him for a thousand rubles, since he kills rats so cleverly, and … O Lord! It seems I've offended you again!]

Fox terriers do not have "long curly brown" hair, so Nabokov endows his canine protagonist with features specific to this breed.[109] A superficially trivial substitution, it is fraught with implications, as this particular fox terrier in *Ania v Strane Chudes* introduces a pack of its relatives that from now on will be present in the background of Nabokov's fiction as well as scoring one important appearance in the foreground of his memoir.

Nabokov's fox terriers frequently come riding on the crest of a surging autobiographical motif. To mention just two representative examples: in *Glory* a fox terrier called Lady belongs to Lida, an early love interest of Martin Edelweiss; in *The Gift* numerous appearances of affectionate fox terriers add to the period veracity of the remembered world of Fyodor Godunov-Cherdyntsev's idyllic childhood, becoming yet another emblem of the lost paradise of that novel.[110] Such seemingly disjointed sightings of fox terriers in the pages of Nabokov's novels come into sharp focus with the aid of the most conspicuous appearance of a dog of the same breed in *Speak, Memory*. Chapter 7 of *Speak, Memory* (as well as its counterpart in *Drugie berega*) revolves around the author's distant recollection of a childish infatuation with a French girl named Colette. In *Speak, Memory* Colette, the neglected daughter of well-to-do Parisian burghers, comes to the sunlit world of the author's harmonious childhood unaccompanied, in an "ordinary coach-train," whereas her parents arrive on the scene in their "blue-and-yellow limousine" ("a fashionable adventure in those days," Nabokov remarks). The loneliness of this unloved child is underscored by one moving detail, namely by the constant presence at Colette's side of her sole confidante, a little dog:

> The dog was a female fox terrier with bells on her collar and a most waggly behind. From sheer exuberance, she would lap salt water out of Colette's toy pail. I remember the sail, the sunset and the lighthouse pictured on that pail, but I cannot recall the dog's name, and this bothers me.[111]

A few paragraphs later the same fox terrier is used by Nabokov as the centrepiece of a carefully orchestrated display of his mnemonic prowess:

> And now a delightful thing happens. The process of re-creating … stimulates my memory to a last effort. I try again to recall the name of Colette's dog – and, triumphantly, along those remembered beaches, over the glossy evening sands of the past, where each footprint slowly fills up

> with sunset water, here it comes, here it comes, echoing and vibrating: Floss, Floss, Floss![112]

Proceeding with all the caution required of retrospective impositions of information obtained from Nabokov's memoir to similar passages in his fiction, we may conclude that the image of a fox terrier enjoys the status of an emblem signalling a strong presence of the writer's emotional involvement with a given episode. From this point of view, Nabokov's transfer to *Ania v Strane Chudes* of the first "dear little fox terrier" (*foksik*) of one of the most cherished of his childhood recollections considerably enriches the emotional colouring of the entire episode, resulting in the creation of an image that transmits the translator's own attitude to the object depicted. As such, it can hardly fail to provoke a direct sympathetic response from the reader at a point in the narrative where the original text may not necessarily be comparable in its emotional intensity. As should become clear from another piece of textual evidence offered below, in *Ania v Strane Chudes* Nabokov is circumspect in his management of the reader's response to his fairytale narrative.

In the chapter entitled "Pig and Pepper" ("Porosёnok i perets") the Duchess violently shakes her child as she sings her famous "Speak roughly to your little boy." In the original, the narrator interrupts the Duchess's singing:

> While the Duchess sang the second verse of the song, she kept tossing the baby violently up and down, and the poor little thing howled so, that Alice could hardly hear the words.[113]

The absence of this paragraph from Nabokov's version is a sign of the translator's discomfort with the violence of this scene. On a notable previous occasion Carroll uses the same expression "poor little thing" to describe Alice's bursting into tears out of fear of "going out altogether, like a candle" after shrinking in size under the influence of the magic potion in chapter 1. In Nabokov's adaptation, *that* "poor little thing" appropriately becomes *bedniazhka* – the epithet he evidently could not bring himself to apply to the Duchess's baby. All this is not to say that Nabokov's version seeks to gloss over some potentially cruel episodes of the story – after all, his rendition of "I speak severely to my boy, / And beat him when he sneezes" reads "To ty sinii, to ty krasnyi, / B'iu i snova b'iu!" (a parody of Lermontov's "Kazach'ia kolybel'naia"). Rather, with its predilection for diminutive forms and its removal of some of the more violent descriptions Nabokov's translation has a tendency to sound more gentle than Carroll's frequently ambivalent original.

Nina Demurova summarizes the impression of many readers familiar both with *Ania v Strane Chudes* and the writer's more mature compositions: "The echoes of *Alice* reverberate in many of Nabokov's works ... and form a subtext in more than one."[114] The covert as well as overt presence of *Alice's Adventures in Wonderland* can be felt in such seminal Nabokovian texts as *Priglashenie na kazn'* (*Invitation to a Beheading*; 1936, English translation, 1959), *Volshebnik* (*The Enchanter*; 1939), and *Lolita* (1955), to mention but a few examples. As Connolly has observed, "the elusive boundary between illusion and reality which is invoked in [*Ania*] will crop up in numerous works by Nabokov, and the realization by Alice's sister that the dream of Wonderland 'would change to dull reality' when she opens her eyes anticipates the discovery of several of Nabokov's protagonists."[115]

There is also quite a bit of Lewis Carroll in the figure Humbert Humbert, that most convincing of all Nabokovian villains: no wonder that along with Edgar Allan Poe's wedding, "Lewis Carroll's picnics" was on Nabokov's list of "scenes one would like to have filmed."[116] Reflecting on Carroll in connection with his most famous work, Nabokov remarked: "Some odd scruple prevented me from alluding in *Lolita* to his perversion and to those ambiguous photographs he took in dim rooms. He got away with it, as so many other Victorians got away with pederasty and nympholepsy."[117]

We have every reason to suspect that already at twenty-three, Nabokov sensed that Carroll's fantasies were saturated with their author's sexual urges. While he may not have been prepared to formulate his aversion to the least savoury aspects of Carroll's agenda at that time, by downplaying some manifestations of Carroll's crudeness in his *Ania v Strane Chudes* and encrusting it with references to his own past, he produced its gentler version. As he sensed that Carroll's narratives amounted to what Will Self has termed "the struggle by a tormented pedophile to keep the manifest object of his desire straitjacketed in a fallacious ... dreamlike realm of sexual ignorance,"[118] Nabokov was not prepared to become a disinterested and disengaged transmitter of Carroll's struggles.

"Abandonné d'une infidèle amante": Translation as Solace

Nabokov's engagement to Svetlana Siewert came to an abrupt end on 9 January 1923, and the circumstances surrounding this event no doubt contributed to the pain of the ordeal.[119] The fact that Svetlana – addressee of so many of his letters, dedicatee of so many of his poems, the inspiration behind his versions of Byron's "Stanzas for Music" and Ronsard's "Quand vous serez bien vieille" – should have accepted her parents' decision to break their engagement was harrowing. Nabokov's response to this blow, however, was that of an artist: the loss of his fiancée compelled him to creation. In January through February 1923 he wrote much verse; his second short story, "Slovo" ("The Word"); his longest poem to date, *Solnechnyi son* (The Sun Dream); all of which, in one way or another, either echoed or dealt directly with what Brian Boyd terms Nabokov's "sense of rejection by Svetlana." So intense a release of creative energy had to have had an effect on Nabokov's translations. The body of work connected with 9 January 1923 expanded with his new translations from Alfred Tennyson, Alfred de Musset, and Charles Lamb as he sought solace in the company of his literary confidants.

It is unlikely that *The Princess: A Medley* by Alfred Tennyson (1847), with its tendentious topicality, could have become a source of inspiration for Nabokov at any point in his artistic career, save for a situation where it would have served the butt of parody.[120] This same verse narrative, however, features the poem "Now sleeps the crimson petal, now the white," an anthology piece that Christopher Ricks rates among Tennyson's "finest lyrics." Translated into Russian on 25 January 1923, this poem opens the cycle of translated works that dealt with Nabokov's loss of Svetlana.

Nabokov's version of the poem appears to have lost its connection with the verse narrative, where it is read by Princess Ida "to herself, all in low tones" and is overheard by the narrator feigning sleep. Nabokov titles his translation "Letniaia noch'" (Summer Night): under this title the original had been anthologized in a number of collections of English poetry, to one of which Nabokov must have had recourse in his search for a poetic utterance reflecting his own state of mind.[121] It opened a mini-cycle of translated works united by the all-pervading motifs of longing, grief, and ultimately, resignation that Nabokov experienced so acutely in the aftermath of his engagement's dissolution.

While the poem itself is not rhymed, each stanza of this fourteen-line piece ends with the word "me," lending "Summer Night" a recurring refrain. In his discussion of the Persian sources of *The Princess*, John Killham reinforces the opinion of Tennyson's contemporaries who recognized in it a *ghazal*.[122] Since Killham is careful to define the form of this poem as a "variation upon the form of ... [a] *ghazal*," one might be justified in seeing in it an exercise retaining a number of formal attributes of a sonnet, especially in view of its linear count, metre, and distinctly non-Persian composition.[123] In a telling departure from his usual practice of preserving the form of the original, Nabokov appears to have focused on capturing his own emotional response to Tennyson's text as it echoed his longing for reunion with his beloved.

In Nabokov's version, the opening stanza of Tennyson's "Summer Night" has been extended, and the quatrain has acquired one additional line and two enjambments (see ll. 3–4 and 4–5 below), becoming a stanza comprising five lines:

Вотъ красный лепестокъ уснулъ, уснулъ и бѣлый,
не дышитъ кипарисъ въ аллеѣ царской;
не вспыхнетъ золотой плавникъ въ купели
[4] порфировой; свѣтящіяся мухи
проснулись: ты проснись со мной.[124]

[Now the red petal fell asleep, and so did the white one, / the cypress doesn't breathe in the royal alley; / the golden fin won't flicker in the font / of porphyry; luminescent flies / have woken: now you awake with me.]

In the remainder of "Letniaia noch'" iambic lines of different length vary in much the same, apparently random fashion as they do in this opening stanza. The general impression that in the Russian Nabokov has heightened the intensity of the rather measured emotional atmosphere of the English poem is strengthened by Nabokov's persistent use of enjambment, a formal feature absent from the original, which accounts for much of the translation's immediate emotional impact.

A closer examination of the translation's manuscript reveals another property of "Letniaia noch'": while appearing an equilinear version of the fourteen-line-long original, this translation of Tennyson's "Summer Night" is incomplete. Having encountered a turn of phrase that was particularly difficult to convey in Russian, Nabokov omitted one line of Tennyson's poem, where lines six and seven (the first of the poem's three unrhymed epistrophic distichs) contain a poetic image that Nabokov's "Letniaia noch'" fails to elucidate.

In the English couplet the exotic vision of a "milk-white peacock" is compounded with Tennyson's "she."[125] Enforcing his use of poetic licence, Tennyson ignores the gender mismatch stemming from his coupling of "peacock" (not "peahen") with "she," gaining instead the pleasing image of a white, ghost-like apparition, feminine in gender, flashing against the twilight background of the approaching night before gradually fading. Although not entirely neuter in English, where it should be qualified as a poeticism, Tennyson's application of "she" to "peacock" would have been very difficult to match in Russian, where grammatical gender can make a joke out of a figure of speech that in the original English can be interpreted as a "rich and strange" image. In a rare manifestation of a lack of concern for the intricate detail displayed by the original, Nabokov ignores this problem. As a result, the four lines of the original have been compressed into three in the Russian version. Where Tennyson has his two distichs –

Now droops the milk-white peacock like a ghost,
[6] And like a ghost she glimmers on to me.
Now lies the earth all Danaë to the stars,
[8] And all thy heart lies open unto me.

– Nabokov makes do with only three lines –

Вотъ призракомъ поникъ павлинъ молочно-бѣлый
Подъ звѣздами земля-Даная разметалась,
и вся душа твоя раскрыта мнѣ.[126]

[Now the milky-white peacock stooped down, ghost-like / Under the stars Danae the earth spread herself, / and your entire soul lies uncovered before me.]

Thus, while Nabokov's "Letniaia noch'" has the appearance of an equilinear version of Tennyson's original, this impression must be attributed to the poem's opening quatrain having one extra line and not to Nabokov's desire to create an exact Russian replica of "Summer Night."

The emotional thrust of this translated piece is contained in the two passionate appeals carried in the closing lines of the poem's first and last quatrains: *ty prosnis' so mnoi* (for "waken thou with me") and *rastvoris' vo mne* (for "dissolve in me"). Nabokov's translation of the gender identification of the poem's two personages, its lyrical persona and the addressee, is resolutely interpreted as an enamoured man's appeal to a beloved woman: Tennyson's "my dearest" is translated by Nabokov as *liubimaia*.[127] Nabokov banishes any trace of the ambiguity contained in the original from his version of "Summer Night," which has become an autonomous lyric addressed by a man to a woman.[128]

In December 1915 Nabokov had translated Alfred de Musset's "La Nuit de décembre" to express his exasperation at the realization that his affair with Valentina Shul'gina had ended. A source of bliss at its outset in the summer of the same year, the relationship proved to be doomed once transplanted from "the sylvan security" of Nabokov's country estates to "grim St. Petersburg."[129] On 1 August 1919, in London, Nabokov translated Musset's "Rappelle-toi" to bid farewell to his homeland and inaugurate a major new theme of his work, that of exile. On 28 January 1923 he turned to Musset again, seeking – and finding – a fitting expression for his feelings associated with 9 January. By doing so he wrote another important chapter in the book of his lifelong relationship with that French poet.

As "La Nuit de décembre," the immediate pretext for "Lettre à M. de Lamartine" ("Letter to Mr de Lamartine") was Musset's liaison and breakup with Caroline Jaubert. With all its vivid imagery and pathos, the verse epistle laments the predicament of a man abandoned by his lover.[130] Based on his personal experience of betrayal, disappointment, and misery, Musset asserts that the poet's fate and vocation is to express pain. Intense amorous suffering is the only human sensation capable of transcending the boundary separating the realms of finite earthly existence from the soul's eternal life, the epistle suggests.

The fragment translated by Nabokov is preceded by Musset's description of an unfortunate seasonal labourer who returns home from his work only to find his thatched cottage burned to the ground and his wife and mother of his children killed by the fire. Apart from a life of begging, all that awaits him and his orphaned children now is famine and death.[131] As it turns out, this matter-of-fact tableau, for all its Nekrassovian colouring, does not have as its end the poet's desire to provoke compassion for the downtrodden: it is an extended metaphor whose real purpose is to give the epistle's addressee and the reader some idea of the intensity of the lyrical hero's suffering in the wake of his lover's betrayal.

The uneven lines of Nabokov's Tennyson translation may give an impression that he was not interested in preserving the regularity of the original iambic pentameter. The deregulated rhythm of his take on Musset's epistle conveys a sense of the disorder and devastation ("horreur et détresse") that reign throughout the fragment he rendered.

Throughout "Iz pis'ma k Lamartinu. A. Miusse" (From a letter to Lamartine. [By] A. Musset), syllabotonic metres are prevented from establishing themselves with any degree of steadiness, as their flow is constantly interrupted by accumulations of unstressed syllables between ictuses. Nabokov's translates Musset's fragment into what he himself would have termed a "broken" metre, which he generally avoided in his original poetry. Coupled with the disturbing depiction of the spurned, devastated lover wandering through the filthy, rowdy streets of Paris ("cet immense égout" – this immense sewer – as Musset disdainfully calls it), the deregulated metre of this fragment makes it one of the most uncharacteristic of all Nabokov's verse experiments. The broken metre of "Iz pis'ma k Lamartinu" stands somewhere in between his *dol'nik* experiments and the much more orderly polymetric structures of two of Nabokov's most accomplished Russian poetic utterances, the long poems "Vecher na pustyre" ("Evening on a Vacant Lot"; 1932) and "Slava" ("Fame"; 1942).[132]

In this Russian version of "Lettre à M. de Lamartine," the mask of Musset's heartbroken lover hides the face of the Russian translator who at a time of personal distress returned to a poetic text he knew well since his days at the Tenishev School.[133] Just as the broken rhythms of this fragment cannot be fully explained in terms of Nabokov's attempt to reproduce the classical metre of the French original, the emotional colouring of the invective directed at the *ledianaia podruga* ("froide et cruelle amie") discloses a good deal of the translator's personal involvement with his material, if only to the reader familiar with the circumstances of Nabokov's biography at the time when this translation was created. The lyrical plot that secretly unites such seemingly disparate works as Tennyson's "Summer Night" and Musset's verse epistle in Nabokov's versions begins to take shape as other translated texts enter its gravitational field. The next poem that was to be pulled into it contributes to a further development of the lyrical plot that unites all the translations brought to life by the aftermath of 9 January 1923.

Charles Lamb (1775–1834) is chiefly remembered as an essayist, critic, and wit. Of his two, perhaps three, poems that have survived ("The Old Familiar Faces," "Hester," "Farewell to Tobacco"), only one remains an anthology piece: "The Old Familiar Faces" (January 1798). This poem is the best representative of that strain in Lamb's verse that Louis Cazamian calls "a note of moving simplicity and tender effusion."[134] An unrhymed piece of twenty-one lines, it comprises seven tercets ending in a refrain – the evocation of the irrevocably lost "old familiar faces." Lamb, who initially included a longer, more personal version of the poem in a collection entitled *Blank Verse*,[135] claimed that his "stanzas" "pretend to little like Metre" and simply portrayed the "Disorder [he] was in" at the time he wrote them.[136]

According to Winifred F. Courtney, "The Old Familiar Faces" "easily" yields its autobiographical substratum. When Lamb writes of his love for the "fairest of all women," he means Ann Simmons, the young woman he loved but had to abandon in the wake of his mother's violent death ("Closed are her doors on me, I must not see her"); one "friend" whom he "left abruptly, like an ingrate" is Charles Lloyd, and the other ("Friend of my bosom, thou more than a brother!") is Lamb's schoolmate Samuel Taylor Coleridge. Lamb's sister Mary, who in a fit of madness had stabbed their mother to death, is among those who are "taken" from the poet.[137]

One surmises that when Nabokov turned to "The Old Familiar Faces" on 30 January 1923, he could not have helped seeing parallels between his own predicament and that of Lamb's lyrical persona. The prevailing mood of the poem was akin to what Nabokov was experiencing at the time; the Russian poet-translator would not even have to have known the story behind the poem to relate to it (it is difficult to imagine that Nabokov would not have been familiar with the story of Lamb's life, his selfless devotion to his sister). Another autobiographical factor that may have contributed toward Nabokov's decision to undertake a translation of "The Old Familiar Faces" was the proximity in age between Lamb, who wrote this poem when he was twenty-three, and Nabokov, who translated it when he was only a year older. The title of Nabokov's translation is "Znakomyia litsa. Iz Ch. Lemb"; Nabokov omits the monosyllabic "old" while retaining – and amplifying – the "familiar."

The opening tercet of the translation contains a few significant differences from the original: Lamb's "playmates" and "companions" become "peers" (*sverstniki*); the "old familiar" faces become "inexpressibly familiar," in a rather dramatic departure from the neutral "old" in favour of the more literary compound *neskazanno-znakomye*. By replacing Lamb's "I have had" with "I remember" (in the emphatically inverted word order *pomniu ia*, l. 1), Nabokov's translation opens with a powerful evocation of one of the fundamental motifs of the writer's art – that of memory and remembrance. Lamb's nostalgic reference to his joyful childhood also found an appreciative reader in Nabokov – a writer who would eventually proceed to immortalizing his happy childhood in *Speak, Memory*.

The opening line of the third tercet contains one of the most radical instances of departure from the original. Whereas in the original, the subject of the poem's lyrical persona's admiration is rather conventionally referred to as "fairest among women" (l. 1), in his translation Nabokov sharply redirects his attention from the subject of passion to passion itself:

I loved a love once, fairest among women;
Closed are her doors on me, I must not see her –
All, all are gone, the old familiar faces.[138]

Зналъ я любовь, разлюбилъ вѣсь міръ для любимой;
дверь закрылась, – видѣть её я не долженъ –
всѣ, всѣ ушли несказанно-знакомыя лица …[139]

[I knew love, for my beloved's sake I fell out of love with the whole world; / the door has shut – I must not see her – / All, all inexpressibly familiar faces have left …]

This asymmetry cannot be explained without taking into account the autobiographical element present in the Russian wording of this tercet's opening line.

In another meaningful alteration, Nabokov subtly but resolutely brings his translation closer to his own exilic predicament. The fourth tercet of Lamb's poem opens with a matter-of-fact recollection of the "haunts of his childhood":

Ghost-like, I paced round the haunts of my childhood.
Earth seemed a desert I was bound to traverse,
Seeking to find the old familiar faces.[140]

According to Lamb's recollection, these lines were inspired by a solitary walk he had taken around the Temple, where he, son of a Bencher's factotum, had been born. Nabokov is attentive to this image of a revisited past, which figures here in conjunction with Lamb's likening himself to a ghost. For Nabokov, Lamb's sad hyperbole "Earth seemed a desert I was bound to traverse" was more than a rhetorical figure – as an émigré, he had a first-hand acquaintance with the meaning of the word "traverse" in the sense that Lamb uses in his poem. Nabokov's translation of this tercet delicately repositions many accents of the original fragment:

Тѣнью блуждалъ я по тихимъ окрайнамъ былого;
міръ казался пустыней, а я былъ скитальцемъ,
ищущимъ васъ, несказанно-знакомыя лица.[141]

[A shadow, I roamed the quiet outskirts of the past; / the world seemed a desert and I was a wanderer, / seeking you, inexpressibly familiar faces.]

In Nabokov's version of the fifth tercet, Lamb's simile "ghost-like" acquires a novel meaning, one that reflects Nabokov's persistent search for a "spectral dimension" of phenomena depicted in a work of art. The instrumental case form of *ten'* ("shadow"), in conjunction with the imperfective past tense form of *bluzhdat'* substantially modifies Lamb's simile: having become a mournful shadow, the lyrical persona of Nabokov's translation traverses the equally ephemeral outskirts of his past, rather than the concrete "childhood haunts" of the original. Nabokov transforms Lamb's pensive ramble around the Temple into a vision.

Having already translated "Quand vous serez bien vieille, au soir, à la chandelle" (*Le Second livre des sonnets pour Helene*, no. 43) as "Kogda na sklone let i v chas vechernii, charam ..." on 16 May 1922 in Berlin, Nabokov returned to Ronsard on 25 August 1923, toward the end of his stay in the south of France. The two sonnets translated by Nabokov on this occasion were "Avant le temps tes temples fleuriront" ("Before their time will your temples bloom")[142] and the famous "Je veux lire en trois jours l'Iliade d'Homère" ("For three days I wish to read Homer's *Iliad*").[143] It is difficult to ascertain exactly what Nabokov intended to do with these translations, although there is a strong indication that he envisaged an entire sequence comprising Ronsard's sonnets in his rendition. At the basis of this hypothesis lies the fact that the Russian translations of the French sonnets are supplied with a numeration that does not appear to follow any of the authoritative editions of Ronsard's poems.[144] No fewer than three sets of the handwritten copies of the would-be sequence appear to have survived among Nabokov's papers.[145]

While it may not be possible to restore the lyrical plot of a presumed sonnet sequence, the precise length of which is unknown, the three extant pieces can be interpreted as parts of a larger narrative unity, especially since it appears to be sustained by a gradual evolution of a unifying theme. The same unity is upheld by a continuous representation of the protagonist's "I," which amounts to a nuanced portrait of the Poet. As suggested by its number and supported by its content, sonnet 1 ("Sonet I" ["Do sroka skorb' tebia oserebrit ...," – Before [it is] time grief will sprinkle you with silver]) may well have been produced with the thought of providing a point of departure for the envisaged sequence.

As was the case with the earlier version of "Quand vous serez bien vieille," Nabokov's translation of this sonnet reproduces the rhyme scheme of its model. The iambic pentameter of Nabokov's Russian version provides a fitting analogy to the shorter line of the French original, as opposed to, say, "Quand vous serez bien vieille," which he reset in hexameters.

As the opening piece of a sonnet sequence, "Sonet I" echoes the melancholic tonality characteristic of the other translations Nabokov created in response to 9 January 1923.[146] The words of a pitiless Nymph ("Ton desastre ira ma destinée, / Pour abuser les poètes je suis née," ll. 6–7), who tries her hardest to instil uncertainty into the Poet's soul, appear to be corroborated by an ill omen, "un dextre éclair" (l. 14), that flashes before the Poet's eyes (l. 14).

According to the numeration the three translated sonnets have been supplied with in the extant manuscripts, "Kogda na sklone let i v chas vechernii charam ..." (the 1922 version of "Quand vous serez bien vieille"), was to follow "Sonet I" as "Sonet VI." Against the background of "Sonet I," "Sonet VI" acquires a novel shade of meaning. The Poet – identified unambiguously in "Sonet VI" as Ronsard ("vesna moia byla proslavlena Ronsarom," "my spring was lauded by Ronsard," l. 4) – appears to have regained his confidence, which had come under such a savage verbal attack from the Nymph in "Sonet I." In Nabokov's "Sonet VI," Ronsard's coy mistress is assured that even in years to come she will be remembered as the woman whose "spring was glorified by Ronsard," which makes it clear that whatever was the curse inflicted upon the Poet by the wrathful goddess, the Poet has been able to overcome it.

The final instalment of the supposed sonnet sequence appears to bring the theme of artistic confidence and self-esteem first articulated in "Sonet VI" to a new level, as the personality of the Poet is deepened with the help of an ostensible self-portrait in a domestic interior. The Poet has already been portrayed once as the victim of a potent adversary impersonated by the wrathful Nymph ("Sonet I"), and as a suave, persuasive, and gallant artist capable of applying his poetic gift to the task of achieving his amorous ends ("Sonet VI"). In "Sonet VIII" ("Tri dnia khochu chitat', mechtat' nad Iliadoi," a version of "Je veux lire en trois jours l'Iliade d'Homère"), he is shown to be enjoying the company of Homer (whom Ronsard would have read in the original), while only a messenger from his beloved (named, appropriately enough, Cassandre) is allowed to disturb the Poet during his self-imposed seclusion with the text of the *Iliad*.

Throughout his version of the sonnet, Nabokov follows the rhyme scheme of the French original. Nabokov conveys the casual tonality of the original without attempting to retain some of the obsolete lexical items to be found in Ronsard's text (it is, nonetheless, telling that Nabokov's equivalent for the obsolete "huis" is *kalitka*, whose obsolete meaning is comparable to that of the French "huis").[147] While the exact lexical expression of the Poet's threat to his porter ("Tu sentiras combien pesante est ma colère") is not matched by that of the translation ("ty poznakomish'sia s krutoi moei dosadoi"), its portent has been transmitted into Russian.[148]

Most important, in "Sonet VIII" there is not a trace left of the fatalistic atmosphere permeating "Sonet I": self-doubt and a premonition of failure have been cast aside by the Poet in "Sonet VIII"; after a period of uncertainty, the Poet has regained his ability to be inspired by literature and love.

So strong was the impact of Nabokov's infatuation with Svetlana Siewert on the young poet and writer's output dating from 1922 to 1923 that it seems fitting to designate the sizeable body of his poetic texts dealing with this infatuation as the "Siewert cycle," following the time-honoured tradition that identifies similar thematic entities within the poetic outputs of Fëdor Tiutchev and Nikolai Nekrasov as the Denis'eva and Panaeva cycles (*denis'evskii tsikl* and *panaevskii tsikl*, respectively). The true magnitude of this impact, however, would not be possible to appreciate without taking into account Nabokov's experiments in translation that were inspired by his courtship of and engagement to Svetlana Siewert, and especially those created in the aftermath of their breakup.

Stressing the immaturity of Nabokov's feelings for Svetlana Siewert, Brian Boyd observes that his love for her "owed more to timing and ripe daydreams than to any profound suitability of character,"[149] and indeed the essential lack of understanding on Svetlana's part of Nabokov's lyrics and emotionally charged translations confirms that the real drama of this infatuation was to a large extent a poetic creation. In losing Svetlana Siewert, Nabokov gained his own Annette Olenina, his own Amalie or Therese Heine – powerful but evanescent infatuations that left a lasting impression on Pushkin and Heine.

Bidding Byron's "Histrionic Tempests" Adieu

On 20 April 1924, the Berlin-based Russian Literary Club commemorated the centenary of Lord Byron's death with a literary evening. V. Sirin, the rising star of émigré literature – a translator, poet, and writer with strong ties to England – took part in this undertaking, reading "some poems in English and some he had just translated into Russian."[150] If Nabokov's participation in the Byron gala serves as any indication, he had not yet begun to favour Keats over Byron, a disenchantment that was to find expression in the memorable lines from *University Poem* (1926) already quoted here. On 18 April Nabokov prepared his versions of "She Walks in Beauty" (1815), "So We'll Go No More A Roving" (1816), and also revised his 1922 translation of "Stanzas for Music" ("There be none of Beauty's daughters," 1816). With the versions of Byron's poems created on 18 April 1924, however, Nabokov's long-standing affinity with Byron began to wane, as his poems – theretofore a staple of Nabokov's translating repertoire – ceased to figure among his translations.

Within the body of work translated by Nabokov, the three 1924 texts represent a fascinating example of versions of foreign poems created with the deliberate intent of acquainting the listener/reader with an English poet whose name had long been proverbial or even notorious, but whose verse was seldom read or valued for its own merit. It is safe to say that in commemorating Byron, Russian Berliners were paying homage to a quintessential exilic poet, a freedom fighter, a liberty-minded man of action, and also a major inspiration for Pushkin and Lermontov. In his annotated *Eugene Onegin* (1964, 1975), Nabokov would argue persuasively that Pushkin's idea of Byron was greatly influenced by the French renditions of his tremendously popular epic pieces, which, with the notable exception of *Don Juan*, hardly represented how Byron the poet was perceived in his homeland. It is noteworthy that in his 18 April 1924 selection, Nabokov favoured not Byron the epic poet (a side of Byron Nabokov could have illustrated by reading excerpts from his reliable version of "The Dream") but Byron the lyrist, the author of "She Walks in Beauty," "So We'll Go No More A Roving," and "Stanzas for Music" ("There be none of Beauty's daughters").

The 1924 trio of Byron texts affords a rare glimpse of Nabokov the poet-translator at work: apart from a fair copy of Nabokov's version of "She Walks in Beauty" there survives a draft bearing traces of extensive revisions, while the 1924 version of "Stanzas for Music" ("There be none of Beauty's daughters") is in itself a revision of the 1922 translation of the same poem.

United by the identical recurring title – "Iz Bairona" – the three translated poems are also thematically connected, each of them presenting a different strain of Byron's amorous verse, from the exalted "She Walks in Beauty" (extracted from the same *Hebrew Melodies* of which Nabokov had already translated "Oh! Snatched Away in Beauty's Bloom," "'All Is Vanity,' Saith the Preacher," and "Sun of the Sleepless!"), to the frivolous "So We'll Go No More A Roving," and finally, to the implicitly erotic "Stanzas for Music" ("There be none of Beauty's daughters").

The comparative dearth of mono- and disyllabic words that represents an inherent impediment to the creation of equimetric translations of English poetry into Russian makes itself felt in Nabokov's take on "She Walks in Beauty." In his line two, Nabokov telescopes "Of cloudless climes and starry skies" into a line that struggles to retain as much of the original as possible in spite of its gain of an extra foot. As a result, the monosyllabic poeticism "climes" contained in the original line has been omitted and the bypartite structure of Byron's phrase (adjective + noun, conjunction, adjective + noun) has been transferred into Russian in a truncated form (*bezoblachnaia i zvezdnaia vyshina*; adjective, conjunction, adjective + noun). The translator's difficult choice, however, is anything but mechanical. In choosing to transpose the meaning of Byron's simile containing a reference to sky ("starry skies") by the Russian *vyshina*, Nabokov has followed the overall elevating vector of Byron's likening of his model to an ethereal being. In the remainder of the Russian stanza quoted here, the increasing inertia of an established rhyming combination begins to dictate its own rules (*nochnaia/sochetaia, vyshiny/sochteny* – it should be kept in mind that the sestet-like stanzas of this poem have only two such combinations each), drastically limiting the translator's freedom in choosing lexical means for preserving the original imagery. The characteristically Nabokovian mode of paraphrastic verse translation is represented by the two concluding lines of the first stanza, where he reconsiders the original, emerging with a synthesis of Byron's imagery.

The English stanza closes with an eloquent expression of Byron's preference for the subdued beauty of night over that of "gaudy day" ("that tender light / Which heaven to gaudy day denies," ll. 5–6). The vividness of Byron's image is assisted by a subtle personification: on the one hand, the "heaven" that denies "tender light" to the "gaudy day" represents the celestial source of illumination; on the other, "heaven" (due to this sentence's grammatical construction, this word occupies the position of subject) represents an implicit reference to a higher power that governs distribution of light in the universe ("heaven … denies … tender light" to "gaudy day"). Nabokov chooses to verbalize the implied reference to a state of being concealed from human perception, exchanging "tender light" for *ottenki raia* ("hues of paradise," l. 5), which fuses the original reference to heaven with the translator's own individual image, one sparked by the picture painted in the matching fragment of the English poem.

Having presented Byron's vision of an ethereal being and heavenly beauty, Nabokov proceeded to display another side of the British poet, namely Byron the libertine and carouser who wrote "So We'll Go No More A Roving," this "masterpiece of non-statement."[151] "Iz Bairona" ("Itak ne budem my s toboiu" – So you and I will not be) is a poem consisting of four quatrains of ternary iambs.[152] The translator of *Colas Breugnon* and "friend of Rabelais and Shakespeare" does not shy away from a signature Byronic innuendo contained in the poem: "the sword outwears its sheath" becomes "no protiraet mech' nozhny" (complete with the archaic final stress in *nozhný*, as Dal' would have it), and the innocuous "the day returns too soon" is made suggestive ("khot' noch' daetsia dlia liubovi [although the night is given for love], "i slishkom skoro den' vstaët" [too soon the day rises]).

Nabokov's mature preference of Keats over Byron did not amount to a total eclipse of the latter poet by the former: Byronic echoes continued to resound throughout Nabokov's writings, not infrequently acquiring undertones of parody; intimate knowledge of Byron facilitated and enriched Nabokov's discriminating appreciation of Pushkin. Nabokov's enigmatic contrasting of Byron's "histrionic tempests" with Keatsean "marble roses" in *University Poem* (1926) – and his unambiguously expressed preference for the latter – may well have been a retrospective acknowledgment of the fact that Keats's steadfast attention to the inner life of "a thing of beauty" (*Endymion*) as embodied in a work of art (see, for example, his "Ode on a Grecian Urn") proved at some point of Nabokov's evolution to be a deeper source of inspiration than Byron's comparatively facile visions of beauty, both sacred and profane.

"в изгнаньи, на землѣ": Baudelaire's "Albatros"

As early as 1937, Vladislav Khodasevich discerned that "the life of the artist … is a theme that can be perceived in nearly all of [Nabokov's] writings."[153] Nabokov's notion of the artist's ambivalent position on the borderline separating the plane of objective reality from that of artistic invention developed over a substantial period of time and, most important, after coming into contact with stimulating alternative expressions of underlying philosophical concerns. Sometime in June 1924, Nabokov rendered in Russian one of the most influential texts ever to deal with the problem of the artist's place in the universe, Charles Baudelaire's "Albatros."

Baudelaire's nameless, intentionally generic and elusive "Poète" can hardly be more different from, say, Ronsard's depiction of Renaissance artistic self-sufficiency in "Je veux lire en trois jours l'Iliade d'Homère." Not only does Nabokov's version of Baudelaire's poem mark an early point in his growing interest in this theme, it points in the direction of one of his most important sources of inspiration for its later, more complex manifestations in such differing works as *The Defense* (1930), *Invitation to a Beheading* (1936), *The Gift* (1938), and *Bend Sinister* (1946) – to limit this list only to those of his subsequent works that can be said to offer a particularly eloquent expression of this rich theme. As Khodasevich was first to point out, however, there can hardly be a single major Nabokov text free of some articulation of this paramount subject.

The opening quatrain of Nabokov's "Albatros" gives some suggestion of the subtle transformations the Baudelaire poem has undergone. Nabokov opens with a poeticized retelling of Baudelaire's rather matter-of-fact introductory description: for example, the phrase *po zybiam skol'ziashchie matrosy* is in fact an imaginative rendition of the first quatrain's closing line ("le navire glissant sur le gouffres amers," l. 4). Noteworthy is the postponed appearance of the vessel that carries the sailors (Nabokov's *matrosy*, Baudelaire's "les hommes d'équipage"), as if the translator has chosen to endow his text with a surrealistic touch by making the sailors glide above the waves without any means of conveyance. In its altered state, the opening line sets the tone for the rest of the poem by elevating the dominant mode in this Russian version of "L'Albatros." Consequently, the coarse intonation of the fragment of reported speech inserted into the last two lines of the third stanza (*mazni ego po kliuvu*; brush him against [his] beak) eloquently underscores the jeering enmity faced by the allegorical bird on the ship's deck once it has been brought down.

The nerve of this poetic rendition of Baudelaire's poem is to be found in the opening line of the second stanza. Nabokov translates "à peine les ont-ils déposés sur les planches" (as soon as they are placed on the planks) as "Kak tol'ko on liud'mi na palubu postavlen" (as soon as he is by people placed on [a] deck, l. 5). Superficially, the introduction of the word *liudi* (here men; instr. plur.) compensates for the lost "hommes d'équipage" of the poem's opening line; within the semi-autonomous context of the translated text, however, it suggests that the antipathy harboured by humanity (*liudi*) toward this angel-like creature is rendered inevitable by the base nature of humankind. As shown by the Russian poem's second stanza, Nabokov's *al'batros* is more angel-like than exotic, since Baudelaire's comparison of the bird's "great white wings" ("grandes ailes blanches") with a pair of oars ("Comme des avirons traîner à côté d'eux") is omitted entirely from Nabokov's version of the poem, which instead features "the white masses of the heavy wings" (*gromady belye otiazhelevshikh kryl*, l. 8).

The closing quatrain of the poem may be interpreted as the condensed expression of the tragic conflict of the poet with an uncomprehending actuality, a vision shared by both Baudelaire and Nabokov:

Поэтъ похожъ на нихъ, – царей небесъ волнистыхъ.
Имъ стрѣлы не страшны и буря имъ мила.
Въ изгнаньи, – на землѣ, – средь хохота и свиста,
[16] мѣшаютъ имъ ходить огромныя крыла![154]

[A poet resembles them – those furrowed kings of the skies. / Arrows don't frighten them and a tempest is dear to them. / In exile – on earth – amid guffaws and jeers, / their gate is encumbered by enormous wings.]

In his subsequent original work, Nabokov was to develop this theme far beyond the itinerary suggested by the powerful conclusion of Baudelaire's poem. In his subsequent novels and short stories, an artistic nature would be manifested in some unpredictable guises: consider, for example, the short story "The Leonardo" ("Korolëk," 1933), featuring a counterfeiter as its protagonist; or in a more sinister vein, *Despair* (1932) and *Lolita* (1955), in which murderers and child-molesters are caught arraying themselves in the white wings of scorned and misunderstood poets. As Khodasevich was quick to point out, not nearly all of Nabokov's artistic protagonists are true artists; some are little more than repulsive and dangerous frauds. Baudelaire's melancholic comparison of the poet to a "prince of the heavens" rudely brought down to earth did not fail to set in motion Nabokov's irony.

"My soul's imaginary sight": Shakespeare's Sonnets 17 and 27

Samuel Schuman has demonstrated that Shakespearean echoes permeate Nabokov's Russian writings, even though he "began making massive use of Shakespearean materials, especially in his novels ... only when he began writing principally in English."[155] The year 1924 witnessed an upsurge of Nabokov's interest in Shakespeare: it was then that he wrote his first major original composition, *The Tragedy of Mr. Morn*, a five-act verse romance teeming with manifestations of his lifelong dialogue with one of his most potent paragons and literary interlocutors.[156] By 26 February 1924, Nabokov had written "Shakespeare," a forty-eight-line affair detailing the author's personal vision of the Bard using the Bard's signature prosodic medium, iambic pentameter.[157] Unabashedly anti-Stratfordian in its treatment of the authorship problem, the poem emphasizes the tantalizingly elusive nature of a genius whose proportions are frankly estimated to have been nothing short of divine. Toward the end of this wry encomium Nabokov bestows upon Shakespeare the title of "a god of iambic thunder ... hundred-mouthed, unthinkably great bard."[158]

In his search for Shakespearean themes and echoes in Nabokov's Russian writings, Schuman naturally turns to Shakespeare's plays, most notably to *Hamlet*, which Nabokov attempted to translate in 1930, to *Othello* (in connection with *Camera Obscura*), and also to *King Lear* and *Romeo and Juliet*. Schuman's admittedly limited overview determines that "Nabokov's engagement with Shakespeare and his works at the beginning of his professional career" was deep and broad in its range.[159] One important instance of a direct creative involvement with major Shakespearean texts must be added to Schuman's list. It comprises Nabokov's translations of sonnets 17 and 27, made on 1 November 1924.

Any attempt to analyse Nabokov's version of an important text should begin with an effort to ascertain the source of such a version. He probably used the same *Oxford Shakespeare* edited by W.J. Craig (1914) that he was to rely on later in his life.[160] Craig's edition tends to omit some of the elisions characteristic of Thomas Thorpe's 1609 Quarto ("heav'n" becomes "heaven") and replaces its Arabic numerals with Roman ones, which is exactly how the original English texts of the sonnets are reproduced in Album 19.[161] Nabokov retained the Roman numerals of Craig's edition when his versions of the two sonnets eventually appeared in the 18 September 1927, issue of *Rul'*.

In Thorpe's 1609 Quarto, sonnet 17 ("Who will believe my verse in time to come") closes a sub-sequence devoted to the task of persuading the poet's fair friend to get married and exercise his conjugal duties ("You had a father, let your son say so"). In a rare reversal of the practice of literary adaptation he had all but abandoned since completing his version of Lewis Carroll's *Alice's Adventures in Wonderland*, Nabokov chose to ignore the implications stemming from the context in which the sonnet originally appeared and re-addressed it to a woman:

Сонетъ мой за обманъ вѣка бы осудили,
когда бъ онъ показалъ твой образъ неземной,
но въ пѣснѣ, знаетъ Богъ, ты скрыта, какъ въ могилѣ
[4] и жизнь твоихъ очей не выявлена мной.[162]

[The centuries would denounce my sonnet for mendacity, / if it showed your likeness as unearthly, / but in a song, God knows, you are concealed as in a grave / and the life of your eyes has not been revealed by me.]

Russian predicative participles (*skryta*) and past tense verbs (*zhila*) unambiguously indicate that in Nabokov's "Sonet XVII" the object of the poet's exhortation is feminine in gender – a major transformation that amounts to a plea to a woman not to neglect reproduction, which in its turn should provide living evidence of the poet's truthfulness in his praise of her beauty: "No esli by nashlos' ditia tvoe na svete, / zhila by ty vdvoine, – v potomke i v sonete" (cf. the closing couplet of the English original: "[but] were some child of yours alive that time, / You should live twice in it and in my rhyme"). It is clear that Nabokov, who – at least in 1924 – was of the opinion that the real poet of genius behind Shakespeare's writings would never become known (see his "Shakespeare"), decided to interpret sonnet 17 as he saw fit, "freeing" it from its dependence on the context in which it first appeared. Later in his career Nabokov was to parody attempts on the part of some over-zealous admirers of Shakespeare to interpret his writings in accordance with their own ideas regarding what they saw as the "true" significance of the Bard's elusive images (in *Pale Fire,* Charles Kinbote uses a phrase from Thorpe's famous preliminary note to the Quarto to further his perverse reading of John Shade's poem).

Except for this gender disagreement, Nabokov's version of sonnet 17 aspires to offer the reader a fair representation of Shakespeare's difficult text not only in terms of its significance but also in terms of its form.

Once again, Nabokov extends the original's metre, seeking to compensate for the comparative inequality in word length between English and Russian. In his "Sonet XVII" Nabokov successfully retains one of the most taxing features of Shakespeare sonnets for a translator, their venturesome wordplay.[163] When Shakespeare attempts to "number in fresh numbers all [his model's] graces" (l. 6), the matching fragment of Nabokov's translation provides an alliterative rendition of this line in Russian: "i chistoe chislo vsekh prelestei tvoikh" (where the repetition of the identically sounding syllable *chis-* in two different words mirrors Shakespeare's "numbers number").

In this duo of translated sonnets, "Sonet XVII" prepares the ground for "Sonet XXVII," which presents the reader with subject matter and portent more complex both in terms of their significance and verbal manifestation. Dream, memory, thought, imagination, and unfulfilled longing all converge in sonnet 27 ("Weary with toil, I haste me to my bed") to give the reader one of the finest examples of Shakespeare's mature metaphysical style.

It is easy to see why this poem would hold such a strong appeal for Nabokov, a lifelong insomniac. The domain of dream – presented here as both an image generated by a slumbering mind (*son*) and as aspirations or ideals people pursue in their waking reality (*mechta*) – was always within the focus of Nabokov's contemplation. Sonnet 27 blurs the line separating one meaning of the word "dream" from the other and paints a detailed picture of a querying mind caught in a limbo between its ability to envisage the object of its longing with utmost vividness and its pathetic incapacity to derive satisfaction from this ability. On a more mundane level, with its reference to tiresome and probably pointless "travel" (l. 2), sonnet 27 would have appealed to Nabokov by adding to its picture another important Nabokovian motif – that of wandering or forced banishment, which later on in the sonnet is to undergo a Shakespearean transformation into a purposeful pilgrimage (l. 6). W.J. Craig's *Oxford Shakespeare* set the example for modern readers and editors of the sonnet who interpret the word "trauaill" (as it was spelled in the 1609 Quarto) as "travel." It is this reading that is reflected in Elena Nabokova's transcript of the English text of the sonnet in Album 19. To translate it, Nabokov evokes a poetic Russian denomination of wandering, *stranstvie*, familiar to the student of his translation from his version of Byron's "Dream" (1918).

Спѣшу я, утомясь, къ цѣлительной постели,
гдѣ плоти суждено отъ странствій отдохнуть, –

но только всѣ труды отъ тѣла отлетѣли,
[4] пускается мой умъ въ паломническій путь.[164]

[I hurry, having worn myself out, toward the curative bed, / where the flesh is fated to rest from travels – / but as soon as all the labours flew away from the body, / my mind launches itself on a pilgrim's path.]

Nabokov's version of sonnet 27 is in many ways a summation of his individual transpositional technique, representative of this particular stage in his development as a translator. The cornerstone of his strategy lay in a selective approach to the original text: Nabokov the translator favoured texts congenial to his own artistic notions and metaphysical concerns. Such congeniality permitted him to view the original in its entirety, which in its turn had a direct bearing on the actual execution of his task. Here Nabokov employs an extension of the original metre, gaining a greater degree of freedom in the transposition of lexical items from English into Russian.

While restricted by his adherence to the formal constraints of the original and its imagery, Nabokov's paraphrastic technique permits a significant number of alterations. Thus, his representation of Shakespeare's image of a "bed, dear repose for limbs with travel tired" (ll. 1–2), which is a single continuous phrase in the English, is divided between two phrases: "curative/healing bed" (*tselitel'naia postel'*, l. 1) and "flesh" (*plot'*, l. 2). He retains the meaning of the original phrase but does away with its exact wording and placement within the matching fragment of the original.[165] At the same time, an important descriptive characterization of the sonnet's setting has remained where it had been placed by the author: Shakespeare's reference to separation between the protagonist and the object of his yearning ("far where I abide," l. 5) appears at the end of the first line of the sonnet's second quatrain (*otsiuda, – izdalëka*, l. 5) in this Russian version. Similarly, one of the central images of the English poem retains its original placement: "my soul's imaginary sight" (l. 9), translated by Nabokov as "moei dushi tainstvennoe zren'e" (l. 9), appears in the opening line of the sonnet's fourth and last quatrain. It is notable, however, that the Russian version of this phrase digresses from the original by introducing into the text a reference to the enigmatic nature of the "soul's sight," which constitutes an important shift in the phrase's meaning: the adjective "imaginary" becomes "mysterious" (*tainstvennyi*).[166] Another important image of the original poem, "a jewel hung in ghastly night" (l. 11), undergoes a similar change in Nabokov's version: it becomes "samotsvet v mogil'noi temnote" (l. 12), where the adjective *mogil'nyi* (sepulchral) links the bleak reality of the poet's actual surroundings with death. The central contrast implied in Shakespeare's sonnet is mirrored in its Russian version: the imagined spectre of a dear beloved appears more vivid and lively than the protagonist's surroundings. Nabokov's version of sonnet 27 omits Shakespeare's reference to the transforming powers of the imagination: whereas Shakespeare speaks of a miraculous transformation of a "ghastly night" into a "beauteous" and rejuvenated one ("my soul's imaginary sight … makes black night beauteous and her old face new," ll. 9, 12), Nabokov refuses to endow his description of the night with any positive connotations ("moei dushi tainstvennoe zren'e … okrashivaet noch'," ll. 9, 11).

In Nabokov's "Speshu ia, utomias', k tselitel'noi posteli," separation from the personified object of the protagonist's yearning is overcome by the force of the imagination, a force that is capable of eclipsing desolate reality with a vision that is much more tangible than the protagonist's actual surroundings. Imagination, artifice beats reality at its own game by turning out to be a phenomenon that possesses more distinctive qualities than its uninspiring rival.

"A great and admirable poet": Gallicizing Tiutchev's "Vernal Thunderstorm"

Nabokov's affinity with Fëdor Tiutchev is of momentous significance, as witnessed by the Tiutchevian allusions that permeate Nabokov's writings.[167] In purely quantitative terms, Tiutchev occupies a prominent place among the poets whom he translated the most, on a par with Pushkin, Lermontov, and Byron. Some time around 1925 Nabokov drafted a translation of Tiutchev's "Vesenniaia groza" ("Liubliu grozu v nachale maia," 1820s).[168] Demonstrating how versatile he could be in his translating experiments, Nabokov rendered Tiutchev's signature poetic utterance into French verse.

In his "J'aime au début de mai l'orage,"[169] Nabokov provides a version of Tiutchev's poem that does justice to the formal characteristics of the original while conveying its meaning. Presaging one of the most distinctive features of Nabokov's English versions of Tiutchev's lyrical pieces, "J'aime au début de mai l'orage" demonstrates a superb comprehension of the finer aspects of the original. The translation survives in a very rough draft but nonetheless amounts to a complete poetic text.

Focusing on a fragment of Nabokov's translation, we may get a feel for this early foray into French.

The closing quatrain of "Vesenniaia groza" starts with a phrase that lends itself to differing interpretations:

Ты скажешь: вѣтреная Геба,
Кормя Зевесова орла,
Громокипящій кубокъ съ неба,
[16] Смѣясь, на землю пролила.[170]

[You would say: flighty Hebe, / while feeding Zeus's eagle, / from the skies a thunder-boiling goblet, / laughingly, spilled on the earth.]

The opening clause may be interpreted as an apostrophe: in anticipation of his interlocutor's enraptured reaction to the majestic spectacle unfolding before their eyes, the poet provides an expressive classical simile of his own. In such a way the closing quatrain of the poem has been interpreted by generations of native speakers of Russian, who encounter this poem at school where they are required to memorize it even before they are capable of appreciating the subtler aspects of Tiutchev's poetics. Not only does Nabokov's reading succeed in providing a close replica of its model, it shows him to be an interpreter whose sophisticated appreciation of a familiar text is free of cliché:

On dirait qu'Héb[é] la légère
qui fai[t] boire l'aigle divin[,]
en riant, laisse choir à terre
[16] sa coupe de feu et de vin.

[It would seem that Hebe the light, / who [provides drink to] the divine eagle, / laughingly lets drop to the earth / her chalice of fire and wine.]

"It would seem" ("on dirait") does away with the apparent apostrophe of the opening clause: while marvelling at a vernal storm, Tiutchev's protagonist talks to himself. Nabokov's choice of "coupe" for *kubok* (goblet, chalice) hints at a quintessential feature of Tiutchev's poetics, his preference for archaisms. Imperfect, hastily drafted, unpublished, Nabokov's "J'aime au début de mai l'orage" is a piece of textual evidence that permits us to discern the earliest stage of his dialogue with one of his favourite Russian poets.

"I dream'd a vision of the dead": The Effects and After-Effects of Tennyson's *In Memoriam*

Although the exact date of Nabokov's version of section 67 of Alfred Tennyson's *In Memoriam A.H.H.* (1833–49, 1850) has not been ascertained, it is difficult not to conclude that his revisiting Shakespeare's sonnets 17 and 27 had facilitated the transition from one canonic poetic sequence to the other. "Shakespeare's *Sonnets* are not only an important source for *In Memoriam,*" Christopher Ricks maintains, "they are its most important analogue."[171] Tennyson's reflections upon the transience of life – along with the homoerotic implications of his celebration of the addressee – link his work with Shakespeare's. Not that Nabokov had to draw deliberate parallels between Shakespeare and Tennyson: *In Memoriam A.H.H.* abounds in traits that carry a strong Nabokovian appeal in their own right.

In section 87 of *In Memoriam A.H.H.*, Tennyson revisits his and Arthur Henry Hallam's alma mater of Trinity College, Cambridge. Both the melancholy atmosphere of this section and Tennyson's description of the college and its environs will be echoed throughout Nabokov's recollection of Trinity in *Speak, Memory*. These echoes crescendo in chapter 13's concluding passages, which portray Nabokov's visit to Cambridge some seventeen years after his graduation, during a fruitless search for an academic appointment in England at a time when for him and his family it was a matter of life and death.[172] Here as elsewhere in chapter 13, Nabokov makes a subtle travesty of Tennyson's fond description of Cambridge, superimposing his own disenchantment with their former college on Tennyson's reverent remembrances of it. This becomes particularly apparent when Nabokov mentions the "sung trees" (called *stol' vospetye derev'ia* in the Russian version of the memoir) that grow around Trinity, the same trees that Tennyson recalls in his verse narrative.

On a more profound level, Tennyson's *In Memoriam A.H.H.* ran parallel to Nabokov's persistent inquiries into the transcendental, especially those characteristic of the earlier stages of his spiritual evolution. If sections 87–89 contain some vivid descriptions of the idyllic student days at Trinity and its surroundings that Nabokov subtly undercuts in his memoir, sections 81, 103, and especially the famous 51 contain articulate verbalizations of metaphysical certainty he could hardly have ignored.[173] It was no accident, then, that Nabokov turned to *In Memoriam A.H.H.* The appeal that Tennyson held for him would have been based on a shared experience while remaining in line with Nabokov's own search for an expression of his intuition of the hereafter.

Nabokov's alteration of Tennyson's title indicates the translator's desire to weaken this text's dependence on its original context: the full title of Tennyson's verse narrative, *In Memoriam A.H.H.*, with its specific reference to a specific addressee, is truncated to acquire a generalized meaning, as Nabokov entitles his version of "When on my bed the moonlight falls" "In Memoriam (Iz Tennisona)." The 23 May 1926 publication of the translation in the Paris-based *Zveno* omitted the section number, as if to suggest that the fragment's original context was no longer as relevant as it was in the English. Nabokov's truncated title was followed by a poem of four quatrains written in iambic pentameter, reproducing one of the most effective unifying formal features of Tennyson's verse sequence, namely its ABBA rhyme scheme.[174]

While the title of Nabokov's version of section 67 endows the translated fragment with more general scope ("In Memoriam" instead of *In Memoriam A.H.H.*), the actual translation displays a greater number of details, some of which are unwarranted by the original. The "ray of moonlight" (*lunnyi luch*) of the stanza's opening line does not simply "fall" on the protagonist's bed, it shines on his blanket; Tennyson's "place of rest" (l. 2) is loftily presented as "there where you are surrendered to earth."

Nabokov's version of the section's second stanza reveals his attitude toward his material. A significant modification of the original, it employs extensive personification:

Thy marble bright in dark appears,
As slowly steals a silver flame
Along the letters of thy name,
[8] And o'er the number of thy years.[175]

Тамъ жизнь твою читаетъ лунный свѣтъ:
Какъ перстъ скользитъ серебряное пламя
По мраморной доскѣ твоей, во храмѣ,
[8] По буквамъ имени и числамъ лѣтъ.[176]

[There moonlight reads your life: / as a finger, silver fire glides / across your marble gravestone, in a temple, / across the letters of your name and number of years.]

The opening line of the English poem's third stanza holds a hint of why Nabokov may have wished to employ such an extensive personification ("lunnyi svet … chitaet tvoiu zhizn'," l. 5) in the second one. Omitted from the translation, the adjective "mystic" ("The mystic glory swims away," l. 9) makes it clear that Tennyson's "moonlight glory" designates a transcendental agency powerful enough to unite the bereft protagonist with the late addressee of his poem by means of a shaft of moonlight that falls both on the protagonist's bed (or blanket, in Nabokov's version) and on the tombstone of the departed loved one.

Skilled renditions of foreign texts, Nabokov's early translations of Shakespeare's sonnets and Tennyson's *In Memoriam A.H.H.* show lack of concern for their contexts. His version of sonnet 17 does away with the complications associated with the gender of the Poet's addressee; his translation of "When on my bed the moonlight falls" makes no effort to inform its Russian reader of the amorous implications of the author's bereavement. In *Pale Fire*, however, Nabokov will highlight these aspects of Shakespeare's sonnets and Tennyson's lyric narrative, where the homosexual narrator Charles Kinbote will be savouring them along with A.E. Housman's *Shropshire Lad*. Here and elsewhere, we find that Nabokov's earlier misinterpretations of original texts have a way of becoming verbal vestiges in their own right, providing him with an opportunity to revisit them and turn them into sources of inspiration.

"Рыданій чистый звонъ," ou les tours de force siriniennes

1927 and 1928 saw the publication of some of the most important and challenging works Nabokov the translator was ever to undertake. Vladimir Sirin, who had already begun his transition from poetry to prose with *Mashen'ka* (1926) and *Korol', dama, valet* (1928), made a considerable effort to create his version of Alfred de Musset's "La Nuit de mai" (May Night) and a new translation of the same "La Nuit de décembre" he had translated and published in Russia in 1916. Were these works mere bravado performances? Why did Nabokov, who was so reluctant to make many of his translation experiments public, decide to publish them at all at a moment in his career when his first novels were gathering general acclaim?

Jane Grayson qualifies Nabokov's version of "La Nuit de mai" as a "technical *tour de force*," "executed with energy and … virtuosity" on a par with Musset's "virtuoso performance, full of stirring sentiment and striking imagery," yet his "renderings of some of the most emotionally charged passages must finally disappoint."[177] "La Nuit de mai" is a dramatic verse narrative that opens the series of Musset's "nuits": "La Nuit de mai," "La Nuit de décembre," "La Nuit d'août," and "La Nuit d'octobre." Generically, Musset's "nuits" belong to the medieval genre of visions or visitations and depict their protagonist, Le Poète, in his encounters with his Muse, the personification of his inspiration.[178] The authoritativeness of Grayson's pronouncement notwithstanding, such evaluations do not bring us any closer to an understanding of what these translations meant for Nabokov, or why he would need to make them at a specific point in his literary career in the first place.

In its quaintly exalted fashion, "La Nuit de mai" (May Night; 1835) examines suffering in its relation to art. Throughout the length of this dialogue, the spiritually frail and disconsolate Poet is shown to be resisting all attempts on the part of the Muse to awaken him to creation. The Muse – Musset's eroticized allegory of inspiration – continually entreats the Poet to "take up his lute and give her a kiss" ("Poète, prends ton luth et me donne un baiser"), which is her way of putting the infinitive "to compose" in the imperative. The Poet, who at first fails even to recognize the arrival of his genius ("Qui vient? qui m'appelle? – Personne. / Je suis seul; c'est l'heure qui sonne; / Ô solitude! ô pauvreté!" [Who comes? Who calls me? – No one. / I am alone; the hour is striking; / O solitude! O poverty!]), is of the opinion that his unspecified suffering (he calls it "martyrdom") is incompatible with art.[179]

The reader may assume that the silence following this melancholy conclusion signifies the Muse's disappearance: the reluctant Poet has squandered his inspiration and along with it his chance to immortalize his grief in a work of art. For all the archaism of Musset's poetic idiom, "La Nuit de mai" is an ingenious rhetorical construct: this poem about grievous silence and the drama of artistic impotence proves to be a flamboyant celebration of Musset's own prowess as a poet, as in no way the vigorous author of this particular "Nuit" can be identified with its pusillanimous protagonist, all the autobiographical parallels notwithstanding.

In "La Nuit de mai," Musset's display of his skill comes with the Muse's lengthy attempts to compel the Poet to composition. Prior to her eventual surrender, the Muse presents him with an array of possibilities for transfiguring his despondency into art. She unrolls before his eyes a magic carpet of the most diverse subjects and modes of self-expression: after all, it is in his power to create an unknown universe ("un monde inconnu"), echo the events of his own life ("les échos de ta vie"), or travel in his verse all of the world, from "green Scotland" and "tanned Italy" to Greece ("la Grèce ma mère," as the Muse refers to it). Historical narrative verse should by no means be off limits to the Poet ("Dirons-nous aux héros des vieux temps de la France?"), and neither is the love lyric or meditative poetry, be it sad, hopeful, or joyous ("Chanterons-nous l'espoir, la tristesse ou la joie?").

As Grayson has pointed out, Nabokov excels in finding exact Russian parallels to the vast majority of concrete lexical items to be found in Musset's evocations, matching not only the various denominations of flora and fauna featured in "La Nuit de mai" but also the impressive catalogue of geographic landmarks and historical allusions.[180] In one instance Nabokov even demonstrates his ability to beat Musset at his own game by introducing his own botanical allegory. In one of her soliloquies the Muse suggests Napoleon – "l'homme de Waterloo" – as one of the many possible objects for depiction:

L'homme de Waterloo nous dira-t-il sa vie,
Et ce qu'il a fauché du troupeau des humains
Avant que l'envoyé de la nuit éternelle
Vînt sur son tertre vert l'abattre d'un coup d'aile,
Et sur son cœur de fer lui croiser les deux mains?[181]

[Will the man of Waterloo tell us his life, / And that he mowed down a flock of humans / Before the messenger of eternal night / Came to his green hillock to knock him down with a blow of his wing, / And on his iron heart crossed his two hands?]

Nabokov's rendition of this fragment is at once faithful and inventive:

Отъ Корсиканца ли про Ватерло услышимъ,
и сколько ковыля людского он скосилъ,
пока не налетѣлъ духъ ночи безразсвѣтной,
не сбилъ его крыломъ на холмикъ непримѣтный
и руки павшему на сердцѣ не скрестилъ?[182]

[Shall we hear from the Corsican about Waterloo, / and how much human feather grass he had reaped, / before the spirit of the dawnless night came in flying, / and swept him to an inconspicuous hillock / and crossed the arms of the fallen one over his heart?]

Not only does Nabokov preserve Musset's ellipsis by referring to Napoleon as "the Corsican" (*Korsikanets*) in a situation where a literal rendering of the original phrase is metrically unfeasible, he also improves Musset's stock description of the countless victims of Napoleon's lust for power. In the original, Musset presents the plight of Napoleon's victims by mixing two similes: he likens Napoleon to a reaper oblivious to the consequences of his actions, and the human multitudes unfortunate enough to get in the way of his ambitious goals to cattle ("ce qu'il a fauché du troupeau des humains"). Accepting the prompt contained in the first part of Musset's double-edged simile and doing away with the second, Nabokov likens Napoleon's victims to *liudskoi kovyl'* (human feather grass; see the line "i skol'ko kovylia liudskogo on skosil" above) which gets mercilessly mowed down by that megalomaniac. As Nabokov was to comment in his later encomium of Aleksandr Blok (1931, 1952), an evocation of *kovyl'* ("feather grass" [*stipa pennata*]) in Russian poetry is frequently tantamount to a reference to Russian *bylinas* and *chansons de geste*, with their mournful commemoration of the fallen.[183]

"V. Sirin" came into being as a writer of exile capable of transforming into art not only his individual experience but also his expatriate milieu. One of the most persistent motifs of Russian émigré literature was that of displacement and nostalgia, and Sirin excelled at doing justice to this theme, first in his poetry and subsequently in his prose. "Maiskaia noch'," with its exploration of the interrelationship between suffering and art, is a programmatic statement that embodies its translator's stance on the crucial dilemma of either succumbing to adversity or deriving strength from it. By sharing his version of "Maiskaia noch'" with his émigré readers, Nabokov was endorsing a point of view articulated by Musset's Muse, that quaint allegory for inspiration: for a true artist bereavement, loss, and indeed suffering is but a pretext for creation, and poets should be grateful to fate for providing them with such rich emotional material. Exiled, destitute but free, émigré artists and poets have no limits placed on their expression, and their muses can lead them to extraordinary discoveries and revelations:

Чьё горе велико, тотъ истинно великъ.
Но если ты позналъ страданіе, не думай,
что должен ты, поэтъ, нѣмотствовать угрюмо.
Чѣмъ горестнѣй напѣвъ, тѣмъ сладостнѣе онъ.
Есть пѣсни вѣчныя, – рыданій чистый звонъ.[184]

[He whose grief is great is great indeed. / But if you have tasted suffering, don't think, / that you, poet, must remain sullenly silent. The more grieving the motif, the sweeter it is. / There are eternal songs – pure ringing of sobs.]

These lines communicate the edifying prescription of the Muse's final monologue:

Rien ne nous rend si grands qu'une grande douleur.
Mais, pour en être atteint, ne crois pas, ô poète,
Que ta voix ici-bas doive rester muette.
Les plus désespérés sont les chants les plus beaux,
Et j'en sais d'immortels qui sont de purs sanglots.[185]

[Nothing makes us greater that a great pain. / But, although you suffer from it, don't think, O poet, / That your voice here on earth must remain silent. / The most beautiful songs are the most desperate ones, and I know some songs that are pure sobs.]

Nabokov endorses Musset's censure of despondency: to assume the posture of Musset's Poet, who is rendered impotent by his fixation on his woes, is to imperil art. Yet it would be a mistake to identify fully Nabokov's stance on the issue with the position formulated and advocated by Musset in his poem.

In her fourth soliloquy the Muse undertakes her first serious attempt to stir up the Poet to creation by presenting him with the infinite possibilities of art, and there ensues an entire chain of verbs in the imperative mood:

Partons, dans un baiser, pour un monde inconnu.
Éveillons au hasard les échos de ta vie,
Parlons-nous de bonheur, de gloire et de folie,
Et que ce soit un rêve, et le premier venu.
Inventons quelque part des lieux où l'on oublie;
Partons, nous sommes seuls, l'univers est à nous.[186]

[Let's leave, in a kiss, for an unknown world. / Let's wake up, randomly, life's echoes, / Let's tell ourselves about happiness, glory, and madness, / And that it be a dream, and the first one to come. / Let's invent somewhere places where one forgets; / Let's leave, we are alone, the universe belongs to us.]

Nabokov's translation of this fragment is noteworthy not for its occasional abandonment of an original image in favour of a new one, more suitable in the metrical context of the Russian verse, as is the case with Musset's "baiser" ("Partons, dans un baiser," etc.), which Nabokov replaced with an "embrace" ("Davai, v bezvestnyi mir, obniavshis', uletim"; see below). The most important alteration of the original text comes further in the translation, when the Muse invites the Poet to invent someplace where one can lose oneself in oblivion ("Inventons quelque part des lieux où l'on oublie"):

Давай, въ безвѣстный міръ, обнявшись, улетимъ.
Разбудимъ наугадъ мы жизненное эхо.
Коснёмся славы мы, безумія и смѣха.
Забвенія страну съ тобою создадимъ.
Сонъ выберемъ любой, лишь былъ бы онъ безцѣленъ.
Умчимся. Мы одни. Вселенная насъ ждетъ.[187]

[Let's, to an unknown world, having embraced, fly away. / Haphazardly, we'll wake a lively echo. / We'll touch fame, madness, and laughter. / We'll create a land of oblivion. / We'll select any dream, as long as it's aimless. / We'll fly away. We're alone. The universe awaits us.]

"Son vyberem liuboi, lish' byl by on bestselen" – the condition upon which the Muse invites the Poet to choose any of the dreams that are available to them both – is not set by Alfred de Musset but by Vladimir Nabokov, the translator of "La Nuit de mai." The dream of a novel universe should be "aimless" (*bestsel'nyi*), which is to say free of any utilitarian purpose. An unmistakably Nabokovian sentiment makes its way into his version of a French poem that has already emerged as an important testament to the translator's own philosophical and aesthetic credo. What first appeared nothing more than a translation tour de force emerges as an important statement of the translator's own well-considered notions and beliefs. The suffering endured by the artist is only an incentive for reaching new creative heights, or "chem gorestnei napev, tem sladostnee on. / Est' pesni vechnye, – rydanii chistyi zvon" (cf. "Les plus désespérés sont les chants les plus beaux, / Et j'en sais d'immortels qui sont de purs sanglots" [the most desperate are the most beautiful songs, / And I know some immortal ones that are pure sobs]). To put it succinctly, those able to distil suffering into art reach immortality.

Grayson, who was the first to point out the true significance of Nabokov's affinity with Musset, has commented on the perceived mutability of Nabokov's attitude toward the French poet: "In his middle career ... Nabokov was to set Musset aside and employ other models for his intellectual and artistic constructions of biography and memory, Proust for one."[188] Indeed, Nabokov's connection with Musset appears to weaken as the writer enters his creative maturity. It may well be true that "other models for ... constructions of biography and memory" had at some point in Nabokov's evolution taken the place once occupied by those provided by the author of the "nuits." What is equally important, however, is that having once declared his allegiance to "dreams devoid of a [utilitarian] goal" (*bestsel'nye sny*) through the medium of a Musset translation, reinforced by the French poet's view of the interrelationship between suffering and art, Nabokov remained faithful to this viewpoint.

In his 1939 eulogy of Vladislav Khodasevich, Nabokov once again reiterated his notion of how suffering relates to art, mocking the opinion of his own and Khodasevich's opponents among the émigré writers belonging to the so-called Parisian school (*parizhskaia nota*), who sought to belittle art in the face of the calamities experienced by modern man. Developing his argument, Nabokov made use of a key phrase from Musset's "La Nuit de mai":

> To speak of his ... "mastery" ... would be meaningless and even blasphemous in relation to poetry in general, and to his own verse in a sharply specific sense, since the notion of "mastery," which automatically supplies its own quotation marks, turns thereby into an appendage, a shadow demanding logical compensation in the guise of any positive quantity, and this easily brings us to that peculiar, soulful attitude toward poetry in result of which nothing remains of squashed art but a damp spot or a tear stain. This is condemnable not because even the most *purs sanglots* require a perfect knowledge of prosody ...[189]

Even the purest of sobs – *purs sanglots* – do not relieve the poet of his duty to attain mastery of his craft; deprivation and suffering should compel him to the creation of stellar works of art, such as those of the late Khodasevich. Nabokov, who explained to his English readers references to Baratynskii and Blok embedded in his eulogy of Khodasevich, did not comment on his use of Musset's *purs sanglots*, understanding, one senses, that it would take too much time and effort to elucidate the intensely personal meaning of this allusion not only to Musset's poem, but to his own version of this poem in his Russian translation.[190]

By way of translation, Musset's *purs sanglots* became an inalienable part of Nabokov's phraseology, as can be attested by a passage from his autumnal masterwork *Ada*: "I had a schoolmate called Vanda. And *I* knew a girl called Adora, little thing in my last floramor. What makes me see that bit as the purest *sanglot* in the book? What is the worst part of dying?"[191]

This fleeting reference to the same fragment of "La Nuit de mai" instantly summons a host of associations, and some of these associations would not be possible to appreciate properly without taking into account a maximally broad context of Nabokov's writings, extending as far as his earlier, Russian experiments in translation, including his version of one quaint French Romantic verse dialogue by Alfred de Musset.

On 7 October 1928, yet another Nabokovian translation of a "Nuit" by Musset appeared in *Rul'*. It was a completely new version of "La Nuit de décembre," the same poem a version of which Nabokov had written in December 1915 and published in 1916 ("Dekabr'skaia noch'. Iz Alfreda de Miusse" – his earliest publication).

Another ostensible "bravura performance," the 1915 version of "La Nuit de décembre" was in fact a literary undertaking with an intensely personal subtext: dedicated to Valentina Shul'gina (with whom Nabokov was in love at the time he wrote his "Dekabr'skaia noch'"), it had substantially refashioned the original, introducing into it a number of subtle references to their waning love affair and specifically to the translator's own predicament.

The evolution of Nabokov's technique since the time he made his first version of "La Nuit de décembre" can be demonstrated by a comparison of a representative fragment from the two versions, one published in 1916, the other in 1928. Below, the eighteenth stanza from the original text of "La Nuit de décembre" is followed by its first Russian incarnation published in *Iunaia mysl'*.

Partout où j'ai voulu dormir,
Partout où j'ai voulu mourir,
Partout où j'ai touché la terre,
Sur ma route est venu s'asseoir
Un malheureux vêtu de noir,
Qui me ressemblait comme un frère.[192]

> [Wherever I wanted to sleep, / Wherever I wanted to die, / Wherever I touched the ground, / On my way came to sit / A wretch dressed in black, / Who resembled me like a brother.]

Having presented a long succession of the Poet's encounters with the mysterious vision (stanzas 1–17), Musset is about to have his protagonist demand an explanation of the ghost, who will eventually reveal his identity in the last line of the poem's final, thirty-first stanza. A chain of anaphoras marks an emotional upsurge that subsides toward the end of the stanza, which contains one of the recurring characteristics of the ghost (this time he is referred to as "a wretch" or "an unfortunate" ["un malheureux," cf. Rus. *zloschastnyi*]).

> Вездѣ, гдѣ хотѣлъ засыпать,
> Вездѣ, гдѣ хотѣлъ умирать,
> Вездѣ, гдѣ ждалъ новаго дня,
> Въ пути мнѣ встрѣчался прохожій,
> Паломникъ вѣсь въ чёрномъ, похожій
> Какъ братъ на меня.[193]

> [Everywhere where I wanted to sleep, / everywhere where I wanted to die, / everywhere where I waited another day, / on my way I met a passerby, / a pilgrim in everything black, resembling / me like a brother.]

Nabokov's first version preserves the anaphoras contained in the stanza's first three lines. The approach of an already established final word in the stanza's closure, which recurs throughout the poem, forces the sixteen-year-old translator to digress from his original in order to locate a rhyming word: as a result, Musset's "wherever I have touched the ground" ("Partout où j'ai touché la terre," l. 3, stanza 18) has given way to a filler "vezde, gde zhdal novogo dnia" ("everywhere where I awaited a new day"), but the translator's ultimate aim, the preservation of the stanza's integrity, has been achieved. Equally alien to the original is the noun "pilgrim" (*palomnik*), which had to be inserted in the stanza's penultimate line to conform to the demands of the amphibrachic measure dominating the 1915 version.

The version published *Rul'* in 1928 takes into account the practical knowledge gained from the 1915 experiment (see, for example, how the formulaic phrase "ves' v chërnom," which, thanks to its succinctness proved to be a true find in the first version, gets carried over to the second one). The 1928 version, however, is strikingly different from its 1915 prototype: for one thing, its iambic basis (stanzas 1–18 are written in tetrameters, stanzas 19–28 alternate pentameters with tetrameters, and the last three stanzas of the poem – the Vision's response – are written in anapestic trimeters) has nothing to do with the amphibrachic rhythm of the first version, and the lexical divergences from the original are far less numerous.

повсюду, гдѣ дрема долила,
повсюду, гдѣ звала могила,
повсюду, гдѣ коснулся я
земли, – садился при дорогѣ,
вѣсь въ чёрномъ, человѣкъ убогій,
какъ братъ, похожій на меня.[194]

[Everywhere where sleep overpowered me, / everywhere where the grave would call me, / everywhere where I touched / the earth – sat by the road, all in black, a wretched man, / resembling me like a brother.]

The translator's vocabulary has expanded considerably, both in quantitative and qualitative terms; his transpositional technique has acquired unprecedented flexibility – he has learnt that it is not necessary to restrict his search for the right word to the same register as employed in the original to preserve its meaning: *povsiudu* replaces the more frequent *vezde* for "partout" and provides a superior aural parallel to the French word in Russian. The second line of the quoted stanza contains an image unlicensed by the original: "povsiudu, gde zvala mogila." This personification, however, allows the translator to retain the aural imprint of his model by employing a number of consonants representative of the sound of the French phrase they replace (cf. "voulu mourir" and *zvala mogila*), and provide an exact rhyming pair for the final phrase of the stanza's first line (*drema dolila* – sleep overpowered). While *drema* is an excellent choice for "dormir" (in addition to their similar sound the two words share the same Indo-European root), the stress that unavoidably falls on the last syllable (*dremá*) due to the iambic rhythm of the line is certainly unusual, as is the word *dolila* (from *dolit'*, archaic; cf. standard *odolevat'*, to overcome, overpower). As it turns out, Nabokov's use of this quaint turn of speech is fully sanctioned by Vladimir Dal':

ДОЛИТЬ арх. Одолѣвать. *Меня долит жажда; долитъ дремá*.[195]

It was not, however, Nabokov's intimate knowledge of the richest lexical depository of the Russian language that had facilitated his search for a resourceful parallel to the French phrase. In the opening line of his second version of the eighteenth stanza, Nabokov is drawing on his individual translating experience – something he lacked in 1915. First encountered by Nabokov in Dal', this unusual and vivid phraseological combination had initially been tested – and internalized – in his adaptation of Romain Rolland's *Colas Breugnon*:

> *Дремота долитъ.* Я засыпаю, плотно усѣвшись, чтобы въ очагъ не упасть.[196]

> [Sleep is overpowering [me]. I'm falling asleep, firmly planting myself [in my chair] so as not to fall into the fireplace.]

The place Musset's "La Nuit de décembre" came to occupy in Nabokov's work and thought is a unique one. Fully aware of Musset's limitations (again one is reminded of that mention of Musset's name in a denigratory context in "Mademoiselle O"), Nabokov remained fond of the French poet, whose verse held for him considerable sentimental value. While "La Nuit de mai" would surely have appealed to Nabokov by providing him, as it did at the time of its publication in 1927, with an opportunity to formulate his stance on a number of philosophical, aesthetical, and ethical problems, the case of "La Nuit de décembre" was different. It is unlikely that so discriminating an arbiter as Nabokov would have wished to treat his readers to a poem he did not value.

The incentive for making a new translation of "La Nuit de décembre" must have come from elsewhere. It is possible that the memory of creating that juvenile adaptation of the poem would have imprinted Musset's imagery on Nabokov's receptive imagination, endowing what was essentially a period piece with a personal resonance and individual significance. It is an astonishing coincidence that Nabokov, who was keen to discern both overt and covert patterns in nature, life, and art, was able to look at one of his first literary endeavours and recognize in it a prefiguration of his own biography to date, as if the act of artistic appropriation he had committed in 1915 – the fusion of the circumstances of his own life with those of the French poet – had an uncanny bearing on how his own future would unfold. In his "La Nuit de décembre," Musset casts a retrospective glance at the three major events of his life: the loss of his father (see stanzas 9–11); his (self-imposed) exile, his wanderings across Europe (stanzas 12–18); and an acrimonious parting with a mistress (stanzas 21–26). Along with such tribulations Musset's poem refers to bouts of youthful intemperance (stanzas 7–8), and, crucially, leads its protagonist toward the realization that he is doomed to solitude. Nabokov was capable of both appreciating the parallelism between his own life and that of Musset's protagonist, as well as seeing the instances demonstrating that the seemingly fateful personal connection with "La Nuit de décembre" had only a limited relevance to his life (Nabokov, after all, was never given to debauchery and knew well that solitude was not to become his lot in life). The cardinal reversal of Nabokov's strategy from personalized adaptation to translation with far less personal investment must at the same time have amounted to an attempt on the part of the translator to disassociate himself from a literary text with a number of unsettling biographical parallels.

Even the briefest catalogue of instances of Nabokov's turning to Musset at various junctures of his life and career in letters will not fail to impress upon the observer the idea that Nabokov's connection with the French poet was not susceptible to the changes that affected his attitude to many other poets and writers whom he had once rated highly. The initial translation of "La Nuit de décembre" (1835) was made some time in January 1915. Nabokov's debut collection of verse (spring–summer 1916) opened with an epigraph from Musset: "Un souvenir heureux est peut-être sur terre / Plus vrai que le bonheur" (On [this] earth, a happy recollection is perhaps / more faithful than happiness, "Souvenir" [Recollection]; 1841). On 1 August 1919, Nabokov translated Musset's "Rapelle-toi" (1842). On 28 January 1923, he put into Russian a long fragment from "Lettre à M. de Lamartine" (1836); his translation of "La Nuit de mai" (1835) was published in October 1927 (the echoes of this poem resonate in Nabokov's French essay "Pouchkine, ou le vrai et le vraisemblable" [Pushkin, or the Real and the Plausible], 1937;[197] in his eulogy of Khodasevich, 1939; and in a concluding passage of *Ada*, 1968). Nabokov's penultimate novel, *Transparent Things* (1972), contains a quotation from Musset's "À Julie" (1832).[198] Last but not least, one is reminded that in March 1977, five months prior to his death, Nabokov urged his son to read Musset.[199] Some of the more intimate aspects of Nabokov's lifelong devotion to Musset may remain obscure; it is clear, however, that Musset never fell out of favour with Nabokov, no matter how much more refined his literary tastes would grow, how much closer he would become to artists whose sophistication Musset could not match.

"Les sanglots longs": Rendering Verlaine's Plaintive Masterpiece

Having published his translation and a retranslation of two of Musset's dramatic verse narratives, Nabokov, now at a peak of his creative activities, turned to poets whose genius and complexity was on a substantially different level from that of the author of "La Nuit de mai" and "La Nuit de décembre." It was as if Nabokov's work on one of the predecessors of the great poets of the following period in the history of French poetry had served him as a laboratory where he tested his ability to rise to new challenges. By the end of 1928 Nabokov could report to Gleb Struve, literary editor of the Paris-based *Rossiia i Slavianstvo*, that he had completed his work on two signature poems of two illustrious French poets: "I've got a couple of rather amusing translations (Rimbaud 'Bateau ivre' and Verlaine 'Les sanglots longs des violons.')"[200]

Nabokov's version of Verlaine's "Chanson d'automne" (*Poèmes saturniens*, 1866) is dated 26 November 1928. Even if all his translating experiments had only led to this eighteen-line-long piece, which has never been published in full, Nabokov's efforts would have been entirely redeemed, for this "Glukhoe vskhlipyvan'e skripki" is a true tour de force of both his translating and verse-making technique.

Is it possible to recreate the refined musicality of Verlaine's short lines, their lulling, languorous intonation in a language different from the poem's native mode of expression? After all, in "Chanson d'automne" mood and alliteration are inseparable, and to attempt to divorce one from the other would be to destroy the poem's effect. An appreciation of the difficulty of transposing this syncretic union of sound, form, and significance into another language, however, can do no more than hope to approach the complexity that should accompany an attempt to perform it.

Les sanglots longs
Des violons
[3] De l'automne
Blessent mon cœuer
D'une langueur
Monotone.[201]

[The protracted sobs / Of the violins / Of the autumn / Shatter my heart / With languor / Monotonous.]

"Chanson d'automne" is written in sestets rhyming aabccb, which adds a considerable impediment for a translation that already has to deal with the maximal terseness of Verlaine's idiom and its alliteration. Nabokov's solution to this challenge is as effective as it is unorthodox.

Глухое всхлипыванье
скрипки
[3] истомной
осенней мутью
ранитъ грудь,
монотонно.[202]

[The muted sobbing / of a violin / langorous // with autumnal gloom / wounds the breast, / monotonously.]

Nabokov's method combined the retention of the general significance of Verlaine's lines with a search for sonorous combinations corresponding to the aural imprint of the French lines. Thanks to the addition of the adjective *glukhoi* to the noun *vsklipyvan'e,* the opening line of the Russian stanza retains the expressive succession of Verlaine's s's and l's (compare "les sanglots longs" and *glukhoe vskhlipyvan'e*). Further into the stanza, Nabokov excels at providing close Russian equivalents to the sound of Verlaine's words: thus *istomnoi* corresponds to "automne" (cf. ll. 3), and *osennei* to "blessent" (cf. ll. 4).

Outwardly, the rhyme scheme of the original poem appears to be merely echoed in the Russian stanza, as the end syllables of its first two lines do not share the same or even approximate sound. Should one recite the poem's opening lines, however, the inventiveness of Nabokov's response to the exigencies of form and sound begins to emerge. The two uneven lines that open his version of "Chanson d'automne" share an internal rhyme that effectively compensates for the lack of its traditional external counterpart (*vSKHLIPyvan'e/SKRIPki*). What is likely to escape the attention of a reader (and may not be consciously appreciated by a listener) is that Nabokov employs this principle of internal rhyming throughout his rendition of the poem. Album 15 preserves an explanatory scheme that explicates his use of this principle:

глухое всхлип –	les sanglots longs
ыванье скрип –	des violons
истомной	de l'automne

осенней муть –
ю ранит грудь
монотонно

blesse<nt> mon cœur
d'une langueur
monotone.[203]

Eschewing the graphic appearance of a translated poem whose effect is contingent upon its sound, Nabokov demonstrates how he has provided a parallel to the rhyme scheme of Verlaine's poem.[204] Nabokov's virtuosity lies in his ability to implement his solution throughout the poem, a fitting achievement for what was then a fifteen-year-long career in translation. By resetting in Russian a French poem composed purely of sobs, Nabokov demonstrated that Musset had solved the enigma of suffering's paradoxical ability to perpetuate art.

"Les yeux horribles des pontons": Arthur Rimbaud's "Bateau ivre" and Its Ports of Call

The names of Paul Verlaine and Arthur Rimbaud are intertwined, and it seems appropriate that Nabokov's version of Verlaine's "Chanson d'automne" should have been created in temporal proximity to Rimbaud's "Bateau ivre." "P'ianyi korabl'. Iz A. Rembo," the other of the two "amusing" (*zaniatnyi*) translations from the French, appeared in the 16 December 1928 issue of *Rul'*.

In a 1964 interview Nabokov recalled that "between the ages of ten and fifteen" he had read and relished "Wells, Poe, Browning, Keats, Flaubert, Verlaine, Rimbaud, Chekhov, Tolstoy and Aleksandr Blok."[205] The name of Jules Verne is also mentioned in the interview, but among the writers who "have lost the glamour and thrill they held for [him]" (this list includes Poe, Emmuska Orczy, Conan Doyle, and Rupert Brooke). While Nabokov's disparaging remark regarding Alfred de Musset in "Mademoiselle O" alerts one to the necessity of taking the writer's later statements regarding the literary tastes of his youth with a pinch of salt, there is no doubt that the numerous echoes of Jules Verne's *Vingt mille lieues sous les mers*, Edgar Allan Poe's "Manuscript Found in a Bottle," "The Narrative of Arthur Gordon Pym of Nantucket," and "Descent into the Maelstrom," as well as James Fenimore Cooper's and Mayne Reid's frontier narratives would have provided enough common ground to spark Nabokov's interest in "Le Bateau ivre" (The Drunken Boat; 1871), not to mention the profound congeniality of the poem's treatment of the themes of inspiration and poetry. Nabokov's imagination, much like that of Rimbaud, was nourished by the fantastic and extravagant tales of these writers. The not-so-distant echoes of Verne, Poe, Cooper, and Reid that resound through "Le Bateau ivre" would certainly have appealed to Nabokov, who was always eager to revisit the haunts of his childhood. The transformations that these allusions undergo in the longest of Rimbaud's poems are at least partially responsible for Nabokov's take on "Le Bateau ivre."

To translate Rimbaud's "Bateau ivre" is to interpret it, and Nabokov seeks to expound many of its riddles. Before attempting to interpret this interpretation, however, one must locate the version of the text on which Nabokov's translation is based. Modern critical editions of Rimbaud's poetry use Verlaine's transcript of the poem, presumably written down at the author's dictation.[206] It would be tempting to conjecture that Nabokov could have anticipated the latest developments in Rimbaud studies and made his translation from a facsimile of Verlaine's manuscript that became available in 1927,[207] but internal evidence indicates that for his "P'ianyi korabl'" Nabokov used an earlier edition of Rimbaud's poetry, based not on Verlaine's manuscript but rather on the variant published in the 1884 issue of *Les Poètes maudits*.[208]

The seventh stanza of "Le Bateau ivre" contains one of the most important textual divergences from the pre-1927 editions not based on Verlaine's manuscript of the poem. In Verlaine's manuscript the third line of this stanza (l. 27) reads:

Où, teignant tout à coup les bleuités, délires
Et rhythmes lents sous les rutilements du jour,
Plus fortes que l'alcool, plus vastes que *nos* lyres
[28] Fermentent les rousseurs amères de l'amour![209]

[Where, suddenly turning bluenesses, deliriums / And slow rhythms under the blazes of the day, / More strong than alcohol, more large than our lyres / Ferment the bitter rednesses of love!]

According to Verlaine's manuscript, Rimbaud compares "les rousseurs amères de l'amour" (see l. 28, the stanza's closing line) to "alcohol" (*l'alcool*) and "our lyres" (*nos lyres*). Verlaine's use of the possessive pronoun *nos* in his manuscript has been questioned by readers and scholars alike;[210] it is not supported by the printed text of the poem that appeared in the 1884 edition of *Les Poètes maudits*, where it reads *vos lyres* ("your" [plur.] instead of "our" lyres).[211] Indeed, it is difficult to reconcile the phrase *nos lyres* (our lyres) with Rimbaud's otherwise consistent use of the first person singular in this egocentric verse narrative that continuously employs "I," "me," "myself," and stresses the individual nature of the protagonist's mysterious quest.

The matching line of Nabokov's translation does not take into account Verlaine's manuscript copy of the poem and presents this phrase as it was conjectured and reproduced in the 1884 edition of *Les Poètes maudits* and then in a string of subsequent editions of Rimbaud's poetry:

гдѣ, въ пламенные дни, лазурь сквозную влаги
окрашивая вдругъ, кружаться въ забытьи, –
просторнѣй *вашихъ* лиръ, разымчивѣе браги, –
[28] туманы рыжіе и горькіе любви.[212]

[where, on fiery days, the translucent azure of moisture / colouring suddenly, circle in a swoon – / more expansive than *your* lyres, more intoxicating than moonshine – / the ruddy and bitter fogs of love.]

Nabokov's "P'ianyi korabl'" is an imaginative rendition of Rimbaud's "Bateau ivre." For all its serene outward decorum effectively mirroring the form of the original, this poem of twenty-five quatrains, written in a Russian iambic hexameter with alternating rhymes, matches the flight of Rimbaud's fantasy, often endowing it with fresh tinges of exuberance.

Evgenii Vitkovskii has commented on a striking difference in Nabokov's rendering of a key image from stanza 9 of "Le Bateau ivre":[213]

J'ai vu le soleil bas, taché d'horreurs mystiques,
Illuminant de longs figements violets,
Pareils à des acteurs de drames très-antiques
[36] Les flots roulant au loin leurs frissons de volets![214]

[I've seen the low sun stained with mystical horrors / light up long purple lumps / Like actors in very ancient dramas, / The swells rolled off their shudders of shutters.]

In Nabokov's translation, the "acteurs de drames très-antiques" (Rimbaud's reference to ancient Greek theatre) become "apparitions from a very old drama":[215]

я видѣлъ низкихъ зорь пятнистые пожары,
въ лиловыхъ сгусткахъ тучъ мистическій провалъ;

какъ привидѣнія изъ драмы очень старой,
[36] волнуясь чередой, за валомъ вѣялъ валъ;[216]

[I saw the spotty conflagrations of low dawns, / in the lilac accumulations of clouds a mystical abyss; / like apparitions from a very old drama, / heaving alternately, one surge followed another;]

Nabokov's asymmetric rendition of the original phrase alerts the reader to the presence of an agenda that is not entirely aligned with the ostensible task of presenting the reader with a close approximation of the meaning of the French poem. Rimbaud's classical allusion ("drames très-antiques") is replaced with an allusion to "a very old drama" (*iz dramy ochen' staroi*), which is much more likely referring to a Renaissance work, quite possibly by Shakespeare (see Nabokov's reference to "apparitions" or "ghosts" from that drama, which can be seen as a reference to either *Macbeth* or *Hamlet*). Qualified as a mistranslation by Vitkovskii, this alteration of the original could hardly have been accidental: Nabokov decided to develop Rimbaud's ambiguous reference to "horreurs mystiques" contained in the stanza's opening line by enriching it with a more concrete additional allusion to the spectral dimension of Shakespeare's dramas.

Nabokov is keen to amplify the transcendental aspect of the wanderings of Rimbaud's drunken boat. The poem's eighteenth stanza opens with the description of the boat's getting lost "sous le cheveux des anses" (an image suggested by a specific passage from Jules Verne's *Vingt mille lieues sous les mers*):[217]

Or moi, bateau perdu sous les cheveux des anses,
Jeté par l'ouragan dans l'éther sans oiseau,
Moi dont les Monitors et les voiliers des Hanses
[72] N'auraient pas repêché la carcasse ivre d'eau;[218]

[Now me, the boat lost under the hair of coves, / Tossed by the hurricane into birdless ether, / Me, [whose] water-inebriated hull / No Monitors no Hanseatic sailboats / Could have fished out;]

Nabokov's translation of the stanza's opening line renders Rimbaud's reference to the state of being "lost under the hair of coves" by radically redirecting the drunken boat's itinerary:

Но я, затерянный въ кудряхъ травы летейской,
я, бурей брошенный въ эѳиръ глухонѣмой,

шатунъ, чьей скорлупы ни парусникъ ганзейскій,
[72] ни зоркій Мониторъ не сыщетъ подъ водой, – [219]

[But I, lost in the curles of Lethean grass, / I, thrown by the tempest into deaf-mute ether, / rambler, whose shell neither the Hanseatic sailboat / or the eagle-eyed *Monitor* will find under water, –]

A discussion of Nabokov's version of "Le Bateau ivre" must mention its last stanza and the problems that arise from his rendition of one of the most famous images of this famous poetic text.

Je ne puis plus, baigné de vos langueurs, ô lames,
Enlever leur sillage aux porteurs de cotons,
Ni traverser l'orgueil des drapeaux et des flammes,
[100] Ni nager sous les yeux horribles des pontons.[220]

[I can no longer, soaked in your languor, O waves, / Follow in the wake of cotton carriers, / Or traverse the haughtiness of banners and flames, / Or sail under the horrible eyes of pontoons.]

"Le Bateau ivre" culminates in an admission of weakness in the presence of the commercial and military vessels eager to brandish their might. As Enid Starkie put it, in the poem's closing quatrain Rimbaud comes to a realization that "this wild journey was over and he must content himself with everyday reality."[221] This reading may contain a key to Nabokov's interpretation of the closing phrase of the poem, which is in striking contrast with everything we know about the ending of "Le Bateau ivre" now:

О, волны, не могу, исполненный истомы,
пересѣкать волну купеческихъ судовъ,
побѣдно проходить среди знаменъ и грома
[100] и проплывать вблизи ужасныхъ глазъ мостовъ.[222]

[O, waves, overcome by languor, I can't / traverse the wake of merchant ships, / progress triumphantly amid banners and thunder / and sail near the horrible eyes of the bridges.]

Nabokov translates "les yeux horribles des pontons," the poem's final phrase, as "terrifying eyes of bridges" and not as "terrifying eyes of convict ships/hulks," as do Rimbaud's translators today.[223] In French the word "ponton" can be used to refer to a "pontoon bridge," or a "bridge of ships," and Nabokov chooses to construe it as a reference to the bridges over the river Meuse in the poet's native town of Charleville (now called Charleville-Mézières; in Rimbaud's time the two towns were separated by the Meuse). At the same time, the phrase can also be construed as a reference to the use of decommissioned ships as floating prisons, also called "pontons," first during the Napoleonic wars and subsequently in the course of retaliation against members of the Paris Commune by the Versaillais. The latter reading provides a satisfactory explanation as to why "the eyes of convict ships" should seem "horrible" to the autobiographic protagonist of "Le Bateau ivre": Rimbaud, who sympathized with the Commune, would have been aware of its bloody suppression even if he had not stayed in Paris long enough to witness it during his escape from Charleville.[224]

By refusing to admit an apparent reference to the political events of 1871 into his version of the final stanza of "Le Bateau ivre," Nabokov puts a finishing touch on his interpretation of the poem. Nabokov's "P'ianyi korabl'" interprets Rimbaud's "Bateau ivre" as a mystical journey of the soul of a seer ("voyant"), a metaphorical wandering toward the remotest corners of the world of the quick as well as those of the world of the dead (see his alteration of "les cheveux des anses" to *kudri travy leteiskoi* in the poem's eighteenth stanza). "The eyes of [pontoon] bridges" seem horrible to the poet because they signify his return to a mundane reality against which he is powerless, his final descent from the realm of inspiration to the prosaic, all-too-familiar surroundings of his native town. After Rimbaud's boat has bathed in the intoxicating waters of "le Poème de la Mer," will he be able to hide his Baudelairean "wings of a giant" (*ses ailes de géant*)? Perhaps, but it will be an effort not devoid of pain.

The story of Nabokov's dialogic engagement with Rimbaud's "Bateau ivre" receives an unexpected archival envoi. Album 23 preserves Véra Nabokov's multiple clippings of her husband's periodical publications, among which we duly find "P'ianyi korabl'" as it appeared in *Rul'*. Next to the poem's last line she writes what presumably is her version of the poem's finale:

и близъ пловучихъ тюремъ проплывать[225]

[and near [the] floating prisons sailed]

The writer's lifelong companion and confidante begs to differ from his interpretation of this crucial image. Her rendition of the poem's concluding line is in iambic pentameter rather than her husband's hexameter; it does not rhyme with the rest of the stanza. It conveys, however, the actual meaning of the original's finale. While the date of its appearance in Album 23 cannot be ascertained, it amounts to a clue for our attempt to understand Nabokov's dissatisfaction with his earlier translations and adoption of literalism. It is also a testimony to the kind of collaborative companionship that united Vladimir and Véra Nabokov. It appears to have been predicated not on Véra's unconditional worship of her husband's genius, but rather on a sense of intellectual equality and shared passion for artistic fidelity and precision.

"I worshipped you": The First Pushkin Translation

Vladimir and Véra Nabokov used the money from the sale of the German rights to Nabokov's second Russian novel, *Korol', dama, valet* (1928), to fund a butterfly-hunting expedition to the Eastern Pyrenées, with the town of Le Boulou, near the French-Spanish border, as their base. There Nabokov revived his draft of an unfinished 1924 short story to write *The Defense* (1930), his first Russian masterpiece.[226] It was in Le Boulou that Nabokov made his first translation of Pushkin into English – an auspicious beginning for a man who would become the most zealous representative of Pushkin's literary estate in the English-speaking world.[227]

Pushkin had composed his "Ia vas liubil: liubov' eshchë, byt' mozhet" exactly one hundred years earlier, in 1829, in full accordance with the tenets of an austere neoclassical poetics that could hardly be more different from the mode of expression characteristic of Verlaine, Rimbaud, or even Pushkin's near contemporary Musset. If Nabokov were to create a close approximation of Pushkin's poem, the exuberance and ingenuity of Nabokov's Russian versions of French proto-symbolist and late Romantic poets would have to be sacrificed to the laconic spirit of Pushkin's poetry; the genius of the English language would have to be appeased as well, all Pushkin's ties with the Gallic literary tradition notwithstanding.

> Я васъ любилъ: любовь ещё, быть можетъ,
> Въ душѣ моей угасла не совсѣмъ;

Но пусть она васъ больше не тревожитъ;
[4] Я не хочу печалить васъ ничѣмъ.[228]

I you loved: love yet, maybe,
in soul mine has gone out not quite;
but let it you more not trouble;
I not wish to sadden you with anything.[229]

Pushkin's statement of resignation is remarkably a-rhetorical. To emphasize the genuineness of the sentiment encapsulated in the poem, he foregoes most of the traditional literary devices in his poetic arsenal, gaining a subtlety of expression that is hard, if not outright impossible, to match even in Russian (today scholars refer to "Ia vas liubil" as an "imageless" – *bezóbraznyi* – poem).[230] Translators who wish to do justice to the poem's originality and yet preserve its formal parameters will require all the ingenuity they can muster.

I worshipped you. My love's reluctant ember
is in my heart still glimmering, may be,
but let it not break on your peace; remember,
[4] I should not want to have you sad through me.[231]

In this version of Pushkin's lyric, Nabokov preserved the metre, rhyme scheme, and even the alteration of masculine (even) and feminine (odd) rhymes. Working under the duress of these constraints, Nabokov recasts the main metaphor implied in the poem's first stanza, an approach that was effective when he dealt with Musset, Verlaine, and Rimbaud. In the second line of the poem's first stanza, Pushkin speaks of his passion in terms suitable to a description of a flickering fire ("liubov' … ugasla ne sovsem" – love … has gone out not completely); Nabokov extends the reach of Pushkin's implied metaphor, introducing "my love's" "reluctant ember" to justify the faint "glimmering" in his stanza's second line. What would have worked well in a translated version of a poem by Tennyson, Rimbaud, or Musset – or perhaps even Shakespeare – leads to rather ambiguous results, as the fire of the translated stanza threatens to become unruly once it has been given too much verbal freedom compared to the original, where it is permitted to flicker only once, then promptly abandoned in favour of a less exalted mode of expression.

A fine lexical rendition of the Russian phrase it echoes, the closing line of Nabokov's version of the poem's first stanza sounds stilted at best ("I should not want to have you sad through me") and lacks the flexibility that is a cornerstone of Pushkin's idiom in general and of this poem in particular. As Nabokov said in connection with his efforts to render in English Pushkin's "Ia pomniu chudnoe mgnoven'e," "What is to be done with this bird you have shot down only to find that it is not a bird of paradise, but an escaped parrot, still screeching its idiotic message as it flaps on the ground?"[232]

Surrender was not among the options this translator was willing to consider. Nabokov never published "I worshipped you," his 1929 version of Pushkin's 1829 lyric. He evidently intended to create other versions, test other languages in his quest for an ultimate translation of the poet to whom he owed so much. Such attempts, along with a discussion concerning the reasons that brought "I worshipped you" into existence one hundred years after its composition, will be considered below.

"Les amis inconnus": Vladimir Nabokov and Jules Supervielle

Like Jules Laforgue and Isidore Ducasse (Comte de Lautréamont), Jules Supervielle (1884–1960) was born in Uruguay, but unlike his predecessors he drew inspiration from his dual identity as South American and European as well as from his first-hand acquaintance with the Atlantic Ocean. Remembered primarily as a poet, he was also a novelist, short-story writer, dramatist, and translator.[233] In the two decades preceding the outbreak of World War II, he gained respect for his tacit but resolute opposition to many of the trends of the day. This is the reason why scholars had considerable difficulty categorizing him until critic Marcel Raymond placed him "en marge du surréalisme."[234] The "cosmic" Supervielle, who not infrequently juxtaposed his subjects with celestial bodies and imagined God's musings, can also be termed a metaphysical poet inasmuch as he attempted to embrace eternity and hint at eternal themes within his depictions of the phenomenal.[235] A staunchly apolitical artist, Supervielle made no secret of his detestation of the theatrical aspects of tyranny, as his sardonic poem "La pluie et les tyrans" (1938) testifies.

Nabokov's letters to his wife delineate a mini-narrative of his friendship with Supervielle, who was instrumental in inducting him into the world of French letters. A thirty-three-year-old Russian Berliner whose fourth novel, *Despair*, was being serialized in a Paris-based émigré journal, Nabokov first rang Supervielle's doorbell on 24 October 1932. By that time the forty-eight-year-old author had published three books of poems: *Débarcadères* (Jetties; 1922), *Gravitations* (1925), and *Le Forçat innocent* (The Innocent Condemned; 1930); released a collection of novellas: *L'Enfant de la haute mer* (The High-Tide Child; 1931); and placed three novels with Gallimard. While we do not know the circumstances preceding their initial encounter, it is clear that Supervielle's Russian visitor gained enough of his host's trust to be invited to discuss his works.[236] By 25 October 1932, Nabokov professed love for his poetry and in a matter of weeks they addressed each other "cher ami."[237] Though Supervielle's name does not figure prominently in the extant chronicles of Nabokov's career in letters, his importance for Nabokov's efforts to transcend the limitations of the émigré world cannot be overestimated. In Supervielle, Nabokov found an enthusiastic champion who introduced him to the editor-in-chief of *La Nouvelle revue française*, Jean Paulhan (1884–1968). It is difficult to imagine the fate of such significant components of the Nabokov canon as "Mademoiselle O" (1936) and "Pouchkine, ou le vrai et le vraisamblable" (1937) without Supervielle's intercession on their author's behalf.[238]

As we observe how the tone of Nabokov's reports of his calls on Supervielle grows less reverential with time, we should not overlook one aspect of their association: in Supervielle he did not merely acquire a useful connection but also found a like-minded contemporary. As such, Nabokov's friendship with the "talented" Supervielle deserves to be elevated to the level of his association with Russian champions Iulii Aikhenval'd and Vladislav Khodasevich. The significance of their professional conversations and discussions of each other's works must be taken into account whenever we attempt to impute the degree of Nabokov's integration into the literary world of his day. Much like Nabokov's association with Khodasevich, which inspired Godunov-Cherdyntsev's conversations with Koncheyev in *The Gift*, Nabokov's artistic intimacy with Supervielle was bound to have an effect on his compositions. As we begin to gauge that effect, Nabokov's translations from Supervielle acquire primary importance.

Nabokov's versions of Supervielle's "Le Sillage" (The Wake ["On voyait le sillage et nullement la barque," Visible was the wake and nothing of the boat]) and "L'Appel" (A Call ["Les dames en noir prirent leur violon," The black-clad women took their violin]) may seem like a minor addition to the sum of our knowledge of his engagement with French literature, but this impression is deceptive. Their appearance on our horizon forces us to reconsider everything we know about this avowed admirer of Baudelaire, Mallarmé, Rimbaud, Ronsard, and Verlaine who never parted ways with his adolescent partiality to Musset. In Supervielle, Nabokov found an older contemporary with a distinctly individual position within the scintillating universe of artistic experimentation that characterized pre–World War II French letters. Like Nabokov's Russian ally Khodasevich, Supervielle distanced himself from the unbridled formal innovation embraced by so many of his contemporaries and worked to deepen, rather than expand, the thematic and expressive range of the French literary tradition. Few of his contemporaries perfected the art of distilling individual metaphysical epiphanies into deceptively accessible poetry with a strong supranational undercurrent to the extent Supervielle did. It is no accident that he exerted a formative influence on the chief Russian surrealist poet Boris Poplavskii (1903–35), whose significance Nabokov acknowledged in a belated and rueful acceptance of his guilt for failing do so in Poplavskii's lifetime.[239]

Among the acclaimed virtuosos of French poetic diction whose verse is enshrined in the Pléiade book series, next to his fellow bearers of the title "Prince des poètes" – Leconte de Lisle, Verlaine, Mallarmé, Fort, and Cocteau – Supervielle cuts a fascinating and mysterious figure. It would be an oversight, however, to attribute this impression to his bicultural identity or enigmatic imagery. As befits a master of his craft, the individuality of his vision matches the formal sophistication with which he subverts the French poetic canon in a multitude of unostentatious ways. The student of French metrics Clive Scott puts it well in his professional evaluation of this poet: "For all the transparency of Supervielle's favouring of the heptasyllable, and indeed the octosyllable, there is much we do not understand about his metrical craft. We are very poor readers of Supervielle's rhythms."[240] How much did Nabokov understand about what may well be the single least transparent aspect of his Parisian friend's hermetic art? Close study of Nabokov's translations shows that he put his expertise in the field of translation of French poetry into Russian in service of Supervielle's furtive genius.

"Eshchë vidnelsia sled lad'i uzhe nezrimoi" (Was visible still the trace of an already invisible barque) is a translation of "Le Sillage" ("On voyait le sillage et nullement la barque"). The watercolour surface of the poem's palette may detract from its implications, but not for long: these thirteen lines relate the fate of two lovers who have committed suicide by drowning, as only a vestige of their happiness lingers in the wake of their abandoned and vanished sailboat. Arrestingly, Supervielle's treatment of this theme eschews all and any expectation of unhappiness or tragedy associated with such an outcome. The poem relates the silent recognition of those who discover this scene's aftermath that the drowned couple whose bodies they find next morning elected to preserve forever the state of the amorous bliss they tasted on their boating trip. A variation on the themes explored in such poems as "Le Survivant" ("Lorsque le noyé se réveille au fond des mers et que son cœur" – When the drowned one wakes up at the bottom of the sea and his heart), "Départ" (Departure ["Un paquebot dans sa chaudière," A steamer in its boiler), "Haute mer" (High Seas ["Parmi les oiseaux et les lunes," Among the birds and the moons]), all from *Gravitations*; such novellas as "L'Enfant de la haute mer" (1928) and "L'Inconnue de la Seine" (The Unknown [Girl] of the Seine; 1929), this poem is characteristic of Supervielle's fascination with the sea and its allure for mortals.

An equivocal nocturnal atmosphere permeates the cryptic imagery of "Damy v chërnykh plat'iakh vziali v ruki skripku," Nabokov's version of "L'Appel" ("Les dames en noir prirent leur violon"). With its faintly sepulchral atmosphere, "L'Appel" exhibits a certain affinity with the experimentation of its author's contemporaries the surrealists. Mysterious women in black play a mournful melody on a marble violin, this melody is quickly silenced, and the stone instrument is revealed to resemble a naked child asleep in an arboreal shadow. This pageant of disconnected images crescendos in an anonymous appeal whispered to the narrator, who presumably is the one experiencing this vision:

> Et ce fut alors qu'au fond du sommeil
> Quelqu'un me souffla: "Vous seul le pourriez,
> Venez tout de suite."[241]
>
> [And it was then that in the depth of [my] sleep /
> Someone whispered to me: "You alone could, / Come at once."]

Dorothy Blair discerns in this mysterious poem a Superviellean variation on the Orpheus myth; it is possible to read it as an appeal to a poet, who alone can break the silent spell by breathing life into the mute and ossified instrument.[242] This fractured, elliptic mini-narrative finds a suitable parallel in Nabokov's "Damy v chërnykh plat'iakh vziali v ruki skripku," which recreates the melancholic atmosphere of the original in a suitably enigmatic Russian poem.

"L'Appel" employs the ten-syllable line, with shorter lines marking its midpoint and then closure. The placement of caesuras in this poem follows no apparent pattern, as if to underscore the surrealistic implications of its imagery. To echo the effect of this poem on the French reader, Nabokov's equilinear version of the poem uses trochaic hexameter. This may not be the obvious choice for an original comprising lines of variable length, yet Nabokov's variant of the poem is replete with distant, distorted echoes of Russian trochaic poems written on the subject of departure and leave-taking, such as Lermontov's "Vykhozhu odin ia na dorogu" (I come out alone on a road; 1841).[243]

Viewed together as components of a bipartite cycle aiming to introduce their author to a Russian audience, the Nabokov translations from Supervielle seek to infect the reader with his fascination with the eerie originals. The subdued tonality of the poems' images gives a fair idea of their author's ability to be as clear or as inscrutable as he wishes to be while communicating a sense of his subtle formal craftsmanship and uncommon demeanour. Made privy to the secrets of Supervielle's art by the writer himself, Nabokov developed an enlightened appreciation of his benevolent patron's world view. These enthralling miniatures raise the inevitable question of the extent of Nabokov's acquaintance with Supervielle's art as a whole. It is at this juncture where we confront the tantalizing possibility that our awareness of the esteem in which Nabokov's held Supervielle work may contribute to our understanding of the most enduring mystery of his art, the origins of the *Lolita* theme.

Motivated as Nabokov was to make inroads into the world of French letters, he was careful in his choice of doors through which to reach his destination. He must have recognized in Supervielle a kindred spirit prior to presenting himself at his Parisian address, and that recognition could have been rooted solely in Nabokov's acquaintance with Supervielle's writings. It is difficult to imagine that Nabokov did not extend every effort to ensure that he appeared knowledgeable about various aspects of Supervielle's art, from his poetry to his novels. If that indeed was the case, Nabokov would certainly have known the story of one of Supervielle's most prominent victims of the sea, Philémon Bigua, the protagonist of *Le Voleur d'enfants* (*The Man Who Stole Children* in Alan Pryce-Jones's translation; 1926).

Colonel Philémon Bigua is a deep-pocketed foreigner – a Uruguayan political exile, to be exact – who roams the streets of European capitals in a chauffeured limousine with the aim of satisfying an odd passion. His wife Desposoria is barren, so the colonel finds an outlet for his frustrated paternal instincts in saving unfortunate children from their delinquent, neglectful parents by abducting and raising them as his own. At the novel's outset we see the colonel separate a seven-year-old Antoine from his nanny and bring him to his spacious Parisian apartment, where Antoine meets his "brothers" – the unruly teenager Joseph, picked up on the streets some years ago, and the English twins Jack and Fred, "saved" from their impecunious parents on a visit to the London Zoo. The reader learns that Antoine's kidnapping was long in the making: after identifying him as the child of a single mother who does not seem to care for her son, Bigua proceeds to shower the boy with gifts. When Antoine finds himself in Bigua's limousine and subsequently his apartment, he is made to realize that the strange older man with a bizzare accent is none other than his mysterious friend who will treat him as his son thenceforth.

Things go surprisingly well for the colonel until he decides to make his family complete by adding to it the only missing piece – a girl-child, a sister to his boys, as it were. An opportunity presents itself soon enough when a Parisian drunkard familiar with the colonel's weakness for child-rearing practically presses him to accept into his family a girl whom he has fathered with a prostitute.

This realization of a long-standing ambition of his becomes the colonel's undoing as he realizes that he has become attracted to the girl Marcelle. The novel descends into an awkward farce, where we have to countenance the colonel's torment at the sight of a girl who is described as pale, sensitive, and trembling when he sees her for the first time. As he brings Marcelle over to his place, Bigua discovers "in spite of himself" that this "child with fine joints and chapped lips" is capable of coquetry and cannot help but notice that Marcelle is beautifully built and that "her expression wore a gentleness which did not belong to childhood." In the course of the ensuing events, no matter how hard he tries, Bigua is unable to drive away unchaste thoughts; he is consumed by fantasies, desire, and guilt. At one particular moment he makes a dreadful fool of himself by showing up for dinner with the fly of his trousers undone and his foreskin exposed for his entire family – including Marcelle – to see. From that moment on he begins to consider suicide as the only way out of his predicament.

As time goes by, Marcelle starts an affair with Joseph, the eldest and rudest of the colonel's "sons," and becomes pregnant. After throwing Joseph out, the terrified colonel decides to take his family to his native Uruguay. Upon discovering that Joseph serves as a sailor on the same transatlantic liner they are travelling on and has resumed his involvement with Marcelle, Bigua throws himself overboard, with all his affairs in disarray. As he drowns he realizes that he has forgotten to leave behind his carefully prepared last will.

The subject of an adult man's attraction to a pre-pubescent girl-child and its dramatic possibilities has become so closely intertwined with Nabokov's *Lolita* that one needs to be reminded of its long prehistory in his oeuvre, from its first formulation in the poem "Lilith," to *The Gift*, to the novella *The Enchanter*, to its eventual realization in the world-famous eponymous novel. So complex is the issue of the theme's gestation and evolution that it cannot be traced to a single source. On more than one occasion, however, we are able to discern entry points of techniques, motifs, and plot twists that find a refracted reflection in that richly allusive novel. Nabokov's proximity to Supervielle's *Le Voleur d'enfants* suggests that he may have discerned the potential of this subject in that imperfect, ambiguous, and unconvincing treatment of a similar theme.

As D. Barton Johnson has noted, Nabokov's acquaintance with Supervielle's 1931 novella "L'Inconnue de la Seine" may have had an effect on his poem of the same title.[244] The Superviellean motif of drowning finds a plethora of parallels in Nabokov's compositions, where it is echoed in what Johnson terms his "preoccupation with the [mermaid] theme."[245] Indeed, from his earliest poems onward, Nabokov's writings contain an impressive gallery of mermaids or naiads, of which Hazel Shade of *Pale Fire* and Lucette in *Ada* are most prominent.

Apart from an influential ally, Nabokov found in Supervielle an artist-interlocutor of the kind he wished he had found when he refashioned Rupert Brooke into the transcendentalist avatar of his own creation. Supervielle, not Brooke, persistently and with "tormented and creative perceptiveness, peered into the twilight of the beyond." In his poems and novellas, Supervielle imagines the afterlives of the dead, suggesting that the moment they cease to exist as people they enter a new realm of being (the novella "L'Inconnue de la Seine" is a striking incarnation of this theme). Supervielle appears to have appealed to Nabokov by his consistent exploration of the theme of life after death, while his *Le Voleur d'enfants* anticipated and possibly encouraged Nabokov's search for his variation on the theme of a child imperilled by adult lust.

Shakespeare's "mortal coil," Pushkin's *vypolzina*, Gogol's *ryzhaia svitka*: A Russian *Hamlet* That Was Not to Be

The letters section of the June–July 1931 issue of *Le Mois*, a Parisian periodical billed as a "synthèse de l'activité mondiale," featured a short essay entitled "Les écrivains et l'époque" by "V. Sirine." The essay was followed by an unsigned piece entitled "Vladimir Nabokoff Sirine, l'amoureux de la vie," which effectively introduced the most important writer of the younger generation of the Russian diaspora to the magazine's readers. Composed by one of the most enthusiastic – and discerning – of Nabokov's Russian critics, this article painted a propitious portrait of a writer whose uniquely broad range of artistic enterprise was happily coupled with industriousness: "Sirine est un grand travailleur. Depuis 1926, il a donné un roman presque tous les ans. Actuellement, il travaille à une nouvelle traduction de *Hamlet*."[246]

Indeed, between 1926 and 1931, Nabokov had published *Mashen'ka*, *Korol', dama, valet*, *Zashchita Luzhina*, a collection of stories and poems entitled *Vozvrashchenie Chorba* (1929), *Sogliadatai* (1930), and *Podvig* (written 1930); he had also completed *Camera Obscura* (1931). Had Nabokov completed his "nouvelle traduction" of *Hamlet*, it would have become a major landmark in the Russian perception of Shakespeare, prefiguring Boris Pasternak's *Gamlet* of 1941, although it would, no doubt, have been vastly different from any other Russian version of the tragedy.

Three fragments from the *Hamlet* translation were in fact published in *Rul'* in 1930. They included "Dva otryvka iz 'Gamleta' 1. (Iz stseny 7 deistviia IV); 2. (Iz stseny 1 deistviia V)";[247] the third and last published fragment was entitled "Gamlet (Deistvie III, iavlenie 1)."[248] As follows from Nabokov's precise indication of the sources of his translations, the first published fragment comprised the Queen's announcement of Ophelia's death from act 4, scene 7 (from "One woe doth tread upon another's heel" to "Pulled the poor wretch from her melodious lay / To muddy death"), while the second presented the verbal skirmish between Hamlet and Laertes as they "grapple." The fragment ran from Laertes's "Now pile your dust upon the quick and dead" to the Queen's melancholy observation on what she perceives as the progress of her son's madness, toward the end of scene 1 in act 5 (until the words "His silence will sit drooping"). The fragment published in the 23 November 1930 issue of *Rul'* comprised the entire "To be or not to be" soliloquy (act 3, scene 1). All in all, in September and November of

1930, Nabokov published his translation of about one hundred lines from Shakespeare's tragedy.

Nabokov's archives preserve drafts of some fifteen more unpublished *Hamlet* fragments. In addition to writing down thoughts for Russian versions of a number of mostly disjointed, scattered fragments, he contemplated an *additional* Hamlet soliloquy containing the prince's morose broodings on his mother's character, written *in English*.

Evidence obtained from both published and unpublished fragments indicates that Nabokov was planning to translate the more inclusive version of the tragedy's text, one based on the Second Quarto edition of *Hamlet*, known to Shakespeare scholars as the "good" quarto or Q2, some copies of which are dated 1604 and some 1605,[249] and not on the First Folio (also known as F) edition of 1623. Thus, Nabokov prepared his versions of Horatio's characterization of "young Fortinbras" (act 1, scene 1); the same character's excursion into the history of ancient Rome "a little ere the mightiest Julius fell" in act 1, scene 1;[250] the King's digression from act 4, scene 1 ("For goodness, growing to a pleurisy, / Dies in his own too-much") – this fragment also appeared only in Q2.[251] Likewise, it is Q2 that attributes the remark on Hamlet's madness after his scuffle with Laertes in act 5, scene 1 to the Queen (from "This is mere madness" to "His silence will sit drooping") – in the published text of Nabokov's translation of this fragment, this short speech was assigned to the Queen and not the King, as it had been done in F (cf. "Koroleva[:] Vsë eto lish' bezum'e… on zamolchit, potupias" [Queen: All this is nothing but madness … he would fall silent, looking down][252]). Such evidence confirms that Samuel Schuman was justified in directing readers of his article examining Nabokov's connection with Shakespeare to the *The Oxford Shakespeare* edition by W.J. Craig, since Craig had based his version of *Hamlet* on Q2.[253] By the same token, for all its impressive apparatus, the G.R. Hibbard-edited Oxford World's Classics edition of *Hamlet* in the Oxford Shakespeare series will prove of limited use to the student of Nabokov's version of *Hamlet*, as it is based on the F edition of the play and relegates all the additional fragments of the tragedy found in Q2 to an appendix.[254] The New Folger Library edition of *Hamlet*, by far the most efficient representation of the Q2 text among the editions of Shakespeare's work in wide circulation, will be used here in lieu of Craig's *Oxford Shakespeare* employed by Nabokov both for his translations of sonnets 17 and 27 and for his work on *Hamlet*.[255]

One of Nabokov's incentives for trying his hand at translating *Hamlet* was dissatisfaction with the works of his Russian predecessors. In "The

Art of Translation," an essay published some ten years after his attempt to create a Russian *Hamlet* of his own making, Nabokov disapproved of what had once been the dominant mode in nineteenth-century translations of Shakespeare into Russian, namely the translators' preoccupation with "eternal problems" and their lack of regard for individual detail:

> It was the rule with Russian versions of Shakespeare to give Ophelia richer flowers than the poor weeds she found. The Russian rendering of
>
> There with fantastic garlands did she come
> Of crowflowers, nettles, daisies and long purples
>
> if translated back into English would run like this:
>
> There with most lovely garlands did she come
> Of violets, carnations, roses, lilies.[256]
>
> The splendor of this floral display speaks for itself; incidentally it bowdlerized the Queen's digressions, granting her the gentility she so sadly lacked and dismissing the liberal shepherds; how anyone could make such a botanical collection beside the Helje or the Avon is another question.[257]

In his published version of the same fragment Nabokov makes a point of preserving the local colour in the Queen's speech, rectifying the mistakes of his predecessors:

> Есть ива у ручья; къ той блѣдной ивѣ,
> склонившейся надъ ясною водой,
> она пришла съ гирляндами ромашекъ,
> крапивы, лютиковъ, лиловой змѣйки,
> зовущейся у вольныхъ пастуховъ
> иначе и грубѣе, а у нашихъ
> холодныхъ дѣвъ – перстами мёртвыхъ.[258]
>
> [There is a willow by the brook; to that pale willow, / bent over lucid water, / she came with gardlands of camomiles, / nettles, buttercups, long purple, / that is called among liberal shepherds / differently and ruder, but among our / cold maids – fingers of the dead.]

In Nabokov's rendition the *Hamlet* fragments retain their original metrical properties: he translates Shakespeare's blank verse into

Russian iambic pentameter, demonstrating the mastery of the medium he had had since his version of Byron's "Dream" in 1919.

While the metrical qualities of a Shakespearean text cannot qualify as a major impediment to the creation of adequate Russian translations of his plays, such a text's lexical richness presents a serious challenge. Shakespeare's writing is extraordinarily varied while remaining firmly within the limits of its time, a time that has been pronounced the Golden Age of the English language; the stylistic range of his characters' speeches is immensely broad both in terms of sheer verbal inventiveness and contrapuntal shifts in register.

For the second fragment included in the *Rul'* publication of 19 September 1930, Nabokov chose the verbal clash between Laertes and Hamlet from the opening scene of act 5 (see the two characters' scuffle in Ophelia's grave):

Что можешь ты?
Рыдать? Терзать себя? Поститься? Драться?
Испить отравы? Крокодила съѣсть?
Всё сдѣлаю. Зачѣмъ пришёлъ? Чтобъ выть?
Чтобъ посрамить меня прыжкомъ въ могилу?
Ложись въ могилу къ ней, – я лягу тоже.
Болтаешь о горахъ? Такъ пусть навалятъ
на насъ съ тобой земли такую груду,
что темя опалитъ она о солнце,
и Оссу обратитъ въ волдырь.[259]

[What can you do? / Tear yourself? Sob? Fast? Fight? / Partake of poison? Eat a crocodile? / I'll do it all. Why have you come? To howl? / To shame me with leaping in her grave? / Go lie in her grave – I'll do it too. / You prattle about mountains? Let them heap, then, / upon you and me such a pile, / which will burn its pate against the sun, / and turn Ossa into a blister.]

The translated fragment of act 5 displays Shakespeare's command of radically different lexical registers in the course of a dynamic exchange (the quotation above represents only Hamlet's response to Laertes's laments over his sister's freshly dug grave). Here Hamlet triumphs over Laertes not because he gains a higher moral ground (which would have been difficult, given the circumstances that lead to his initial confrontation with Laertes), but because Hamlet is able to undermine Laertes's grandiloquent evocations of classical images with his vehemently sarcastic mockery of such rhetoric and focus on the intensity, the immediacy of his own grief.

Most important – and Nabokov was acutely aware of this quality in Shakespeare's language – the vividness of Shakespeare's writing expands thanks to his ability to conjure up verbal images that frequently seem to assume a life of their own, an existence seemingly independent of the apparent theme of a given soliloquy, dialogue, or sentence, and yet connected intrinsically with a delicate and complex network of motifs within the larger context of a given play.

One of Nabokov's drafts demonstrates his awareness of this phenomenon as well as his approach to rendering it in Russian.

> POLONIUS: I did enact Julius Caesar. I was killed i'th' Capitol. Brutus killed me.
> HAMLET: It was a brute part of him to kill so capital a calf there. – Be the players ready?[260]

> <POLONIUS> Я игралъ Цезаря. Я былъ убитъ въ Капитоліи. Убивалъ Брутъ.
> <HAMLET> Весьма брутально съ его стороны было убивать этакую цесарку. Что, готовы актёры?[261]

> [<Polonius> I played Caesar. I was killed in the Capitol. Brutus did the killing. <Hamlet> Rather brutal on his part to kill such a [guineafowl]. Well, are the actors ready?]

Nabokov's draft version of Hamlet's double-edged remark is equally in tune with the Prince's mockery of Polonius's haste to avoid any ambiguity in his words and with Hamlet's desire to advance his secret agenda before the inception of the carefully orchestrated play-within-the-play. Unbeknownst to either character, Hamlet's punning remark presages the circumstances of his accidental murder of Ophelia's and Laertes's busybody of a father soon thereafter, and Nabokov chooses to amplify the hidden portent of Hamlet's words by replacing Shakespeare's "capital calf" with "helmeted guineafowl" (*tsesarka; Numida meleagris*). The irony of this substitution lies in the fact that Hamlet will kill Polonius thinking that he has killed the King, or "Caesar" – the root of the Russian name for *tsesarka*, which is a large domesticated bird related to the turkey. This comparison is full of implications for our understanding of Polonius's appearance and character, the same Polonius who is sliding toward his gruesome end as a pathetic, if not altogether innocent, victim of Hamlet's thirst for revenge. The murderer who may wish to compare himself to Brutus will be butchering an old man who is as capable of self-defence as he is of fathoming the consequences of his dimwitted attempts to understand and interpret the "method" in Hamlet's madness.

Nabokov published his version of the "To be or not to be" soliloquy in the 23 November 1930 issue of *Rul'*. As far as is possible to judge from the surviving fragments from the Berg collection, the published version of the soliloquy was preceded by a search for different ways of rendering Hamlet's reflection in Russian.[262] The published version of the soliloquy renders "When we have shuffled off this mortal coil" as *kogda osvobodimsia / ot shelukhi suet*, whereas the draft attempted to render the implied comparison of the separation of human consciousness from the body it once inhabited with a snake's shuffling off its skin: *kogda zemnuiu vypolzinu sbrosim*. In accordance with one of the tenets of Shakespearean and, for that matter, Nabokovian poetics, the translator sought to render Shakespeare's implied likening of human life to the existence of a lowly, despised, and dangerous creature by means of a play on words, substituting a component in the phrase *zmeinaia vypolzina* (approx., [discarded] snakeskin) with a like-sounding adjective *zemnaia* (*vypolzina*). Russian literary mythology ties the word *vypolzina* to Aleksandr Pushkin, who, according to the recollections of Vladimir Dal', jokingly referred to his newly tailored frock coat as *vypolzina* on the eve of his fatal duel (the same frock coat, which Pushkin intended to wear for a long time, had to be cut from his body so not to disturb the mortally wounded poet).[263] If Nabokov did indeed cancel this literary allusion in the text of his published version of Hamlet's soliloquy (assuming that the draft version of "shuffled off this mortal coil" preceded the published text of the soliloquy in Nabokov's translation rather than following it), this choice can be interpreted as a reconsideration of Nabokov's translating method: to an adaptation-like version of the phrase, which would have been endowed with a resonance understandable only in a Russian literary context, Nabokov preferred a more neutral version that presented Hamlet's soliloquy as a genuinely foreign text, one devoid of alien literary associations.

In the published version of the soliloquy, Nabokov renders the phrase "whips and scorns of time" as *bichi i glum vremën*, which conveys the lexical meaning of the phrase. The draft version of the same phrase provides a phonetic rendition of Shakespeare's alliteration as *podkhlëst i khokhot veka*, which employs an expressive accumulation of fricative consonants. While it is impossible to say with utmost certainty whether the published fragment represents the final version of the translation, it is likely that Nabokov discarded the more asymmetric, alliterative variant in favour of the less expressive published variant, as it rendered the meaning of the original phrase closer to its English source, thus conforming to the more mature principles of Nabokov's translating methodology.

Equally daring was Nabokov's punning rendition of Hamlet's "miching malicho," with which in act 3, scene 2 Hamlet sums up the import of the dumb show for the benefit of the unsuspecting Ophelia.[264] Nabokov translated the phrase as *zlo podpolzlo*, demonstrating at once his understanding of its meaning and aesthetic value. Shakespeare's phrase and Nabokov's version of it successfully balance on the verge of meaningless nonsense and the profoundest of meanings, given the aim of the dumb show (as well as that of the entire play-within-the-play episode) in the context of the tragedy.

Nabokov's active work on a Russian translation of *Hamlet* may not have been completed, but it directly informed *Bend Sinister*, his novel of 1947, the first of his novels to be written in America in English. Nabokov's *Bend Sinister* makes extensive use of *Hamlet*; in fact, it features an entire chapter that deals directly with the aesthetic and ethical aspects of translation in general and with the task of rendering *Hamlet* in a foreign language in particular. The significance of the *Hamlet* imagery in the context of *Bend Sinister* has been studied by a number of scholars; it should be stressed, however, that chapter 7 of *Bend Sinister* is also Nabokov's contemplation of both his role as a translator of Shakespeare and of his incomplete Shakespearean project.

As it turns out, the only fragment from Nabokov's drafts of his Russian *Hamlet* that appeared in print is to be found in the Shakespearean chapter 7 of *Bend Sinister*, in the guise of a sample quotation attributed in the text of the book to Ember, the novel's most unfortunate translator of *Hamlet*, who has to carry out his task while living under a totalitarian regime. Nabokov transliterates this fragment, and presents a piece of his own translation as though it had been made by this character of his:

> *Ne dumaete-li vy, sudar', shto vot eto* (the song about the wounded deer), *da les per'ev na shliape, da dve kamchatye rozy na proreznykh bashmakakh, mogli by, kol' fortuna zadala by mne turku, zasluzhit' mne uchast'e v teatralnoí arteli; a, sudar'?*[265]

Nabokov transferred this transliterated quotation verbatim from one of the index cards he had used while at work on his Russian *Hamlet*. In the text of the original it corresponds to the following fragment from act 3, scene 2:

> Would not this, sir, and a forest of feathers – if the rest of my fortunes turn Turk with me – with two Provincial roses on my razed shoes, get me a fellowship in a cry of players, sir?[266]

Having performed a quatrain of a ballad featuring a "stricken deer" and in high spirits after the success of his *Murder of Gonzago* ruse, Hamlet invites Horatio to pay tribute to his dramatic potential. Nabokov translated both the balladic quatrain and Hamlet's appeal to his friend; the translated fragment had to await publication until it made an appearance in a context at once different from the one it was meant to appear in initially and eerily similar to the paranoid atmosphere of Elsinore, as powerfully evoked by Nabokov in *Bend Sinister*.[267]

In the text of chapter 7 of *Bend Sinister*, the fragment cited above is followed by a lengthy digression dealing with different aspects of the translator's art, its glory and its inherent ambiguity. Adam Krug, the novel's protagonist, is distracted from his thoughts by Ember the translator, who asks Krug to share his opinion of his work:

> "I think it is wonderful," said Krug, frowning. He got up and paced the room. "Some lines need oiling," he continued, "and I do not like the color of dawn's coat – I see 'russet' in a less leathery, less proletarian way, but you may be right. The whole thing is quite wonderful."[268]

Krug is somewhat dissatisfied with Ember's rendition of Horatio's "But look, the morn in russet mantle clad / Walks o'er the dew of yon high eastern hill" (act 1, scene 1). But what exactly does Krug mean by his "leathery, proletarian way" of translating Shakespeare's "russet [mantle]"? Can it be *krasnyi* or *alyi*, with their all-too-obvious political associations? Perhaps Krug does not like the alternative variant that can be found in Nabokov's preparatory drafts for his Russian *Hamlet*, where the same phrase is rendered as follows:

> Но глянь-ка утро въ рыжей свиткѣ ходитъ
> ужъ по росѣ восточной той горы.[269]

[But look now, the ruddy-shirted morning is treading / already the dew of that eastern mountain.]

While *ryzhii* (red/ginger/ruddy) may not be as "proletarian" as *krasnyi* or *alyi*, the phrase *ryzhaia svitka* would certainly have elicited Adam Krug's raised eyebrow. Much like *uzhasnye glaza mostov* for "les yeux horribles des pontons" in the final line of Nabokov's version of Rimbaud's "Bateau ivre," the choice of the obsolete and regional noun *svitka* for Shakespeare's "mantle" is bound to strike the bilingual reader as odd, considering the difference in the two words' lexical register (cf. Krug's characterization of Ember's choice as "proletarian" in the fragment cited above). *Svita* or *svitka* may indeed be compared to "mantle" inasmuch as it denotes a long article of clothing that was worn on top of other clothes, yet as such, it also denotes the wearer's social status, since it was worn by peasants in Russia and Ukraine.[270] The path that took Nabokov from "mantle" to *svitka,* however, may be traced, given its pronounced literary associations. A red *svitka* (cf. Shakespeare's "russet mantle") figures prominently in Gogol's "Fair at Sorochintsy" (1831), where it once belonged to a fiend that had been expelled from hell, bringing misfortune to all people who chanced to come into possession of it.[271] To a literate speaker of Russian, therefore, *svitka* evokes definite associations with Gogolian demonology, a link not altogether irrelevant in the text of a tragedy that deals with diabolic temptation.

Adam Krug is not happy with some of the choices made by both Ember and his creator in his Russian hypostasis as Vladimir Sirin. By the time *Bend Sinister* was published, its author had long abandoned his attempts to put *Hamlet* into Russian, having substantially re-evaluated his former approach. Should our hypothesis be correct, and should the unpublished fragments have been written earlier than the three fragments published in *Rul'*, it would clarify the trajectory of Nabokov's thought regarding his Russian *Hamlet*. In the unpublished fragments, Nabokov evidently experimented with a mode of translating Shakespeare into Russian that permitted indirect allusions to Russian literature, a move that, if implemented, would have been tantamount to a reversal of his method to one of adaptation. The published fragments, however, avoided allusions to Russian literature and culture (consider Nabokov's exclusion of such a marked term as *vypolzina* from the published version of the "To be or not to be" soliloquy), and soon after the publication of the fragments Nabokov abandoned the project altogether. In *Bend Sinister*, however, he revisited the drafts of his Russian

Hamlet, this time to cast a retrospective glance at his unfinished project at a time when his work as a translator had entered a new phase in its evolution. Along with the composition of *Bend Sinister*, Nabokov was working on his English versions of Russian authors from Zhukovskii to Khodasevich, some of which make up the kernel of *Three Russian Poets: Translations of Pushkin, Lermontov, Tyutchev* (1944). In all likelihood this combination of translation and original creation prompted Nabokov's intense reflection on translation as an artistic pursuit and contributed to the rapidly unfolding evolution of his views on translation.

"De la Nuance avant toute chose": Verlaine's Restless Spirit Appeased

When Nabokov entered the most intensive phase of his Russian literary career, translation ceased to occupy a dominant place in his creative enterprise. Yet though the composition of original novels, short stories, poems, and dramatic works left little room for so labour-intensive a pursuit as translation, he never abandoned it, even during his heyday as a Russian writer in the period between 1929, the year he wrote *The Defense*, and 1939, the year he wrote *The Enchanter*. The fact that the translations belonging to this period were made by a mature master of the Russian language renders them a fascinating aspect of his artistic activities, while the circumstances under which Nabokov made these translations provide valuable insights into both their genesis and their place in his life and art.

In June 1930, the émigré translator and conservative thinker Ivan Tkhorzhevskii (1876–1951) issued an anthology of "new" French verse in his Russian translations. The anthology brought together no fewer than seventy-three poets (one of them, Léon Dierx, had been born as early as 1838). Tkhorzhevskii, a quintessential representative of the old school of Russian literary translation in exile, sought to draw a "general line of the development of French poetry," discerning in it a movement from "ennui and faithlessness to a thirst for happiness, accompanied by a simultaneous [and] spontaneous strengthening of religious sensitivity." Unafraid of sweeping generalizations, Tkhorzhevskii traced a direct line from Rimbaud, with what he saw as "the aimless wanderings of 'The Drunken Boat,'" to "the steadfast and bold 'Rower' ['Le Rameur'] by Paul Valéry."[272]

In mid or late 1930, Gleb Struve asked Nabokov to review Tkhorzhevskii's anthology, an opportunity that Nabokov, who had already written a critical response to Tkhorzhevskii's versions of Edward FitzGerald's *Rubáiyát of Omar Khayyám* in 1928, did not take.[273] Once he had read Tkhorzhevskii's translations more closely, however, Nabokov revisited the idea in a letter to Struve dated 8 November 1930. As follows from his letter, Nabokov took particular issue with Tkhorzhevskii's version of Verlaine's "Art poétique." Tkhorzhevskii had given the poem a new title ("Nakaz poetam"), retained its dedication to Charles Maurice, but misinterpreted its polemical thrust: the dedication had not been there when the poem was published for the first time in *Paris-Moderne* on 10 November 1882 and appeared only subsequently, after Maurice had attacked the principles of Verlaine's poetics in an article signed "Karl Mohr," accusing the poet of hermeticism and contempt for rhyme.[274] In his letter to Struve, Nabokov vowed "to appease Verlaine's spirit" by retranslating the poem into Russian.

Written as early as 1874, Verlaine's "Art poétique" was by no means a work of an acknowledged *maître*, someone who was in a position to issue an ukase (cf. Tkhorzevskii's title for the poem). In "Art poétique" Verlaine, whose own poetics had undergone a considerable rejuvenation under the influence of Rimbaud (it is ironic that "Art poétique" should have been composed during Verlaine's imprisonment in Mons), challenged many anachronistic assumptions about how French poetry should be written and proceeded to demonstrate that his unorthodox approach to the art of verse-making could be as effective as that of many of his Parnassian contemporaries. Verlaine's choice of prosodic medium for his programmatic statement was anything but accidental: the enneasyllabic verse (*rythme ennéasyllabique*) of "Art poétique" deliberately scorns the alexandrine, French poetry's medium of choice for centuries. The uneven syllabic count of Verlaine's lines was in agreement with the poet's persistent search for a novel mode of expression whose chief aim was musicality, an objective that is boldly announced in the poem's opening stanza:

De la musique avant toute chose,
Et pour cela préfère l'Impair
Plus vague et plus soluble dans l'air,
Sans rien en lui qui pèse ou qui pose.[275]

[Music above all things, / And to that end favour *l'Impair* / More vague and more soluble in the air, / With nothing in it that burdens or strikes a pose.]

In "Art poétique," the *impair* that Verlaine urges his colleagues to prefer is a poetic line consisting of an odd number of syllables, a demand that would eventually lead French poetry away from the dictates of the alexandrine toward the adoption of *vers libre*.[276] The imprecision, the fluid vagueness of the *impair*, its freedom from the affectation characteristic of a tired literary form are among the qualities that compelled Verlaine to make so strong a case for its adoption. Again and again throughout "Art poétique," Verlaine demonstrates that irregularity, deliberate lack of order, as well as freedom from excessive rationalization of artistic endeavour may prove to be among the vital resources for French poetry in the near future.

Tkhorzhevskii's "Nakaz poetam" shows that this translator had failed to comprehend the importance of Verlaine's choice of metre. Tkhorzhevskii's version employs regular dactylic tetrameters with truncated clausulas, which misrepresents the pathos of Verlaine's appeal to his readers. Tkhorzhevskii's take on stanzas 2 and 4 reveal his misunderstanding of his model's individuality.[277] In the original Verlaine urges his colleagues not to be afraid of choosing their words even if they *do* have some kind of flaw ("il faut aussi que tu n'ailles point / choisir tes mots sans quelque méprise"); Tkhorzhevskii, by contrast, tells his readers to be especially careful with their lexical choices. Ironically enough, in his Russian *nakaz*, Tkhorzhevskii employed a Gallicism that could hardly be more alien to the spirit of Verlaine's manifesto: the second line of the stanza quoted above instructs the reader-poet to be *izyskannyi* (refined) in his vocabulary. Since the Russian *izyskannyi* is, in its turn, based on the French participle *recherché*, this word choice becomes a striking example of Tkhorzhevskii's misrepresentation of the original, since being recherché is precisely what Verlaine, the champion and connoisseur of artistic naiveté, was against.

Tkhorzhevskii's miscalculations may be glaring, but how is one to render in Russian a poem that makes such explicit use of the realia typical of a specific situation in the history of French verse? It is not difficult to criticize the monotonous regularity of Tkhorzhevskii's metre, but what is one to do about the fact that the very concept of the *impair* is irrelevant in a Russian prosodic context? Having rejected the edifying tonality of Tkhorzhevskii's version on 8 November 1930, Nabokov succeeded in finding a solution to the riddle of a Russian "Art poétique."

Да будетъ музыка первой заботой,
предпочитай же нечётный счётъ, –

онъ, въ воздухѣ тая, смутнѣе течётъ,
въ нём что-то простое, лёгкое что-то.[278]

[Let music be your primary concern, / so favour then an uneven count – / as it melts in the air, it flows more vaguely, / in it there's something simple, something light.]

The fact that Nabokov translates Verlaine's "Et pour cela préfère l'Impair" as *predpochitai zhe nechëtnyi schët* (approx., do prefer an uneven [odd] count), immediately tells the reader that he is aware of the theoretical implications of the French poet's appeal. On the one hand, the enneasyllabic verse of "Art poétique" implies an odd number of syllables in a line; on the other, the phrase *nechëtnyi schët* is relevant in the context of the evolutionary changes in the history of Russian prosody characteristic of the symbolist and post-symbolist eras, a period of Russian literature that owed a good deal of its inspiration to none other than Paul Verlaine. Throughout the length of his "Iz Polia Verlena" ("Da budet muzyka pervoi zabotoi"), in each one of its nine stanzas Nabokov prevents the amphibrachic tetrameter from dominating the poem's metre by shortening the number of unstressed syllables between ictuses from two to one, which is to say that the overall number of unstressed syllables situated between stressed ones varies from line to line, effectively becoming "uneven" or "odd" in purely symmetric, quantitative terms (cf. Nabokov's *predpochitai zhe nechëtnyi schët*). Using an amphibrach-based *dol'nik* as a phenomenon peculiar to the development of Russian poetry when it sought to replace the rigidity of the five classical syllabotonic feet by the admission of "mongrel" rhythms that had long been considered impermissible, Nabokov succeeds in providing his Russian reader with a meaningful parallel to Verlaine's *impair*, a phenomenon indicative of the development of French syllabic poetry in the early stages of its gradual adoption of prosodic units comprised of an odd and variable number of syllables per line.

In Nabokov's version the fourth stanza of "Art poétique" retains many of its idiosyncratic properties. Where Tkhorzhevskii's translation had been unable to meet the demands of Verlaine's delicate and deliberate construction, Nabokov offered a seemingly impossible reflection of the French word order and inner rhyming. Below, the fourth stanza of the original is reproduced, this time followed by Nabokov's translation:

Car nous voulons la Nuance encor,
Pas la Couleur, rien que la nuance!

Oh! la nuance seule fiance
Le rêve au rêve et la flûte au cor![279]

[For we also want Nuance, / Not Colour, only nuance! / Oh! Nuance alone weds / Dream to a dream, and flute to horn.]

Вѣдь только оттѣнокъ важен. Цвѣта, –
Богъ съ ними. Намъ только оттѣнка нужно.
О, это нужно, чтоб встрѣтились дружно
рожокъ со свирѣлью, съ мечтою мечта.[280]

[For only the overtone is paramount. Colours – / God be with them. All we need is the overtone. / Oh, what needs to happen is a friendly encounter / between a shepherd's horn and a reed-pipe, between one dream and another.]

In concert with his earlier injunction ("Il faut aussi que tu n'ailles point / Choisir tes mots sans quelque méprise"), Verlaine places "nuance" first in the rhyming position of this stanza's second line, and next in the internal rhyming combination contained in the stanza's third line ("la nuance seule fiance"). In his *rhyming* version of the stanza, Nabokov successfully mirrors the effect of Verlaine's distinctive word order without compromising the overall rhyme scheme of the stanza: abba. Nabokov preserved this stable rhyme scheme throughout the poem's nine quatrains, one of the effects of Verlaine's "Art poétique" that Tkhorzhevskii in his version of "Nakaz poetam" had failed to represent.

When in 1973 Gleb Struve reminded Nabokov of his 1930 translation of Verlaine's "Art poétique," the writer recalled it as being "poor" (*nevazhnyi*).[281] That Nabokov the literalist could no longer see the value of this work in the literary mode he had by then abandoned and denounced is regrettable. Made competitively and on a whim, apart from successfully conveying the meaning of the original this translation infuses its form with significance redolent of the cultural context from where this statement originated. As such, this little-known work qualifies as a high point of Nabokov's Russian period.

"Вы снова близко, рѣющія тѣни": Seeing past Goethe's *poshlust*

In a deservedly famous passage from *Nikolai Gogol* (1947), Nabokov introduces and discusses the Russian concept of *poshlust* (his transliteration) for which "the other three European languages" he knew "possessed no special term."[282] To both Gogol and Nabokov this native notion seemed especially apt to designate a breed of base vulgarity that found a ripe expression in some aspects of German life and thought. "It takes a super-Russian," Nabokov proceeds, "to admit that there is a dreadful streak of *poshlust* running through Goethe's *Faust*."[283] It appears, however, that he was of a different mind when his translation of Goethe's "Zueignung" (Dedication) to *Faust* was published in an issue of the Paris-based *Poslednie novosti* dated 15 December 1932, although what happened in the temporal gap separating 1932 from 1947 may have altered more than one aesthetic evaluation.

In his "Iz Gëte. Posviashchenie k 'Faustu'" (From Goethe. Dedication to *Faust*) Nabokov transferred the four aBaBaBCC octaves of iambic pentameter that make up Goethe's "Zueignung" with the utmost accuracy, as if to indicate that this version of the poem is little more than a copious reproduction of the original.

Ihr naht euch wieder, schwankende Gestalten!
Die früh sich einst dem trüben Blick gezeigt.
Versuch' ich wohl euch diesmal fest zu halten?
[1.4] Fühl' ich mein Herz noch jenem Wahn geneigt?[284]

[You approach again, wavering forms! / On one early occasion you showed yourselves to gloomy sight. / Am I trying to capture you now? / I feel my heart is still inclined to that illusion.]

Вы снова близко, рѣющія тѣни.
Мой смутный взоръ уже васъ видѣлъ разъ.
Хочу-ль теперь безумія видѣній?
[1.4] Запечатлѣть попробую ли васъ?[285]

[You're close again, soaring shadows. / My beclouded sight already discerned you once. / Do I want now the madness of visions? Shall I attempt to depict you?]

In the absence of the monumental piece of closet drama that follows the original poem in its German version, even the most precise of translations is bound to endow it with a novel meaning, one not necessarily equal to that of the prefatory piece it is meant to be. In this stand-alone Russian incarnation, "Posviashchenie k 'Faustu'" underscores the nostalgic tonality of the poem. This impression is confirmed by a number of shifts discernible in the second stanza of the poem.

Nabokov's version of Goethe's "Zueignung" ends with a statement that is in agreement with what had always been a powerful aspiration in Nabokov's art – to recreate and recapture the past: "vsë nastoiashchee vdali propalo, / a proshloe deistvitel'nost'iu stalo" (all that is present has vanished in a distance, / while the past has become the reality; cf. Goethe's "Was ich besitze, seh' ich wie im weiten, / Und was verschwand, wird mir zu Wirklichkeiten" – What I possess, I see as if from afar, / And what has vanished, has become reality for me). Freed of any reference to ownership ("Was ich besitze"), the conclusion of Nabokov's version reiterates the dichotomy between "present" and "past" so relevant to his own original work. One remarkable feature of Nabokov's "Iz Gëte. Posviashchenie k 'Faustu'" is that the digressions from the original do not render it a poetic appropriation of the German poem. The form, the overall melancholy tonality of Goethe's "Zueignung" have been faithfully transmitted in "Posviashchenie"; it is the rich though hardly conspicuous nuances of this translated text that betray the presence of Nabokovian motifs.

In his post-*Lolita* interviews, Nabokov famously denied knowing German and claimed to have no appreciation for German literature and culture. His sensitive and eloquent rendition of Goethe's exordium tells a different story and serves as a reminder that his pronouncements on literary matters were not devoid of contradiction.

"Comme le roi d'un pays pluvieux": Claiming the Crown of Baudelaire's Imaginary Kingdom

The two late Russian fragments "Solus Rex" and "Ultima Thule" (1940), which were meant to become chapters of a novel, foreshadow *Bend Sinister* and especially *Pale Fire*. A probable origin of the story of an imaginary kingdom and its hapless autocrat may well be located in a French poem that Nabokov translated in the early thirties, quite possibly in close temporal proximity with his unpublished versions of "Le Sillage" and "L'Appel" by Jules Supervielle.

The opening passages of "Solus Rex" present its protagonist as a languorous, reluctant king who wakes up in his bed and props "a white fist under his cheek, on which the blazon embroidered on the pillowcase had left a chessboard impression."[286] As in *The Defense*, chess imagery was to play a prominent role in Nabokov's last, unfinished Russian novel, which was to deal with illusion and madness. The reader of these two loosely connected stories is left to ponder whether the island realm depicted in "Solus Rex" is a fictional phenomenon that is entitled to an existence of its own, or whether it is merely an illusion, a figment of the protagonist's distraught imagination. Be that as it may, the image of a lonely king who rules over a distant northern land endowed with a rich history and a grey climate finds a precursor in the protagonist of Baudelaire's "Spleen":

> Je suis comme le roi d'un pays pluvieux,
> Riche, mais impuissant, jeune et pourtant très vieux,
> Qui, de ses précepteurs méprisant les courbettes,
> S'ennuie avec ses chiens comme avec d'autres bêtes.[287]

[I'm like a king of some rainy country: / rich, but impotent, young and yet very old, / Who despises the bows of his tutors, / Bored with his dogs as well as other beasts.]

Like the protagonist of "Solus Rex," that of "Spleen" finds himself in a bed decorated with a heraldic emblem: "son lit fleurdelisé se transforme en tombeau" (cf. the reference to an "embroidered blazon" in "Solus Rex").

The hexametric, caesural lines of Nabokov's "Splin. Iz Bodlera" echo both the intonation and atmosphere of Baudelaire's fantasy:

> Я – словно властелинъ въ сырой странѣ тумана:
> сей немощный богачъ, увядшій очень рано,
> скучаетъ, не терпя наставниковъ своихъ,
> равно среди собакъ и тварей остальныхъ.[288]

[I'm like a sovereign of [some] damp country of fog: / that impotent man of wealth, who has waned very soon, / he pines not being able to tolerate his mentors, / equally among [his] dogs and sundry other beasts.]

Nabokov's "Splin" offers a subtly stylized version of the original: the artificial quality of the imagined world of Baudelaire's protagonist is underscored by Nabokov's use of such archaic forms as *sei* (see l. 2 above), *mladoi* ("uvy, im ne prel'stit' mladogo mertvetsa" – alas, they won't attract the young dead man – for "pour tirer un souris de ce jeune squelette," l. 12), which reinforce Baudelaire's references to alchemy and the Roman practice of taking blood baths as a remedy for old age.

In "Spleen" ("Je suis comme le roi d'un pays pluvieux"), Baudelaire creates an intricately detailed mirage of an imagined parallel universe – behind the spectre of an ennui-plagued monarch rises an entire country with a climate of its own ("un pays pluvieux"), its own court customs ("Et les dames d'atour, pour tout prince est beau"), population, and even architecture ("son peuple mourant en face du balcon"). As this deceptive, self-parodying illusion takes on a life of its own, what seemed to be a conventional literary device – a simile – turns out to be the confident demonstration of an artist's power to create new worlds. For all their differences, the imagined universes of *Pale Fire* and *Ada* find a parallel and quite possibly a model in Baudelaire's mocking vision of his protagonist as ruler of a distant northern land, endowing Nabokov's version of "Spleen" with the status of a tangible, important dialogic encounter of two artists who delighted in the creation of minutely detailed artificial universes of their own.

"Ce labeur ingrat": Verity in Verisimilitude

Interpretation and translation converge in "Pouchkine, ou le vrai et le vraisemblable" (Pushkin, or the Real and the Plausible; 1937), a Nabokovian essayistic masterpiece and the pointed summit of his earlier, predominately Russian, forays into explicatory and meditative nonfiction.[289] Like many earlier Nabokovian essays, "Pouchkine" was conceived as a public talk. Seeking to secure an escape route from Germany, Nabokov gave readings in England, where his own English version of *Otchaianie* – *Despair* – was to be published in London in 1937; in 1936–7 he was also looking for a job in France and gave a number of public readings there and in Belgium. Along with the French version of Fëdor Tiutchev's "Vesenniaia groza" (ca. 1925), "Les écrivains et l'époque" (1931), and "Mademoiselle O" (1936), "Pouchkine" proves that Nabokov could have become a major Francophone writer.

"Pouchkine" features French versions of four Pushkin poems. They are "Tri kliucha" ("V stepi mirskoi, pechal'noi i bezbrezhnoi," 1827), "Ne poi, krasavitsa, pri mne" (1828), "Stikhi, sochinënnye noch'iu, vo vremia bessonnitsy" (1830), as well as stanza 13 of the unfinished and untitled narrative poem known alternately as "Rodoslovnaia moego geroia (Otryvok iz satiricheskoi poemy)" or "Yezerskii" (1832–3). While scholars have kept these translations in sight, it was not until the publication of Nabokov's correspondence with his wife that it became apparent that prior to their publication, Nabokov had sought help from a native speaker of French. Acting on the advice of Jean Paulhan, who felt that the translations did not "soar" ("envolée"), Nabokov had them edited by another member of the *Nouvelle revue française* circle, Mélot du Dy.[290]

Nabokov's selection opens with "Tri kliucha," as the poem was known at the time when he wrote his essay, introduced as "a famous poetic work where the Russian verb seems to stream happiness, but when translated, it becomes a mere shadow of itself."[291] In "Dans le désert du monde, immense et triste espace," he offers his French reader not an equilinear version of the poem but its truncated variant (his translation omits ll. 6 and 8 of the original):

Dans le désert du monde, immense et triste espace,
trois sources ont jailli mystérieusement;
celle de la jouvence, eau brillante et fugace,
[4] qui dans son cours pressé bouillone éperdument;
celle de Castalie, où chante la pensée.
Mais la dernière source est l'eau d'oubli glacée ...[292]

[In the world's desert, immense and sad expanse, / three springs have mysteriously sprung up; / one of youth, its water brilliant and fleeting, / the flow of which seethes madly; / one of Castalian water where the thought sings. / But the last spring is the icy water of oblivion ...]

Nabokov's commentary on the poem in which "the Russian word appears to be streaming with the joy of living" ("où le verbe russe semble ruisseler du bonheur de vivre") sounds paradoxical, if not deliberately provocative, given the overall tonality of the original, the concluding line of which stresses unequivocally that the heat of a burning heart can be quenched only by the sweet, cool water springing from the source of oblivion. Neither Nabokov's commentary nor the translated fragment, however, is concerned with the feeling of sadness that is evoked by the poem as a whole. In his short introduction to the translated fragment, Nabokov emphasizes first and foremost the unprecedented agility of Pushkin's poetic line, the versatility of his verbal art. The translation concludes with an ellipsis: Nabokov is aware of the omitted lines, as he is aware of the rich evocative power of the poem written in close temporal proximity to such iconic

Pushkinian utterances as "Arion" ("Nas bylo mnogo na chelne," There were many of us in [that] boat) and "Vo glubine sibirskikh rud" (In the depth of Siberian mines), poems that dealt with Pushkin's sense of disappointment and disillusionment at the collapse of the lofty ideals of his freedom-loving youth in the aftermath of the Decembrist uprising. The absence of these two lines from this version of "Tri kliucha" (Three Sources) is another reminder that in 1937 Nabokov the literalist had not yet arrived.

"Dans le désert du monde, immense et triste espace" is followed by "Ne me les chante pas, ma belle" ("Ne poi, krasavitsa, pri mne"). Nabokov translates Pushkin's poem into French octosyllabics that provide a favourable environment for the creation of a French poem that follows the original Russian text.[293] Nabokov introduces this poem as "a poetic work of divine simplicity in Russian; the words, perfectly simple by themselves, are all a little larger than life":[294]

Ne me les chante pas, ma belle,
ces chansons de la Géorgie,
leur amertume me rappelle
[4] une autre rive, une autre vie.[295]

[Do not sing them to me, my beautiful / those songs of Georgia, / their bitterness reminds me of / another shore, another life.]

The "sadness" of Georgia has been replaced with the "bitterness" ("amertume") of her songs; for the sake of the rhyme the wording of the concluding line of the first stanza has been modified, too: what was once "another life and a distant shore" (*drugaia zhizn' i bereg dal'noi*) becomes "another shore, another life" ("une autre rive, une autre vie"). In the second stanza the "cruel singing" of the poem's female addressee (*zhestokie napevy* – cruel chants) is replaced by "ton langage cruel" (your cruel language, ll. 5–6), and the "features" of the "distant, poor maiden" (*cherty dalekoi, bednoi devy*) by her "visage" ("le visage / d'une pauvre fille lointaine," ll. 7–8). Another important difference is in the manner in which the ghost of the poet's forsaken love presents itself to the protagonist: in the original, it happens as a result of the protagonist's effort (*ego ia vnov' voobrazhaiu* – I envisage it anew, l. 12); in the translation, it "resurfaces" before the poet of its own accord ("Cette ombre fatale et touchante, / lorsque je te vois, je l'oublie, / mais aussitôt que ta voix chante, / voici l'image ressurgie" – This shadow, fatal and touching, /

when I see you, I forget, / but as soon as your voice sings, / here comes the resurgent image).

Nabokov employed the same French octosyllabic verse to render the trochaic tetrameter of "Stikhi, sochinënnye noch'iu vo vremia bezsonitsy." The first, incomplete version of the poem appeared in the text of "Pouchkine"; the full, equilinear version was published in a Francophone almanac dedicated to the poet. Entitled *Hommage à Pouchkine,* this almanac was edited by Zinaïda Schakhovskoy and published in Brussels. It included articles by Modeste Hofmann, Gleb Struve, Vladimir Weidlé, and Schakhovskoy herself.

Pushkin's trochaic piece is remarkable in many ways, not least in its rhymes: the opening rhyme combination recurs throughout its length like some troubling thought that its sleepless protagonist finds himself incapable of shaking off – aBBaCCaaDDaFFgg. Nabokov's first, incomplete version of the poem does not retain the rhyme scheme but simplifies it to abbaccddeed. The later, equilinear version develops this scheme, arriving finally at abbaccddeedffgg. André Monnier, who discusses the first, incomplete version of the poem, commends Nabokov's "talent" for echoing Pushkin's onomatopoeia with his alliterations.[296]

The trajectory of alterations that runs from the earlier version to the later one evidences Nabokov's desire to bring his translation closer to the original text. Thus, ll. 6–8 of the initial version – "frisson de l'ombre, instant qui passe, / Bruit du destin trotte-menu, / léger, lassant, que me veux-tu?" (shiver of the shadow, the instant that passes, / the noise of destiny's petty trotting, / light, weary, what do you want from me?) – omits Pushkin's direct reference to *zhizni mysh'ia begotnia* (life's mouse-like scurrying), replacing it with a reference to a comparable aural effect. The revised version of these lines succeeds in approaching the wording of Pushkin's phrase by the inclusion of a direct reference to a mouse ("une souris") and increases the emotional tension implied in Pushkin's rhetorical question: "frisson d'ombre, vie qui passe, / comme une souris! bruit menu, / dis, pourquoi me tourmentes-tu?" (shiver of the shadow, life that passes, / like a mouse! petty noise, / Tell, why do you torment me?).

Another noteworthy development fails to conform to the tendency described above, representing instead his personal imprint on the translated text. Not only does he replace Pushkin's generic reference to one of the fates by her proper name (cf. *Parki bab'e lepetan'e* [wench-like murmuring of a Fate] – and Nabokov's *Lachésis, commère loquace* [Lachesis, voluble tattletelling], l. 5), in the later, complete version of the poem,

Nabokov represents Pushkin's premonition by means of a reference to another personage of Greek mythology (cf. *Ty zovësh' ili prorochish'?* [Do you summon or prophesy?] and "Est-ce un appel? Est-ce Cassandre?" [Is it a summons? Is it Cassandra?]). The detail is remarkable since it anticipates another such replacement in Nabokov's later version of another of Pushkin's lyrics, his English version of "Chto v imeni tebe moëm?" (1830). Nabokov's "The Name" ("What is my name to you?") replaces Pushkin's reference to recollection with the evocation of yet another Greek deity: in the closing line of the poem's third quatrain, where Pushkin evokes *chistye, nezhnye vospominaniia*, Nabokov refers to "Mnemosyne's pure tender beams."[297]

Nabokov's replacements of Pushkin's Fate with Lachesis, of foreboding with Cassandra ("Je ne puis m'endormir. La nuit"), and remembrance with Mnemosyne ("The Name") are characteristic of Nabokov's translating method prior to his transition to the "literal" technique made famous by the *Eugene Onegin* translation and the polemics that ensued from it.[298]

As can be gleaned from these examples, Nabokov's "poetic" translating method was far from constricted by some narrowly understood concept of fidelity to the original. While striving to preserve a representative number of his model's formal features, Nabokov remained faithful to his own personal vision of the original – a characteristic that bespoke the artist in the translator. Nabokov the poet, however, placed faithfulness to detail and precision above many other qualities traditionally associated by the uninitiated with the art of verse-making, a trait that must have facilitated his frequent transitions from original composition to translation.

In "Pouchkine," Nabokov's selection of Pushkin's poems in his translation closes with a version of what is now known as stanza 13 of Pushkin's unfinished "Pedigree of My Hero" ("Rodoslovnaia moego geroia"/"Ezerskii"). When Nabokov introduces this stanza as "l'une des plus belles strophes d'*Eugène Onéguine*,"[299] he clearly uses this attributive construction as a shorthand for "one of the most beautiful stanzas of the *Eugene Onegin* type," avoiding what would otherwise have become a discussion of this stanzaic form's afterlife in Pushkin's oeuvre. Nabokov's version of "Zachem krutitsia vetr v ovrage" mirrors the intricate rhyme scheme of the original composed in the *Onegin* stanza and presents the reader with a close approximation of the Russian poem's content. A rhymed version, "Pourquoi le vent troublant la plaine," naturally digresses from the original: for example, the closing couplet of this *Onegin* stanza urges the poet to be proud – "Gordis': takov i ty, poet, / I dlia tebia uslovii net." Even though Nabokov's version of the stanza arrives at the same destination via a different route – "Lève ton front, poète élu; / rien ne t'enchaîne, toi non plus"[300] – the meaning, if not the wording, of this sonorous couplet is in full agreement with that of its Russian model.

Nabokov was aware of the shortcomings of his poetic transpositions.[301] "Pouchkine," however, inaugurated a new stage of his development as a translator. While these Pushkinian renditions remain poetic approximations of the originals, the purpose of these translating efforts is quite different from that of Nabokov's earlier, predominantly Russian versions of foreign poets. First and foremost, the translations of these four poems were made to acquaint their French readers with the unique qualities of Pushkin's artistic individuality. As such, their function was practical in nature, and it was no accident that in his introduction to the first translation included in the text of the essay, Nabokov called translation "ce labeur ingrat."[302] The kind of responsibility that comes with a translated work that presents itself not as another facet of a verbal artist's creative pursuit but rather as that of a translator whose chief aim is to deliver to the reader the single most accurate version of the original text is hardly comparable to that of a poet who, as Nabokov was to term it later, occasionally relaxes "in the company of a foreign confrère."[303] The master craftsman responsible for translations of the kind included in the text of "Pouchkine" himself begins to resemble a scholar "who is eager to make the world appreciate the works of an obscure genius as much as he does himself."[304] The genius of Nabokov's translation technique throughout its evolution lies in his ability to combine a passion for exactitude that is decidedly scholarly with a verbal mastery that is purely artistic. Nabokov's English versions of various Russian poets, from Batiushkov to Fet, from Blok to Khodasevich, inherit much of their virtuosity from his versions of the Pushkin poems from "Pouchkine, ou le vrai et le vraisemblable."

Chapter Three

BEFORE *EUGENE ONEGIN*: "SINNING LOVINGLY, SINNING TENDERLY" (1940–1955)

Viewed superficially, Nabokov's earliest English-language translations amount to little more than an extension of the practices he established before coming to the United States.[1] Closer study of the literary translations of this period – unmistakably poetic in their execution and diction – shows them to be informed by a different understanding of the task of rendering foreign literary works into a different language. The whimsically appropriative renditions that became an outlet for the translator's creativity or camouflaged his jealously guarded emotions are gone; Nabokov's individuality, however, finds new ways to shine through his translations.

Even a cursory glance at the translations Nabokov made for publication and teaching testifies to the breadth of his curiosity and his earnestness as educator. Between 1940 and 1955 he translated Akhmatova, Avvakum, Baratynskii, Batiushkov, Blok, Fet, Griboedov, Karamzin, Khodasevich, Kol'tsov, Lermontov, Nekrasov, Tiutchev, Turgenev, Pushkin, and Zhukovskii, among others. Wanting to demonstrate to his students the extent of these Russian authors' integration into European culture, he translated some particularly influential works by Schiller and lectured on Russian adaptations of Southey and Walter Scott. Translation itself becomes the focus of his scrutiny, and not only in his pre-literalist manifesto "The Art of Translation" (1941). It is examined in *Bend Sinister* (1947) and *Pnin* (1957), both of which were conceived and composed before the watershed publication "Problems of Translation: *Onegin* in English" in 1955. Last but not least, Nabokov tackled translation head on in "Rimes" ("Pity the elderly gray translator," 1952) and "On Translating *Eugene Onegin*" (1954).

The ensuing survey proves that during this decisive period, translation came to define the fabric of Nabokov's creativity to a greater degree than ever.

"The very deep waters of English verse": *Mozart and Salieri, The Covetous Knight,* and *A Feast during the Plague*

Nabokov's English translation of Pushkin's *Mozart and Salieri* (1826–30) was among his earliest literary activities in America. Inspired by Edmund Wilson, it was one of the earliest and happiest results of their exhilarating, if doomed, bond. This is how Nabokov recapitulated a conversation they had before 2 December 1940: "Your suggestion regarding *Mozart and Salieri* has worked havoc with me. I thought I would try with the idea – and then suddenly found myself in the very deep waters of English verse. After a week of hard work I have finished the first scene."[2] On 9 April 1941, he thanked Wilson for going over the finished text: "[It] is quite perfect now – you have played your Mozart to my Salieri."[3] When the translation appeared in the 21 April 1941 issue of the *New Republic*, Wilson's preamble stressed the lasting relevance of Pushkin's diminutive masterwork and assured its readers that "it has never been properly translated."[4]

Fluid and inventive, Nabokov's translations were no mere stylizations of antiquated English idioms, lexical equations of a Russian bard with his Anglophone contemporaries. Infused with his awareness of the Lake Poets, Pushkin's imaginative appropriation of the Shakespearean dramatic idiom in his "little tragedies" is idiosyncratic: the Russian in which the poet expresses himself may be dated in some instances but it is timeless in its plasticity. The brand of English poetry Nabokov affects here is not defined by his confident blank verse alone – with its "adieus," "nays," "perchances," "thines," and "thous" – the lexis of his *Mozart and Salieri* harks back to a wide range of English models. Along with his general knowledge of English poetry, Nabokov's perusal of Shakespeare in general, and his study of the sonnets and *Hamlet* in particular, makes itself apparent at every step in his renditions of Pushkin's "little tragedies." In the "coils and crucibles" of his translating laboratory, Nabokov begins to accumulate the critical mass of intelligence that will propel him toward a radically new vision of the Pushkin phenomenon – and the translation technique uniquely suited for its representation in foreign languages. Nabokov's command of Russian, however, becomes the source of many felicitous translating choices as well.

In those instances where the language in which Pushkin composed *Mozart and Salieri* differs from modern usage, Nabokov guides his reader to the meaning of the original. Thus when Salieri speaks of his ability to suppress his urge to retaliate against his rivals, Pushkin uses the adjective *zleishii* not in the modern superlative sense of "the most wicked [enemy, insult]," but rather as a comparative. Nabokov's translation accounts for that nuance and communicates Pushkin's meaning precisely:

perchance, I'd muse, I'll find an enemy
more hateful still; perchance a sharper insult ...[5]

"Precision" is too vague a term when applied to creative approximations of foreign texts. In line with Nabokov's earlier literary translations, *Mozart and Salieri* amounts to an incisive and at times ingenious interpretation of the original. The soliloquy in which Salieri expounds the perverse logic behind his decision to become the implement of fate whose goal is to rid the world of Mozart's supernatural genius contains a fragment seemingly free of all ambiguity:

Быть можетъ, новый Гайденъ сотворитъ
Великое – и наслажуся имъ ...[6]

The obvious interpretation of this phrase has the pronoun *im* refer back to the noun preceding it: "[when] new Haydn creates something great, I will delight in *it*." Since here the instrumental case forms of the masculine and neuter pronouns *on* and *ono* overlap after a reflexive verb governing them, the reader has every reason to treat it as a neuter singular pronoun agreeing with the nearest neuter substantive, *velikoe*. This, however, is not how Nabokov interprets this phrase. His version of the fragment is both unexpected and noteworthy:

perchance another Haydn may achieve
some great new thing – and I shall live in him ...[7]

Nabokov's Salieri anticipates how a part of him will survive in "another Haydn," a fellow professional, another one of "the priests, the ministers of music" to whose guild he believes he belongs and to whose existence Mozart's extraordinary creativity is a living reproach. As Salieri contemplates poisoning Mozart, this interpretation suggests, he is dreaming of the new lease on life – perhaps even immortality – his villainous deed will afford him. Nabokov redirects his readers' attention from Salieri's ability to delight in a fine – though not inspired – musical composition to the suspicion that the enormity of his crime might render it a creative act in its own right. Is this interpretation too liberal in its whimsicality? Does it lead the reader astray from the apparent lucidity of Pushkin's message?

It appears that Nabokov is inviting his readers to focus on this "little tragedy's" proverbial leitmotif – proverbial in its native environment but not in a foreign-language rendition, where it requires reinforcement. In scene 2, the simple-hearted genius queries his future murderer, whom he repeatedly mistakes for his "brother": "villainy and genius / are two things that don't go together, do they?"

As it acquires all the features of a solipsistic rant, Salieri's concluding soliloquy revisits this query. After pouring poison into Mozart's wine glass, he feverishly tries to grasp the significance of his victim's simple words: "Villainy and genius, / two things that do not go together." Significantly, Nabokov's English rendition of this fragment's context is longer by two lines, even though it turns two opening Russian lines into one. Nabokov's version amplifies Salieri's condemnation of the mob: to one phrase ("skazka / tupoi, bessmyslennoi tolpy") he has multiple ("a legend, but a lie, / bred by the stupid mob, by their inane / vulgarity"). The asymmetries of Nabokov's version of *Mozart and Salieri* point to a conceptual understanding of the original that highlights the ambiguity between the obvious baseness of Salieri's deed and his conviction that by committing it he soars above the pedestrian aspirations of earnest craftsmen.[8] As the burden of answering Salieri's formulation of Mozart's original query shifts to the reader, Nabokov makes it difficult to ignore its context. As such, it confronts the reader with a tantalizing possibility.

Can Salieri be privy to the grand design of Mozart's fate in the way that some apocrypha make Judas privy to the predestined path of Christ's passions? In scene 2, Mozart abandons his gaiety as he senses that his end is near but is unable to profit from his premonition. The cerebral "mathematician" Salieri may well be able to grasp the grander design of things, but that does not bring him any closer to either Mozart's sunny pre-*Requiem* disposition or his ineffable genius. Salieri does express some unsettling truths about the vulnerability of a genius – such notions could not fail to reverberate with someone with an intimate familiarity with Baudelaire's "Albatros." The murderer's cerebral perspicacity notwithstanding, the baseness of his deed renders him a member of the mob he despises so much, and this is the notion that Nabokov highlights for his Anglophone readers.

Mozart and Salieri is largely free of marginalia in Nabokov's "bedside" Pushkin.[9] In Salieri's opening soliloquy, which gives voice to his rage at Heaven's bestowal of genius on Mozart, however, Nabokov heavily underlines the word "envy" ("Net! Nikogda ia *zavisti* ne znal!") that precipitates Salieri's descent into villainy. The poison in Salieri's hollow ring, "the last gift of [his] Isora," is the only force that can check Mozart's ascent to unprecedented heights of creativity. After furnishing *The Gift* with a fleeting reference to this evocative image, in his translation Nabokov conducted a thorough study of the contexts in which it occurred and gained a novel understanding of its significance and complexity.[10]

Encouraged by Wilson, from *Mozart and Salieri* Nabokov proceeded to two more Pushkinian "little tragedies." In a letter dated 25 May 1941, Nabokov warned Wilson: "I am afraid I am sending you another translation. *The Scoopoy Ritzer*'s monologue. This time I have tried to follow Pushkin's rhythm as closely as possible. Even mimicking some of the sounds. And the so-called *alliteratio puschkiniana.*"[11] On 18 July 1941, Nabokov informed his friend: "I have now translated the little *Feast During the Plague.*"[12]

Nabokov's "Scene from *The Covetous Knight*" is reductive indeed: for all the vividness of his version of the Baron's self-implicating soliloquy in front of his gold-laden coffers, one scene cannot represent the totality of this distillation of Pushkin's filial insecurities. Nabokov was aware of Vladislav Khodasevich's explication of the personal subtext of *The Covetous Knight*, according to which the conflict between the miserly Baron and his impecunious son Albert was a re-enactment of Pushkin's quarrel with his tight-fisted father.[13] On this particular occasion, however, to a holistic interpretation of a given text Nabokov preferred highlighting one specific feature of it.

Unlike *Mozart and Salieri*, *The Covetous Knight* is an exact equimetrical replica of its source fragment, which demonstrates Nabokov's desire to surpass the earlier work in terms of representative faithfulness to its model. The fragment he selected for scrutiny in his copy of Pushkin's work exemplifies his command of the English iambic pentameter with particular vividness. The soliloquizing Baron Fillip equates the power of money with omnipotence; the lifelong miser makes no mistake as to the extent to which avarice brings out the worst in people.

The catalogue of his abilities closes with an invocation of his power to murder without getting his hands dirty – and in his Pushkin volume Nabokov highlights the following four lines:

Я свисну [,] и ко мнѣ послушно, робко
Вползётъ окровавленное Злодѣйство,
И руку будетъ мнѣ лизать, и въ очи
Смотрѣть, в них знакъ моей читая воли.[14]

[I'll whistle, and to me obediently, meekly / Will come crawling bloody Villainy, / and [it] will be licking my hand and into my eyes / look, in them reading a sign of my will.]

Nabokov writes in the comma after "Ia svisnu" (I'll whistle) missing from the 1937 edition, which shows the extent to which he cares about the rhythmic properties of this key fragment. In his translation of these four lines he strives to retain their original cadence:

I'll whistle, and behold: low-bending, cringing
in creeps Assassination, blood-bespattered,
and while it licks my hands it will be watching
my eyes to read in them the master's order.[15]

As to *alliteratio puschkiniana*, the mock Latin term Nabokov invents in his letter to Wilson, it is best illustrated by his rendition of the Baron's euphoria at the sight of his coffers. The following three lines are remarkable in a number of respects: they contain a rhyming couplet, which challenges the dominance of unrhymed blank verse in this "little tragedy," and feature an expressive accumulation of sibilants, which foreshadow a sharp turn in the Baron's mood:

Я царствую! – Какой волшебный блескъ!
Послушна мнѣ, сильна моя держава;
Въ ней счастіе, въ ней честь моя и слава![16]

[I am reigning! – What a miraculous glitter! / Obedient to me, powerful is my stronghold; / In it is [my] happiness, in it is my honour and glory!]

Nabokov's translation is fully attuned to the original's specificity. The phrase "enchanting shine" retains and amplifies the orchestration of the fragment's last line, which diverges from the meaning of the original with a clear aim of achieving that expressive aural effect:

> Now I am king! What an enchanting shine!
> A mighty realm has now become my manor;
> here is my bliss, my blazon, and my banner![17]

The triad of explosive "b's" explains the reasoning behind Nabokov's departure from the meaning of the original: this approximate interpretation of the line – it is worth noting that the original sanctions it only partially – makes room for this aural effect. As such, it exemplifies the kind of liberty Nabokov permits himself in his outwardly faithful rendition of this fragment – to the extent it was possible in an equimetric rendition. On closer inspection, Nabokov's early English-language translations of Russian poetry prove to be quite indulgent when it comes to their retention of the translator's personal view of the works he translated. This brings us closer to the issue of Nabokov's treatment of the textual integrity of this "little tragedy."

Why did Nabokov not translate *The Covetous Knight* in its entirety? His workload did not obstruct his translating *Mozart and Salieri* and *A Feast during the Plague* in their entirety. If the length of *The Covetous Knight* was not an impediment, what could possibly have prevented him from supplying his readers with a complete version of Pushkin's dramatic miniature?

In all likelihood, the answer to this question lies in the content of this "little tragedy," namely in its treatment of the Jewish theme. The text of Pushkin's *Covetous Knight* may not be the earliest text in the Russian literary canon to make this distinction, but it is the most significant literary text to document the vacillation between the neutral ethnonym *evrei* and the pejorative *zhid*. Unlike Shakespeare's Shylock, the usurer Solomon who suggests that Albert poison his father to repay his debts and enjoy life is no nuanced portrayal of a Jewish character. Likewise, Pushkin's stage remarks introduce Solomon as *zhid*, whereas Solomon refers to himself as *evrei*. Nabokov was unable to bring himself to translate this "little tragedy's" first scene with its clichéd portrayal of a Jewish character as a scheming and cowardly crook. By omitting the first and last scenes of *The Covetous Knight* from his translation, Nabokov refused to deal with the problem posed by the lexical differentiation between the two ethnonyms, a linguistic quandary he could not qualify as anything but offensive.

The incomplete translation of *The Covetous Knight* shows the limits of Nabokov's regard for the original's integrity. This sensitivity to the offensive nature of Pushkin's usage represents the most jarring example of life's meddling in the affairs of high art to be found in his canon. Nabokov's fascination with Pushkin may seem to know no bounds, but a closer look at his translation of this "little tragedy" proves once and for all that it was anything but unlimited. Translating *The Covetous Knight* in 1941, he could not ignore the atrocities committed by anti-Semites on the other side of the Atlantic, the atrocities he and his immediate family barely avoided when they made their escape from Europe. On this occasion Nabokov, who spoke so eloquently in defence of the ivory tower as a temple of artistic freedom, permitted his scruples to dictate the course of action in the realm of art. The writer who claimed that his compositions had "no moral in tow"[18] here makes a choice influenced by his ethics. The fact that he did not compose this particular text is not relevant: as we shall see, at this point Nabokov firmly believed that translation was a form of artistic self-expression.

A Feast during the Plague was the last "little tragedy" Nabokov translated. In and of itself, Pushkin's ameliorative adaptation of John Wilson's *City of the Plague* (1816) is a fascinating example of translation's ability to foster independent creativity on a par with Shakespeare's reworkings of his sources. After enjoying moderate popularity at the time of its publication, Wilson's three-act blank-verse tragedy sank into obscurity. Pushkin's liberal reimagining of it does not merely save it from oblivion, it turns, in Henry Gifford's words, Wilson's "dross" into "pure gold."[19]

Nabokov's version of this "little tragedy" is far from his first creative engagement with this centrepiece of the Russian literary canon. In *The Eye* (1930), one of Smurov's numerous paraphrases of literary sources includes the sentence "It is difficult to put into words the musical delight that the singing of bullets gives us,"[20] which echoes the proverbial opening lines of the fifth stanza of the Chairman's death-defying dirge; in *The Gift* the pretentious critic Christophor Mortus publishes an article entitled "The Voice of Pushkin's Mary in Contemporary Poetry," which refers to the mournful Scottish ballad from the "little tragedy."[21]

Nabokov's *Feast during the Plague* is more than an attempt to mirror the original and mimic its alliteration. The curtain of its exactitude hides a critical interpretation of Pushkin's stylization of an English literary work. Once again, this feature of Nabokov's translation is made apparent by the asymmetries distinguishing the Pushkin's take on Wilson from its Nabokovian English reincarnation.

A bevy of young people in a plague-stricken city elects a chairman to lead their merrymaking as they drown their fear of death in debauchery.

One of their wittiest comrades has recently succumbed to the disease, so the Chairman invites a Scottish girl, Mary, to sing "something dolorous and plaintive" as the revellers "revert more madly" to their impious "merriment," for which they will be rebuked by an elderly clergyman.

Pushkin's Chairman calls Mary's Scottish ballad "a simple shepherd song" ("prostaia pastush'ia pesnia"), and it appears to have all the features required by the genre. It is composed in trochaic tetrameter, which James Bailey identifies as a major prosodic medium for folk lyric songs.[22] What may be the standard in one folk tradition, however, may be devoid of any significance in another, and this is where Nabokov begs to differ. He contrasts Pushkin's trochaic tetrameter, with alternating masculine and feminine rhymes, with iambic trimeters featuring a similar alternation in the rhyming lines. The reason behind this striking departure from the original becomes apparent once we have had a chance to process the cadence of Nabokov's take on Pushkin's song:

In times agone our village
was lovely to behold;
our bonny church on Sundays
was full of young and old;
our happy children's voices
rang in the noisy school;
in sunny fields the reaper
swung fast his flashing tool.[23]

The choice of the metre is every bit as significant here as the lexical markers Nabokov chooses to reinforce this song's intended social (the folksy form "agone") and ethno-geographical (the conspicuously Scottish modifier "bonny") attribution. The iambic trimeter into which Nabokov resets Pushkin's song has a strong semantic halo in English prosody: it is only one metric foot away from English common meter, which is used in literary imitations of folk songs and ballads, such as Willliam Wordsworth's "A Slumber Did My Spirit Seal" or A.E. Housman's "When I Was One-and-Twenty." Nabokov's translation highlights and compensates for the dearth of Pushkin's understanding of the subtleties of the English poetic tradition.

Nabokov's version of *Pir vo vremia chumy* is no mere translation. Much like Salieri's attempt to "verify harmony by algebra," it is a critical study of Pushkinian poetics that favours analysis over admiration. If Nabokov's handling of the textual integrity of Pushkin's *Covetous*

Knight revealed his inability to go against his ethical principles, this improvement on the authenticity of Pushkin's prosodic choices foreshadows the analytical approach he would evolve in his critical study of *Eugene Onegin*. In his "Notes on Prosody" (1964), Nabokov takes Pushkin to task for a metrical irregularity he first noted in the margin of his personal collection of the poet's works:

> The *only* time Pushkin himself, by an unfortunate and incomprehensible oversight, uses a duplex reverse tilt is in l. 21 of his *The Feast at the Time of Plague* (1830) ... The trochaically tilted word is *ego* ("his"), which is iambically stressed in speech:
>
> *Ya predlagayu vïpit' v ego pámyat'.*
> In memory of him I suggest drinking.[24]

The reason for Nabokov's dissatisfaction with this prosodic lapse is clear: the iambic metre of this line mandates the shift of the stress on *ego* from the second to the first syllable. Nabokov's metrical rendition of this line makes it clear that this is a violation of the fixed stress position occurring in natural speech. The literary 1941 translation glosses over this blemish, which serves as another reminder that at that point Nabokov had yet to evolve a way of endowing his translations with the qualities of analytical examinations of the original. The subsequent evolution of his translation practice and theory demonstrates that that was the direction in which he was moving.

Nabokov's translation of two-and-one-third of Pushkin's *malen'kie tragedii* is a mere episode of his dialogue with these texts. They had become integrated into his individual referential field long before he decided to translate them into English; each one of them has a history of functioning as a starting point of Nabokovian encounters with Pushkinian creativity. It is here, however, where we see how Nabokov's general inquisitiveness regarding all things Pushkinian begins to give way to a much more probing approach toward the mysteries of Pushkinian "genius." Nabokov never abandoned this speculative term. His Pushkinian translations, however, mark a turning point in his engagement with the poet. It was a point of no return, after which the hero worship of his early years would be replaced by an incisive analysis of Pushkin's creations as constructs quickened not so much by a Mozartian divine genius as by a sophistication unmatched in Russian letters.

Nabokov's personal copy of Pushkin's collected works steers us toward those aspects of his admiration of the poet that were immune to change. Pushkin, and no other poet, provided Nabokov with the most precise formulation of their mutual understanding of art as a non-utilitarian pursuit. It occurs at the finale of *Mozart and Salieri*: these are the last words Mozart utters. The inspired composer and simple-hearted man is unable to recognize his bitterest enemy in the man whom he considers his best friend and equal, yet he is capable of verbalizing the difference between himself and those incapable of partaking of the ultimate happiness available to man:

> If all could feel
> like you the force of harmony! But no;
> the world would crumble then; for none would care
> to bother with the baser needs of life;
> then all would seek art's franchise. We are few,
> the chosen ones, the happy idlers, we
> who have no use for what is merely useful,
> who worship only beauty ...[25]

In the margin next to this Russian fragment Nabokov writes and underlines the Russian word *prelest'*. No matter how hard he would try to uncover the sources of Pushkinian inspiration, how deeply he would dig down Pushkin's "secret stem," how voraciously he would try to "feed upon its root," he would never break the spell of these lines' charm.

"The Art of Translation": The Translation Manifesto and Its Satellites

Few aspects of Nabokov's thinking on the subject of translation emphasize the fluidity of his position as well as the extent to which his earliest translation manifesto, "The Art of Translation" proves to be a palimpsest.[26] For more than a decade after its publication in 1941 the essay continued to contract, expand, and morph into various documents that served as basis for numerous talks and public appearances. As he reworked the initial published version, he continued to put an ever-growing emphasis on the indispensability and contradictions of translation.

Indispensable as it is, translation is a minefield of technical pitfalls and ethical contradictions. That "the world of verbal transmigration" is "queer" is an axiom at this stage of Nabokov's thinking on the subject, hence the opening line of the essay's earliest, published iteration. Human frailty, incompetence, and conceit are the root causes of no fewer than three degrees of evil – and it is here where Nabokov makes blunderers who "live in solecisms like others live in sin" run the gauntlet of his irony. Willing as he is to forgive and accept as inevitable honest mistakes, he pulls no punches as he makes cruel fun of those practitioners of the art who usurp authorial privileges to become petty tyrants. If they decide to become arbiters of their author's style by editing it according to their own taste, translators betray both the author and the reader by jamming the frequency on which the two could communicate. Should they be motivated by their prudery or politics, translators will do more harm than good as they become impostors who betray their authors and take advantage of their readers' trust. Manifestations of such usurpation are various and many, so Nabokov enlists all his humour and irony to ensure that his readers make no mistake in recognizing in the violations of authorial privileges anything but a form of tyranny. As he appeals to his American readers' Puritan legacy, he half-jokingly qualifies it as "a crime, to be punished by the stocks, as plagiarists were in the shoebuckle days."

If we were to separate a principle unifying all Nabokovian pronouncements on translation, we would see that whenever he objects to violations of authorial will, he does so on ethical grounds. Translation for him is another front line in his personal defence of individual creativity. Would it be correct to assume, then, that the 1941 essay in all its iterations effectively amounts to an advocacy for "the translator's invisibility" that anticipates Lawrence Venuti's pithy formulation of the single most enduring assumption regarding translation? Far from it. Focused as they are on his subsequent, literalist pronouncements, Nabokov's critics tend to disregard the direction in which the author of "The Art of Translation" is taking his readers. In one paramount respect all the various iterations of the 1941 essay cannot be more different from the doctrine at the basis of the *Eugene Onegin* project.

Toward the end of the essay Nabokov presents his readers with a summary of his struggles with a particularly difficult translating task, but before he does that he declares his allegiances with maximal clarity. In the ranks of translators he finds scholars, drudges, and artists, and while none of them are immune to common human weaknesses, he isolates a criterion, a rule that separates "ideal" translators from those who are merely good or frankly vile:

> The scholar commits fewer blunders than the drudge; the point is that as a rule both he and she are hopelessly devoid of any semblance of creative

> genius. Neither learning nor diligence can replace imagination and style ... We can deduce now the requirements that a translator must possess in order to be able to give an ideal version of a foreign masterpiece. First of all, he must have as much talent, or at least the same kind of talent, as the author he chooses. In this, though only in this, respect Baudelaire and Poe or Zhukovski and Schiller made ideal playmates. Second, he must know thoroughly the two nations and the languages involved and be perfectly acquainted with all details relating to his author's manner and methods; also with the social background of words, their fashions and period associations. This leads to the third point: while having genius and knowledge he must possess the gift of mimicry and be able to act, as it were, the real author's part by impersonating his tricks of demeanor and speech, his ways and his mind, with the utmost degree of verisimilitude.[27]

According to the author of "The Art of Translation," the single most important criterion by which literary translation ought to be judged is "creative genius." As he looks back on his work in translation in anticipation of new challenges coming his way in 1941, Nabokov mounts an impassioned defence of translation as a medium of artistic expression not altogether dissimilar from original creation. Important as knowledge and mimicry are, they cannot compensate for the absence of "genius." This dictum is the 1941 essay's essence, and no matter how much its text mutates from one version to another in the decade following the year of its publication in *The New Republic*, this feature remains immune to change.

No rules, techniques, or craftsmanship can replace "genius." Like "genius," "perfection" dwells in a realm unattainable to rationalization. This is the import of that parodoxically anti-climactic but profoundly Nabokovian dénouement of "The Art of Translation." One of Nabokov's earliest statements of purpose on American soil, this essay is as much of a contemplation on the nature of translation as it is a formulation of his understanding of what art is and what its guises are, and at this point in his evolution he refused to consider translation anything but art, all its conundrums and contradictions notwithstanding. A true artist may disappear, but no true artist can ever become invisible.

"The Art of Translation" is the centre of a small, but not negligible constellation of pronouncements on the same subject in various stages of completion. Apart from the various iterations of the 1941 essay that continued to expand until at least 1951, this constellation includes an identically entitled talk, which can be approximately dated 1954.[28] With the earlier text it shares a conviction that translation is an art and that such a phenomenon as "the perfect translator" is no mere intellectual construct. From its eponymous precursor it differs in scope and purpose, which was to introduce a series of Russian poetic masterpieces in Nabokov's literary versions. This short document introduces an amusing nomenclature by inviting the listener to imagine "two fair countries, *From* and *Into*, the far hills of *From* and the translator's homeland *Into*":

> The perfect translator should know the *From* language as well he does the *Into* language. He should also be acquainted with the manners, traditions, fauna, flora and times of both countries. He should have a special knowledge of the works of his author, John From, and a deep insight into the literature of which he is part. He, John Into, should have genius, style, vision, and wit. He should be absolutely honest, should not bypass difficulties, should never let down poor John From (who is generally dead, anyway, and cannot hit back).[29]

The speculative category "genius" continues to be the heart of Nabokov's translation theory well into the early fifties, preceding the formulation of his literalist doctrine. Faithful as he is to this aspect of his views on the subject, the signs of his dissatisfaction with the speculative nature of that component of his stance become increasingly palpable. The subsequent expanded version of the 1941 essay proclaims translation a "pathetic business" and a "controversial" topic. The various iterations of the 1941 essay and its satellites never cease to put forward the suggestion that "the world of verbal metamorphosis" is inherently "queer." What is the source of this dissatisfaction, why does it continue to undermine the apparent harmony of Nabokov's proud reiterations that translation is an art and another avenue for the expression of genius that manifests itself in the dialogue of equally gifted minds capable of transcending the physical limitations of time and space? Nabokov's insistence that "honesty" and "faithfulness" are integral components of a sum he dubs "the ideal translation" increasingly come into conflict with such speculative, individual, and ultimately indefinable notions as "genius" and "perfection." This is the source of that "contradiction" that he cannot prevent from haunting his thinking on this subject, and it is the growing critical mass of this incongruence that leads to his eventual rupture with the settled way of looking at translation that proved reliable until he concentrated on *Eugene Onegin*. This rupture, however, was not to happen until the early fifties, and the received wisdom that translation is an art would continue to underpin his experiments in translation well past his first decade on American soil.

All its incongruities notwithstanding, the dialogue-driven adoration of artistic genius that is the premise of "The Art of Translation" and its satellite statements on the subject provides us with a perspective from which to survey and evaluate translating experiments dating from the same period. For all the romanticism and pathos it encompasses, this vantage point does enable us to evolve a perspective on a sizeable body of translated texts empowered and united by this vision of translation's specificity.

"The greatest poet of our time": Vladislav Khodasevich in Nabokov's English

Nabokov's pre-1955 statements on translation emphasize the communicative, indeed dialogic, aspect of this endeavour. No stretch of imagination is required, however, to appreciate the fact that the majority of such encounters presuppose the need to establish a contact with the deceased. Nabokov was aware of this – hence his emphasis on the dubious ethics of interpreting the words of those "who are generally dead … and cannot hit back" and his comparison of translation to the "profanation of the dead" ("On Translating *Eugene Onegin*").[30] In this regard his translations of Vladislav Khodasevich (1886–1939) represent a special case: not only do they extend the companionship Nabokov formed with this author prior to his death, they continue a conversation that began prior to their actual encounter. Khodasevich was among those critics who did not merely greet the younger writer – his responses to him amount to some of most insightful and durable interpretations of his art. Nabokov allied himself with Khodasevich during their mutual opposition to Georgii Adamovich, Georgii Ivanov, and the writers of the "Parisian school"; a fellow Pushkinist, Khodasevich remained for Nabokov an authority on all things Pushkin. Nabokov's eulogy of Khodasevich pronounces him "the greatest Russian poet of our time, Pushkin's literary descendant in Tyutchev's line of succession," who "shall remain the pride of Russian poetry as long as its last memory lives."[31] That Nabokov should continue his efforts to enshrine his émigré ally according to his exalted notion of his stature is understandable; what is remarkable is the sense of urgency that permeates Nabokov's effort to extend Khodasevich's memory into a different linguistic dimension.

Scarcely a year after Nabokov's arrival in America he published his versions of a trio of Khodasevich's poems, making certain that the surge of interest in all things Soviet that accompanied the war would not omit that émigré writer. That Nabokov was fighting an uphill battle can be gleaned from the contents of James Laughlin's *New Directions in Prose and Poetry 1941*, where these translations appeared under the heading of "Soviet Russian Poetry," which grouped Khodasevich the inveterate anti-Soviet exile with the likes of Nikolai Aseev and Vladimir Maiakovskii.[32] Nabokov's translations of Khodasevich, therefore, are a part of his lifelong resistance to the ignorance of those Western observers who overlooked émigré culture while fawning over the Soviets.

Nabokov's selection from Khodasevich's sparse poetic output includes "Obez'iana" ("The Monkey"; 1919), "Ballada" ([A Ballad], "Orpheus"; 1921), and "Ni zhit', ni pet' pochti ne stoit" ([It's almost worthless to live and to sing], "Poem"; 1922). The selection showcases Khodasevich's range, proceeding from the Pushkinian blank verse narrative of "The Monkey" to the partially rhymed ternary-metre-based stanzas of "Orpheus" and closing with the diminutive iambic "Poem." The English translations present their author as a master of the form, echoing Nabokov's critical assessments of Khodasevich's art in general and the 1939 eulogy in particular, which emphasized his "craftsmanship."[33] Faithful as these translations are to the form of their originals, they also contain a number of shifts that inevitably betray their translator as no humble emulator of his model. These texts' close proximity to "The Art of Translation" is not accidental: they illustrate Nabokov's enthusiasm for both the letter and the spirit of the transpositional technique he believed to be most effective at the time. On the one hand, they strive to retain as much of the form, stylistic register, and imagery of the originals as possible; on the other, they are not averse to compromise. The calculated liberties they take, however, reveal the presence of a considered agenda. The asymmetries distinguishing the translations from their models are no mere shortcuts – they represent a feature that may well be unique among Nabokov's translations of others. These English renditions augment the demeanour, the personality of the original lyrical "I" in such a way that their reader may wonder if the translator has not self-identified with the poet whose words he relays to a new audience.

"The Monkey" is the earliest and longest piece in Nabokov's selection, and the English iambic pentameter of these unrhymed lines echoes the iambic tetrameters employed in his translation of Pushkin's *Mozart and Salieri*. Like Salieri's soliloquies in Nabokov's rendition, Nabokov's take on Khodasevich's first-person account of the summer of 1914 compacts the original: to Khodasevich's fifty-six lines Nabokov has forty-seven. The poem's high point, the moment when the lyrical hero experiences an epiphany after shaking hands with a monkey belonging to an itinerant street performer, shows how the translation leaves out conventional phrases and similes:

И видит Бог, никто в мои глаза
[38] Не заглянул так мудро и глубоко,
Воистину – до дна души моей.

[And God knows, no one into my eyes / Has ever peered so wisely and deeply, / Indeed – to the bottom of my soul.]

The conventional turns of speech "God knows" and "the bottom of my soul" give way to Nabokov's terser variant:

[33] and no man's eyes had peered into my soul
with such deep wisdom ...[34]

Nabokov's choice of the opening poem in his selection is not mechanical – it is topical. A versified summary of a seemingly evanescent event in its narrator's life, "The Monkey" closes with a coda that endows the poem's contents with universal significance: "That day the war broke out, that very day." The epiphany experienced by the narrator was a dark one: to him the outbreak of World War I foreshadowed the triumph of the beast that had for so long seemed to be subdued by civilization. David Bethea comments on this ending's irony: "The monkey ... has turned the tables and is sitting atop its master's shoulders like a Maharajah on its elephant."[35] Nabokov's placement of this and no other poem at the beginning of his selection could not but invite its Anglophone readers to draw parallels with another, seemingly distant global conflict as it encroached on their sense of harmony and order in 1941. In his translation Nabokov joins forces with his ally Khodasevich to communicate their shared understanding of the bitter historical irony that undercuts the placidity of the narrator's ordered life in the poem. The "wretched" Serb who disrupts the narrator's summer holiday is a harbinger of the unthinkable disasters that will affect the lives of private individuals in the same way that Russia's decision to defend

Serbia in 1914 upended the life of the narrator. Nabokov's translation casts Khodasevich – and implicitly, himself – in the role of a wretched exile from a strange distant land whose seemingly insignificant appearance amid someone's placid existence may prove to be full of portent. The exiles Nabokov and Khodasevich have a vitally important experience to share with their audience; the only question is whether their message will be heeded.

If "Orpheus," the second poem in this selection, has acquired the status of Khodasevich's "finest lyric" (Bethea), it is in no small degree due to Nabokov's pronouncing it in a 1927 review a work that "attains the limits of poetic craftsmanship."[36] Mikhail Gasparov has used this poem's example to demonstrate how the often speculative, indeed arbitrary, notion of poetic perfection may be quantified if we account for a poetic text's ability to absorb multiple "semantic hues" (*semanticheskaia okraska*).[37] Nabokov, who did not merely profess his admiration for this poem but also commented on its choice of metre no fewer than fourteen years prior to translating it, was intimately familiar with its minutest details, which makes the alterations he introduces into his translation particularly intriguing.

Nabokov, who once remarked on the rarity of "Orpheus's" amphibrachic trimeter in Khodasevich's prosodic repertoire, retains the original's partial rhyme scheme but renders it in ternary anapests. Dispensing with some of the poem's signature features, he willfully retains, augments, and alters others. Khodasevich's period reference to the "sixteen candle" light bulb (*solntse v shestnadsat' svechei*) is accurately rendered with "a sixty-watt sun," the sixty-watt bulb being the modern equivalent of the obsolete Russian description of the source of light in the protagonist's dingy surroundings. Khodasevich's somnambulistic murmur, however, is replaced with a strikingly American "crooning," memorable to *Lolita* readers as a reference to contemporary U.S. mass culture. Khodasevich's "visual punning" (Bethea) on the word "foot" and its two meanings, anatomic and prosodic, does not survive in this translation either. Most remarkably, perhaps, the translation develops and interprets a key image contained in the poem's penultimate line:

And the room and the furniture slowly,
slowly start in a circle to sail,
and a great heavy lyre is from nowhere
handed me by a ghost through the gale.[38]

Khodasevich is more equivocal as to the identity of the force that hands his protagonist the lyre (*The Heavy Lyre* was the title of his 1922 verse collection) in the poem's penultimate stanza, where to Khodasevich's "someone" (*kto-to*) Nabokov has "ghost." It is here where the reader may begin to wonder whose ghost may be getting in touch with the poem's narrator and where the action of the poem may be taking place. So specific are the details of the narrator's surroundings that he can be placed in the America of the 1940s. One of the signature features of the original poem is its identification of the narrator with its author, who contemplates the rift that splits his existence into two realms, that of his quotidian surroundings and that of otherworldly inspiration. The ghostly apparition that materializes in Nabokov's version of the poem may be taken for the shadow of a dead friend who visits the translator in his new surroundings. This may well be the import of Nabokov's resolute renaming of Khodasevich's "Ballada" as "Orpheus."

Nabokov's selection closes with the three-quatrain-long "Poem." This translation confirms the reader's impression that Khodasevich's lyrical hero is a visionary who claims the liminal state between the sensed and the imagined as his domain. The world of everyday cares is *eto tlen'e* – this putrefaction – which Nabokov interprets as "this mortality and blight." The only source of consolation in the midst of the insubstantial coarseness (*neprochnaia grubost'*) that constitutes our life is the intuition of "a completely different existence" (*sovsem inoe bytie*) that sets the narrator apart from the "tailors" and "builders," the results of whose work are doomed, all their apparent durability notwithstanding. Unsubstantiated as it is, this intuition instils in the narrator a degree of metaphysical optimism inaccessible to those preoccupied with the phenomenal. This is the source of his trust in so diaphanous a pursuit as poetry.

On 28 November 1943, Nabokov wrote to Wilson: "I am so glad you enjoyed Khodasevich. He was a splendid personality."[39] Nabokov's selection of Khodasevich's poems aimed at much more than a mere "introduction" of this poet to a new reading audience. His translations aspire to convince their Anglophone readers that that poet's private revelations and individual epiphanies are as valuable as the infectious pathos of the Soviet poets at the forefront of those readers' attention. Nabokov feels free to compress and alter Khodasevich's images, as if being certain that he has the late poet's full confidence in his ability to do justice to his legacy. The ghost that materializes in the penultimate quatrain of "Orpheus" to hand the lyrical hero a heavy lyre is likely that of the late poet himself, who comes into contact with the translator in his manifestly American surroundings. If, according to Nabokov's conviction, in some cases translation may amount to "the profanation of the dead," it also has the potential to summon the spirits of the departed from oblivion – provided the translators are sufficiently inspired to hold meaningful conversations with their "confrères." Such a communicative act forms the subtextual plot of "Orpheus," a characteristically Nabokovian "ghostly" variation on a theme provided by Khodasevich's "Ballada."

Three Russian Poets (1944), *Pushkin, Lermontov, Tyutchev* (1947) – and Beyond

If the Nabokov canon can be likened to a constellation of celestial bodies in the manner of the astral metaphor in *Speak, Memory*'s chapter 14, these two booklets of translated verse would be wayward meteors. Made to the whimsical standards proclaimed in "The Art of Translation," they found no place in the sombre reality of the "literalist" doctrine. Once lovingly cited in their author's correspondence with his relatives and proudly performed in public, these translations' very existence became a liability when Nabokov's opponents in the *Eugene Onegin* debate cited them as a glaring inconsistency in his literalist stance. As major chapters in his relationships with his Russian predecessors, these translations tested the outer limits of the traditional – literary – methodology and contributed to the eventual development of the literalist doctrine. First and foremost, however, they are fascinating in and of themselves.

Anyone wanting to make sense of *Three Russian Poets* and its expanded version *Pushkin, Lermontov, Tyutchev* should bear in mind that these booklets skim the surface of a pool of materials produced at the dawn of Nabokov's American teaching career. As far as his vision of the three poets' significance was concerned, this selection amounted to a minimalistic representation of the Russian poetic canon, aimed primarily at students.[40] Had he chosen to do so, he could have augmented it with his translations from their contemporaries and near-contemporaries Batiushkov, Baratynskii, Fet, Nekrasov – or their literary descendants Blok and Khodasevich – since, as we shall see, he had at his disposal enough material to create a more inclusive anthology of Russian poetry in his literary renditions.[41] Nabokov's ordering of the poets within his mini-anthology is notable as well. It exemplifies his disregard for chronology while demonstrating his desire to impress on the reader the idea that Tiutchev, while worthy of Pushkin's company, cannot occupy his younger contemporary Lermontov's place next to the master.[42] The ordering of poems within each section is full of significance as well.

Nabokov's translation "The Upas Tree (*Antiaris toxicaria*, Lesch. 1810)" is among the earliest included in the two booklets (1941) and one of its centrepieces.[43] Pushkin's "Anchar" (1828) is a masterwork of allegory. On its surface the poem offers an eloquent and incisive contemplation on the perils of absolute power;[44] its undercurrents, however, are rife with autobiographical implications for a poet tormented by a seemingly benevolent but crassly authoritarian ruler.

The expansive title of Nabokov's "Upas Tree" presents the results of an inquiry into the mysteries of Pushkin's imaginative use of a scientific legend. The tale of an exotic toxic tree came to Pushkin from an English source, but to arrive at its English variant Nabokov had to tackle the problem of Pushkin's naming his poem with a word unprecedented in Russian usage. Nabokov's predecessors D.S. Mirsky (1926) and Babette Deutsch (1936) had already established a minor tradition of equating the sonorous noun *anchár* with "the upas tree," as it was known to Pushkin's European contemporaries, but Nabokov made the actual plant's taxonomical Latin name part of the title – along with a reference to the author of its original scientific description, Jean-Baptiste Leschenault de La Tour (1773–1826).[45] The Latin *Antiaris* is a variation on the same Javanese word that engendered the striking Pushkinian *nomen omen, anchár*. Nabokov's taxonomic perfectionism answers his own call on "the perfect translator" to be "acquainted with the manners, traditions, fauna, flora and times" of the countries and languages he is dealing with in his work.[46]

For all its reticence in preserving the original's imagery and metre, however, Nabokov's "Upas Tree" adheres to his practice of presenting his readers with subtle interpretations of the original.[47] Such interpretations turn this translation into a composite image of the translator's individual notions of the original.

Nabokov's notes to *Eugene Onegin* hint at the rich autobiographical substratum of this seemingly abstract reflection on power and powerlessness. Pushkin's drafts referred to his involvement with the poem's predicament, as they metonymically equated its author's ancestral homeland of Africa with Russia.[48] In concert with an important leitmotif of the *Eugene Onegin* project, the subsequent commentary stressed Pushkin's dependence on his French intermediaries. The exegetic facade of this speculative extrapolation does not obscure the fact that

Nabokov's earlier, literary translation of the poem amounted to more than a mere illustration of Pushkin's debt to the French. The earlier poetic paraphrase provided its reader with a holistic interpretation of the original, which did justice to the rich significance of the allegory at its conflicted – "toxic" – root. As such, it was a Nabokovian response to a Pushkinian challenge, an attempt to unravel the mystery of a cryptic poetic statement with the aim of presenting its new audience with a faithful reproduction of that enigma. To accomplish this task, Nabokov sought to enrich his reading of the original with a deeper understanding of the intention behind it, and it is to this end that he kept probing the various aspects of its composition and significance. It is difficult to avoid the impression that Nabokov's scientific investigation into the botanical aspects of Pushkin's allegory inspired his metaphor for translation being "a kind of V movement: down one stem and up another," which began with "sympathy" and culminated in "impersonation and expression."[49]

It may seem surprising, but Nabokov's ties to Pushkin's variation on the theme of Horace's "Exegi monumentum aere perennius" may be even firmer than they appear. It was Horace's *Carmina* that inspired the title of his unpublished collection of literary juvenilia "Carmina lucis" (1918); it was the portent of Pushkin's "Exegi monumentum" that Nabokov laboured to unravel for decades. Already in 1931 he presented an early interpretation of the poem as he addressed his fellow émigrés in Berlin after citing its third quatrain:

> Perhaps written in mockery of poets' vain aspirations, these lines have proven the purest prophecy, as incidentally have those very lines Pushkin was freely imitating here. Right was old Derzhavin, right was Horace, in their anticipation of the schoolchildren's stumbling reading, in other lands, in other centuries. But it may well be that Pushkin alone of all the world's poets has aroused in succeeding generations such blissful, such reverential adoration.[50]

Preparing to plunge into his Pushkinian masterpiece *The Gift*, Nabokov confronted his Berlin listeners with an unorthodox reading of one of the most famous poems in the Russian literary canon. Eschewing the traditional interpretation of it as a straightforward imitation of its predecessors, he stressed the parodic effect of this Pushkinian dissection of poetic self-aggrandizement. That the 1931 interpretation was a mere stage in the development of a characteristically Nabokovian take on the poem is demonstrated by a later expostulation of the poem's significance:

> In 1836, in one of the most sublime compositions in Russian literary history, Pushkin parodied Derzhavin['s "I've set up to my myself a monument," 1796] stanza by stanza in exactly the same verse form. The first four have an ironic intonation, but under the mask of high mummery Pushkin smuggles in his private truth. They should be in quotation marks, as Burtsev pointed out some thirty years ago in a paper I no longer can trace. The last quatrain is the artist's own grave voice repudiating the mimicked boast. His last line, although ostensibly referring to reviewers, slyly implies that only fools proclaim their immortality.[51]

The 1943 translation of Pushkin's "Exegi monumentum" is the middle point connecting these two interpretations, each of which engendered a different translation based on a different methodology. The addition of the quotation marks, which Nabokov introduces into his translations to signal his acceptance of the interpretation proposed not by Vladimir Burtsev but by Mikhail Gershenzon in his *Mudrost' Pushkina* (1919), permits the reader to understand the not-altogether-obvious portent of the poem.[52] The four opening stanzas restate Derzhavin's straightforward assertion of his artistic accomplishments à la Lomonosov and Horace; it is the poem's last stanza where Pushkin's addition makes it clear that above fame and recognition, one should place individual freedom:

> Велѣнью Божию, о Муза, будь послушна:
> Обиды не страшась, не требуя вѣнца,
> Хулу и похвалу пріемля равнодушно,
> И не оспоривай глупца.[53]

> [To God's command, O Muse, be obedient: / Unafraid of insult, not demanding a wreath, / Abuse and praise accepting with equanimity / And do not contest a fool.]

> Obey thy God, and never mind, O Muse,
> the laurels or the stings: make it thy rule
> to be unstirred by praise as by abuse,
> and do not contradict the fool.[54]

A closer study of Nabokov's 1943 translation shows that it follows the text reproduced in the 1937 edition of Pushkin's collected works.[55] The poem's penultimate line features a gerund (*priemlia*), and not the imperative (*priemli*) featured in modern editions of "Exegi monumentum." This minor digression is significant for our understanding of the evolving nature of Nabokov's translating methodology – as well as his relationship with Pushkin. The 1943 literary translation enshrines the version of the text based on Nabokov's personal copy of Pushkin's collected works. Far from being an authoritative reproduction of Pushkin's texts, up to a certain point in Nabokov's evolution it held for him considerable sentimental value. The subsequent – literal – translation of the same poem will not simply shed such trappings of a literary translation such as rhyme and elevated vocabulary. It will be based on a textually sound Soviet academic edition that accurately reproduces Pushkin's imperatives contained in the two closing lines.[56]

The tension displayed by these seemingly minor discrepancies between the two translations belonging to two distinctly different stages in Nabokov's evolving relationship with Pushkin is telling. The sentimental attachment to one of Nabokov's most cherished possessions, his émigré edition of Pushkin's collected works, gives way to a detached scientific contemplation of a source superior in its reliability. The vision of the Pushkin phenomenon behind Nabokov's translations and interpretations of the Russian national poet made prior to his conversion to literalism in 1955 is that of an émigré clinging to his notion of Russian culture's unspoiled, non-Soviet variant. It was Nabokov who, following the lead of his older contemporary and ally Khodasevich, proclaimed his allegiance to that quixotic notion, first in his poems, public talks, and subsequently in the most majestic Pushkinian paean of his Russian years, *The Gift*. When Nabokov complained to Wilson of the difficulties he was having with the 1943 version of "Exegi monumentum," he referenced not only the technical complexities associated with creating a close poetic replica of its model but also those associated with his desire to instil his translation with the émigré ethos of Pushkin worship. This impression is strengthened by close reading of the expanded selection of Pushkin's poems reproduced in the *Pushkin, Lermontov, Tyutchev* booklet of 1947. Before proceeding to examine the remainder of that Pushkinian selection, we must dwell on two fascinating manifestations of the Nabokovian brand of dialogism, namely his responses to Pushkin's contemplation of fame and immortality.

Nabokov presented his initial poetic take on Pushkin's "Exegi monumentum" to Wilson on 9 November 1943. The difficulties he was having with his literary rendition of Pushkin's programmatic statement overlapped with the composition of at least two original statements in a similar vein, the Russian poem "Slava" (Fame; 1942) and the English poem "A Discovery" (early 1943).[57]

"Slava" deals with the temptation of immortality as suggested by Pushkin's "Exegi monumentum." According to the authorial explanation appended to the poem, in it "a certain devil … is tempting a free poet with all manner of material rewards."[58] "A free poet" is a reincarnation of Nabokov during his first years on American soil, and what that devil is tempting him with is the prospect of fame and recognition in his native land – in exchange for his freedom.[59]

As Nabokov points out in the same explanation, the two closing lines of this quatrain paraphrase quatrain three of Pushkin's "Exegi monumentum," which in Nabokov's 1943 version reads as "Throughout great Rus' my echoes will extend, / and all will name me, all tongues in her use: / the Slavs' proud heir, the Finn, the Kalmuck, friend / of steppes, the yet untamed Tunguz."[60] Nabokov's engagement with Pushkin's "Exegi monumentum" in translation begins to emerge as a pivotal dialogic encounter marking a turning point in his artistic career, his transition from Russian to English as his main vehicle of self-expression. To the extent that "Slava" amounts to a reflection on the consequences of his separation from his native tongue, this poem cannot be fully appreciated without taking into account its dialogic orientation toward Pushkin. The significance of this dialogue with Pushkin for Nabokov is underscored by the fact that it continued in English in his English-language manifesto "A Discovery."

"A Discovery" picks up the theme of achievement and immorality where Pushkin left it in his "Exegi monumentum" to present a variation different from the one found in "Slava." Nabokov subverts the Horatian tradition of conceiving of one's achievement in solely aesthetic terms: he takes pride in being the first to break free of that tradition's strictures to expand into the universe of scientific inquiry. The pursuit of verifiable knowledge, the expansion of the limits of the known, and the thrill associated with one's ability to leave an individual imprint on a scientific breakthrough, he suggests, offer delights comparable to those coveted by the poets since time immemorial.

Nabokov's "Discovery" is a polemical piece brought into existence not only by his joy at making his long-awaited scientific discovery but also by his dialogue with Pushkin's ironic manifesto. While it may have been prompted by the reservations he had regarding the durability of his artistic achievement prior to the universal success of *Lolita*, first and foremost this poem is a celebration of his freedom from the tradition that confined Pushkin and his predecessors to a single medium of expression, in much the same manner as their language confined them to a monoglot audience.

In addition to "Exegi monumentum," "The Upas Tree," "A Scene from *The Covetous Knight*," *A Feast during the Plague*, and *Mozart and Salieri* included in *Three Russian Poets* (1944), its expanded 1947 version features the newly translated "I value little those much-vaunted rights," "Epigram (On Vorontsov)," "The Name," and "Winter Morning." Each one of these additions enlarges the reader's notion of Pushkin's individuality, augmenting it with various shades of his artistic temper. The translator, whose introductory note teases the reader with the assertion that Pushkin's "life was as glamorous as a good grammarian's life ought to be," continues to be in charge as he proves that Pushkin's short lyrics display "a precision of expression and a melody of tone that Russian literature had never known before."[61]

In a reversal of Nabokov's subsequent translating practices, his 1947 version of Pushkin's "Iz Pindemonte" (1836) was based on a close lexical variant of the original.[62] "I value little those much-vaunted rights," the sonorous poetic rendition of the original, amounts to reiteration of the point Pushkin made in the last stanza of his "Exegi monumentum." This time, however, Pushkin proudly displays his disdain for conventional ideas and notions by asserting his independence from the opinion of others.

After demonstrating Pushkin's mastery of the iamb in the quatrains of "Exegi monumentum" and "The Upas Tree" on the one hand, and of iambic blank verse in the "little tragedies" on the other, Nabokov showcases Pushkin's formidable command of the iambic hexameters encased in rhyming couplets, the form traditionally serving as the Russian equivalent of the French alexandrine. The rebellious spirit of Gallic rationalism brims with ebullience as Pushkin refuses to be bound by the traditional notions of freedom as a communal project:

Иныя, лучшія мнѣ дороги права;
Иная, лучшая потребна мнѣ Свобода …
Зависѣть отъ Властей, зависѣть от народа –
Не всё ли имъ равно? Богъ съ ними![63]

> [Different, better rights are dear to me / Different, better Freedom I require ... / To depend on the authorities, to depend on the people – / Isn't it all the same to them? God be with them!]

> My spirit fights
> for deeper Liberty, for better rights.
> Whom shall we serve – the people or the State?
> The poet does not care – so let them wait.[64]

A translation of a quintessential Russian expression of the stance "above the fray," "I value little those much-vaunted rights" becomes another centrepiece of Nabokov's representation of Pushkin the independent thinker. It is, however, full of significance for understanding its translator's intellectual lineage. Few poems in his versions come closer to the spirit of Nabokov's defence of individual freedom. This poem and its English translation get tantalizingly close to expressing Nabokov's own credo to the extent that he can be said to have had one.

The single-quatrain "Epigram (On Vorontsov)" is a surprising but not illogical addition to a small selection of Pushkin's poetry that seeks to convince its reader of the richness of his repertoire. This epigram is not to be found in Nabokov's personal copy of Pushkin's collected works: it follows the variant reproduced in another émigré edition of Pushkin's compositions, *Sobranie zapreshchënnykh stikhotvorenii A.S. Pushkina* (ca. 1920). While it savages its highborn, immensely influential target as a "half-merchant and half-prince, / half-scholar and half-dunce,"[65] this epigram does not merely show Pushkin's combative side – it contributes a novel variation on the theme of artistic independence, a major leitmotif of Nabokov's selection. The freedom to attack a more powerful adversary, the ability to get even with him rhetorically, is a guarantee of the poet's eventual triumph.

Nabokov's translation of "Chto v imeni tebe moëm" permits us to mark the moment when Mnemosyne, the muse of memory, becomes associated with his effort to preserve his past. Viewed in the context of Nabokov's contemporaneous projects, "The Name" reveals itself a variation on the theme of metaphorical immortality suggested in "Exegi monumentum," developed in "Slava," and finalized in "A Discovery." At a crucial point in Nabokov's version of this poem, Pushkin's dolorous but hopeful appeal to a woman in whose heart a memory of him may still dwell undergoes a surprising transformation. Musing on how his name, so rich in associations in his native tongue, should appear to be devoid of any significance when viewed through foreign eyes, the poet poses a rhetorical question in the poem's third and penultimate stanza:

Что въ нёмъ? Забытое давно
Въ волненьяхъ новыхъ и мятежныхъ
Твоей душѣ не дастъ оно
Воспоминаній чистыхъ, нѣжныхъ.[66]

[What's in it? Forgotten long ago / In tribulations new and tempestuous / To your soul it will not give / Recollections pure, tender.]

While remaining close to the original's melancholic tonality, Nabokov's version of this stanza, along with his take on this poem in its entirety, proves to be an exercise in double vision. Without betraying the original and its agenda, it emerges as a reflection on the nature of a foreign memoirist's relationship with his audience, a sentiment at the core of Nabokov's nascent autobiographical project:

What is it, then? A long-dead past,
lost in the rush of madder dreams,
upon your soul it will not cast
Mnemosyne's pure tender beams.[67]

Nabokov's "The Name" is where Mnemosyne makes her first appearance in his Anglophone oeuvre. In purely technical terms, this personification is a reprise of a tactical solution that proved helpful when Nabokov translated into French Pushkin's "Stikhi, sochinënnye noch'iu, vo vremia bessonitsy" in 1937, where he adjusted Pushkin's impersonal invocation of one of the three Moirai into a direct mention of Lachesis. There is more to this move than its ingenuity. Whereas Lachesis's presence in "Je ne puis m'endormir. La nuit" was sanctioned by the original and permitted by the logic of literary methodology employed therein, Mnemosyne's appearance in "The Name" is difficult to justify in terms of sheer interlingual equivalence. As we shall see, Nabokov was fully cognizant of the fact that such instances of translation asymmetry violated the integrity of the original text, coming dangerously close to becoming offences against authorial will. Mnemosyne, however, is a Nabokovian plenipotentiary in the world of Pushkinian invention, a manifestation of the interconnectedness between the two poets. This is precisely what Nabokov meant when in "The Art of Translation" he described such sublime occasions when "professional writers" "relaxed" in the company of their "confrères."

The expanded selection of Pushkin's poems in *Pushkin, Lermontov, Tyutchev* closes with "Winter Morning" ("Zimnee utro," 1829). As this careful reproduction of Pushkin's sestets completes the picture of the poet's formal virtuosity, its subject matter demonstrates his acuity. Lest this assembly of predominantly contemplative, reflective, and imaginative pieces convince the reader that Pushkin was a romantic dreamer rather grave in his disposition, Nabokov closes it with a paean to the phenomenal. A counterbalance not only to such cerebral pieces as "Exegi monumentum," "The Upas Tree," and "The Name," but especially to the "little tragedies," the light-hearted "Winter Morning" is a bacchanal of sensuous detail. Brimming with colour and passion, this translation emphasizes Pushkinian vivaciousness. The teleology of this interpretation is thrown into sharp relief by student class notes taken in Nabokov's Harvard Pushkin course, which singled out "Winter Morning" as an example of the poet's "Dynamism."[68]

Apart from being the moon to Pushkin's sun in the universe of Russian letters, Lermontov was one of Nabokov's lifelong literary companions. An unavoidable presence on the intellectual horizon of any educated Russian,[69] Lermontov did not merely enter Nabokov's Trinitarian doctrine of Russian poetry, he remained a permanent source of fascination for him. "Though decidedly patchy, he remains for the true lover of poetry a miraculous being whose development is something of a mystery": originally formulated in 1941,[70] this dictum held its value in both *Three Russian Poets* and *Pushkin, Lermontov, Tyutchev*.

"The Lermontov Mirage" offers fascinating material for a study of Nabokov's relationship with his interlocutors far beyond his engagement with the essay's protagonist. It features a sizeable "verbal vestige" of Nabokov's engagement with Vladimir Solov'ëv, from whom he borrowed his interpretation of "Son" ("V poldnenvyi zhar, v doline Dagestana," 1841). Nabokov's presentation of the "most fatamorganic," "perfectly unique" "Triple Dream"[71] – it would reappear in his introduction to *A Hero of Our Time* (1958) – was appropriated from Solov'ëv's 1901 survey of Lermontov's life in art. While Nabokov readily acknowledges Bertrand Russell's definition of solipsism,[72] his debt to Solov'ëv goes unrecognized.

Its low profile notwithstanding, "The Lermontov Mirage" prefigures that brand of literary allusiveness which was to become a hallmark of

Nabokov the Anglophone writer. The essay teems with unacknowledged references to various literary sources, some of which have their roots in his translations. In addition to A.H. Housman, Russell, Shakespeare, Solov'ëv, and even the twelfth-century travelogue writer Daniel the Traveller, Nabokov's commentary on Lermontov's relationship with his homeland features an invocation of "an unofficial English rose".[73] This imprecise quotation from Rupert Brooke's "The Old Vicarage, Grantchester" (1912) is more than a fugitive echo of the English poet Nabokov once loved. It signals that he did not abandon the Brooke-Lermontov connection he had made in his 1922 essay,[74] where his version of Brooke's "Vision of the Archangels" retold its English model in terms of Lermontov's "Angel" ("Po nebu polunochi angel letel," 1831).

In "The Lermontov Mirage" "Farewell," a truncated version of "K*" ("Prosti! My ne vstretimsia bole," 1832), illustrates the presence of a "superficial" Byronic influence on his Russian admirer.[75] In all likelihood, Nabokov means to connect it with "Fare Thee Well" (1816), which enjoyed such popularity in Russia that Pushkin used its opening lines as an epigraph to *Eugene Onegin*'s chapter 8. Out of twenty-five lines found in the original, Nabokov preserves only twelve: the omission of the poem's core, so Lermontovian, so un-Byronic in its qualities, facilitates the Byron connection. Nabokov's careful transposition of Lermontov's amphibrachs, however, underscores the degree of Lermontov's independence from his English paragon.

"The Triple Dream," Nabokov's take on "Son," is yet another illustration of the transpositional technique advocated in "The Art of Translation." Not content with borrowing Solov'ëv's justification for this poem's being "perfectly unique," in his essay Nabokov corrects what he identifies a Lermontovian "solecism" and explains the reasoning behind his choice. If his rendition of the poem's closing quatrain

И снилась ей долина Дагестана …
Знакомый трупъ лежалъ въ долинѣ той,
Въ его груди, дымясь, чернѣла рана,
И кровь лилась хладѣющей струёй.[76]

[And she dreamed of a valley of Daghestan … / A familiar corpse was lying in that valley, / In his chest, steaming, a wound shone black, / And blood poured [in a] chilling stream.]

as

For in her dream she saw a gorge, somewhere
in Daghestan, and knew the man who lay
there on the sand, the dead man, unaware
of steaming wound and blood ebbing away.[77]

cannot be justified as a faithful rendition of the original, it is due to the translator's unequivocally expressed desire to improve the original by "omitting" the purported solecism.[78]

Not content with pointing out this "solecism," Nabokov chooses to "correct" it – out of fear, he indicates, of subjecting Lermontov – and his translation – to ridicule. Solecisms and imperfections have no place in Nabokov's literary versions of Russian classics. At this point in his development as translator, the same man who would castigate others for making their versions of foreign texts sound "fluid" or "smooth" had no difficulty performing this same operation. In a thought-provoking preview of the complexities Nabokov was to face after his conversion to the literalist doctrine, his 1956–7 translation of the same poem glosses over the issue of the alleged solecism. That partially rhymed "literal" version follows the original closer than the fully rhymed variant of 1941, yet eliminates the conundrum pointed out in "The Lermontov Mirage."[79]

Nabokov's introduction to the 1958 translation of *A Hero of Our Time* retains a condensed version of his appropriation of Solov'ëv's analysis of the poem. Most striking of all, perhaps, it qualifies this poem as "prophetic," suggesting a greater continuity in Nabokov's evolving views on Lermontov than his exposition of his weaknesses as a prose writer may imply.[80]

Like both versions of "The Triple Dream," "My Native Land," Nabokov's rendition of "Otchizna" (1841), is equimetric; additionally, it mirrors the original rhyme scheme where a sestet is followed by five quatrains. This exactitude disguises a uniquely individual understanding of the poetic text in question: according to "The Lermontov Mirage," above all else it is an illustration of an "emotional paradox": "The Russian poet talks of the view from his window as if he were an exile dreaming of his land more vividly than he ever saw it."[81] This interpretation is as good a reminder as any that Baudelaire's vision of poets as eternal exiles in "L'Albatros" never lost its relevance for Nabokov.

Pushkin, Lermontov, Tyutchev expanded the initial selection of Lermontov's works in *Three Russian Poets* with the addition of "Imitation of Heine," "The Sky and the Stars," "The Wish," "The Sail," "Thanksgiving," "The Angel," and "The Rock."[82] Nabokov ran these translations by Wilson, who voiced his disagreement with a number of his friend's choices and solutions. On 1 February 1946, Nabokov defended himself against Wilson's criticism: "Lermontov is banal … and as I am rather indifferent to him, I did not go out of my way to debanalize the passages you question."[83] Everything that we know about Nabokov's lifelong engagement with Lermontov indicates that on this occasion he was less than forthright.

"Imitation of Heine," the two-quatrain miniature that opens the expanded selection of Lermontov poems in *Pushkin, Lermontov, Tyutchev*, renders "Sosna (Iz Geine)" (1841). As follows from its subtitle, the poem is an adaptation of a German source, Heinrich Heine's "Ein Fichtenbaum steht einsam." This poem occupies a special place in the history of Russian poetics: together with Lermontov's own "Oni liubili drug druga tak dolgo i nezhno" (1841), it is one of the earliest Russian attempts to echo Heine's deregularized prosody.[84] Lermontov's variable-length amphibrachs amount to a standardization of the irregular rhythm of the original, which, in addition to refusing to follow a single metrical scheme, features only a single rhyming combination. The poem is famous for its transformation of the Heinean erotic allegory – where a masculine "ein Fichtenbaum" longs for a feminine "einer Palme" – into a depiction of alienation universal in its proportion.

While preserving Lermontov's partial rhyming, Nabokov's "Imitation of Heine" resets the original in a far less rigid metre. Superficially puzzling, this decision is informed by his intimate understanding of the semantic implications of this prosodic adjustment. Nabokov's decision to endow his version with features common not only to its Russian original but also to that original's German source is significant. The surface of a straightforward-enough translation hides import unmistakably personal in its essence. Apart from honouring Lermontov, this translation revisits Nabokov's own engagement with the author of *Buch der Lieder*. "Imitation of Heine" revisits Nabokov's Crimean renditions of Heine's *lieder* as well as his imitations of the singer of Lorelei. By deregularizing the metre of Lermontov's original and turning the two quatrains into a composite image of Heinean rhythmicity, Nabokov succeeds in concealing an intricate prosodic mechanism capable of generating a series of delicate and meaningful sound effects redolent of not only Lermontov's dialogue with Heine but also his own lifelong engagement with the German poet.

"The Sky and the Stars" ("Nebo i zvëzdy") may date back to 1831, but here it follows such late pieces as "The Triple Dream" and "Imitation of Heine." The poem presents its seventeen-year-old author not merely as a metaphysical poet of uncommon promise, it shows him an intrepid experimenter. Nabokov's rendering of Lermontov's unrhymed dactyls with alternating foot count is not as precise as it could have been. While it retains a number of dactylic lines, it does not reproduce Lermontov's metre consistently. The translation seeks to convey the meaning of the original poem first and foremost, introducing the reader to another facet of this young poet's extraordinary personality, his ability to envy celestial bodies ("People are envious / of one another. I, on the contrary, – / only the beautiful stars do I envy").[85]

If "The Sky and the Stars" is a bold formal experiment and a demonstration of Lermontov's prodigious promise, "The Angel" (1831) is an early masterpiece to which Nabokov was partial.[86] Challenged by Wilson, he was quick to recognize the "banality" of Lermontov's characterization of this world as "a vale of tears and strife."[87] Wilson's objection notwithstanding, Nabokov retained his rendition of "on dushu mladuiu v ob'iatiakh nës / dlia mira pechali i slëz" as "he carried a soul in his arms, a young life / to the world of sorrow and strife." "The Lermontov Mirage" demonstrated his genuine appreciation of this poem's sentimental charm. In that essay Nabokov spoke of its remarkable melodiousness, and his subsequent rendition of the poem aspired to reproduce this same effect as closely as possible in a rhyming translation. Nabokov does away with Lermontov's alternation of four- and three-feet amphibrachs in favour of a more varied and accommodating prosodic medium that follows the general outline of a ternary metre. Nabokov had every reason to be proud of his work, and one can only imagine how offended he was by Wilson's failure to look past his careful reproduction of the least impressive features of this poetic text.

At twenty-seven lines, "The Wish" ("Zhelan'e," 1832) is the longest piece in the entire selection. The "jet-black mane," which Nabokov conceded was a superior choice to the one he had sent Wilson, appears in the poem's first stanza – Nabokov heeded his friend's criticism. The original showcases Lermontov's mastery of trochaic tetrameter, which is meant to stylize the metre of a folksong. In his version, Nabokov captures the ebullience of the poem, its unadulterated lust for life and love, which presents a different side of Lermontov the metaphysical visionary and prophetic somnambulist.

"Parus" (1832) – "The Sail" – may well be Lermontov's signature piece, his single most famous lyric utterance. This paean to the way rebellious romantic individuality asserts itself in the face of adversity is composed in iambic pentameter, which readily lends itself to an equimetric rendition, in contrast with some of its forerunners in this selection. Instead of Lermontov's third-person description, Nabokov's version of the poem leans heavily on apostrophe ("What do you seek in a far country? What have you left at home, long sail?"). Nabokov's rendition of the closing line of "The Sail," "as if in tempests there *was* peace" (emphasis added), provoked Wilson's reproach: "Your last line of Белеет парус одинокий is a conspicuous example of your failure to master the English subjunctive." Nabokov's justification for his wording of that line allows us a rare glimpse of the aesthetics behind his poetic renditions of Russian poetry, which were very much in concert with the sentiments expressed in "The Art of Translation": "the 'was' in the last line of the 'Sail' was intentional as 'there were' seemed cacophonic to me and sagging."[88] Nabokov omitted to mention that in the magazine publication of 1946, that line read "as if in tempests there *were* peace" (emphasis added).[89] Aesthetic considerations, rooted as they are in this translator's individual appreciation of the original, become the decisive factor that determines its appearance in the target language.

"Thanksgiving" renders "Blagodarnost'" (1840) in a strikingly asymmetric fashion: it doubles the original line count from eight to sixteen while making no attempt to preserve Lermontov's anaphoras. The sardonic catalogue of all the slights the lyrical hero has had to endure culminates in a direct challenge to the Almighty to rid him of his life. The only rhyming combination this translation retains appears to be random, and the translation itself emerges as a loosely rhythmical prose retelling of the two quatrains of rhymed verse. Indubitably effective as a recreation of Lermontov's fervour, "Thanksgiving" stands out in this selection of resolutely poetic texts due to its failure to give the reader any idea of the original's form.

"The Rock" ("Utës," 1841) closes the expanded selection of Lermontov's poems in *Pushkin, Lermontov, Tyutchev*. Nabokov captures the lyrical specificity of the original allegory: after spending a night on the "breast" of an old "great rock," a "little golden cloud" playfully speeds off, unaware of a host of emotions stirred in the seemingly unmovable, soulless mass of stone. Unlike "Thanksgiving," this two-quatrain miniature retains the original rhyme scheme, but it foregoes the trochaic pentameter – for which Lermontov was deservedly famous – in favour of a far-too-generic iambic pentameter.

This selection of Lermontov's poems succeeds in creating a vision of a formally enterprising and prodigiously gifted poet with a remarkably broad thematic range. From the metaphysical insight of "The Sky and the Stars" and "The Angel," Nabokov's Lermontov shifts to the earthiness of "The Wish"; from the extrasensory perception of "The Triple Dream" to the doleful amorous allegory of "The Rock." The compromise with the original that distinguishes Nabokov's "Thanksgiving" may be at odds with his overwhelming desire to retain as much of his originals' features as possible, but more often than not, when faced with the choice between the significance and the form he sacrifices the former for the latter. Merely a feature of a given selection of poems in Nabokov's translation, this points in the direction he was moving in his thinking on translation methodology, presaging the eventual triumph of sense and reason over rhyme and matter in his literalist doctrine.

Nabokov may be pouring scorn on stale academic conventions in his translator's preambles, yet his selection of the three greatest Russian poets extends the lease on life for one of Russia's most durable mythologems, that of the Golden Age of Russian literature. The two booklets of translated poems that put Lermontov after Pushkin and made Lermontov's senior contemporary Tiutchev wait in the wings vary in their scope, but they do not waver in their presentation of the Russian poetic canon as something impervious to change. The fabulous nineteenth century, as it was termed in *Invitation to a Beheading*, was the time when Russian poetry reached its pinnacle, this selection implies, and that will never change.

Tiutchev is the only member of Nabokov's holy trinity of Russia's lyricists whose selection did not expand from *Three Russian Poets* to *Pushkin, Lermontov, Tyutchev*. Both booklets include "Nightfall," "Tears" ("Friends, with my eyes I love caressing"), "The Journey," "Silentium," "Last Love," "Dusk," "The Abyss," "Autumn," "Appeasement," and "Tears" ("Human tears, Oh the tears! you that flow"). In an early indication that Nabokov's relationship with Tiutchev represented a special case in the annals of his Parnassian predilections, the number of Tiutchev poems in his translation continued to grow after these booklets were published: apart from revising "The Journey" twice, Nabokov would share with his Harvard students "My soul would like to be a star," "Through the azure haze of the night," "She sat on the floor," and "The sky is overcast with slow." Among Nabokov's papers we also find "One cannot understand her with the mind," his version of one of Tiutchev's most famous – and much mocked – utterances.

No account of Nabokov's relationship with Tiutchev can afford to forego a discussion of a seemingly extraneous circumstance that proves to be full of significance for our understanding of his fondness for this poet. For the entirety of the Russian portion of his career in letters, Nabokov relied on a specific edition of Tiutchev's poems, the Berlin-published, pocket-sized *Stikhotvoreniia* put out by his émigré publisher Slovo (1921). Along with the Modeste Hofmann edited collected works of Pushkin, the Tiutchev volume was one of Nabokov's most cherished possessions. Apart from affecting Nabokov's understanding of the poet's place in the history of Russian letters, that small book became embedded in his fiction, forever linking on one important occasion the writer and one of the meekest of his creations.

Nabokov's dialogue with Tiutchev forms one of the most significant subtextual currents running through "Cloud, Castle, Lake" (1937), where a gang of German amateur torturers brutalizes the gentle, defenceless protagonist, Vasiliy Ivanovich. That he should nourish a weakness for Tiutchev's poetry adds a particularly piercing detail to Nabokov's presentation of his character; that the lines from Tiutchev's "Silentium" should provide a chillingly ironic commentary on Vasiliy Ivanovich's predicament makes that presentation doubly unsettling for the reader, since it goes to the core of the most disturbing aspect of that short story.

The readers of "Cloud, Castle, Lake" have every reason to suspect its omniscient narrator of indifference to, if not complicity in, the cruel treatment of Vasiliy Ivanovich. On more than one occasion the narrator oversteps the boundaries of his privileges, only to conclude the story with the following dénouement:

> He called on me … kept on repeating that he must resign his position, begged me to let him go, insisted that he could not continue, that he had not the strength to belong to mankind any longer. Of course, I let him go.[90]

Such grandstanding on the part of a narrator – whose status and responsibilities appear to overlap with those exclusive to his creator, the author – makes one wonder why he does nothing to save "one of his representatives," as he introduced Vasiliy Ivanovich, from humiliation and suffering. The conundrum at the centre of "Cloud, Castle,

Lake" is complicated by the fact that Vasiliy Ivanovich, the narrator, and the author are lovers of Tiutchev's poetry. This is not where their affinity ends, however. As it turns out, Nabokov shares with Vasiliy Ivanovich his own "little volume of Tyutchev."[91] This same "little volume" accompanied the Nabokovs on all their travels from the Old World to the New and back, as indicated by a French security services stamp authorizing its export from the country before the Nazi invasion; this same volume was the source of all the extant translations from the poet. Rich in Nabokov's marginalia, this document provides us with a priceless opportunity to trace these translations to their source texts and follow his work on their English-language reincarnations.

On 29 April 1941, Nabokov informed Wilson "I … will soon have to tackle Tute-chev."[92] Simon Karlinsky notes that Nabokov kept playing with the sound of Tiutchev's surname, and when on 20 March 1952 he gave a public reading of his translations at Harvard University, he spelled out the poet's surname letter by letter to liken it to "a kind of moist twitter."[93] Translating Tiutchev was high on his list of teaching priorities, to be certain, yet one senses that Nabokov's partiality toward Tiutchev was uncommon indeed.

As Wilson found out on 23 November 1943, Nabokov, whom he knew as a formidable opponent in matters relating to Russian poetics and politics, was a passionate admirer of Tiutchev. While the two friends planned their anthology, Nabokov showed Wilson his translations and Wilson shared with Nabokov his essays. After reading the proofs of Wilson's "note on Russian poetry" dealing with Tiutchev, Nabokov did not mince his words, sensing that his friend had failed to grasp that poet's essence.[94]

Nabokov's regard for Tiutchev underwent an evolution of its own. On the one hand, it was profoundly influenced by the way Tiutchev was interpreted by Andrei Belyi and his disciples, who laid the foundations for systematic studies of Russian poetics. On the other, Nabokov developed a personal understanding of the way Tiutchev's poetry was integrated into a global literary context. Apart from being convinced that a single Tiutchev poem was a focal point where the past and future of Russian poetry converged, he discerned in Tiutchev unexpected parallels with other writers.

"Nightfall" ("Letnii vecher," 1826–8) and "Tears" ("Liubliu, druz'ia, laskat' ochami" [I love, friends, to caress with [my] eyes]; 1823) open the Tiutchev selection. The fact that in these equimetric, equilinear renditions of fully rhymed originals only the odd lines rhyme points to the translator's desire to retain the meaning of the original. Nabokov uses this leeway to convey the exuberance with which Tiutchev paints his verbal landscapes. As is the case with all of his translations, these English variants abound in ingenious solutions to the problems posed by the originals and felicitous interpretations of their imagery.

According to a marginal note in Nabokov's personal copy of Tiutchev's poems, "Tears" ("Friends, with my eyes I love caressing") expresses his "credo." The poem inaugurates a Tiutchevian way of endowing nature with his individual pantheism. The translation's second quatrain encapsulates the manner in which Nabokov alerts his reader to this aspect of the poet's individuality: to Tiutchev's somewhat cryptic "creation" (*sozdan'e*) Nabokov has "Nature," and instead of introducing another noun to refer to the same concept as Tiutchev does in the second part of the quatrain, he continues with the sensuous personification he had already introduced:

> I love to look around when Nature
> seems as it were immersed in May;
> when bathed in redolence she slumbers
> and smiles throughout her dreamy day.[95]

As Nabokov metonymically equates "spring" with "May," he condenses Tiutchev's references to the world of creation into one sensuous personification, implying that Tiutchev sees nature as an attractive woman; this quatrain paves the way for the appearance of Aphrodite in the subsequent lines. The marginal notes in Nabokov's volume of Tiutchev's poems show that his attention was drawn to the seemingly prosaic way Tiutchev introduced his simile with the rather pedestrian turn of speech *kak by*. Instead of suppressing it, however, Nabokov goes to great lengths to ensure that his translation preserves this feature: it is to accommodate its English equivalent "as it were" and similar hallmarks of Tiutchevian poetic diction that he refuses to follow his model's rhyme scheme.

"Nightfall," a version of the earlier "Letnii vercher," expands the reader's idea of Tiutchev's mastery of the verbal landscape. This is another instalment in the series of his sensuous personifications of nature. Not content with depicting nature as a vividly imagined voluptuous Greek goddess in "Tears," in "Nightfall" Tiutchev makes this image still more tangible by endowing his personification with anthropomorphic physiology. Nabokov's version of the concluding quatrain seeks to mirror the tangibility of Tiutchev's vision:

> And now there goes through Nature's veins
> a liquid shiver, swift and sweet,
> as though the waters of a spring
> had come to touch her burning feet.[96]

As he read his versions of Tiutchev's short lyrics on 20 March 1952, Nabokov confessed that "one would have liked to render all his poems." His marginal notes to multiple Tiutchev poems identify the effects he sought to replicate in those versions of Tiutchevian verbal landscapes he did translate: "merging of sounds, images; meaning and grammar!" ("Vecher"), "makes the compressed style correspond to the burden of passion" ("Liubliu glaza tvoi, moi drug"), and "vision corresponding to sound" ("Son na more").

Transfixed by Tiutchev's depiction of chthonic fear in "Pesok sypuchii po koleni" (1830), Nabokov produced three radically different versions of "The Journey." Two of them predate his conversion to literalism, and one exemplifies the essence of literalism in a nutshell. Does the intensity of Nabokov's engagement with the poem help us appreciate his fascination with this seemingly minor component of Tiutchev's legacy?

The initial incarnation of "The Journey" opened Nabokov's "Four Poems by Tyutchev" published in the *Russian Review* (1944). Here the two quatrains of regular Russian iambic tetrameter disintegrated into English distichs of uneven length, while the partial rhyming connecting the poem's even-numbered lines remained the only vestige of its original structure ("Knee-deep, this powdery sand ... We ride / late in the murky day").[97]

Nabokov's marginalia shows that he placed great value not only on Tiutchev's orchestration of the original, but also on the syntax decelerating the tempo of so fluid a prosodic medium as iambic tetrameter. The original features an accumulation of ellipses and elliptic sentences – to experience this effect, Nabokov readers have to be content with his measured delivery of the poem's sentences in small, couplet-like parcels. Not happy with that solution to the problem of conveying the original's effect in English, Nabokov retranslated it for *Three Russian Poets* and *Pushkin, Lermontov, Tyutchev* ("Soft sand comes up to our horses' shanks / as we ride in the darkening day").[98]

Both versions of the poem preserve Nabokov's helpful clarification of Tiutchev's concise but potentially ambiguous reference to the journey being conducted on horseback; both versions preserve the exclamatory sentence declaring the surroundings "a comfortless neighborhood." Nabokov's fondness for this interpretation of Tiutchev's "kakie grustnye mesta" (lit., such sad surroundings, emphatic) is palpable: his translation underscores the unnerving effect the poem's crepuscular atmosphere has on the travellers, possibly harbouring a threat. The poem crescendos in the invocation of an Argus-like monster: the same Tiutchev who was so keen to discern in nature the features of Aphrodite in "Slëzy" ("Tears") is acutely aware of the terrors associated with darkness.

Nabokov's commentary to *Eugene Onegin* incorporates the third and final version of the poem. As follows from the gloss, the "curious" parallelism between Pushkin's phrasing of a certain clause and Tiutchev's exclamation in the second stanza of "The Journey" cannot be explained by one poet's awareness of the other's work, yet the annotator seizes this opportunity not only to present his reader with an unadorned "literal" replication of Tiutchev's original, but also to comment on its putative relationship with a foreign-language source:

> As has been pointed out by Russian critics, the image in ll. 7–8 ["Grim night like a hundred-eyed beast / looks out of every bush"] is an improvement upon a metaphor in Goethe's *Wilkommen und Abschied*: "Wo Finsternis aus dem Gesträuche mit hundert schwarzen Augen sah."[99]

Nabokov's fascination with the concluding metaphor permits us to put the translator's partiality toward this poem into the context of his lifelong preoccupation with the question of nature's relationship with humankind. A dark variation on Tiutchev's depiction of nature as an animate being, "The Journey" invites us to ponder the possibility of nature's inherent hostility to our venturing into its mysteries. On more than one level, Nabokov's numerous attempts to employ his artistic sensitivity to justify his sense of nature's fundamentally benign attitude toward us, his desire to relate to the creative element at the root of all things with his individual creativity may be interpreted as an answer to the sentiment formulated in "The Journey." Its appearance in the temporal vicinity of such Nabokovian explorations of this theme as *Conclusive Evidence/Speak, Memory*, *Bend Sinister*, *Lolita*, *Pnin*, and *Pale Fire* ceases to appear accidental when we qualify the impetus behind his constant attempts to refine his version of the poem as an activity profoundly dialogic in its essence.

In "Cloud, Castle, Lake," Vasiliy Ivanovich's failure to follow the injunction at the core of Tiutchev's "Silentium" precipitates his undoing: had he heeded his favourite poet's imperatives, conveyed by his creator in English as "speak not, lie hidden, and conceal / the way you dream, the things you feel," he could have escaped his tormentors into the serenity of his fulfilled dreams. Even if we take into account the prodigious breadth of Nabokov's literary interests across the six languages at his disposal and augment it with our awareness of his lifelong devotion to Pushkin, we will have to acknowledge that no other literary work commanded Nabokov's attention with the urgency matching that of Tiutchev's paradoxical call to honour the sanctum of one's inner world. Nabokov's version of "Silentium" is an indubitable pinnacle of his pre-literalist period, an achievement in which he took considerable pride. After investing serious effort into creating his version of the poem, Nabokov made it a centrepiece of his public talks, during which he accentuated its painstakingly devised rhetorical effects.

"Speak not, lie hidden, and conceal" ("Silentium" ["Molchi, skryvaisia i tai"]; 1825–9) extends and, one senses, exhausts the potential of the traditional – poetic, literary – mode of translation. Willing and able to give himself a wide berth when tackling a demanding literary text, here Nabokov refuses to cut any corners. The translation strikes a balance between replicating both the form and the significance of the original poem, down to recreating its circular composition, opening and ending on the same verb in the same imperative mood (cf. Tiutchev's "Molchi … i molchi" and Nabokov's "Speak not … and speak no word"). An inevitable companion to any equimetrical and equilinear rhyming translation, Nabokov's poetic paraphrase adheres to the lexis stylistically congenial to that of Tiutchev's original even when he needs to depart from its wording. Appreciative of the archaic flavour of Tiutchev's register yet faced with the impossibility of reproducing the flavour of Tiutchev's Slavonicized Russian, Nabokov delves into the King James Version of the Bible to mimic the needed effect. Nabokov echoes Tiutchev's query "Poimët li on, chem ty zhivësh'?" with "Will he discern what quickens you?" Superficially, the decidedly bookish verb "quicken" clashes with Tiutchev's neutral Russian vocabulary in this context. The justification for this paraphrase lies elsewhere. "Quicken" has strong associations with a number of memorable biblical passages;[100] its stylistic register is an imperfect but effective parallel to

Tiutchev's Slavonicism *vnimat'* – to hark – "vnimai ikh pen'iu i molchi." As he paraphrases Tiutchev, Nabokov stays stylistically congruent.

How could Nabokov turn his back on this translation? Why did he disown it, refusing to reproduce it in his lifetime? The answer to this question may lift the veil over the transformation he was to undergo – his transition from someone who viewed Russian culture through the optics of national mythologems to someone equipped with an analytical perspective on such phenomena.

"Notes on Prosody" (1964) draws a line under Nabokov's lifelong fascination with the technical aspects of versification.[101] While it focuses on the syllabotonic system of versemaking, which was Pushkin's – as well as Nabokov's preferred medium of poetic expression – it features a discussion of its dissolution, a development he witnessed as he was staging his first experiments with meter and rhyme. This discussion concerns a tectonic shift in Russian prosody, which saw the triumphant emergence of "non-classical," asymmetrical accentual versification as an accepted medium of literary poetry, and assigns "Silentium" the position of honour:

> In Russian [accentual verse] did not come into general use until Blok … composed a number of magnificent short poems in it. But Tyutchev, as early as 1832 (in the poem *Silentium*, first published that year in *Molva*) had already inaugurated the musical gasp of mixed or broken meter, which he followed up by his Heinean *Last Love*, first published in 1854 (*Sovremennik*).[102]

While stressing the paramount importance of "Silentium," this statement contradicts everything we know about this poem in Nabokov's own previous literary, "paraphrastic" translations. As it was translated in *Three Russian Poets*, reproduced in *Pushkin, Lermontov, Tyutchev*, read at numerous public talks in both English and Russian, "Silentium" was a poem written in regular iambic tetrameter. The gap between its appearance in the earlier, "poetic" translation of 1941–3 and the same poem's description in 1964 is jarring. The solution to this problem comes from a close study of Nabokov's source text, the 1921 pocket-sized edition of Tiutchev's poems. The émigré edition he had trusted unconditionally until the 1950s was a reproduction of pre-revolutionary editions of Tiutchev's poems, which in their turn were based on earlier standardizations of that poet's irregular rhythms. Particularly noteworthy in this respect was the fate suffered by "Silentium": until Georgii Chulkov located the poem's autographs and restored the authorial version of its text and prosody in the 1920s, it was universally known in variants compromised by Tiutchev's well-meaning but incompetent editors. Sequestered as he was from the latest developments in Tiutchev studies in Soviet Russia, Nabokov did not doubt the authenticity of the text available to him until the late 1950s. It was then that he discovered that his translation of so influential a poetic text was based on a faulty source.

This episode helps us understand the ease with which Nabokov turned his back on not only the poetic versions of Russian classics but also such a successful work as "Speak not, lie hidden, and conceal." By transposing a compromised version of Tiutchev's text into sonorous English iambs, Nabokov unwittingly upheld a long-standing tradition of treating "Silentium" as a pinnacle of Tiutchev's meditative lyric poetry, but not as a runaway masterpiece of accentual prosody that presaged the fall of syllabotonic versification as the sole medium of Russian literary poetry. The idea that the syllabotonic system was the medium sanctified by Pushkin's authority and that departures from its five matrices were "broken" metres was the bedrock of the speculative notion of the Golden Age of Russian poetry. It was this notion that permeated and influenced Nabokov's individual cultural eschatology, according to which the emergence of "broken," "non-classical" metres not favoured by Pushkin or his illustrious contemporaries foreshadowed the fatal rupture of the continuum of Russian civilization in 1917.

Along with "Speak not, lie hidden, and conceal," "Love at the closing of our days / is apprehensive and very tender" – Nabokov's translation of Tiutchev's "Posledniaia liubov'" (1852–4) – is another pinnacle of his work in the literary, poetic, or "paraphrastic" mode. Like his version of "Silentium," "Last Love" is also incorporated into Nabokov's individual mythopoetics.

According to "Notes on Prosody" (1964), "Last Love" "followed up" on "Silentium's" employment of "the musical gasp of mixed or broken meter." As the discussion of "Silentium" has shown, Nabokov was not always aware that it was the earlier "Silentium" that became one of the earliest examples of a successful use of accentual verse in literary Russian poetry.[103] According to the incomplete knowledge at his disposal at the time when he worked on the *Three Russian Poets / Pushkin, Lermontov, Tyutchev* translations, however, it was "Last Love" – and emphatically *not* "Silentium," which he knew in a compromised and standardized version reproduced in his beloved *Stikhotvoreniia* – that "inaugurated the musical gasp of mixed or broken meter." In the alternative reality of Nabokov's individual mythopoetics, this error gave rise to a series of haunting images found in some of his most accomplished creations.

As late as 1952, when he addressed a group of New York–based Russian émigrés with an updated version of his 1931 Aleksandr Blok speech, Nabokov was firm in his understanding of the place "Last Love" had in the history of Russian poetry and poetics.[104] It was this poem and no other, he assured his listeners, that set into motion the sequence of events that enabled Blok's legitimization of accentual versification in his poetic praxis at the outset of the twentieth century. This certainty compelled Nabokov the university instructor to allot considerable time to the study of Tiutchev's introduction of an additional syllable into the second line of "Last Love" in his Russian literary courses as the earliest manifestation of the changes to come. The learning materials he prepared for his students show how much effort he invested in explicating the nature of this phenomenon and its consequences for Russian letters.[105] Based as it was on the erroneous assumption that "Last Love" was the point where the classical Pushkinian versification converged with its Nemesis accentual ("pausative," "broken" in Nabokov's emotional terminology), this certainty had a far-reaching effect, and not only on Nabokov's teaching and translation. *Invitation to a Beheading* (1935–6) illustrates this point with exceptional efficacy.

The action of the novel unfolds in Russia's distant future, long after the civilizational breakdown that was 1917 took its debilitating toll on the country's soul, depriving it of its creativity. Among the characteristics distinguishing Cincinnatus from his fellow citizens is his ability to experience poetry on a level inaccessible to his tormentors. It is with the aid of Tiutchev's "Last Love" that Nabokov demonstrates his protagonist's "atavistic" gift. As he reaches the second line of the poem that features the metrical aberration altering its initial iambic cadence into non-metrical – "broken" – accentual verse, Cincinnatus trips over the extra syllable introduced into the line and gasps, consumed by a "horror of death."[106] To grasp what the elusive image "passionate syncope" designates in Nabokov's individual mythopoetics, we should turn to the expanded 1952 version of his 1931 eulogy of Aleksandr Blok. Apart from letting us in on the secret of Nabokov's partiality to "Last Love," it introduces us to the entire host of associations that defined his cultural eschatology for decades. This individual eschatology forms a powerful subtext that runs through *Invitation to a Beheading* and affects an entire series of his most consequential compositions, including his Russian masterwork *The Gift*.[107]

The 1952 variant of the Blok speech proves that even five years after the publication of *Pushkin, Lermontov, Tyutchev*, Nabokov continued to labour under the misapprehension that "Last Love" held the key to the subsequent evolution of Russian poetics by prefiguring Blok's revolutionary changes via Afanasii Fet's mediation. Made prior to Nabokov's discovery of the actual place of "Posledniaia liubov'" in the history of Russian poetics – it was to be one of the many discoveries of his *Eugene Onegin* project – his English version "Last Love" carries that misapprehension in its compositional DNA. Irrelevant in the context of Anglophone poetics, in an English rendition of the poem this effect was impossible to replicate and had to be implied. In his "Last Love" Nabokov struggled to create a euphonious approximation of a prosodic feature to which he assigned so much significance:

> Love at the closing of our days
> is apprehensive and very tender.
> Glow brighter, brighter, farewell rays
> of one last love in its evening splendor.[108]

In his comparison of various English-language versions of this poem, Barry P. Scherr has shown that Nabokov, in striking contrast with the tenets of his subsequent literalist dogma, strives "to imitate nearly 'every formal element'" of the original, "down to the extra syllables in lines two and four." In Scherr's estimation, "the net effect" of Nabokov's translation creates "a quite different and less nuanced rhythm," which prevents him from "attaining perfection."[109] Scherr's comparison of no fewer than twelve versions of "Posledniaia liubov'" demonstrates that Nabokov's version was not merely that poem's first "formally precise [English] rendition" but also shows "the greatest sensitivity to the metrical quality of the original."[110]

No extant comparative analysis of the English versions of "Posledniaia liubov,'" however, accounts for the responsibility Nabokov assumed when he undertook to create his rendition of a poetic text he was so partial to due to his individual understanding of its aesthetics and significance. Scherr is justified in rebuking Nabokov for the wording of his translation's second line when he opines that "the 'very' before 'tender' in line 2 is not only unnecessary but strikes an immature note."[111] Yet the introduction of the adverb "very" into the line in question is no mere formal device permitting Nabokov to mimic the effect of the added syllable to what would otherwise have been a line of regular iambic tetrameter. Apart from lending itself to a translingual aural wordplay of *suevernyi* and "very," this intensifier grants the reader some sense of the aesthetic impact this metrical aberration had on the translator, his compatriots, and contemporaries. Imperfect and approximate as it is, this is a rendition of the "passionate syncope" – "passionate hiccupping" in the Russian original of *Invitation to a Beheading* – that Nabokov called "a sob that alters the entire history or Russian letters" in the 1952 version of his encomium to Aleksandr Blok. This is the reason behind Nabokov's placement of this superficially gratuitous adverb in this particular place in this particular line. Its excessiveness, its oddity is intentional and represents a calculated aural, lexical, and metrical effect that aims to prevent its English reader from treating it as any other line of verse.

Even against the background of "Speak not, lie hidden, and conceal" ("Silentium") and "Last Love," "Dusk" ("Sumerki," 1830–5) stands out as a singularly successful replication of its Russian model. Apart from preserving the original's trochaic tetrameter and its two-octave alternating rhyme structure, this translation conveys to the reader the poem's exuberant alliterativeness. Not content with a lexical description, Tiutchev depicts the arrival of darkness with a succession of devoiced consonants and sibilants, only to augment their hushing effect with a careful arrangement of recurring vowels dominated by drawn-out "oo's." As the second octave introduces and develops the theme of sleep and oblivion, Tiutchev's aural palette expands to an accumulation of recurring "l's."[112]

It is not an exaggeration to qualify Nabokov's solution to the challenge posed by this original as a triumph of his mode of poetic transposition. The aural imprint of the Russian poem is carefully transferred into the English in such a way that the succession of the same and similar sounds replicates the effect of their Russian counterparts with haunting efficacy.[113] This display of interlingual alliteration is a means to an end: "Sumerki" depicts a willful dissolution of discrete personhood in elemental non-existence. The poem's lyrical hero entreats "twilight" to absorb his consciousness until it ceases to reflect upon its own existence as an entity separate from primordial cosmic darkness. There is no mistaking Tiutchev's *unichtozhen'e* – "obliteration" – for anything other than death. What is remarkable about this interpretation of this eternal theme is its certainty that the dissolution of a thinking and feeling subject in nature is devoid of tragic implications.

Nabokov the lepidopterist could hardly have ignored the moth, heard and not seen in Tiutchev's first octave. Whereas "Sumerki" does not ascribe the distant noise to any specific source, "Dusk" connects this image with the humming of that unseen creature. It is not surprising that in the margin next to the poem's text Nabokov would draw a stout-bodied airborne insect, its wings rotating in a decidedly un-butterfly-like fashion, its proboscis probing a flower. The marginal note that appears below this picture and closer to the poem's mention of "obliteration," however, forces us to reconsider this seemingly insignificant detail.

The laconic note placed next to the Russian poem's two closing lines reads:

Joyce
Г.XV[114]

The name of the author of *Ulysses* is followed by the Cyrillic "G," which in conjunction with the Roman numerals "XV" signifies a Russian abbreviation of "G.[lava] XV," "Chapter XV." Incredible as it may seem, in "Sumerki" Nabokov discerned a parallel with so dissimilar, so distant a literary phenomenon as *Ulysses*. It may well be, however, that Tiutchev's invocation of a moth brought Nabokov closer to solving what he identified as one of the greatest mysteries of Joyce's novel.

Nabokov's *Ulysses* lectures follow the structure familiar to any modern reader of the novel, which numbers the chapters within its three parts. When numbered consecutively, however, "Chapter XV" corresponds to the novel's "bordello scene," or chapter 12/episode 15 ("Circe"). Nabokov's lectures brim with enlightening interpretations, but even he could not discern a reason behind the phantasmagoric manifestations accompanying Bloom's and Stephen's arrival at "the house of ill fame" in Nightown's Mabbot Street. To his students he explained this chapter as "a grotesque exaggeration of thoughts passing through the mind of Bloom: broken thoughts acting on a dim stage in a nightmare comedy" before confessing, "I do not know of any commentator who has correctly understood this chapter."[115] Nabokov's marginal notes to Tiutchev's "Sumerki" permit us to advance our idea of his personal appreciation of this episode's key sequence.[116]

In his lectures Nabokov breaks chapter 12/15 into a number of scenes, proceeding to summarize "scene 4" as follows: "In the house of ill-fame Bloom meets Stephen and Lynch. Various visions appear. The author conjures up Bloom's grandfather Leopold Virag."[117] Whether this is a mere apparition along the lines of Hamlet's vision of his vengeful father, whether Joyce wanted us to see this visitation as yet another one of the numerous grotesque jokes that crowd this scene, one thing is indubitable: this episode suggests that individual human consciousness survives death. More to the point of Nabokov's lifelong metaphysical concerns, the Leopold Virag scene depicts a discourse with a dead man. Virag's arrival is as grotesque as the rest of the scene: he "chutes rapidly down through the chimneyflue and struts two steps to the left on gawky pink stilts."[118] Nabokov had every reason to believe that this ghost's arrival was announced earlier in the chapter.

Following in Zoe Higgins's wake, Bloom crosses the threshold of Bella Cohen's establishment and proceeds to the music room. Joyce's "stage directions" provide the first detail of its decor as follows: "A shade of mauve tissuepaper dims the light of the chandelier. Round and round a moth flies, colliding, escaping."[119] After staying out of the narrator's focus for a few pages, the moth re-enters our field of vision as Virag prepares to weigh in on the subject of sex – more specifically, concerning men's fatal attraction to the opposite sex, which he delivers in his Hungarian-inflected English.[120]

Tiutchev's Russian moth put Nabokov in mind of the way its Irish relative was attracted to the mauve chandelier shade in Bella Cohen's brothel. Nabokov may have warned his students against "seeing in Leopold Bloom's humdrum wonderings ... a close parody of the *Odyssey*,"[121] but it is worth keeping in mind that Cohen's "house of ill-fame" corresponds to the palace of the enchantress Circe, who instructs Bloom's Homeric counterpart on the mysteries of the underworld. Superficially dissimilar to Joyce's *Ulysses*, Tiutchev's "Sumerki" delves into the same mysteries.

Ulysses's chapter 12 retains many of its secrets, yet some details of "scene 4" can be ascertained. Apart from Virag's parallel between the power of sex over men and the perilous attraction of artificial light sources to moths, this fragment features a discourse with a dead man and depicts a case of metempsychosis involving a moth. Whether Nabokov's parallel between Tiutchev's "Sumerki" and this aspect of Joyce's *Ulysses* advances our understanding of either text is open to question. What is indisputable, however, is that Nabokov discerned in them both a subject that was close to the heart of his metaphysical inquiry. This affords us a rare opportunity to move closer to the intentionality behind his painstakingly precise, yet individualized reproduction of "Sumerki."

"Dusk" takes a cue from Tiutchev's metaphysical poem to envision a situation where human consciousness may continue to exist past the point of its dissolution in the impersonal universal darkness. Furthermore, the kinship Nabokov discerned between "Sumerki" and *Ulysses* suggests that "Dusk" interprets Tiutchev's poem as a depiction of a ghostly visitation in which a flying insect impersonates the incorruptible soul of a dead person in the manner of a Shakespearean "glow-worm" (directly referenced here) and that of Virag's song ("I'm a tiny tiny thing," etc.).[122] "Sumerki" reconciles individual consciousness with death, its ostensible limit, by suggesting that it is in fact a liberation that leads to a reunification with the universal soul. "Dusk" develops this theme by resolutely interpreting Tiutchev's moth as a Joycean vision of a metempsychic visitation, and this is the point of both Nabokov's marginal notes to his Russian source text as well as its English reincarnation.

"The Abyss" ("Sviataia noch' na nebosklon vzoshla"; 1850) develops the subject of "Sumerki" still further. Sunset confronts the individual contemplating it with the "abysmal pit" hidden under the "golden carpet" of day. Unlike "Speak not, lie hidden, and conceal" ("Silentium"), "Last Love," and "Dusk," this equimetrical and equilinear English replica of a Russian model stops short of following the alternating rhyming of its Russian model, in a sign that Nabokov wanted more freedom to reproduce the original's meaning. The second stanza of "The Abyss" follows its model in focusing the reader's attention on the limitations of human reason in its confrontation with unfathomable universal mysteries:

> Gone vision-like is the external world,
> and man, a homeless orphan, has to face
> in utter helplessness, naked, alone,
> the blackness of immeasurable space.[123]

Like "Dusk," the poem's closing quatrain suggests a resolution of this tension:

> All life and brightness seem an ancient dream –
> while in the very substance of the night,

unraveled, alien, he now perceives
a fateful something that is his by right.[124]

This quatrain's concluding lines imply that the greater formal freedom gained from Nabokov's replacing the alternating rhyming of the original with the partial one of his translation did not permit him to sustain its lexical cohesion throughout. "Something" is too pale a contextual equivalent to "legacy" (*nasled'e*), impoverished as it is by its appearance after so elevated a modifier as "fateful."

"Autumn" is Nabokov's take on Tiutchev's masterpiece in the verbal landscape genre, "Est' v oseni pervonachal'noi" (1857). The poem offers respite from the symbolism of the previous depictions of nature in this selection, as its portrayal of Indian summer is unburdened by metaphorical significance. While this translation does put on display Nabokovian attention to form when it follows Tiutchev's variable iambs and mirrors his two quatrains of alternating rhyming with one featuring enclosed rhymes, it misses the opportunity to convey one Tiutchevian mannerism. Nabokov was aware of Tiutchev's habit of introducing similes and comparisons with the prosaic turn of speech *kak by*: after noting it in his copy of *Stikhotrovreniia* next to the second quatrain of "Slëzy," Nabokov made a point of preserving it with the aid of the English cliché "as it were."[125] With its "Ves' den' stoit kak by khrustal'nyi" ("All day looks as if it were made of crystal"), the opening quatrain of "Est' v oseni pervonachal'noi" provides the translator of "Tears" with an opportunity to represent this same feature of the authorial style in another translation. Without ignoring the feature altogether, in "Autumn" Nabokov settles on "All day 'tis like some precious prism," with "'tis like" being the equivalent of *kak by*.

This translation highlights Tiutchev's verbal acuity: the second quatrain of his miniature landscape zeroes in on a single spider web sparkling on an "vacant furrow" (*prazdnaia borozda*). After highlighting this stanza in *Stikhotvoreniia*, Nabokov provided it with a graceful rendition: "Alone a silky filament / across the idle furrow gleams." This luminous detail notwithstanding, "Autumn" does not succeed in preserving its model's melancholic tonality, becoming a rather matter-of-fact replication of Tiutchevian scenery.

Like its predecessor "Est' v oseni pervonachal'noi," "Uspokoenie" (1830) depicts nature's creativity in action. Unlike its predecessor, it conveys no melancholy mood. This poem is a triumphant paean to nature's magnificence, which shows a different angle of the quintessentially

Tiutchevian personification of nature. A sign of Nabokov's heightened partiality toward a translated work, the two-quatrain-long "Appeasement" is a precise metrical and strophic replica of the model that preserves its rhyme scheme. The lexical asymmetry of this translation manifests itself already in the opening line, which replaces Tiutchev's Slavic mythological reference to "lightening bolts" as *peruns* with Thor, the Norse god of thunder and weather.

On 20 March 1952, at Harvard University, Nabokov read a selection of his translations as well as their originals, one of which was "Appeasement." In his spoken afterword he admitted taking liberties with the original and explained his decision to "specify" some of the original images:

> I have done something here that a perfect translator should not do. I have sinned in this translation, but I have sinned lovingly, I have sinned tenderly. For reasons of connotation and association, I have preferred to specify the "feathered creatures," which is all the original has in the way of birds, because I wanted the actual birds of the Russian woodland that Tyutchev had in mind, to burst into song here, as they would at this point in a Russian reader's perception. Moreover, I have improved upon the closing rainbow by throwing wide open its iridescent parenthesis. The sound of the Russian word for "rainbow," which is *raduga,* shimmers with allusions to radiance, gladness, paradise – which the sound of the English "rainbow" does not do. Despite the meaningful prism of its seven different letters (for the seven colours), English "rainbow" suggests an umbrella rather than a sunshade.[126]

What is striking about this afterword is that more than a decade following the publication of "The Art of Translation" (1941) and only three years before the appearance of "Problems of Translation: *Onegin* in English," Nabokov remained loyal to the speculative and elusive notion of "the perfect translator," that earlier proclamation's centrepiece. Equally noteworthy is his admission that his digressions from the original barred his work from attaining "perfection." Similarly notable is his couching of this admission in the sanctimonious rhetoric of "sinning" and "tender love."

Nabokov continues to imply that he and his author are intimate interlocutors; that, coupled as it is with a superb understanding of the original's context and implications, his "tender love" for the original absolves him of the sin of infidelity to it. As he clings to the notion of a special relationship that connects the artist-translator with his confrère, he admits that it is premised on a major fallacy. If a translation is a work of art, it is autonomous from its model and cannot be criticized for infidelity. While his special relationship with the author absolves him of his "sins," the boundaries where such sinning ceases to be a product of love and tenderness become too loose to be defined with any degree of certainty. This point is best illustrated by the one liberty Nabokov chooses not to discuss, his replacement of the Tiutchevian Slavonicism *peruny* with "Thor" in the poem's opening quatrain. Both Perun and Thor belong to the pre-Christian pantheons of two related pagan traditions, yet it is difficult to imagine Tiutchev the Slavophile giving his confrère a beyond-the-grave blessing to replace a Russian deity in what that translator himself admits to be a depiction of a quintessentially Russian backdrop. No rainbow can distract us from the realization that this liberty takes the translation one step too far from the original.

"Tears," which closes the Tiutchev selection in *Three Russian Poets/ Pushkin, Lermontov, Tyutchev*, renders the single-stanza "Slëzy liudskiia, o, slëzy liudskiia" (ca. 1849). In his 1975 survey of the extant English translations from Tiutchev, R.C. Lane called Nabokov's work "remarkable" but noted that "it falls short of its author's usual standard of fidelity to the original."[127] The "usual standard" signifies literalism – like so many others before and after, this critic turns Nabokov's subsequent methodology against a translation that adheres to a radically different, earlier set of principles.

"Tears" is part of a selection that spotlights Tiutchev's ability to relate to nature while making nature relevant to the cycles of human suffering. In more than one respect it counterbalances the earlier eponymous piece: where the expansive earlier poem exemplified the author's youthful exuberance, its later, terser counterpart bids the reader farewell with a "song of experience." "Tears" particularizes Tiutchev's vague references to the recurrence of suffering in human life: to his "l'ëtes' vy rannei i pozdnei poroi," Nabokov has "you that flow / when life is begun – or half-gone."[128] As was the case with "Appeasement," in "Tears" Nabokov sought to develop a potential concealed in Tiutchev's image according to his individual understanding of that image: this translation is an imaginative depiction of a Tiutchev who surveys his past as he senses the approach of his life's end.

Three Russian Poets and *Pushkin, Lermontov, Tyutchev*, with their witty biographic cameos and vivid versions of the originals, are fine learning tools for those with little or no Russian. They would have continued to enjoy this status had not the logic of Nabokov's development as translator put them at odds with his later, far less forgiving standards. Behind the backs of the three poets whose busts adorn the *Pushkin, Lermontov, Tyutchev* cover,[129] this development was well underway as the work on these English versions of Russian classics propelled their translator and compiler further along in his reconsideration of his methods. Any discussion of the results of this reconsideration, however, must take into account not only the published works but also the pool of materials from which they emerged. The published selections distilled a prodigious amount of the translations Nabokov had produced during his years of teaching at Wellesley, Harvard, and Cornell without exhausting that pool. Those numerous works constitute a body of documents no study of Nabokov's life in translation can afford to ignore.

Nabokov's surveys of Russian poetry revolved around Pushkin, but he made a great effort to equip his students with a good idea of the poet's context, his forerunners and contemporaries. His commentary on *Eugene Onegin* absorbed many but far from all attempts to that end. Expansive as it was, it could not include the side effects of these efforts, some of which are as fascinating as the works themselves.

In his *Eugene Onegin* commentary, Nabokov mentions Konstantin Batiushkov (1787–1855) as a literary pioneer and Pushkin's senior contemporary "to whose idiom Pushkin owed at least as much as he did to the style of Karamzin and Zhukovski."[130] A Batiushkov translation incorporated into the *Eugene Onegin* commentary is a reminder that there is much more to such a bastion of literalism as the *Eugene Onegin* four-volume set than meets the eye.

Nabokov's translation of Batiushkov's "little masterpiece"[131] "Do you recall the cry" ("Ty pomnish, chto izrek" [Do you recall what uttered]; ca. 1821) is a fine introduction to the lesser-known materials of his preliteralist period. It is also a perfect miniature model that shows how translation motivated him to create. Nabokov was clearly captivated by the legend behind this separate-standing stanza: Batiushkov allegedly composed it during a brief spell of lucidity amid a long period of mental illness. This epigram is a grave pronouncement on the lot of human beings who live and die in bondage and whose demise provides them with no reason for their suffering. Upon creating a striking equimetric, equilinear, and rhymed version of the poem, Nabokov felt compelled to respond to it with the least likely parody this poem could engender – a political one:

Said old Melchizedek: the tyrant Nero
was born a zero and will die a zero,
and none can tell why in this vale of tears
he governs, grunts, oppresses, disappears.

This miniature may have been entitled "parody,"[132] but it is more than a humorous take on Batiushkov's original. While we may never be able to ascertain the exact date of its composition, dating it "soon after 4 March 1953," cannot be far off: it is safe to assume that what we are dealing with here is Nabokov's response to the news of Joseph Stalin's death.

The selection that Nabokov presented in response to a suggestion of the British Broadcasting Corporation (BBC) to make an audio recording of his Pushkin translations in 1954 is both surprising and revealing. In the script of that radio talk, the shorter "Upas Tree" and "No hands have wrought my monument" ("Exegi monumentum") frame an expansive rendition of "Vnov' ia posetil" (1835). Made in late 1948 at the bidding of Nicolas Nabokov, who wanted to set it to music, this translation furthers our understanding of "The Art of Translation."[133]

Those familiar with this poem in modern editions will discover that Nabokov's version reads nothing like the ruminative but optimistic piece that ends in a famous salutation of a young generation: "Zdravstvyi plemia / Mladoe, neznakomoe!" (Hail to thee, young, unfamiliar tribe!). Nabokov's version extends the length of the poem's "familiar" text by some seventeen lines, transforming it into a "morose brooding" on a "misspent youth" and "censure well deserved, despite its harshness." It closes with what may be seen as the most un-Pushkinian of pronouncements: "and deep in me there welled most bitter feelings."[134] Pushkin as a morose, embittered man, Pushkin who accepts that his banishment to his ancestral seat Mikhailovskoe was "well deserved" is a Pushkin that few of his admirers would accept, used as they are to the simplistic image of the sun-god of Russian letters.

This version of Pushkin's blank-verse soliloquy resurrects and improves the variant found in Semën Vengerov's 1910 edition of the poet's collected works, which Nabokov would have known from his youth.[135] Could it be that by turning to Modeste Hofmann's study of Pushkin's unpublished texts of 1922, which featured an overview the poem's surviving fragments, Nabokov sought to breathe new life into a long-superseded reading of the poem he knew and perhaps preferred as a young man?[136]

Before he shared this translation with his BBC listeners, Nabokov alerted them to its prosodic fidelity: "I have followed here very closely the cut of Pushkin's unrhymed iambic pentameter."[137] Unburdened by the exigencies associated with a rhyming original and encouraged by the expansive range of Pushkin's pentameters, Nabokov created a translation that took full advantage of his formidable experience of rendering Pushkinian blank verse into English. Such lexemes as "meseems" and "but yesternight" (for *vechór eshchë*) build a stylistic bridge between this later text and the earlier versions of the "little tragedies" to form a distinct linguistic personality; further on Nabokov demonstrates that he continues to view the Pushkinian art of alliteration an integral part of the poet's style. The poem's second fragment contains a scintillating example of Pushkinian onomatopoeia: the line "znakomym shumom shorokh ikh vershin" creates the aural image of a rustling sound made by pine trees in the wind. Not content with the initial version of "[the tall pines'] friendly summits soughing in the wind," Nabokov the translator casts aside any pretense at his invisibility to enter Pushkin's text in person:

> (Or even closer to the poet's text:
> "So old a sound – the soughing of their crests" …
> Here, incidentally, to interrupt
> my version for an instant, I have tried
> to match Pushkinian alliteration –
> "znakómïm shúmom shóroh ih vershín
> menyá privétstvoval …" or in my version:
> "So old a sound – the soughing of their crests").[138]

Nabokov made this interpolation at least twice: when he read this translation at Harvard in 1952, and in his 1954 radio talk for BBC. He does not break his promise to follow "very closely the cut of Pushkin's unrhymed iambic pentameter" – it is as if the patchwork nature of this text licensed him to enter it lest his listeners miss the point of Pushkin's onomatopoeic prowess. Entertaining and edifying in equal measure, this display of Nabokovian showmanship hardly elucidates his decision to show Pushkin at his most morose and pessimistic. Does he set this textual Frankenstein free without worrying about the consequences of misrepresenting Pushkin to those without an extensive knowledge of the poet?

Nabokov's version exhibits a slight semantic asymmetry when it interprets "the little dwelling of disfavour" (*opal'nyi domik*) as a "modest house of exile" at the beginning of the poem's second section. In this translation "banishment," "exile," and "nostalgia" (for *grust'*, sadness) join forces to remind us of a major thematic link between Pushkin and his translator Nabokov – the fact that they are both poets of exile. Much like Nabokov's short story "The Visit to the Museum" (1939), this expanded version of "Vnov' ia posetil" confronts its reader with a strong suggestion that any attempts to recapture one's past are not merely futile but fraught with peril. The lyrical hero of Nabokov's "Return of Pushkin" gives in to nostalgia and falls victim to the least productive of emotions, longing for something irretrievably gone. Nabokov, who at the same time was working on his memoir, was careful not to let himself be carried away by nostalgia, insisting instead that his exploration of his past was aimed at determining life's hidden patterns. The narrator in *Eugene Onegin* rejoices at every opportunity to point out differences distinguishing himself from his protagonist; Nabokov, who enters "The Return of Pushkin" in person, maintains a similar distance from the overall emotional tonality of the poem, which swallows its narrator whole at its end.

The *Eugene Onegin* commentary introduces Vasilii Zhukovskii (1783–1852) as "Pushkin's life-long friend, a prudent mediator in our poet's clashes with the government, and his amiable teacher in matters of prosody and poetical idiom."[139] To Nabokov, Zhukovskii was no mere face in the crowd of Pushkin's contemporaries. Coupled with a genuine poetic talent, Zhukovskii's inability to generate original content and a constant quest for subject matter in translation fascinated Nabokov, who, in a constant quest for subject matter in translation, made his students analyse the various ways in which Zhukovskii's transformative adaptations had a strong ameliorating effect on Russian poetry. While Nabokov the teacher spared no effort demonstrating the ways in which Zhukovskii's renditions of Thomas Campbell, Walter Scott, and Robert Southey became different and in some ways finer than their originals, Nabokov the thinker observed how Zhukovskii's individual spirituality percolated through such retellings. This is what happened when he confronted his students with his explication of "Golos s togo sveta" (Voice from Another World; 1815), Zhukovskii's version of Friedrich Schiller's "Wo ich sei, und wo mich hingewendet."[140]

Nabokov rendered two key quatrains of Schiller's twenty-four-line piece into an artless lexical crib that made no attempt to sound poetic. Its purpose was to show the thematic potential not only irresistible to Zhukovskii the translator but congenial to Zhukovskii the spiritualist.

In Schiller's original, the spirit of a dead woman assuages the fears of those left wondering what has happened to her soul after her death; according to her, death is an eternal union with the deceased. Zhukovskii develops it into a much more elaborate and affecting vision – and this is precisely what Nabokov strives to highlight to his students. In "Golos s togo sveta," a dead woman addresses the quick not simply to dispel their fear of dying but to affirm faith in the ultimate benevolence of the universe. As befits a revelation, the poem is not without its cryptic moments, and at one such point Nabokov comes to his students' aid to elucidate a metaphysical key point:

Нашла ли их? Сбылись ли ожиданья?
Без страха верь; обмана сердцу нет;
Сбылося всё; я в стороне свиданья;
И знаю здесь, сколь ваш прекрасен свет.

[Have you found them? Have [our] expectations been confirmed? / Fearlessly believe; the heart will not be deceived; / Everything has been realized; I am in the land of rendezvous; / And I know *here* how beautiful *your* world is.]

What is the logical antecedent of the "them" found in the first line of the poem's second quatrain? Intriguingly enough, the preceding quatrain provides no explanation. Since Zhukovskii's poem is the dead woman's response to the questions posed by her implied interlocutors, readers must work this riddle out by themselves. The solution toward which Nabokov steered his students can only be taken as a manifestation of his lifelong fascination with the question of whether human individuality could preserve its integrity after death:

Have I found them [the dead]? Have hopes been realized?
Fearlessly believe; no deception awaits the heart;
All has been fulfilled; I am in the land where soul meets soul
and I know *here* how beautiful *your* world is.

It may seem artless due to its lack of effort to mimic the majority of the original formal attributes, but this translation communicates more than a simple crib might have, or perhaps should have, done. Nabokov elaborates a theme singularly close to his heart, that of communication with the dead. His students did not need to worry about the significance of the mystery pronoun; Zhukovskii's evasive "meeting place" becomes a vast "land where soul meets soul." Apart from illustrating the movement and development of a given theme from Schiller's original to Zhukovskii's adaptation of it, the ostensibly unpoetic crib proves to be a statement of interest on the translator's part by recalling one of the earliest translations Nabokov ever made, his version of Petrarch's "Se lamentar augelli, o verdi fronde."

According to Nabokov, Pushkin regarded Evgenii Baratynskii (1800–44) "with a tender and grave respect … unique in the annals of the greater poet's literary sympathies";[141] to his students he introduced him as "the victim of intellect, of analytical knowledge," a pessimist affected by mankind's "inexorable movement away from nature."[142] To illustrate this point Nabokov prepared prose renditions of his "Na chto vy, dni! Iudol'nyi mir iavlen'ia" (1840; "What use are ye, Days! The earthly world will not change its phenomena") and "Vsë mysl' da mysl'! Khudozhnik bednyi slova!" (1840; "Ideas and nothing but ideas! Poor artist of words").

To facilitate his students' appreciation of Baratynskii's intellectualism, Nabokov strips these masterpieces of Russian contemplative poetry of all their verse decorum. Far from losing their poetic qualities, however, the resulting texts become effective specimens of prose poetry. Shorn of their stanzaic and metrical properties, these translations continue to shine as distillations of Baratynskii's thoughts. The second stanza of "Na chto vy, dni! Iudol'nyi mir iavlen'ia" provides a particularly eloquent example of this transformation:

> Не даром ты металась и кипела,
> Развитием спеша;
> Свой подвиг ты свершила прежде тела,
> Безумная душа![143]

In Nabokov's version Baratynskii's apostrophy loses nothing of its poetic sheen; if this is prose, the intensity of its tropes, its elevated lexical register ensures that it cannot be mistaken for anything but poetry:

> Not in vain, oh my foolish soul, hast thou tossed and seethed, madly hurrying on in thy development: thou hast outrun the body in this race.[144]

Those seeking to trace the logic of Nabokov's development as translator will not fail to recognize in these prosaic retellings of poetic originals the signposts marking the outer limit of the lengths he was prepared to travel in search of the perfect way to render poetry in a foreign language. Such a bastion of Nabokovian literalism as *Eugene Onegin* retains more of its model's form than these radical experiments, whereas these two translations refocus their readers' attention on the ideas they formulate.

Before his conversion to the literalist dogma, however, Nabokov was not prepared to dwell in the rarified atmosphere of the world of ideas for long. "To His Wife" (ca. 1949), his version of Baratynskii's "Svoenravnoe prozvan'e" (1831–2), renders into sprightly English trochees one of that poet's sunniest pieces. As Nabokov's title makes clear, this poem is a celebration of conjugal bliss: without giving anything away, the poet shares with the world his joy at finding a fitting pet name for his beloved wife. Baratynskii would not have been himself, however, had even the most light-hearted of his works not disclose at some point or other a rich metaphysical substratum. A pet name that means nothing beyond the poet's household – or perhaps even beyond the closed doors of his and his wife's bedchamber – may prove to be immeasurably more useful at performing the task words are supposed to perform in the first place:

In the world beyond the tombstone …
thus Eternity I'll welcome,
thus 'mid stars will I exclaim,
and your soul to mine will flutter
on the light wings of that name.[145]

Baratynskii the metaphysical poet shows his true colours as soon as his gaze shifts from domestic bliss set in the phenomenal world to that realm whose existence cannot be ascertained empirically. Love and tenderness are the only means of projecting one's metaphysical certainty that pure reason cannot validate, and it is here where Baratynskii happily surrenders his scholarly judgment to irrational faith.

If Nabokov's version of Zhukovskii's "Golos s togo sveta" displays a curious affinity with that of Petrarch's "Se lamentar augelli, o verdi fronde," then his sonorous poetic translation of Baratynskii's "Svoenravnoe prozvan'e" bears close similarity with the translations he made with no intention of getting them published. There is every reason to suspect that the impetus to translate this poem came not from his classroom, but rather from his recognition in Baratynskii's celebration of his wife the kind of spousal affection Nabokov was blessed with himself. His translation of Baratynskii's paean to his beloved Anastasiia Baratynskaia, née Engelhart, may well have in mind another poet's wife, Véra Nabokov.[146] As a vestige of Nabokov's dialogic encounter with Baratynskii, this emulation of Baratynskii's celebration of his eternal union with his wife displays early signs of things to come, such as John Shade's celebration of his wife Sybil in *Pale Fire*. It is in that poem's canto 2 where Baratynskii's "fanciful caress" from "To His Wife" will inspire John Shade's call to Sybil, "Come and be worshiped, come and be caressed," in what is one of the most transparently autobiographic, if fictional, expressions of the writer's love for his wife.[147]

It is *Lolita* that preserves the most prominent trace of Nabokov's dialogic engagement with Baratynskii's "Svoenravnoe prozvan'e." As that novel moves toward its dénoument, its protagonist Humbert Humbert has to grapple with a revelation that iterary refinement, as he realizes to his dismay, is far from being a characteristic distinguishing this self-appointed "bewitched traveller" from the unsophisticated. This occurs when Humbert's fortunate doppelgänger, Clare Quilty, taunts him by leaving a trail of literary allusions in a series of motel guestbooks where Quilty had stayed during his pursuit of Humbert and Dolores Haze. In chapter 23 Humbert discovers that Dolores – the "Lolita" of his nightmarish "confessional" narrative – divulged the pet names that Humbert had lavished upon her to Quilty:

> … my Carmen had betrayed my *pathetic endearments* to the impostor.[148]

Nabokov's autotranslation of *Lolita* (1967) discloses the Russian substratum of the phrase "pathetic endearments" by employing a conspicuous allusion to Baratynskii's "Svoenravnoe prozvan'e":

> … моя маленькая Кармен выдала негодяю жалкий шифр ласковых имен и *своенравных прозваний*, которые я ей давал.[149]

The expansively assymetric Russian rendition of a sparse English phrase approximates the brand of literary allusiveness that forms such an inalienable feature of *Lolita*'s evocative style. Unbeknownst to the Russian reader, it crowns an entire series of references to Baratynskii's "Svoenravnoe prozvan'e" in Nabokov's usage.[150]

The problem of the sources of Nabokov's translations during his period of "gentle and loving sinning" looms large on the horizon of every student of his legacy in this field. Today we know of and have access to his personal copies of Pushkin and Tiutchev and are aware of the fact that his sentimental attachment to these objects sometimes ran against his better judgment. Believing that translation was a form of intellectual *confrérie,* Nabokov frequently acted on his emotions when he chose to translate this or that specimen of Russian verse for his classes. This is best illustrated by his translation of Aleksei Kol'tsov's "Chto ty spish', muzhichok?" (1839).

Nabokov's referential field may have stretched across no fewer than six literary traditions, yet the multilingual writer and scholar who explicated Austen's *Mansfield Park,* Joyce's *Ulysses,* Kafka's *Verwandlung,* and Proust's *À la recherche du temps perdu* never lost site of a Kol'tsov peasant ballad he had known since childhood.[151] When he included "Chto ty spish', muzhichok?" in his survey of Russian literature, he did not merely seek to introduce his students to this specimen of folk literature, he was sharing with them a prominent source of inspiration for his own compositions. Nabokov's attachment to Kol'tsov transpires from his introductory remarks on the poet, whom he considered worthy of mention "even in the most concise survey of early nineteenth century on account of his not very strong but very authentic and original genius."[152] So entranced was Nabokov by "Chto ty spish', muzhichok?" and its tale of otherworldly intrusion into the life of an unremarkable human that he attempted to reset Keats's "La Belle Dame Sans Merci" into a similar idiom on account of the two ballads' similarity in 1921; so affected was he by its distinct formal characteristics that he reserved a place for it in *The Gift.*[153]

Nabokov drafted "Why do you sleep, little peasant?," his unrhymed lexical version of "Chto ty spish', muzhichok?," in the margins of a humble intermediate Russian language reader compiled by George Z. Patrick (1945).[154] Fond as he was of its "elementary anapaests," he wanted his students to focus on "that delightful poem's" story rather than its form. The entire ballad is an appeal "addressed 'to the little peasant' – 'mujichok' – not a young peasant of course, but to a shabby, undersized poorish farmer who inexplicably sleeps through the spring when all farm work should be begun. The *domovoi,* the house goblin, manages the house, dusting the barns, giving away the peasant's horses for the debts he owes his neighbors."[155] The unrhymed, lexical translation also gave Nabokov a chance to dwell on the minutia of peasant existence: when in the final stanza the ballad's speaker mentions how the protagonists' neighbours drink homebrew from traditional cups ("brazhku kovshikom p'iut"), in addition to translating this line as "fill their dippers with ale," Nabokov drew a *kovsh*. By translating the ballad and emphasizing its unique features to his students, Nabokov the teacher addressed a minor but remarkable literary phenomenon, while Nabokov the writer revisited an old confrère. "Chto ty spish', muzhichok?" is one of the least appreciated literary pretexts of Nabokov's extraordinary interest in ghost stories. A key component of the optics through which he examined Keats's "La Belle Dame Sans Merci," this modest ballad sent far-reaching ripples detectable in such complex and accomplished works as *Lolita* and *Pale Fire*.[156]

Nabokov's selection of Tiutchev translations grew considerably from *Three Russian Poets* to *Pushkin, Lermontov, Tyutchev*, but as if to prove that he meant business when he said in a public talk that "one would have liked to render all his poems – at least, all his non-political ones,"[157] he continued to work in that direction even after the publication of the two booklets. His SLAVIC 150 study materials expand the existing selection with the addition of "My soul would like to be a star" ("Dusha khotela b byt' zvezdoi"; 1829), "Through the azure haze of the night" ("Al'py" ["Skvoz' lazurnyi sumrak nochi"]; 1830), "She sat on the floor" ("Ona sidela na polu"; ca. 1859), and "The sky is overcast with slow" ("Nochnoe nebo tak ugriumo"; 1865). Even if we ignore the sundry shards of Tiutchev's lyrics in the *Eugene Onegin* commentary, we cannot overlook "One cannot understand her with the mind," Nabokov's rhyming take on the notorious "Umom Rossii ne poniat'" (1866), omitted from his teaching materials but surviving in his copy of Tiutchev's poems and also in a letter to Mikhail Karpovich.[158] Even with the notable omission of "Umom Rossii ne poniat'," Nabokov's 1952 teaching materials augment his students' idea of Tiutchev the visionary and Tiutchev the nature worshipper with a glimpse of Tiutchev the man of passion.

"The sky is overcast with slow" is not to be found in either of the published booklets, but in his public talks Nabokov made a point of introducing it as a translation of his "favorite Tyutchev poem – the one about the deaf-mute daemons." This poem is an outstanding example of a Tiutchevian way of personifying nature's awesome forces along the lines of Hellenic pantheism. It captures the onset and outbreak of a violent rainstorm; occurring at night, it inspires the poet with its terrifying show of thunder and lightning. It takes a Tiutchev, however, to interpret such an event as a non-verbal discourse of titanic proportions. "Kak demony glukhonemye, / Vedut besedu mezh soboi" – "As deaf-and-mute demons / Conduct a conversation among themselves" – the striking simile that concludes the poem's first octave is deservedly famous. By taking a cue from his confrère Tiutchev's book, Nabokov the lifelong synaesthete develops this simile still further: his translation features "demons deaf and dumb" conversing "in alphabetic light."[159]

Nabokov's "alphabetic light" is no mere variation on a theme provided by Tiutchev's simile. Interplay of lights and colours as a form of communication – it should not be forgotten that while Nabokov possessed "a fine case of colored hearing," before he assigned colours to sounds, he spoke of the letters of the alphabet – brings Nabokov's readers closer to his personal convictions regarding this gift's significance. In chapter 2 of *Speak, Memory*, where he introduces his readers to his synaesthesia, he refers to its manifestations as "leakings and drafts" in the less-than-solid "walls" that surround his being.[160] If these "leakings and drafts" brought him a vague sense of a wider world beyond the walls of his existence, his development of Tiutchev's "alphabetic" outbursts of sheet lightning expresses a premonition that the "very secret thing" that is "being settled in the sky" of the poem's second and closing octave is a sign that nature is full of meaning. Nabokov's translation of his "favourite" Tiutchev in itself becomes a communicative act, a discourse conducted by two metaphysical thinkers who seek to find a fitter description of the secret language discernable in nature by the means available to them as poets.

Next to the equimetrical, equilinear, rhyming translation of "Nochnoe nebo tak ugriumo," Nabokov's version of "Ona sidela na polu" seems barren, prosaic. This poem's subject matter makes it a fitting addition to a selection of Tiutchev's poems that puts so much emphasis on "Posledniaia liubov'." A crown jewel of the "Denis'eva cycle" Nabokov alludes to in his preamble to his Tiutchev selection, it showcases Tiutchev's ability to discern metaphysical import in life's least inspiring phenomena. "She sat on the floor" depicts a woman who pores over some love letters, only to be reminded that they are mere embers of an extinguished passion. It is Tiutchev's comparison of her gaze to the expression that must be discernible in the eyes of souls abandoning this world that renders this poem unforgettable.

It is difficult to avoid the impression that Nabokov came to the conclusion that this extraordinary poem's union of form and significance could not be recreated in another language. This experienced poet-translator with a sophisticated palette of time-proven strategies at his disposal could have experimented with partial rhyming, an extended or curtailed metre. Instead he proceeded with a stark equilinear recounting:

> She took those familiar pages
> and passing strange was the way she looked at them:
> so spirits look from above
> at the bodies they have shed …
> In silence I stood apart
> and was ready to fall on my knees
> full of awe and sadness,
> as if I were in the presence of some dear ghost.[161]

Stark as this foreign-language deconstruction of Tiutchev's poem is, its readers will discern that it is not altogether devoid of Nabokovian artifice. Tiutchev's single adverb *divno* (marvellously, wonderfully, miraculously) balloons in this version into an entire idiom, "passing strange." Appearing in a translation of a Russian poem, this haunting phrase invokes a host of associations, showcasing the way a Bakhtinian "alien word" transfigures a text into which it has been introduced as a "verbal vestige." By incorporating into his translation a lexeme unique to Othello's story of Desdemona's love ("She swore, in faith, 'twas strange, 'twas passing strange," act 1, scene 3), Nabokov sought to convey to his students the intensity of Tiutchev's tragic pathos – and also place it on the level of artistic perfection where it belonged.

"Through the azure haze of the night" renders "Al'py" ("Skvoz' lazurnyi sumrak nochi") in what is a penultimate instalment of the second – expanded – selection of Tiutchev's poems in Nabokov's translation not published in his lifetime. This juxtaposition of "the snowy Alps" – their "dead glazed eyes" expressing "icy horror" as they sleep in a "terrible slumber" of "fallen kings" – with the vivifying rays of the sunrise coming from the east has more to it than meets the gaze of a reader used to interpreting Tiutchev's depictions of nature as grand metaphysical parables. Nabokov professed a strong dislike for Tiutchev's political poems, but made an exception for this allegory of the confrontation between the east and the west, where the former is a source of light and rejuvenation and the latter of apathy and decline. A characteristically Tiutchevian choice of the Slavonic lexical register, the phrase "ventsy iz zlata" in the poem's second and last octave reinforces the metonymical association of the east with the source of the "legitimate" monarchic order which in the original "stands resurrected" ("I blestit v ventsakh iz zlata / Vsia voskresshaia sem'ia"). Lecture notes taken by Nabokov's Harvard students show that he was much more interested in drawing their attention to the "unusual imagery" of Tiutchev's contrasting of night and day, of east and west, than on the political implications of this allegory so close to the heart of the Slavophile poet. Like the previous component in this selection, this translation makes no attempt to echo the trochaic tetrameter carefully scanned in Nabokov's copy of Tiutchev's poems.[162]

Nabokov took the same approach to the last poem in his expanded selection, "My soul would like to be a star" ("Dusha khotela b byt' zvezdoi"; 1829). Not exactly a prose recounting of the original along the lines of Baratynskii's philosophical pieces discussed above, Nabokov's translation of this octave-like miniature preserves its line count without venturing to carry over its iambic tetrameter and rhyme. Nabokov instructed his students to pay close attention to Tiutchev's subtle eroticization of his juxtaposition of "naked night vs. veiled day" while inviting them to compare its astral imagery with that of William Blake in such pieces as "To the Evening Star" (1783).

The expanded selection of Tiutchev's poems ends with a melancholic piece expressing the soul's longing for absolute and sublime serenity in the astral realm. The sum of these poems does succeed in attaining the goal Nabokov set for himself when he declared Tiutchev a kindred spirit to Blake, Hopkins, and Housman. Nabokov's Tiutchev joins their club as an equal, an avid worshipper of nature and passionate lover with a sensitive soul, a poet capable of verbalizing his individual insight into the areas inaccessible to reason. On the one hand, Nabokov the translator downplays other aspects of Tiutchev's personality, setting aside his nationalism and conservatism, but on the other, he assigns much significance to his groundbreaking formal experimentation.

The prevalence of unrhymed translations among later pieces suggests that what we are dealing with here is not an aberration or a whim, but perhaps a tendency. In a sure sign of a major change underway, unrhymed recountings of poetic works become increasingly frequent toward the end of Nabokov's fifteenth year on American soil.

Autumn of 1943 saw the publication of a trio of poems from Afanasii Fet (1820–92),[163] a leading representative of the "pure art" school and, one suspects, Tiutchev's close rival for third place in Nabokov's pantheon of Russia's greatest lyric poets. Like Fyodor Godunov-Cherdyntsev in *The Gift*, Nabokov inherited his love of Fet from his father;[164] like that protagonist, he could not forgive and forget the injustice Fet had suffered at the hands of "our oafish school-of-social intent writers."[165] When he introduced Fet to his students, Nabokov could not help lapsing back into the excited style of his poetic juvenilia ("Fet – the spirit of the air, a wispy cloud, a butterfly fanning its wings"), insisting that "up to the present day it is a good way to test whether a Russian understands poetry or not by finding out whether he appreciates Fet."[166] Writing of his passion for the study of butterflies in *Speak, Memory*'s chapter 6, Nabokov assigns Fet a place of honour as one of only two Russian poets in whose works he found "lepidopteral images of genuinely sensuous quality."[167]

As befits translations dating from the dawn of the period of "loving and tender sinning," the three poems in the 1943 selection are rooted in Nabokov's conviction that poetry should be translated as poetry by poet-translators who immerse themselves in the world of their confrères. As far as Fet was concerned, Nabokov hardly needed to do any research to uncover the mysteries of that poet's inspiration and imagery: these translations expressed a sense of kinship he felt had existed between them since his boyhood. On one specific occasion, however, his search for the source of an epigraph in the writings of a certain German thinker Fet had championed led Nabokov toward a contemplation of a subject prominent in his thought.

The 1943 selection opened with "Alter Ego" ("As a lily that looks at itself in a stream" – "Kak lileia gliaditsia v nagornyi ruchei"; 1878). The rhythm of Nabokov's rendition may be less regular than that of Fet's anapestic tetrameter, yet this is a sonorous poetic translation that replicates the original rhyming and stanzaic structure in an English poem with a recognizable melody. The translation carefully mirrors the import of the poet's profession of eternal love for a beloved who, he is certain, is only temporarily separated from him by her untimely death. The poem concludes with the following statement:

У любви есть слова, те слова не умрут.
Нас с тобой ожидает особенный суд:
Он сумеет нас сразу в толпе различить,
И мы вместе придём, нас нельзя разлучить.[168]

[Love has [its] words, those words will not die. / A special trial awaits us: / At once will it manage to distinguish us in a crowd, / And together we will come, we cannot be parted.]

Fet's relevance for the formation and verbalization of Nabokov's metaphysical intuitions merits a separate study, but even a cursory glance at these translations' immediate vicinity in his compositions from the same period confirms the existence of a strong semantic aura connecting the two confrères. Timofey Pnin's belief in "a democracy of ghosts," in which "the souls of the dead ... formed committees, and these, in continuous sessions, attended to the destinies of the quick"[169] echoes Nabokov's take on Fet's otherworldly resolution of the two lovers' separation in "Alter Ego":

Love has words of its own, these words cannot die.
Our singular case special judges will try:
in the crowd they will notice us right from the start –
for as one we will come – we whom nothing can part.[170]

This poem's "verbal vestige" extends far beyond *Pnin* as Nabokov's partiality to "Alter Ego" turns this translation into a manifestation of a link between his metaphysical intuitions and those verbalized by his precursor Fet.

"When life is torture, when hope is a traitor" ("Izmuchen zhizn'iu, kovarstvom nadezhdy" [Tormented by life, by the perfidy of hope]; 1864) was a poem of profound personal significance for Nabokov. On the one hand, according to his sister Elena's testimony, it belonged to a two-poem cycle their father adored.[171] On the other, this poetic text figures prominently in Nabokov's individual mythopoetics. As evidenced by the 1952 additions to his 1931 speech on Aleksandr Blok, his understanding of the gradual emergence of accentual versification in the history of Russian poetry featured a direct line from Tiutchev's "Last Love" to Blok's triumphant use of such metres via this "logaoedic" piece by Fet.[172]

Nabokov's "When life is torture, when hope is a traitor" includes a translation of Fet's epigraph from Arthur Schopenhauer's *Parerga and Paralipomena* (1851). Not only did Nabokov translate this epigraph, he identified its source, not provided by Fet. The effort Nabokov invested in ascertaining the source of Fet's quotation from Schopenhauer is indicative of more than his scrupulousness as a translator. The poetry of Russia's most committed champion and translator of Schopenhauer linked Nabokov with the chief proponent of irrationalist philosophy. "The uniformity of the passage of time in the minds of all men proves more conclusively than anything else that we are all plunged in the same dream; indeed, that it is one Being that dreams it,"[173] runs the epigraph to a poem that eloquently spells out the view that irrational epiphanies allow poets to immerse themselves in a continuous dream that lends the universe its creative energy. Viewed in conjunction with "The Texture of Time," the speculative centrepiece of Nabokov's magnum opus, *Ada*, this poem's synthesis of Schopenhauer's ideas concerning one's notion of and relationship with so mysterious an elemental force as time proves an important pretext for one of Nabokov's richest and most demanding texts. Even though Fet's "secret weakness," his "rationality" and fondness for "antitheses," earned him a rebuke in *The Gift*,[174] Nabokov's apophatic contemplation of time's essence in *Speak, Memory* was informed by Fet's distillation of Schopenhauer's ideas on the matter in so important a pretext as "When life is torture, when hope is a traitor" and elsewhere in his poetry.

The last instalment in the trio is "The Swallow" ("Lastochki"; 1884). Like all the Russian poems Nabokov translated into English during his first fifteen years in the United States, this text throws open a new vista on his earlier oeuvre. Fet's swallow that skims the surface of a pond and comes dangerously close to being devoured by water explains the genesis of a key metaphor in *The Gift*: "When young people of his age, lovers of poetry, followed him on occasion with that special gaze that glides like a swallow across a poet's mirrory heart."[175] Fet's image of a fearless being deriving excitement and pleasure from getting close to traversing the perilous border between two planes of existence appealed to Nabokov's imagination and fed into his contemplation of the poet's place in the world, providing an alternative to Baudelaire's "Albatros."

Like "When life is torture, when hope is a traitor," "The Swallow" presents one of those rational antitheses that Nabokov considered a distinct feature of Fet's thinking. This partially rhymed rendition of a fully rhymed, four-quatrain piece emerges as a likely source for the title of Nabokov's earliest novelistic work written in first person, *The Eye* (1930). When revisited in light of that novel's presentation of a ghostly observer surveying the world of the living, the poem's opening line, "Prirody prazdnyi sogliadatai" ("An idle spy of Nature"), along with the subsequent development of its subject – the suggestion that creativity is a manifestation of the urge to "to scoop from a forbidden / mysterious element one scoop"[176] – emerges as a major reference illuminating the import of one of the earliest of Nabokov's "otherworldly" compositions.

Next to the likes of Lermontov, Tiutchev, and Fet, Nikolai Nekrasov (1821–77), Russia's chief champion of the downtrodden and the darling of Soviet ideologues, may appear an oddity. The four Nekrasov poems singled out for a separate treatment, however, highlight what Nabokov considered that poet's greatest achievement, his "success" at transcending, "in a few great poems, the journalist in him."[177] This transcendence became the focus for Nabokov the interpreter of Russian literature and culture, while Nekrasov the poet of passion provided material for Nabokov the translator and performer.

As was the case with so many Russian poems Nabokov dwelt on in his university surveys of Russian literature, Nekrasov's "A heavy cross is her allotted burden" ("Tiazhelyi krest dostalsia ei na doliu"; 1855) was a text with a long history of assimilation into the referential pool of Nabokov's compositions. Introduced as a "passionate cry of [Nekrasov's] love poetry," this poem figured prominently in *The Gift*, where its iambic pentameter was lauded for its power to "enchant" "by its hortatory, supplicatory and prophetic force and by a very individual caesura after the second foot, a caesura which in Pushkin, say, is a rudimentary organ insofar as it controls the melody of the line, but which in Nekrasov becomes a genuine organ of breathing."[178] It is only fitting that this poem would make a strong comeback at a time when Nabokov worked at weaving the results of his engagement with Russian literature into the allusion-rich fabric of his English-language compositions.

On at least one occasion Nabokov used his translation of "Tiazhelyi krest dostalsia ei na doliu" as a powerful crescendo to a public reading of his translations. Counting on a sympathetic response from his listeners, Nabokov diverted their attention from the cornerstone of Nekrasov's popularity as Tsarist Russia's leading voice of dissent: "Buried and forgotten are Nekrasov's journalistic jingles, his rhymed reactions to the social evils of his day a hundred years ago." It comes as no surprise to readers of *The Gift* – to which Nabokov's Anglophone audience had no access at that time – that Nabokov favours a different kind of poet in Nekrasov, Nekrasov the lyricist: "But the gasp and the sob in his romantic verse endure. His words, the well-worn words of conventional poetry, are of little importance; but I wonder whether my English version of a famous love poem of his does manage to convey its emotional impact, the echo behind the words, the resounding hollows in which the vanished words had been cupped."[179] Tentative as he was regarding his ability to convey the poignancy of Nekrasov's lyricism in his English translation, Nabokov supplied his listeners with a full equimetric, if partially rhymed, rendition of the "famous poem" in seven quatrains of soulful iambic pentameters.

The SLAVIC 150 materials also include "As I hearken to the horrors of the war" ("Vnimaia uzhasam voiny"; 1855–6) and two excerpts from the narrative poems *Who Can Be Happy and Free in Russia* (*Komu na Rusi zhit' khorosho*; 1876) and *Red-Nosed Frost* (*Moroz, Krasnyi nos*; 1864). "As I hearken to the horrors of the war," Nekrasov's "topical" response to the news of Russia's humiliating losses in the Crimean War, is another poem with a distinct place of its own in Nabokov's writing. With its help, Smurov tries to impress Marianna with his non-existent military exploits in *The Eye*.[180] This reference to Nekrasov's "Vnimaia uzhasam voiny" enhances Nabokov's characterization of his protagonist's self-aggrandizement, going to the heart of his need for attention and affection. Free of its integration into the playful texture of that novel – an aspect Nabokov's American students could not appreciate in 1952 – it emerges as a stark formulation of Nekrasov's disdain for the hypocrisy with which people shield themselves from contemplating the human toll of military conflicts waged in their name on distant theatres.

Disdainful as he was of the narrow-minded glorification of Nekrasov's civic poetry, in his translation of "Vnimaia uzhasam voiny" Nabokov makes no effort to undermine the seriousness of this poem's focus on individual suffering and its dilution by patriotic rhetoric and human indifference. The inclusion of "Vnimaia uzhasam voiny" expands the notion of Nekrasov as passionate love lyricist by demonstrating him to be capable of exposing hypocrisy as a cynical distraction from the inconsolable grief of bereft mothers. Nekrasov's subdued pathos reveals itself as a pretext for Nabokov's poetic masterpiece "The Mother" ("Mat'"; 1925), with its contrast between what the believing multitudes interpret as the tidings of great joy and the grief of a single woman who will never see her firstborn son again.

Non-specialists among today's readers of Nabokov's "Russia" (from *Who Can Be Happy and Free in Russia*) will be puzzled to discover that his presentation of one of most famous poems in the Russian canon opens with an entire stanza absent from all of its modern reproductions. An effective and memorable folksong stylization, in *Who Can Be Happy and Free in Russia* it is ascribed to Grigorii "Grisha" Dobrosklonov, a fanciful Nekrassovian impersonation of a "people's intercessor" (*narodnyi zastupnik*). Nabokov's translation retained the stanza Nekrasov composed to appease Tsarist censorship with its depiction of Russia's absolute ruler as a paragon of geopolitical good husbandry.[181] What follows after this decoy is the Nekrassovian characterization of Russia's duality, her richness and poverty, inertia and dynamism. Nabokov introduced this poem to his students not only as an "optimistic satire" but also as an expression of "well-meaning optimism" regarding Russia's potential. The reason he retained the opening stanza so familiar to Nekrasov's pre-revolutionary Russian readers and unknown to their Soviet and post-Soviet counterparts becomes clear when we discover the source for his translations of both "Vnimaia uzhasam voiny" and "Rus'." Nabokov penned his equilinear paraphrases of the two poems using the same *Intermediate Russian Reader* by George Patrick he used to make his translation of Kol'tsov's "Chto ty spish' muzhichok?" Hardly caring for the populist tendency displayed in Patrick's presentation of his language-learning materials, Nabokov shared his fellow émigré's detestation of the bias found in Soviet learning materials.

Red-Nosed Frost ("Not a sound! The soul leaves the world") shows "a young peasant woman" freezing "to death in a winter forest." In the context of the SLAVIC 150 selection, Nabokov's "Ni zvuka! Dusha umiraet" develops the theme of man's relationship with nature so prominent in his teaching materials. Daria is but one representative of the suffering heroines of Nekrasov's consciousness-raising poetry. She typifies the plight of Russian peasantry: a young widow and mother, she is doomed by the circumstances condemning her and people of her social class to slavery. Along with a frank portrayal of his protagonists' wretched existence, Nekrasov's depictions of majestic natural scenes, his plaintive intonations and appeals are all means to an end: this verse narrative seeks to compel the more fortunate, literate Russians to address the social injustice that relegated the majority of the country's population to slavery. The chief enemy against whom Nekrasov went into battle in his civic poetry, the main vice he chastised in his satires was not so much the unjust social order he definitely opposed but the indifference that permitted that status quo to retain its sheen of normality. Keen as he was to emphasize the aesthetic properties of Nekrasov's poems, Nabokov equipped his students with a reliable sense of Nekrasov the scourge of smug complacency.

Such was the calculated effect of Nabokov's selection of Nekrasov's poems that closed with the portrait of a woman falling victim to the frost amid a vivid depiction of nature's grandeur. One detail of this static verbal picture arrests the attention of readers familiar with Nabokov's original compositions dating from this period. No one but the poet and his reader are here to witness the scene of Daria's death – unless, of course, we take notice of a squirrel whose movements cause "a lump of snow" to fall on the dying woman ("a chance sound, a kind of little rustle: / it is a squirrel passing from tree-top to tree-top").[182] For all its beauty and "mysterious attraction," the nature that surrounds Daria is *gluboko-besstrastna* – "deeply impassive" in Nabokov's rendition. One of the later additions to the body of the translated texts dating from this period, "Not a sound! The soul leaves the world" inaugurates the key image that holds together the fragmentary narrative telling the quintessentially Nabokovian tale of suffering from indifference and injustice, that of Timofey Pnin. Begun in early 1953, *Pnin* absorbed many aspects of Nabokov's experience as an American university instructor of Russian language and literature. Nabokov's attention to Nekrasov's portrayal of nature's indifference to the suffering of a human being permits us to focus on the dialogic aspect of his introduction of a similar image into the novel being composed at the time.

Much like Nekrasov's portrayal of nature in *Red-Nosed Frost*, the squirrels that haunt the pages of *Pnin* are "mysteriously attractive"; much like the squirrel that appears toward the end of the translated fragment, they taunt us with our inability to grasp their significance. In his interpretation of the "spectral dimension" of Nabokov's fiction, W.W. Rowe has suggested that the squirrels that appear before Pnin at times of crisis reincarnate his boyhood sweetheart Mira Belochkin.[183] To appreciate the extent to which "the great 'Squirrel Theme,'" as the novel's annotator Gennady Barabtarlo has designated it, is a response to Nekrasov one needs to focus on the most remarkable of its manifestations.

Chapter 5 opens with a description of the protagonist as a rookie driver getting lost on Vermont's forest roads. This presentation of Pnin's difficulties incorporates an *invisible* squirrel, whose appearance heralds his finding his destination. The fact that this episode constitutes a response to Nekrasov's depiction of nature's indifference to human suffering, however, has not received the attention it deserves:

> Our luckless car operator had by now lost himself too thoroughly to be able to go back to the highway, and since he had little experience in maneuvering on rutty narrow roads ... his various indecisions and gropings took those bizarre visual forms that an observer ... might have followed with a compassionate eye; but there was no living creature in that forlorn and listless upper region ... The wind had subsided. Under the pale sky the sea of treetops seemed to harbor no life. Presently, however, a

> gunshot popped, and a twig leaped into the sky. The dense upper boughs in that part of the otherwise stirless forest started to move in a receding sequence of shakes or jumps, with a swinging lilt from tree to tree, after which all was still again.[184]

"Not a stir!" of the Nekrasov fragment in Nabokov's English translation is mirrored by "the otherwise stirless forest" depicted in *Pnin*; the squirrel that passes "from tree-top to tree-top" with "a kind of little rustle" in the fragment is mimicked by its American relative animating the "the sea of treetops" that only seem to be harbouring "no life."

The significance of this "verbal vestige" of Nabokov's engagement with Nekrasov extends far beyond its involvement in a light-hearted game of literary echoes. As it recounts the story of its protagonist's misfortunes, *Pnin* forces its readers to grapple with the problem of empathy. Vladimir Vladimirovich N., the novel's narrator, does everything in his power to make the reader laugh at his protagonist's appearance, marital problems, as well as the difficulties associated with his need to survive in an environment he is ill-equipped to navigate. While *Pnin*'s smug narrator rests in his certainty that no "compassionate eye" follows his protagonist's travails, in the manner of the indifferent environment that destroys Nekrasov's Daria, the novel's author invites his reader to exercise superior judgment. We cannot be sure that the squirrel that escapes the gunshot immediately before Pnin finds his way represents Mira Belochkin's compassionate ghost, but Nabokov's reversal of the forest's indifference to Daria's plight makes this episode a repudiation of Nekrasov's understanding of nature's attitude toward his heroine's plight. By this same token, it nullifies the narrator's contention regarding the absence of compassion in Pnin's fictional universe. Nabokov's challenge to Nekrasov's pessimism affirms that all the misfortunes Pnin has endured by the time he gets to chapter 5 are redeemed by the ultimately compassionate design of the world he inhabits.

If Nabokov's evolving attitude toward Aleksandr Blok (1880–1921) has become the subject of numerous studies, it is because Blok's figure never ceased to be a towering presence on the wide horizon of Nabokov's literary imagination. Nabokov's lifelong passion for the single most important of his senior literary contemporaries undergoes fascinating transmutations as youthful idolization gives way to the shock associated with Blok's endorsement of revolution in *The Twelve* (*Dvenadsat'*; 1918), only to be superseded by a more measured appreciation of his mastery that in time yields to a realization that Blok may have been at least partially responsible for the post-revolutionary decline of Russian culture. In *Invitation to a Beheading* Nabokov subjects Blok's legacy to intense mythologizing; in *The Gift* he casts a wistful glance at his adolescent admiration for the poet; in *Speak, Memory* he charts his past with the help of Blok's diaries; and in *Lolita* and *Ada* he reshapes Blok's images into the richly allusive visions of his own creation. So fervent was Nabokov's partiality to Blok that it has invited scholars to interpret it as "a classic example" of the "anxiety of influence" along the lines of Harold Bloom's substantiation of this influential literary-critical concept.[185] Recently published testaments show that Nabokov's attitude toward Blok was at once less adversarial and more nuanced. In 1944 Nabokov did indeed call Blok's legacy "a heterogeneous mixture of violas and vulgarity" and the man himself "a superb poet with a muddled mind," suggesting that "something somber in him and fundamentally reactionary (remindful sometimes of Dostoevsky's political articles), a murky vista with a bonfire of books at the end, led him away from his genius as soon as he started to think."[186] In the revised and reconsidered 1952 version of the 1931 eulogy of Blok he never published in his lifetime, however, Nabokov emphasized his admiration for Blok's genius at realizing the potential of accentual versification foreshadowed by Tiutchev and Fet and fondly reminisced about the ways in which Blok's lyricism became the backdrop for his youth.[187]

SLAVIC 150 teaching materials include three equiliniar paraphrases of Blok's poems, including "The Strange Lady" ("Neznakomka"; 1906), "The Railroad" ("Na zheleznoi doroge"; 1910), and "Again, as in my golden years" ("Rossiia" ["Opiat', kak v gody zolotye"]; 1908). Among Nabokov's teaching materials we discover "All is disaster and loss," a rhyming translation of the five-line stanza that forms the refrain of Blok's drama *The Rose and the Cross* (*Roza i Krest*; 1913), and "You were truer than others, and vivid, and sweet," a poetic rendition of "Byla ty vsekh iarche, vernei i prelestnei" (1914). While "All is disaster and loss" may be the earliest of these translations, we have every reason to believe that "You were truer than others, and vivid, and sweet" is among the latest rhyming translations of the pre-literalist period.

"In the evening, the sultry air above the restaurants / is both wild and torpid, / and drunken vociferations are governed / by the evil spirit of spring," begins Nabokov's take on "The Strange Lady," a central poem in the Russian canon. Nabokov made no apparent effort to introduce his SLAVIC 150 students to the formal intricacies of the original: the surviving lecture notes make no mention of the poem's virtuosic use of the dactylic rhyme. "Notes on Prosody," however, qualifies "The Incognita" – Nabokov's search for a superior rendition of its title in English betrays his fondness for this poem – as "the most famous short poem in long rhyme."[188]

A non-rhyming paraphrase, it foregrounds the poem's imagery. The original offers a tragic incarnation of the major leitmotif of Blokian poetry, that of the Beautiful Lady, as in his drunken stupor the narrator makes out the silhouette of a slender young woman. What is in all likelihood a distorted reflection of a streetwalker plying her trade, "always escortless, alone," amid the din of a local dive is a manifestation of the narrator's abandoned dreams and aspirations. Nabokov may have withheld from his students his take on Tiutchev's "Umom Rossiiu ne poniat'," but he focused their attention on Lermontov's "strange" love for his native land and Nekrasov's brand of optimistic patriotism. So important was Russia for Blok's brand of eroticized adoration of the eternal feminine that it would have been a major omission not to include his poetic statements to that effect. Nabokov's equilinear paraphrase of "Russia" ("Opiat', kak v gody zolotye") exemplifies this major theme of Blok's individual mythology. The second stanza of the translation renders Blok's invocation of his motherland into unadorned lines of unrhymed English paraphrase:

Russia, beggarly Russia,
your grey hovels,
your wind-borne songs
are to me like the first tears of love.[189]

Apart from being another example of Blok's masterful use of dactylic rhymes, "The Railroad" ("Na zheleznoi doroge") exemplifies the brand of narrative-rich lyric poetry Nabokov strove to produce during his Russian years. The story of a maiden who throws herself under a train after frequenting a railway station in search of emotions she craves but cannot attain merges Nekrassovian pathos with a kind of tragic lyricism that distinguishes Blok's type of decadence from that of his contemporaries in the symbolist camp.

Nabokov assigned a place of honour to "the dreamy stutter of Blok's rhythms" (*The Gift*), this phrase being one of his numerous denominations of the kind of accentual versification that forever changed Russian poetry, rendering its Golden Age history. On the one hand, the so-called Blokian revolution in Russian poetry spelled the end for the poetics associated with Pushkin; on the other, it became one of the most exhilarating impressions of Nabokov's youth. Nabokov's individual mythopoetics semanticized what he called Blok's "pausative" or "broken" metres, endowing them with an ability to convey specific notions. In his 1931/1952 eulogy of the poet he referred to this phenomenon as "that stumbling with agitation meter" and singled out "Golos iz khora" ("Voice from a Choir" ["Kak chasto plachem – vy i ia"]; 1910–14) as a prophecy of the nearing eclipse of Russian civilization. To acquaint his students with Blokian "pausative" verse, Nabokov first translated "All is disaster and loss," composed in the kind of three-ictus *dolnik* that distinguished Blok's work in this metre. "You were truer than others, and vivid, and sweet," with its evocation of railway travel and Gypsy singing, offered another, more representative sampling of all the quintessential attributes of Blok's lyricism as expressed in his signature metre. A translation of "Byla ty vsekh iarche, vernei i prelestnei," "You were truer than others, and vivid, and sweet" is a superb poetic transposition of the original's formal features, including its rhyme scheme and intricate destabilized – "broken," "pausative," "breaking with agitation" – metre. A fine impersonation of all the quintessential characteristics of Blokian lyricism, Nabokov's translation of the poem succeeds in rising to the level of his finest poetic renditions of Russian poetry in English dating from this period.

"I am frankly homosexual on the subject of translators": Nabokov, Anna Akhmatova, and "The Grey-Eyed King"

Nabokov's attitude toward women writers can hardly be called progressive.[190] Even though he overcame what Simon Karlinsky terms his "typically Russian prejudice against women novelists" with regard to Jane Austen and recognized in Marina Tsvetaeva "a poet of genius,"[191] the sum of his assertions on the subject reads as not only intransigent and inflexible, but oddly out of step with his aesthetic sensitivity.

Writing to James Laughlin on 16 July 1942 to discuss an English translation of *The Gift*, he quipped: "I need a man who knows English better than Russian – and a man, not a woman. I am frankly homosexual on the subject of translators."[192] One could argue that this was a private joke that concerned his own work, but his public statements on the subject indicate otherwise. On at least one occasion during the period of "loving and tender sinning," he rephrased this same sentiment when he shared with his listeners his vision for "the perfect translator":

> He, John Into, should have genius, style, vision, and wit ... He should be of the same sex as his author ... when I think of the misguided and miscast ladies who translated Tolstoy and Pushkin in the past, I can say that at least in the present case I belong to the right sex, and know the right language.[193]

Impersonal on their surface, this dictum's implications are pointed enough: it leaves such predecessors and rivals of his as Constance Garnett and Babette Deutsch no chance.

Nothing we have known so far about Nabokov's attitude toward Anna Akhmatova (1889–1966) suggests that his treatment of Russia's foremost woman poet diverged from this general line in any significant way. In his published critical evaluations of the works of her émigré followers, he refused to qualify her influence on them as anything but disastrous. While Nabokov's Russian fiction contains such unsparing portrayals of Akhmatova's imitators as Alla Chernosvitov in *Glory*, it is Liza Bogolepov in *Pnin* who becomes the pinnacle of his parodic assaults on the cult of "Anna of All the Russias." His portrait of this deceitful, manipulative, and vulgar character is complemented by "quotations" from her poetry, which prove to be "a mosaic ingeniously composed of bits of Akhmatova's early lyrics, drawn mainly from the *Vecher* (1912) and *Chëtki* (1914) collections."[194]

If Liza Bogolepov can be read as an English-language reprise of the caricature of the numerous followers of the Akhmatova cult among émigré women poets, taking Alla Chernosvitova's characteristics to a new level, the samples of Liza's poetry appear to go after Akhmatova herself. As Gennady Barabtarlo has pointed out, Akhmatova saw this parody as a personal insult, so close were Liza's "Ia nadela tëmnoe plat'e" and "Samotsvetov krome ochei" to the diction and imagery of Akhmatova's early verse. The similarity between Liza's poems and some of Akhmatova's most famous lyrics does not end here. Barry P. Scherr has shown that Nabokov's introduction of the poetic measure in which Liza's poems are composed as "more or less anapestic trimeter"[195] alludes to the "three-stress dolnik meter with variable anacrusis" characteristic of Akhmatova's prosodic repertoire.[196]

Nabokov's archives preserve a translation of Akhmatova's early masterpiece "Seroglazyi korol'" (The Grey-Eyed King; 1910). Unattributed to its source, this translation has lingered among Nabokov's teaching materials until Barabtarlo ascertained its significance and provenance in 2017.

One poetic gem among many distinguishing Akhmatova's debut *Vecher* (Evening; 1912), "Seroglazyi korol'" comprises seven rhyming couplets of dactylic trimeter. The dimensions of this finely wrought miniature are deceptive: it manages to encompass an entire drama complete with a love triangle and a violent conflict fuelled by infidelity and jealousy. Told in the voice of a married woman who experiences acute heartache at the news of the death of one "grey-eyed king," the poem relates a complicated affair involving the narrator, her husband, her daughter, as well as the deceased man and his grief-stricken wife. A masterpiece of narrative economy, the poem implies much more than it states: the protagonist's husband's appearance, mood, and words hint that he killed the "king" after ambushing him during a hunt. Unable to express her pain openly, the protagonist promises herself to wake up her daughter so that she can see again the eyes of the murdered man, the child's true father.

Nabokov's treatment of Akhmatova's original suggests that the curtain of mockery and dismissal occluded his genuine admiration for her indisputable mastery as both poet and storyteller. "Unallayable anguish, thy praises I sing" invests considerable energy in preserving the form and significance of "Seroglazyi korol'." In what may be a nod to Nabokov's constant association of Akhmatova with untraditional versification, it deregularizes her dactyls. Taken as a whole, however, this translation amounts to a close match for the Russian poem it represents, effectively becoming a testament to Nabokov's admiration of Akhmatova's mastery.

The significance of this translation cannot be underestimated. It shows Nabokov capable of overcoming his bias against a poet whose mastery he could not but recognize. Contrary to his disparaging treatment of Akhmatova in *Pnin*, contrary to his distaste for the influence she exerted on the poetry of her day, Nabokov treated her masterpiece "Seroglazyi korol'" with the care and attention reserved exclusively for the poets he considered first-rate. His long-lost translation of the poem places her work alongside that of Pushkin, Lermontov, Tiutchev, Fet, Blok, and Khodasevich. Without redeeming the less palatable aspects of Nabokov's sustained mockery of Akhmatova, this translation does become a tacit recognition of the fact that her achievement secures for her a position in the ranks of Russia's best poets. The significance of this document for our understanding of Nabokov's attitude toward women writers and toward Akhmatova herself remains to be ascertained, especially since his unpublished lecture notes provide further evidence that his literary pose with regard to Akhmatova contradicted his fair scholarly assessment of her eminent stature.

"Yah pom-new chewed-no-yay mg-no-vain-yay": A Translation Lost and Found

Few pieces of textual evidence show the abyss separating Nabokov the "loving and tender sinner" from Nabokov the translator and annotator of *Eugene Onegin* better than the way Aleksandr Pushkin's "K ***" ("Ia pomniu chudnoe mgnoven'e" [I remember a wondrous instant]; July 1825) fares in his pre- and post-literalist praxis.

As it draws closer to its dénoument, the published version of "The Art of Translation" manifesto (1941) catalogues difficulties associated with rendering into English a certain Pushkinian masterpiece. So complex, so rich is this poem that relating all the problems associated with an earnest attempt to mirror the effects of its opening line alone spills from one paragraph into another.[197] Nabokov's ability to explicate something as ineffable as the "paradoxical combination" of sound and meaning that produces a literary artefact of rare aesthetic value – along with his appeal to "artists" who cannot fail to appreciate this – makes it clear that in him the reader is dealing with an outstanding translator. After such an introduction it is difficult to imagine that the essay can crescendo into anything but a display of the fruits of a genius's labour. But before the essay reaches its terminus, the expectation gives way to suspense and then to disbelief, fuelled by a suspicion that no demonstration can possibly meet the requirements outlined herein:

> I was confronted by that opening line, so full of Pushkin, so individual and harmonious; and after examining it gingerly from the various angles here suggested, I tackled it. The tackling process lasted the worst part of the night. I did translate it at last; but to give my version at this point might lead the reader to doubt that perfection may be attained by merely following a few perfect rules.[198]

The translation does exist but cannot be shared with the reader here and now. Anyone interested in Nabokov the artist-translator is welcome to see his translations for themselves, but to accomplish that they must make an effort to follow his activities and publications. No other early English-language composition makes it clearer that Nabokov the performer and trickster has firmly set his foot on American soil fully prepared to claim the attention of a new reading audience. Was this baffling crescendo another Nabokovian trick?

Amusing as Nabokov's description of his difficulties with Pushkin's poem was, ample evidence proves that it was based on a true story of his struggle to evolve that poem's English equivalent. The marginal notes found in his personal copy of Pushkin's collected works testify to his effort to understand, interpret, and translate this poem's opening line – to translate it into no fewer than three languages at his disposal:

I remember a wonderful moment
Ich erinnere mich eines wundervollen Augenblick
Je me souviens d'un moment merveilleux

Any attempt at translating such a poem should be accompanied by an exploration of its sources of inspiration – Nabokov's marginal notes do not merely identify the poem's hidden addressee as Anna Kern and the circumstances under which the poet met her, but supply her psychological portrait:

прелестная и легкомысленная женщина
гостившая у родственников в соседнем имении
когда Пушкин жил в Михайловском[199]

[Enchanting and frivolous woman / who was visiting her relatives at a neighbouring country estate / when Pushkin lived at Mikhailovskoe]

An explication of any artistic phenomenon benefits from providing it with a context. To this end Nabokov turns to an authority he trusts: John Keats, whose opening line to book 1 of *Endymion* not merely provides Pushkin's famous first line with a close English equivalent but describes this poem's overall effect on its Russian reader:

ср. [cf.] Keats[:] a thing of beauty is a joy for ever
прекрасная вещь есть вечная радость

The marginal notes to the poem indicate that Nabokov does not lose sight of his overarching goal: the creation of a foreign-language version that would mirror the poem's effects in the original. It is at this point that we hear an early warning – the sound of this alarm will be reverberating far beyond the 1941 manifesto that is "The Art of Translation":

> diffic.[ult] to translate

The most expansive marginal note to the poem contains the earliest definition of these difficulties, which Nabokov will subsequently transform into the polished, ironic, and baffling formulation familiar to every reader of "The Art of Translation." As he writes down his thoughts, Nabokov vacillates between the old and new Russian orthographies; unable to stay within the limits of one language, his description switches from Russian to English – this stream of unbridled polyglot consciousness reads nothing like his finalized thoughts on the same subject:

> Цепь простых слов изъ которыхъ каждое, однако, бросает отсвет на соседнее, волшебно меняя его. Есть русская поговорка "не место красит человека[,] а человек красит место." В поэзии наоборотъ, место красит слово[.] It is the position of the word which is more important than the words themselves.[200]

> [A chain of simple words [yet] each out of them, however, throws a tinge on its neighbour miraculously transforming it. There is a Russian proverb: "A position cannot beautify a person, [only] a person can beautify a position." In poetry it is the other way around, the position beautifies a word [continued in English].

It is hard to avoid the impression that after beginning to translate the poem in the margins of his edition of Pushkin's works, Nabokov ran into the considerable difficulties he would subsequently relate in "The Art of Translation." After translating the poem's opening line into English, German, and French, he tackled its closing stanza, only to begin to erase the variants that could not satisfy him. He did translate the poem in its entirety, but the resulting translation does not read like any one of his translations from the period of "loving and tender sinning."

Nabokov's beloved "gofmanskii Pushkin" preserves a separate index card containing "To [Anna Kern]" ("I recall a wondrous moment"). Coupled with the marginal notes, the traces of heavy revising visible on the index card prove that if anything, Nabokov was reticent in his report that his "tackling" of this poem cost him "the worst part of the night." More to the point, the effort associated with this work could not but have demonstrated to him all the limitations of the translation technique he advocated with such flair in "The Art of Translation."

"I recall a wondrous moment" is a literal, and not literary, translation along the lines of those found in *Three Russian Poets* and *Pushkin, Lermontov, Tyutchev*. Preserve as it does the linear count of the original, it cannot be qualified as anything but unrhymed prose. The only traces of poetic artifice are detectible in the English idiom into which Nabokov renders the original, but here too he steers clear of the kind of Wordsworthian, Coleridgean register that distinguishes his earlier, literary English versions of Pushkin's lyrics.

Setting aside for the moment the problem of Nabokov's drastic change of opinion regarding a poem he once called "one of Pushkin's most prodigious" only to dismiss it as an "overrated madrigal" on a later occasion,[201] we can say that his well-documented struggle with "Ia pomniu chudnoe mgnoven'e" became a focal point of his struggle for a deeper understanding of translation, its glories and its miseries, its epistemology and teleology. "Art," "artist," "genius," "mimicry," "perfection," and so on – the entire vocabulary Nabokov developed to put his practice of poetic translation on a solid theoretical footing proved to be of limited use when he confronted a phenomenon whose specificity and rich semantic aura could not be adequately reflected in a literary, poetic translation alone. Nabokov's struggle with "Ia pomniu chudnoe mgnoven'e" confirmed his growing suspicion – one borne out by his work on numerous other poems during the period of "loving and tender sinning" – that "the perfect translator," "the artist," "the genius," "the confrère" could be helpless to do justice to a madrigal of twenty-four iambic pentameters.

"Pity the elderly gray translator": Boxing Himself into a Corner

"The Art of Translation" (1941) is a spirited defence of the artist-translator's right to conduct a dialogue with his "confrères" on his own terms – even if he risks "drowning the foreign masterpiece under the sparkling ripples of his own style." As far as rights go, Nabokov's emphatic use of such qualifiers as "ideal" and "perfect" leaves no room for misunderstanding: no "drudge," no "laborious lady," no "scholar," no matter how "exact and pedantic," can rival "creative genius," as "neither learning nor diligence can replace imagination and style." For all the risks associated with the freedom that "creative genius" affords its possessor, it is unassailable and sacred. The poetic translations executed at the time of this essay's conception and after its publication in *The New Republic* take full advantage of this freedom on the chivalrous assumption that Nabokov's integrity and talent would shield his confrères from the abuse they had suffered at the hands of his less scrupulous, less gifted predecessors.

Nabokov did not take long to realize that the promise of freedom associated with this approach clashed with the harsh reality of its realization. Its pivot on a speculative, indefinable, and often indefensible notion of "creative genius" hindered his endeavours "to imitate the meter and rhyme while retaining the exact sense." "Creative genius" proved of limited use when the stark choice between unique significance and the language-specific means of its communication – essentially a choice between rhyme and reason – forced him to compromise either one of these two aspects in pursuit of a stylistically sound poetic translation.

The only reason Nabokov could ignore this contradiction for some time was his staunch belief in his artistic ability to redeem its detrimental effects. Until the end of his first decade on American soil, this belief permitted him to ignore a number of complexities associated with the task of interpreting someone else's work without possessing an exhaustive knowledge of its inception, evolution, and context. On 1 November 1946, for example, he confessed to Edmund Wilson that he did not ascertain the exact nature of the original's relationship with its source prior to making his 1941 translation of Pushkin's *Feast during the Plague*.[202] This admission demonstrates that in concert with the doctrine propagated in "The Art of Translation," Nabokov relied on his "creative genius" to craft a version of the "little tragedy" that would first and foremost satisfy his own "artistic" sense of fidelity to his confrère Pushkin. This same assumption permitted him to develop emotional ties to his source texts. His reliance on the pocket-sized edition of Fëdor Tiutchev's collected poems may have resulted in the creation of some haunting passages from *Invitation to a Beheading*, but this mainstay proved to be unreliable, as it had not been informed by the advances in Tiutchev scholarship made in the Soviet Union. Nabokov's acknowledgment in "Notes on Prosody" (1964) that Tiutchev's "Silentium," and not "Posledniaia liubov'," became a successful demonstration of the potential of accentual versification for literary poetry shows his belated realization that one of his assumptions about Russian poetics was based on a compromised edition of that poet's works.

Since "The Art of Translation" is a title that Nabokov used for a number of his statements on the subject from this period, it is fascinating to see how his presentation shifts from humorous to sardonic. "I thought I might say a few words about this pathetic business of translating," opens a shorter, later, version of the 1941 essay he used as an opening for a public reading of his translations from the Russian poets (after 1941). Confronted with the need to discuss the asymmetries of his poetic version of Tiutchev's "Uspokoenie," he attempted to cling to the notion of the freedom his "creative genius" afforded him, excusing his "sins" against the original's integrity not by citing his unsurpassed understanding of it but by confessing that these "sins" were sanctified by his "loving, tender" treatment of the poem. It is difficult to imagine Nabokov being satisfied with such excuses for long.

Our study of the pool of materials from which *Three Russian Poets* and *Pushkin, Lermontov, Tyutchev* emerged demonstrates that the 1941 "The Art of Translation" marked a point of departure for Nabokov's gradual movement away from the "artistic" criteria outlined in that essay. A gradual increase in the number of unrhymed – from merely equilinear to frankly prosaic – retellings of the originals toward the end of the decade shows that his rupture with the practice of an "artistic," poetic mode of translation had a logic of its own. His dissatisfaction with the artistic mode of translation, however, reached a high point, prompting him to verbalize it in a poem composed on 17 March 1952 in anticipation of a public reading at Harvard University. "Rimes" ("Pity the elderly gray translator") was composed for the purpose of closing his public readings of such poetic translations as Pushkin's "Exegi monumentum," "The Return of Pushkin," "The Upas Tree," Tiutchev's "Appeasement," "The Journey," "Last Love," "Silentium," "The sky is overcast with slow," "Tears," and Nekrasov's "A heavy cross is her allotted burden." The 20 March 1952 reading began with a recapitulation of the assumptions presented in "The Art of Translation," included the admission of "tender and loving sinning" with regard to Tiutchev's "Uspokoenie" ("Appeasement"), but concluded with "Rimes." Before Nabokov proceeded to read the poem he admitted that it had been prompted by the "psychological difficulties" associated with the need to conform to the standards of "artistic" translation; in another version of the same talk he spoke of "boxing himself into a corner":[203]

Pity the elderly gray translator
who lends to beauty his hollow voice

and – choosing sometimes a second-rater –
mimes the song-fellow of his choice.
To sacred sense for the sake of meter
he is seldom traitor as traitors go.
But pity him when he quakes with Peter
and waits for the *terza rima* to crow.[204]

When forced to re-evaluate the balance between form and sense, between the signifier and the signified, between rhyme and reason, Nabokov chose the signified, sense, reason. This choice was not an easy one. Extensive experience with literary translation persuaded him of the inevitability of compromise between these two hypostases that comprise any work of verbal art, and it is this inevitability, this determinism that he rebelled against in his "Rimes." The poem's vein may be jocular, but its implications are anything but facetious: if violations of the integrity of the original text constitute "sinning," then its sense must be "sacred" indeed.

Nabokov was realistic in his evaluation of the translations executed during his period of "tender and loving sinning." When writing to his sister on 25 October 1945 – which is to say prior to the publication of *Pushkin, Lermontov, Tyutchev* in 1947 and the composition of "Rimes" in 1952 – he ranked all his work to date. As things stood then, he did not hesitate to mention his translations from Russian into English alongside his best original compositions, but it was his translations from Tiutchev that he singled out for special praise:

> The best I have written in verse (in both Russian and English) I have written here. In prose – in English – I have published a novel and a booklet of translations (from Tiutchev, etc.).[205]

Based though they are on the compromised versions of the original poems, "Silentium" and "Last Love" remain the indisputable pinnacles of his work in the traditional – "artistic," "poetic" – mode of translation. These haunting English poems take the principles of "collaborative *confrérie*" defended in "The Art of Translation" to their limit, becoming aesthetic phenomena in their own right. Their fraught relationship with their sources of inspiration cannot be blamed on Nabokov's insufficient knowledge of their history and context alone. The "original sin" at the root of the problem was the belief that creative genius could overcome the contradiction between rhyme and reason inherent in any poetic reimagination of a work of verbal art in a foreign language. When this contradiction threatened Nabokov's greatest translating ambition, his attempt to render in English Aleksandr Pushkin's verse novel *Eugene Onegin,* he made the only choice that seemed viable to him given his history of struggle with the Scylla of rhyme and the Charybdis of reason. "Sacred sense" was to take precedent over treacherous form, and if following this choice meant parting with the notion of artistic freedom, Nabokov was prepared to take that last step.

Chapter Four

Eugene Onegin in Its Element (1955–1965)

"Problems of Translation: *Onegin* in English": From Literary to Literal

"The Art of Translation" (1941) and "Problems of Translation: *Onegin* in English" (1955) advocate two different approaches to translation and represent two distinct stages in Nabokov's evolution as translator and translation theorist. The two essays were written by the same man, but nothing could be more different than the two mutually exclusive methodologies espoused in each one of them, the latter work being a repudiation of the earlier one both conceptually and stylistically. This section shows that citations from the two essays cannot be used out of context to create a composite image of Nabokov's stance on the issue. By underscoring the disparity between the two works, I aim to put an end to the long-standing practice of using the two essays as a continuous narrative, devoid of conflict and contradiction. My effort to highlight their disparity also prepares the ground for discussing a thornier issue: Nabokov's search for a synthesis of the two conflicting methodologies.

"The Art of Translation" is a paean to artistic freedom that seeks to wrestle translation from "downright deceivers," "well-meaning hacks," and "laborious ladies" so that "creative genius" may claim dominion over it. If there is one area where Nabokov's pugnacious, though mostly jocular, rhetoric can be said to betray a degree of hesitation, however, it is in those paragraphs of the 1941 manifesto that concern themselves with "the professional writer's" most formidable antagonist – "the scholar who is eager to make the world appreciate the works of an obscure genius." This scholar, Nabokov hopes, "will be exact and pedantic: footnotes – on the *same* page as the text and not tucked away at the end of the volume." Meeting this condition, however, will not make the author of the 1941 essay change his position with regard to the hierarchy he establishes. As far as he is concerned, "the scholar" and "the laborious lady translating at the eleventh hour the eleventh volume of somebody's collected works" are equally ill equipped to perform the task. The reason? "As a rule both he and she are hopelessly devoid of any semblance of creative genius."[1] Let us consider how the later essay's answer to the same question differs from this unambiguous formulation of that ambiguous criterion.

Those able to get past the spectacle of the fifty-six-year-old Nabokov overcome with "spasms of helpless fury" at the incompetent accolades accorded "smooth" translations will be met with the following expostulations in the essay's second paragraph:

> "Rhyme" rhymes with "crime," when Homer and *Hamlet* are rhymed ... The clumsiest literal translation is a thousand times more useful than the prettiest paraphrase.[2]

The modifier "useful" is the key to the sea change undergone by its author's stance on translation. Before 1955 the majority of his translations rhymed – among the practitioners of "the *art* of translation," he was one of the most dedicated. He may not have taken on Homer or realized his plan to translate *Hamlet* (or Joyce's *Ulysses* into Russian, or Tolstoi's *Anna Karenina* or Dostoevskii's *Brothers Karamazov* into English), but whether he tackled the prose of Romain Rolland or Lewis Carroll, his versions of their novels rivalled the most frivolous of poetic paraphrases in their willful treatment of their models. Youthful exuberance and lack of experience alone could not account for their failure to meet the new key requirement. Made only a few years prior to the publication of "Problems of Translation: *Onegin* in English," his rhymed English translations of the Russian poets paraphrased and interpreted their models. They may have been made with the aim of aiding students of Russian literature – this point was made abundantly clear in Nabokov's introductions to his translations from Pushkin, Tiutchev, and Lermontov – but "usefulness" was never a criterion sanctioned by the author of "The Art of Translation." Can a work of art, "a thing of beauty," be useful? Colas Breugnon's witty comeback at Count Maillebois's defence of "useless beauty" compelled Nabokov to formulate his resolutely negative response to this question as early as 1919, and after that he never budged in his defence of non-utilitarian art.

Until 1955, that is.

The absence of the word "art" next to "translation" in the 1955 essay can only be interpreted as evidence that Nabokov stopped recognizing in translation an art form. The implications of this recognition are momentous for those tracing the evolution of his views on translation. Understood as an applied – "useful" – craft, translation becomes a level field on which any "laborious lady" can challenge "the professional writer" who possesses "creative genius." The rules have changed to spell the end of the beautiful epoch of the sublime *confrérie* between poets separated by time and place but united by genius. By all implications, the heroic age of Parnassian matches involving the likes of Baudelaire and Poe, of Zhukovskii and Schiller – and, by the inevitable extension, of Nabokov and his confrères – comes to an end on the pages of the essay that often reads like an eviction notice served to a creative genius used to calling the Paradise of artistic licence his home.[3] Who is it, then, who comes to replace "the professional writer," the possessor of "creative genius"?

If translators continue to have duties to perform, none of those duties qualifies as "sacred." Another famous fragment from the essay recasts Nabokov's vision for the "person" who can be trusted to perform the job required of a literary translator:

> The person who desires to turn a literary masterpiece into another language, has only one duty to perform, and this is to reproduce with absolute exactitude the whole text, and nothing but the text. The term "literal translation" is tautological since anything but that is not truly a translation but an imitation, an adaptation or a parody.[4]

The masquerade featuring the allegorical representations of the various "degrees of evil" associated with translation is over. Gone are the "stocks" with which in "shoebuckle" days were rectified "blunders and boners," gone are the "types of translators," gone is the "John Into" who, in addition to being "of the same sex as his author," was required to possess "style, vision, wit," and above all else, "genius." With all the might of his rhetoric Nabokov endorses the humble scholar, the same scholar whose eagerness to introduce an "obscure genius" he previously refused to see as sufficient to carry out the translator's duty.

Only those familiar with the evolution of Nabokov's methods and thinking on the issue will be able to appreciate the degree to which the following key passage summarizes his personal struggles with the contradictions inherent to translation:

> The problem, then, is a choice between rhyme and reason: can a translation while rendering with absolute fidelity the whole text, and nothing but the text, keep the form of the original, its rhythm and rhyme? To the artist whom practice within the limits of one language, his own, has convinced that matter and manner are one, it comes as a shock to discover that a work of art can present itself to the would-be translator as split into form and content, and that the question of rendering one but not the other may arise at all.[5]

"The artist" to whom the necessity to separate rhyme from reason comes as a shock is no abstraction, no allegory: we have no ground to suspect that this realization was not shocking to Nabokov, who had laboured to keep the two together since 1916. The "person" who "quakes with Peter" in "Rimes" as he abhors the need to compromise "sacred sense" at the inexorable approach of a rhyme is the epitome of an autobiographical character. The initial shock associated with this realization, however, must have given way to relief. This rebellion against the dictatorship of form over content, rhyme over reason, matter over mind liberated the energy Nabokov needed to reinvent himself as a scholar-translator. The radical nature of this reinvention is underscored by the growth of the academic apparatus Nabokov had come to recognize as a required attribute of any translation worthy of the name:

> I want translations with copious footnotes, footnotes reaching up like skyscrapers to the top of this or that page so as to leave only the gleam of one textual line between commentary and eternity. I want such footnotes and the absolute literal sense, with no emasculation and no padding – I want such sense and such notes for all the poetry in other tongues that still languishes in "poetical" versions, begrimed and beslimed by rhyme.[6]

Those familiar with the road Nabokov had taken to this juncture cannot accept Lawrence Venuti's interpretation of the fervour fuelling his attack on the "artistic" mode of translation. The eminent translation theorist maintains that "Nabokov's views on translation are very much those of a Russian émigré writer living in the United States after 1940. He nurtures a deep, nostalgic investment in the Russian language and in canonical works of Russian literature and disdains the homogenizing tendencies of American consumer culture."[7] Setting aside the issue of Nabokov's investment in canonical works of Russian literature, we can say that "Problems of Translation: *Onegin* in English" represents a rupture with neoromantic notions concerning the special status of the Russian émigré writer, to which Nabokov did cling for a considerable period of time, defending them in "The Art of Translation." In the later essay Nabokov drops all pretense at that writer's exclusivity to enter a level field of academic expertise where his scholarship may be assailed with the same vigour he demonstrates when he criticizes the works of his predecessors. The radicalism of Nabokov's transformation had far-reaching consequences for his translating magnum opus, his upcoming "scholarly" version of Pushkin's novel in verse. None of these consequences, however, could rival the devastating effect the implications of the 1955 essay had on the results of his experiments in the "artistic" mode of translation. To them they tolled the death knell.

Barren of footnotes, less than invincible in their retention of "absolute literal sense," "begrimed and beslimed by rhyme" and "poetical" to a fault, Nabokov's ingenious versions of poems by Akhmatova, Blok, Fet, Lermontov, Nekrasov, Pushkin, and Tiutchev, among so many others, were to become the first victims of the literalist doctrine. Disowning them was the only way out of the "corner" into which Nabokov had "boxed himself." This is what happened in 1964, when Walter Arndt cited them as an obvious inconsistency in Nabokov's criticism of Arndt's "poetical" translation of *Eugene Onegin*.[8] Nabokov's admission of his old, "poetical" translations' incompatibility with his current views may have been publicized on the pages of the *New York Review of Books*, but it was the uncompromising rhetoric of the 1955 essay that made this decision inevitable. When on 12 March 1958, poet and translator Irwin Peter Russell requested Nabokov's permission to republish his "poetical" translations, Véra Nabokov responded on her husband's behalf: "As to his own translations from Pushkin, Lermontov and Tyutchev, he does not want to reprint them … He does not believe in verse translations any more."[9]

The logic, the evolution of Nabokov's development as translator, and not the polemic surrounding his literalist methodology in *Eugene Onegin* – and still less so his being a Russian émigré writer in 1940s America – led him to the formulation of his literalist doctrine. To miss this point is to overlook the specificity of Nabokov's most ambitious and consequential foray into translation, his four-volume translation and commentary to Pushkin's novel in verse.

The questions that need to be answered in connection with this sea change arise from elsewhere. Is it possible to convey the "absolute literal sense" of a work composed in one language in another? To what extent does a practical application of the literalist doctrine redeem the need to compromise the original when transferring it from its native linguistic and cultural context to an alien one? And more to the point of this current study, how did the advent of literalism affect Nabokov's lifelong dialogue with the erstwhile tutelary deity of his life in art, Aleksandr Pushkin? *Eugene Onegin*, however, cannot provide answers to these questions alone, requiring us to consider it in its element, the new reality created by "Problems of Translations: *Onegin* in English."

"The first exact translation of this curious book": *A Hero of Our Time*

With all the delays affecting the *Onegin* project, it was Dmitri and Vladimir Nabokov's translation of Lermontov's novel (1958) that served as the testing ground for the literalist doctrine of 1955. Made to the same specifications as *Eugene Onegin*, this translation never generated the excitement provoked by the literalist masterwork. Object as he did to the Nabokovs' inaccuracies in the use of English tenses and injudicious use of Gallicisms, J. Thomas Shaw found it to be "so generally successful and accurate" as to become "definitive for our time."[10] Formulated in 1959, Shaw's prognosis held its value as recently as 2010, when Boris Dralyuk singled out this translation from more than a dozen rival works for being a "surpassingly readable ... schoolroom favorite."[11]

Writing in 1941, Nabokov praised "the crisp, colorful, economical style that in Lermontov's time was a complete novelty."[12] Made at the dawn of the period of "tender and loving sinning," this comment contrasts with a much more reserved evaluation from the literalist era. While allowing that Lermontov's narrative "surges on with ... speed and force," the 1958 introduction catalogues numerous instances where Lermontov's underdeveloped craftsmanship threatens its cohesion. Finding it difficult to forego his emotional attachment to his subject where Pushkin was concerned, Nabokov the co-translator and annotator did develop a sufficiently dispassionate perspective on Lermontov. He shows him to be a novelist of prodigious promise but does not shy away from pointing out all the inconsistencies, platitudes, and incongruities that tend to go unquestioned. The few prose fragments from "The Lermontov Mirage" of 1941 make for an instructive comparison with the literalist version of 1958 – and presage an inevitable juxtaposition between Nabokov's rhymed versions of the select Onegin stanzas of 1945 and their literalist renditions of 1964/75.

All of the fragments included in the 1941 essay ranked high on Nabokov's list of Lermontov's successes, but eager as he was to prove his author's extraordinary "virility, beauty, and tenderness,"[13] Nabokov appeared not averse to boosting the vim and vigour of Lermontov's prose. The following dynamic sequence from "Bela" shows the difference in Nabokov's approach to his material before and after his conversion to "literalism":

> "Me?" cried Azamat in mad fury, and the steel of a child's dagger rang against the man's armor. A vigorous hand pushed him away, and he crashed backwards into a fence with such force that the fence rocked. In a minute or two there was a terrific hullabaloo: Azamat had run in with his coat all torn, shrieking that Kazbich had tried to kill him. Everybody rushed out, rifles were gripped ... Screams, tumult, gunshots. But Kazbich was already on his priceless horse and twisted and wheeled among the crowd in the street as he struck out in defense with his sword.[14]

> "Throw me?" screamed Azamat in a rage, and the iron of a child's dagger rang against chain-armor. A strong arm pushed him away, and he hit the fence so hard that it shook ... Two minutes later, there was a terrible uproar indoors. Here's what happened: Azamat had burst in, his *beshmet* torn, saying that Kazbich had wanted to cut his throat. Everybody dashed out, grabbed their rifles ... There was shouting, noise, rifle shots; but Kazbich was already on his horse and was wheeling in the midst of the crowd along the street, like a devil, swinging his sword in defense.[15]

The 1941 and 1958 versions of the same fragment differ from each other in number of subtle and not-so-subtle ways. "The *steel* of a child's dagger" hides the author's negligence in identifying the dagger's material (*zhelezo detskogo kinzhala*), and it is this peculiarity that the subsequent version reflects with its "iron of a child's dagger." The 1941 version shows Kazbich wearing generic "armor," which not only misrepresents the specificity of Lermontov's description but also risks suggesting that the author was careless in his arrangement of this animated scene. The Nabokovs diffuse this issue by equipping Kazbich with a "chain-armor," in a precise rendition of Lermontov's *kol'chuga*. The 1941 version gave way to the temptation to make Maksim Maksimych's description more realistic by introducing "in a minute or two," but the subsequent version reverts to his precise "two minutes later" (*cherez dve minuty*). The thinking behind the phrase "there was a terrific hullabaloo" prevented the initial version from giving a precise indication of its locus, but the adverb at the end of its subsequent variant restores the clarity (cf. "there was a terrible uproar *indoors*" and "v sakle *byl uzhasnyi gvalt*"). Azamat's "shriek" and "priceless" in relation to Kazbich's horse were frank embellishments on the translator's part, the latter having no precedent in the Russian text and the former compensating for the pallid gerund derived from "to say" (*govoria*). "Like a devil" (*kak bes*) may or may not have been excessive in reference to Kazbich's frantic "wheeling," but no literalist worth his salt can afford to let go of this vivid, if platitudinous, interpolation.

The 1941 version of another episode from the same novella offers further examples of a methodology Nabokov would later denounce as "paraphrase," as it ran afoul of his literalist definition of an "honest translation."[16] If the initial version of the passage below reads better as an English text, it is because it renders Lermontov's prose with "slick English clichés by means of judicious omission, amplification, and levigation":

> I led him out of the room where Bela had just died, and we went up to the rampart of the fortress. For a good while we walked together up and down without speaking a word, our hands behind out backs. His face did not express anything particular, and this angered me: were I in his place, I should have died of grief there and then. At length he sat down on the ground in the shade and began to scrawl something on the sand with a bit of stick. Well, you know, just for decency's sake, I thought, I had better offer him some consolation: I started speaking; he lifted his head – and laughed. That laugh sent a shiver down my spine. I got up and went to order the coffin.[17]

In his introduction Nabokov declares that he has "gladly sacrificed to the requirements of exactness … good taste, neat diction, and even grammar" in an attempt to convince the English reader that "Lermontov's prose style in Russian is inelegant."[18] It is difficult to come to the same conclusion, however, if all one has is the 1941 fragment. Maksim Maksimych may be justified to be "angry" at Pechorin's lack of remorse after Bela's death, and this is what the earlier version has. Pechorin's laughter may be sending a "shiver" down the narrator's spine in concert with the demands of idiomatic English. Likewise, Nabokov takes an educated guess that when Pechorin sits down Maksim Maksimych follows suit – this explains why he needed "to get up" before leaving. The literalist version of the same passage leaves this thinking behind to confront the reader with Lermontov the "energetic, incredibly gifted, bitterly honest, but definitely inexperienced young man" whose "Russian is, at times … crude"[19]:

> I led Pechorin out of the room and we went on to the rampart; for a long while we walked up and down, side by side, without saying a word, our hands behind out backs; his face did not express anything unusual, and this annoyed me; in his place, I would have died of grief. Finally he sat down on the ground in the shade and began to trace something in the sand with a bit of stick. I wanted to comfort him, mainly for the sake of propriety, don't you know, and started to speak; he lifted his head and laughed. A chill ran over my skin at this laughter. I went off to order the coffin.[20]

Indeed, Maksim Maksimych is not "angered" by Pechorin's apparent cynicism – "annoyed" is a happier match for Lermontov's *dosada.* Rather than supplying his reader with a more idiomatic English equivalent of *moroz probezhal po kozhe,* Nabokov chooses to render it literally ("a chill ran over my skin"); in another close replication of the original, the narrator leaves the scene without getting up first.

As befits a work dating from the early days of the period of "tender and loving sinning," the earlier fragments adapt their model to make it a better fit for its new environment. The subsequent literalist retranslation integrates the experience gained in the course of the initial attempt but diverges from it in the overarching understanding of its task. No longer smoothing out the rough edges of Lermontov's evolving style, it presents the reader with a critically sound rendition of its source. Nabokov's ability to infuse his and his son's literalist version of Lermontov's novel with his critical perspective is what makes this translation unique. The fact that the Nabokovs' version does not shirk from representing Lermontov's prose style as a work in progress has not impeded its becoming the de facto standard among the numerous Anglo-American versions the novel. Thanks to its rigidity of vision and execution, subsequent versions have gained from the Nabokovs' version the freedom of an educated choice between following their path in creating still more literal renditions, or reverting to the more adaptive – pre-Nabokovian, as it were – approach to the task. In this sense, the translation is a success. It offers ample proof that the literalist approach – the twinning of lexical precision and critical insight – has all the potential of being a winning combination.[21]

Juxtaposed with the *Onegin* opus, *A Hero of Our Time* strikes one as a triumph of restraint. Nabokov's introduction and notes to the novel are not devoid of personality; on the contrary, the clarity with which they represent their author's vision facilitates our acceptance of their authority. One has to be reminded that Nabokov's interpretation of the otherworldly arithmetic that accounts for the unique quality of Lermontov's "Triple Dream" owes its inspiration to Vladimir Solov'ëv – in a prefiguration of the more controversial aspects of the *Onegin* commentary, he makes no mention of his source. Indeed, it is easy to forget that the analytical perspective distinguishing this translation's apparatus owes its insight to Nabokov's thorough integration of Lermontov's artistry of fluid interplay of authorial perspectives into his own fiction. In this sense, this work is a masterpiece of mimetic disguise. Those without interest in the origins of Nabokov's perspective will have no trouble accepting it as a result of a traditional academic investigation.[22] Those interested in Nabokov's fruitful dialogue with Lermontov should augment their understanding of the Nabokov-Lermontov nexus with "The Lermontov Mirage" and his poetical translations of Lermontov's lyrics, each of which carries a distinct verbal vestige of Nabokov's discourse with the author of "Triple Dream." Nabokov may have disowned these works, but his subsequent work on Lermontov proves that he never ceased to consider him "a miraculous being whose development was something of a mystery."[23]

From "The Discourse" to *The Song of Igor's Campaign*

Given the amount of academic work Nabokov shouldered during his first two decades on American soil, the steady stream of publications stemming from this facet of his activities astonish by their range and depth, especially when one considers that it was also the time when he composed and published his most consequential original compositions and scientific papers. Another mammoth undertaking he conceived in the 1940s was his annotated translation of *The Song of Igor's Campaign* (1960).

Chapter 14 of *Speak, Memory* may be a memoir of the author's student days, but it features an echo of his ongoing work on the epic: "I invited to my Cambridge rooms the vermillion shields and blue lightning of the *Song of Igor's Campaign* (that incomparable and mysterious epic of the late twelfth or late eighteenth century)."[24] "Vermillion shields" (*chervlënye shchity*) and "blue lightning" (*sinii mlenii*) are his renditions of key epithets from his successive versions of the *Slovo*. They are as much a reference to the 1920s as to the forties and fifties, when sections of his memoir and his translation of the *Slovo* shared room on his writing desk. Apart from being an immediate source of inspiration for *Pale Fire, The Song of Igor's Campaign* is a major undertaking whose significance for the evolution of Nabokov's views on translation awaits proper contextualization.

Slovo o polku Igoreve is another literary artefact with a long history of integration into Nabokov's literary pursuits. To see this one only needs to turn to his version of Alfred de Musset's "La Nuit de mai," which employs a simile alien to Musset but close to Nabokov's heart. A striking image from Euphrosyne's incantation is the origin of Nabokov's phrase *liudskoi kovyl'* (human feather grass) in reference to the loss of life associated with Napoleon's military adventures.[25] Ever since the *Slovo* made its triumphant entry into the Russian literary canon in 1797 via Mikhail Kheraskov's classicist epic *Vladimir*, Euphrosyne's likening of the fate of the fallen warriors to that of crushed feather grass has become a stock metaphor. Aleksandr Blok's masterful employment of it as a reference to folkloric and medieval literature in "Opustis', zanoveska linialaia" (1908), "Na pole Kulikovom" (1908), and "Novaia Amerika" (1913) found an appreciative connoisseur in Vladimir Nabokov. A text he considered "a magnificent literary masterpiece, half poem, half oration,"[26] a plentiful source of popular epithets and images, the *Slovo* was at the centre of a web of associations and cross-references that made it a part of a greater Russian literary tradition.

By creating an English translation of the *Slovo*, Nabokov fulfilled a long-standing ambition – and established himself vis-à-vis not only Bernard Guerney, Roman Jakobson, Samuel Hazard Cross, but an entire history of this text's interpretation and adaptation. As early as 12 September 1930, Nabokov disparaged Konstantin Bal'mont's "atrocious" (*bezobraznyi*) poetic paraphrase of the *Slovo* in a letter to Gleb Struve,[27] and since 1940 – the year when André Mazon's attack on the traditional dating of the *Slovo* launched a global polemic regarding its authenticity[28] – it had come to the forefront of Nabokov's pursuits. On 8 February 1944, Nabokov wrote to Guerney to express his admiration for the "creative thought and poetical care" evident in his *Lay of the Host of Igor* (1943) and to outline a competing vision for its English translation presented in a review published in the *New Republic*.[29] A college instructor in need of a text he could trust, he was soon engrossed in making that vision a reality.

Nabokov's correspondence with Edmund Wilson, his sister Elena, and various colleagues and publishers reflects different stages of his work on his versions of the *Slovo*.[30] Brian Boyd has narrated the story of Nabokov's acrimonious falling out with his prospective collaborator, Roman Jakobson,[31] while Galya Diment has summarized the effect this quarrel had on their co-author, Marc Szeftel.[32] The story of Nabokov's evolving vision of the *Slovo* and his translation of it, however, remains untold.

Those familiar with the circumstances surrounding Nabokov's adoption of the literalist doctrine will see parallels with the evolution of the *Slovo* translation. On 1 November 1948, he informed Wilson that he was working on a new translation of the epic. That translation differed from everything Nabokov had done previously to meet his teaching needs and owed its novelty to the Jakobson-initiated joint academic effort *La Geste du Prince Igor'* (1943). In no small degree a repudiation of Mazon's attacks on the *Slovo*'s traditional attribution and dating, the volume contained Samuel Hazard Cross's English translation of the epic's text as conjectured, edited, and presented by Jakobson. Jakobson's text became the source for "The Discourse of Igor's Campaign," Nabokov's initial English version of the epic. In a replication of the transformation that affected his vision of his sources of Lermontov, Pushkin, Tiutchev and others, Nabokov changed his mind regarding the reliability of Jakobson's edition. Nabokov's letter to Wilson of 2 March 1959 reflects this change:

> I am working hard on my *Discourse on* [sic] *Igor's Campaign* which I once translated but now have completely revamped. The commentary to it has inherited a Eugene gene and is threatening to grow into another mammoth.[33]

The pun "Eugene gene" seems to confirm a logical inference that if the earlier "Discourse" was a typical work of the period of "loving and tender sinning," then the subsequent *Song* – much like its predecessor *A Hero of Our Time* – would be another translation in the literalist vein. This impression is confirmed by Nabokov's disclaimer: "In my translation of *The Song* I have ruthlessly sacrificed manner to matter and have attempted to give a literal rendering of the text as I understand it."[34] The following clarification amplifies this disclaimer's tenor:

> I made a first attempt to translate *Slovo o Polku Igoreve* in 1952. My object was purely utilitarian – to provide my students with an English text. In that first version I followed uncritically Roman Jakobson's recension as published in *La Geste du Prince Igor*. Later, however, I grew dissatisfied not only with my own – much too "readable" – translation, but also with Jakobson's views. Mimeographed copies of that obsolete version which are still in circulation at Cornell and Harvard should now be destroyed.[35]

The degree to which a comparison of the two translations of the *Slovo* should contradict these unambiguously worded statements, the extent to which *The Song of Igor's Campaign* is different from Nabokov's other literalist works is revelatory.

"The Discourse of Igor's Campaign" does indeed owe its existence to Jakobson's conjectures per his "édition critique du *Slovo*."[36] It breaks the raw material from the *editio princeps* into two parts. The sections within the two parts bring thematic order to the text of the *editio princeps* by largely ignoring the paragraph breaks introduced by its first editors while leaving the text itself intact. "The Discourse" enumerates each complete sentence without making any attempt to suggest any kind of strophic structure – here too Nabokov follows Jakobson's "édition critique."[37]

The most remarkable feature that distinguishes Nabokov's *Song of Igor's Campaign* from its antecedent, "The Discourse of Igor's Campaign," is not the ordering of its fragments based on a vision that contradicts Jakobson's[38] but its visual and aural presentation. In concert with Nabokov's decision to designate the *Slovo* a "song" and not a "discourse," it is patently, uncompromisingly poetic. After classifying the *Slovo* "as a 'chanson,' a gest, a heroic song"[39] and its anonymous author as a "bard," Nabokov endowed his translation with a number of attributes that transfigure the dry, if florid, prose of Jakobson's "édition critique" into a masterful stylization of a syncretic, pre-literary work of verbal art. The new version's syntax, together with the intonation it conjures, has the strophic structure of a verse narrative. All the extraordinary metaphors, wordplay, and the subtly suggested rhythmic figures of the new version come together to suggest that this translation abandons the frankly prosaic trappings of Jakobson's conjectures to create a text that can only be defined as poetic. Nabokov acknowledges as much in his notes when he decides not to follow what he sees as an excessively prosaic elucidation of a particularly mesmerizing image on the grounds that doing so "would abolish the poetry."[40] Being confronted with the choice "between rhyme and reason," in his creative interpretation of this source text Nabokov chose to go with the "rhyme" – in the broad sense of poetic artifice – and not the "reason" of Jakobson's cautiously austere "scholarly" conjecture.

Sandwiched between such bulwarks of literalism as *A Hero of Hour Time* and *Eugene Onegin*, *The Song of Igor's Campaign* amounts to a major digression from the fundamental principles of the literalist doctrine. Instead of presenting its readers with a "crib," it offers them a superbly readable poetic text of haunting beauty. Where "The Discourse" offered the sense of the text as Jakobson deduced it using the *editio princeps*, *The Song* consistently and deliberately transfigures that information into poetic rhetoric. Two versions of the same fragment from Vsevolod's speech demonstrate the extent and teleology of that transfiguration:

21. saddle, brother, your swift steeds;
22. for mine are ready, all saddled ahead, near Kursk.
23. And as for my men of Kursk, they are famous warriors; swaddled under the war-horn, nursed under the helmet, fed from the tip of the spear.
24. They know the trails; they are at home in the prairie ravines; their bow strings are tight, their quivers agape, their swords sharpened.
25. Akin to grey wolves they lope in the plain, seeking honor for themselves and glory for the prince.[41]

Saddle, brother, your swift steeds.
As to mine, they are ready,
saddled ahead, near Kursk;
as to my Kurskers, they are famous knights –
swaddled under war-horns,
nursed under helmets,
fed from the point of the lance;
to them the trails are familiar,
to them the ravines are known,
the bows they have are strung tight,
the quivers, unclosed,
the sabers, sharpened;
themselves, like gray wolves,

they lope in the field,
seeking for themselves honor,
[90] and for their prince glory.[42]

Focused as it is on the meaning of its source, only occasionally does "The Discourse" resort to rhetoric unambiguously expressive in its purpose, and when it does ("for mine are ready"), the effect of such tropes is offset by prosaic renditions clarifying the meaning of a given term ("my men of Kursk"). *The Song* re-envisages the same material to liberate the poetry obscured by the previous version's excessive concentration on the matter. As a result, the manner in which it is expressed soars to an unprecedented height. As presented in *The Song*, Vsevolod's speech is a resounding soliloquy in which anaphoras and epistrophes act as both rhetorical and structural devices responsible for the organization of this fragment into a segment of unrhymed verse. Nabokov's purposeful employment of such and similar effects throughout *The Song* leads to the inevitable conclusion: all Nabokov's protestations to the contrary notwithstanding, in this translation manner often reigns supreme over matter.

The transformative energy unleashed by Nabokov's work on *The Song of Igor's Campaign* set into motion his creative imagination. The germs of a tale of "a distant northern land" found in his imitations of Elizabethan and Jacobean verse dramas were to bloom in *Glory*, "Solus Rex," "Ultima Thule," *Bend Sinister*, and *Pnin*. Nabokov's long-standing aspiration to compose a modern equivalent of a traditional epic came to full fruition only after his effort to transform Jakobson's scholarly reading of the *Slovo* into an imaginative stylization of a medieval *chanson de geste*, paving the way for *Pale Fire*.[43]

Juxtaposition of "The Discourse of Igor's Campaign" (1952) with *The Song of Igor's Campaign* (1960) demonstrates that the later work was a digression from the strictures of the literalist doctrine. Nabokov resolves the issues associated with the problem of its authenticity on a creative plane, asserting the primacy of poetic artifice over historical and scholarly considerations. By highlighting the poetic nature of this document, Nabokov shows the *Slovo* to be a work of art whose inherent authenticity breaks free of temporal and material constraints. In an early indication of the complexities that lurk under the surface of his seemingly unambiguous stance on literalism, the reworking of "The Discourse" into *The Song* shows him willing and eager to make an exception from his literalist practices. Contradictory on its surface, this decision proves to be in line with the fundamental principles of Nabokov's aesthetics.

The Slovo asserts the primacy of creative artifice over mundane factuality. It is no coincidence that Nabokov dismissed André Mazon's sceptical stance as that of a historian who uses "sincerity" as a criterion for the evaluation of a work of art.[44] Aesthetic criteria, unambiguously subjective in their essence, afforded Nabokov much-needed freedom from dogma where translation was concerned in quite the same way as they did in the realm of original creativity. The publication of the *Onegin* opus – along with the belligerence that characterized his rhetoric in defence of literalism – was to highlight the contradiction stemming from Nabokov's ultimate commitment to the freedom of aesthetic judgment.

Onegin Dissected and Mounted: Toward "Absolute Literal Meaning"

"Diana's bosom, Flora's dimple" goes Nabokov's 1945 "poetical" rendition of "Diany grud', lanity Flory," the opening line of *Eugene Onegin*'s chapter 1, stanza 32 – the same rendition Nabokov would deride as a "lame paraphrase" in response to Walter Arndt's counter-attack in the *New York Review of Books* in 1964. "Diana's bosom, Flora's cheeks" reads the finalized and revised "literal" version of 1975.[45] While fulfilling its promise of providing the "absolute literal meaning" of the original, Nabokov's translation does not alert its reader to the fact that in certain contexts, Pushkin avoids the Russian equivalent of the English word "cheek" in favour of a far less common and unmistakably bookish Slavonicism, *lanity*. Nabokov's commentary, where one would expect it to be of help with regard to Pushkin's persistent use of such markedly quaint units impenetrable to a Russian with no philological schooling, proves to be equally useless to those who wish to be informed of the significance of the author's choice. Judging by this isolated example alone, Nabokov's *Eugene Onegin*, for all its promise of clarity, is a complex phenomenon with its own share of contradictions built into it. What was gained – and lost – in the aftermath of Nabokov's transition to the literalist method?

Nabokov's finalized preface to the published translation renews its commitment to "absolute literal meaning." His nomenclature of translating methods, as Kristine Anderson and Michael Eskin have shown, recasts John Dryden's three types of translation – metaphrase, paraphrase, and imitation – to legitimize one of the extremes not as one methodology among many, but as the only technique able to convey the significance of the translated text.[46] Meaning, significance – "reason" – behind rhyme is what Nabokov promises his reader:

Attempts to render a poem in another language fall into three categories:

> (1) Paraphrastic: offering a free version of the original, with omissions and additions prompted by the exigencies of form, the conventions attributed to the consumer, and the translator's ignorance. Some paraphrases may possess the charm of stylish diction and idiomatic conciseness, but no scholar should succumb to stylishness and no reader be fooled by it.
>
> (2) Lexical (or constructional): rendering the basic meaning of words (and their order). This a machine can do under the direction of an intelligent bilinguist.
>
> (3) Literal: rendering, as closely as the associative and syntactical capacities of another language allow, the exact contextual meaning of the original. Only this is true translation.[47]

Even though Nabokov initially thought that the iambic rhythm was helpful to the task of rendering *Eugene Onegin*, the finalized version cedes this last bastion of formal fidelity to his overarching pursuit of "complete meaning":

> In transposing *Eugene Onegin* ... I have sacrificed to completeness of meaning every formal element including the iambic rhythm, whenever its retention hindered fidelity. To my ideal of literalism I sacrificed everything (elegance, euphony, clarity, good taste, modern usage, and even grammar) that the dainty mimic prizes higher than truth.[48]

Nabokov succeeded in imbuing his English rendition of Pushkin's text with an understanding that even the harshest of his critics accept as "superb." That the authors of the acclaimed "literary" versions of Pushkin's novel, from Charles Johnston (1977) to James E. Falen (1990), acknowledge their debt to Nabokov testifies to the endurance of his achievement – as does Douglas Hofstadter's desire to prove him wrong in *his* translation (1999). If Nabokov's most persuasive critic, Aleksandr Gerschenkron, however, grants that his is "the most correct translation imaginable," he finds this to be true only in the narrowest sense of the term "exact" or "lexical."[49] It is in the "contextual" significance of Pushkin's word choices, his deliberate play on the diverse aesthetic effects of their combinations, where Nabokov's translation has most frequently been found wanting ever since Gerschenkron demonstrated how Nabokov's aspiration to the "absolute" was checked by the exigencies of its execution in 1965.

If Nabokov's "sacrifices" were to redeem the excesses of his "loving and tender sinning," it seems appropriate to try to trace this line of development from his 1945 poetical renditions to the literalist reincarnations of 1965–75. The attention he allots to stanza 33 of chapter 1 in "Problems of Translation: *Onegin* in English" provides us with an opportunity to ascertain how his vision of this specific task evolved along with his understanding of translation methodology.

The stanza in question constitutes one of Pushkin's celebrated authorial digressions: instead of relating the story of his protagonists, his narrator becomes the most fascinating actor in his own show. It is in such digressions where Pushkin achieves something that no one had done before him in the Russian language: he captures the ambivalent, contradictory, evanescent, fluid energy of humanity. As Pushkin's protagonist reminisces, he reflects on the ways his being became a battlefield of passions and emotions. His voice grows palpably nostalgic when his choice of verbs begins to vacillate between infinitives and finite past tense forms:

Я помню море предъ грозою:
Какъ я завидовалъ волнамъ,
Бѣгущимъ бурной чередою
[4] Съ любовью лечь къ ея ногамъ!
Какъ я желалъ тогда съ волнами
Коснуться милыхъ ногъ устами!
Нѣтъ, никогда средь пылкихъ дней
[8] Кипящей младости моей
Я не желалъ съ такимъ мученьемъ
Лобзать уста младыхъ Армидъ,
Иль розы пламенныхъ ланитъ,
[12] Иль перси, полныя томленьемъ;
Нѣтъ, никогда порывъ страстей
Такъ не терзалъ души моей![50]

Nabokov's poetical paraphrase of this stanza provides a vivid snapshot of Pushkin's original. It gives the reader a reliable sense of this stanza's structure, which includes an incomplete echo of its consistent interplay between masculine and feminine rhymes (see ll. 1, 2, and 9, 12). This is an equimetric, equilinear, and rhymed version of the stanza in question:

> I see the surf, the storm rack flying …
> Oh, how I wanted to compete
> with the tumultuous breakers dying
> in adoration at her feet!
> Together with those waves – how much
> I wished to kiss what they could touch!
> No – even when my youth would burn
> its fiercest – never did I yearn
> with such a torturing sensation
> to kiss the lips of nymphs, the rose
> that on the cheek of beauty glows
> or breasts in mellow palpitation –
> no, never did a passion roll
> such billows in my bursting soul.[51]

The creation of an English equivalent of so idiosyncratic a stanzaic medium results in the introduction of a number of images not present in the original. Easy as they are to point out (Pushkin's waves did not "die," his youth did not "burn," his nymphs are not anonymous, etc.), it is fair to say that even in those instances where rhymes force Nabokov to depart from the lexical meaning of Pushkin's words, his compromises never stray too far from the wording of his model. If this snapshot is somewhat smudged, it retains enough specificity to remain a recognizable depiction of a specific scene. What is it about this superficially adequate translation that fails to satisfy its maker?

Nabokov's 1955 literalist manifesto singles this stanza out as "untranslatable" – which is to say untranslatable in antiquated – "neo-Drydenian" – terms of the "Art of Translation" period. According to Nabokov the literalist, if one sets out to capture an array of semantic connotations in rhymed verse, the quest for a golden mean between its strictly lexical transposition and a variation on its themes will quickly override the goal, as the fragment below seeks to demonstrate:

> Another good example of a particularly "untranslatable" stanza is XXXIII in Chapter One:

I recollect the sea before the storm:

O how I envied
the waves that ran in turbulent succession
[4] to lie down at her feet with love!

Russian readers discern in the original here two sets of beautifully onomatopoeic alliterations: *begushchim burnoy* … which renders the turbulent rush of the surf, and *s lyubov'yu lech* – the liquid lisp of the waves dying in adoration at the lady's feet. Whomsoever the recollected feet belonged to … the only relevant fact here is that these waves come from Lafontaine through Bogdanovich. I refer to "*L'onde pour toucher … [Vénus] à longs flots s'entrepousse et d'une égale ardeur chaque flot à son tour s'en vient baiser les pieds de la mère d'Amour*" (Jean de la Fontaine, "*Les Amours de Psiche et de Cupidon*," 1669) and to a close paraphrase of this by Ippolit Bogdanovich, in his "Sweet Psyche" (*Dushen'ka*, 1783–1799) which in English should read "the waves that pursue her jostle jealously to fall humbly at her feet."

Without introducing various changes, there is no possibility whatsoever to make of Pushkin's four lines an alternately-rhymed tetrametric quatrain in English, even if only masculine rhymes be used. The key words are: *collect, sea, storm, envied, waves, ran, turbulent, succession, lie, feet, love*; and to these eleven not a single addition can be made without betrayal. For instance, if we try to end the first line in "before" – *I recollect the sea before* (followed by a crude enjambment) – and graft the rhyme "shore" to the end of the third line (*the* something *waves that storm the shore*), this one concession would involve us in a number of other changes completely breaking up the original sense and all its literary associations.[52]

Nabokov's explication of his goals permits us to close a sizeable gap in our understanding of his evolving vision. His understanding of the term "contextual" does not concern itself with the lexical context of the words of varying register. It focuses instead on the *literary* context of Pushkin's imagery: at this stage of his career in translation, the hidden machinery of literary artifice is more precious to him than the text's relationship with extra-textual reality. Not rendering the rhyming facade of Pushkin's invention should prepare the ground for an explication of the artistic reasons that set the poet's imagination in motion in the first place. How does the improved and finalized "literal" rendition bring us closer to that goal?

The 1975 version of the same stanza demonstrates the extent of Nabokov's subjugation of the translation to its model:

I recollect the sea before a tempest:
how I envied the waves
running in turbulent succession
with love to lie down at her feet!
How much I longed then with the waves
to touch the dear feet with my lips!
No, never midst the fiery days
of my ebullient youth
did I long with such torment
to kiss the lips of young Armidas,
or the roses of flaming cheeks,
or the breasts full of languishment –
no, never did the surge of passions
thus rive my soul![53]

In a fulfilment of his promise to eschew elegance for the sake of accuracy, the ostensibly English syntax of the translation has been modified to mimic that of an inflected language: the line "with love to lie down at her feet" is not inelegant, it is foreign sounding. The same literalist technique, however, permits Nabokov to regain much of what was lost in the 1945 variant, including Pushkin's truncation of the adverb *sredi* to *sred'* in l. 7, and "Armidas" in the "rhyming" position at the end of l. 10. One can imagine how difficult it was for Nabokov, who was used to expanding on the original mythological references, not contracting them, to produce a translation that deprived its reader of an opportunity to engage with Pushkin's onomastics.[54] These gains notwithstanding, this succession of lines cannot stand on its own as a specimen of English poetry. The reader who wishes to be spared the trouble of considering the original has no choice but to look elsewhere: this translation does sacrifice its independence to uphold that of its model. The literal variant urges its readers to consult Pushkin's text – along with Nabokov's notes to it – making it indispensable.

This was the essence of Nabokov's radicalism as far as his mature vision for translation was concerned. When, as Brian Boyd puts it, "[Nabokov] surprised himself by evolving a new theory of translation,"[55] it was his realization that he could no longer consider translation an art that was most shocking. "Creative genius," which he for such a long time deemed a prerequisite for success in translation, generates a reality of its own rather than imitating something already in existence. The success of any given work of art may be measured by the degree of its independence from the circumstances that prompted its germination and realization. A translation that obscures its model may become a work of art in its own right, but in doing so it risks closing the door that leads to that plane of existence where a different work of art inhabits its discrete dimension. It is difficult not to associate this realization with the discoveries Nabokov made about his "poetical" English renditions of Tiutchev's "Posledniaia liubov'." Based as it is on his personal – mistaken – understanding of the poem's place in the history of Russian letters, Nabokov's translation is as likely to lead the reader to those passages in his *Invitation to a Beheading*, where this mistaken understanding gives rise to a fictional existence of its own, as it is to Tiutchev's unique individual vision for his work and its position within the unity of his art.

Since J. Thomas Shaw's 1965 observation that Nabokov's translation was "written in a language of his own," much ink has been spilt in an effort to conceptualize this effect.[56] Did Nabokov seek to "estrange" Pushkin and by doing so elevate him to the level of the "creative genius" he believed he was? If no "poetical" paraphrase can do justice to Homer or Shakespeare, as he states in "Problems of Translation: *Onegin* in English," no translation can attain the level of Pushkin's perfection. Tempting as it is to follow this ennobling interpretation, it proves to be based on a misunderstanding.[57] As Brian Boyd has pointed out, not only did Nabokov never intend for his translation to stand on its own, he laboured to underscore its dependence on the original by interspersing Pushkin's lines with his. It was only due to the technical difficulty of achieving such an effect that "the translation was *not* printed ... in interlinear fashion, beneath Pushkin's transliterated lines."[58] As Judson Rosengrant has shown, however, no matter where it is reproduced, Nabokov's English may never become altogether neutral and transparent. As if to compensate for its inability to recreate the stylistic interplay of its model, it seeks to become a "concoction," "a hybrid of modern British and American English (with Gallic and archaic admixtures) ... a pastiche of Pushkin's early nineteenth-century Russian."[59] This quality of Nabokov's English proves that it may never be separated from its Pushkinian model.

Where Nabokov's translation does succeed is in its subjugation of itself to the needs of an enlightened appreciation of the original – as long as that appreciation is predicated on a knowledge of the Russian language. Boyd said it all when he stated that "placed under Pushkin's line, approximating Pushkin's order and rigorously faithful to his sense, Nabokov ... is simply and typically illuminating."[60] So powerful is the charge of his illuminating technique that even modern readers of Pushkin's novel in verse whose native language is Russian will benefit from consulting it. One does not have to read further than line 4 of Pushkin's "prefatory piece" to stumble across a difficulty stemming from the fact that Pushkin's Russian differs from modern usage. In modern Russian, the phrase "zalog dostoinee tebia" means "a token worthier *than* you," which renders it meaningless. With its "gage worthier *of* you," Nabokov's translation sets the record straight on two levels: by providing an informative equivalent of *zalog* and by eliminating potential for misreading. Modern editions silently suppress the typo found in stanza 27 of chapter 3 in the 1837 edition, but even then, when Pushkin writes "ia shlius' na vas, moi poety," few modern readers will understand that this line should be read as "my poets, I appeal to you."[61] Such and similar situations where the translation performs its promised task of aiding one's appreciation of the original *without the commentary* are not negligible. By refusing to stand alone and attaching itself to its source, the translation ensures its lasting relevance as an aid, not an independent work of art.[62]

Where does Nabokov's translation fall short of its promise? Setting aside such eccentricities as rendering *krivoi* by "curvate" (1:24), *obez'ian* by "sapajou" (4:7), and *malinovyi* by "framboise" (8:17), it is difficult not to agree with Gerschenkron that when it comes to Pushkin's play on different stylistic strata, the translation that sets out to provide "the exact *contextual* meaning of the original" all too often elevates lexical exactitude at the expense of a paramount stylistic effect. Neither "dimple" nor "cheek" does justice to Pushkin's erotically charged use of the Slavonicism *lanity* in the opening line of the stanza Nabokov introduces as "untranslatable," yet he remains surprisingly mum on the issue of this stylistic nicety throughout his commentary. Damning as Gerschenkron's censure of Nabokov's failure to account for Pushkin's archaisms is, his criticism of Nabokov's inability to convey social speech differentiation between Tat'iana and the nurse is all the more bracing.[63]

If, apart from illuminating its readers, Nabokov's translation does a good deal to puzzle them, it is because not infrequently instead of supplying "absolute literate sense"[64] or "exact contextual meaning,"[65] it becomes a goldmine of the translator's personal insights. Absolute exactitude is unattainable; the ideal of literalism is bound to remain in the world of ideas. Latinism in English cannot convey the stylistic effects of the Slavonicisms encrusting Pushkin's Russian, so Nabokov chose to abstain from attempting to recreate their effect. Yet after making a valiant effort to subdue his creativity, after attempting to transform himself into a selfless scholar in the employ of Pushkin's genius, Nabokov failed to become someone he was not. This becomes apparent when one consults the "Correlative Lexicon," in which his locution "a Russian ear" comes too close to proving to be a contextual synonym of "creative genius":

> Very often, as in the case of *shum*, the obvious translation, "noise," is absurdly incapable of following the Russian word though a contextual maze where a Russian's ear can hear versatile *shum* echo all sorts of humming, murmuring, sighing sounds that the word "noise" would simply drown.[66]

As the example of Nabokov's "Return of Pushkin" demonstrates, it was his ear that discerned in Pushkin's alliterative line "znakomym shumom shorokh ikh vershin" the potential for its English echo: "so old a sound – the soughing of their crests."[67] Nabokov's creativity – his genius, for want of a better word – encompasses not only his composition and writing, it illuminates his reading of others. As the single greatest distinguishing feature of his literalist translation, it ensures its continued relevance. Elevated to the status of an absolute, however, it proves to be its vulnerability.

Worship, Sacrilege, and Dialogue: Nabokov, Pushkin, and *Eugene Onegin*

Notwithstanding its quiddities, Nabokov's translation of *Eugene Onegin* is phenomenally useful. The majority of those who benefit from it are foreigners, but even Anglophone Russians find in it a shortcut to the meaning of their literature's most over-interpreted text. Notwithstanding Nabokov's denunciation of literary translation – or perhaps thanks to it – his literal rendition has galvanized proponents of rhymed translations.[68] The usefulness of a translation he intended to become a "trot" is unquestionable.

That the same cannot be said of Nabokov's commentary to Pushkin's novel is a major conundrum. A labour of stupendous dedication and learning, a trove of valuable information, it has come under fire ever since its publication in 1964. Why? Nabokov's disdain for academic decorum – his refusal to accept that his scholarly commentary is a compilation – can be cited as one reason. J. Thomas Shaw recognized in the commentary Nabokov's "chief contribution" but was taken aback by its "unexpected *personal* quality" that turned so much of it into a work of "*individual* … impressionistic criticism."[69] Brian Boyd has highlighted Nabokov's achievement in demonstrating Pushkin's "uniqueness all the more convincingly because he never exaggerates it in the wrong place,"[70] but acknowledges that the commentary is not without defects. While refusing to see the commentary as either "aimless pedantry" or "covert art," Boyd concedes that it "reveals as much about Nabokov as many of his novels."[71] If this concerned any one of Nabokov's works, it would never be a problem. The fact that it concerns someone else's composition, and in his version, disturbs for all the right reasons. Coupled with his refusal to render Pushkin's poetry by poetry, Nabokov's desire to tower above his commentary can be construed as an attempt to complicate, not facilitate, communication between the author and the reader. If Nabokov's translation refuses to be transparent – "invisible" – on so many levels; if his commentary amplifies his personal, individual point of view to the extent that it begins to obscure Pushkin – for what is Nabokov's insistence that Pushkin was incapable of appreciating English poetry independently if not obscurantism? – then it must be a manifestation of Nabokov's fraught relationship with Pushkin.[72]

Since 1964 there has been no shortage of interpretations elucidating the paradox of this work's unconventionality. Edmund Wilson laid the foundation for one school of thought. "A drama in his *Evgeni Onegin* is not Onegin's drama," he opined in 1965, "it is the drama of Nabokov himself attempting to correlate his English and his Russian sides."[73] When Douglas Hofstadter, Caryl Emerson, and David Bellos contend that Nabokov mutilates Pushkin to appease the demons of his artistic inadequacy, it is Wilson's pithy formulation that they develop. Subtler, better-informed explications have been proposed as well. Accepting that "the role of an impartial erudite-annotator … was … too humble … for Nabokov's artistic temperament," Alexander Dolinin interprets his drive "to elevate Pushkin to the status of a universal genius" as an attempt "to represent *Eugene Onegin* for English readers as both the alien, unfamiliar, uniquely Russian phenomenon that cannot be fully appropriated by the foreign language" and a work that remains "an integral part of the overall West European poetic sensibility." To this scholar, Nabokov failed to separate egocentric art from altruistic scholarship: "Accustomed to dictatorial power over his fictional worlds, he evidently tried to gain the same supreme authority in respect to Pushkin's masterpiece … to assert himself as his sole exegete and peer." In presenting so individual a perspective, Nabokov perpetuated the long-standing Russian tradition of formulating one's personal relationship with the poet by composing a "my Pushkin" piece of his own.[74] Marijeta Bozovic has taken Dolinin's interpretation still further by arguing that Nabokov joins the tradition of moulding "*his* Pushkin" to legitimize his own claim to a position of honour within a "transnational literary canon," "clearly intending … to wrest himself a space in the canon" while aiming "for literary immortality."[75] Different as they are, all of these interpretations converge in one point: an artist determined to leave his mark on the world, Nabokov used Pushkin to fulfil his own ambition – and dictate the terms of a posthumous appreciation of his own work.

While identifying the intensity of Nabokov's engagement with Pushkin's novel as a manifestation of Nabokov's personal, individual relationship with his paragon, such and similar interpretations tend to present his *Eugene Onegin* project as something static. It is true that it is the pinnacle of his intense engagement with the poet, yet a study of its development may shed additional light on or perhaps even revolutionize our understanding of Nabokov's personal stakes in the project of his lifetime. Below, I formulate an alternative point of view that treats Nabokov's *Eugene Onegin* as an elaborate speech act, a verbal vestige associated with Nabokov's dialogic struggle to overcome personal impediments associated with his search for a unique idiom suitable for addressing Pushkin.

Nabokov came to literature with a strong sense of allegiance to Pushkin. During his poetic apprenticeship he established an entire vocabulary to profess his love for the poet, a vocabulary that comprised complimentary similes in line with the Russian tradition of Pushkin worship. This passion gave rise to a singularly strong attachment, a relationship of which Nabokov was protective. As a poet and writer, Nabokov depended on Pushkin for a sense of unique exilic identity, first in the Crimea, subsequently in Berlin and Paris. As a maturing novelist he found in Pushkin a source of inspiration not only for his debut *Mary*, but for the highest point of his career in Russian letters, *The Gift*. As an American writer and scholar, he turned his translation of and commentary to *Eugene Onegin* into his most cherished academic ambition, one on a par with lepidoptery. The *Onegin* project may be best understood as a successor to a line of speech acts, a liberating ascent from tradition-prescribed impersonal worship to an inquiry-driven private investigation.

Nabokov was initially inclined to treat Pushkin as an inexplicable mystery he could only address with impersonal generic metaphors ("Pushkin is a rainbow all over the earth" opens a typical piece of his poetic juvenilia on the subject). That the findings and conclusions of Nabokov's research on *Eugene Onegin* could not be further removed from such simplistic praises is understandable. What is easy to overlook is the fact that the language of his mature statements on Pushkinian subjects targets uncritically accepted platitudes to assert his point of view with a resolute use of the first-person pronoun "I":

> I shall now make a statement for which I am ready to incur the wrath of Russian patriots: Alexandr Sergeyevich Pushkin (1799–1837), the national poet of Russia, was as much a product of French literature as of Russian culture; and what happened to be added to this mixture, was individual genius which is neither Russian nor French, but universal and divine.[76]

No longer an exiled poet used to deriving his sense of his Russianness from his ability to admire Pushkin unconditionally, the author of "Problems of Translation: *Onegin* in English" takes issue with received knowledge concerning Pushkin's uniqueness. Such elusive modifiers as "universal" and "divine" are still present, but over an entire decade prior to 1964 there is a growing sense of a mystery solved, a discovery made. The tonality of this quotation echoes that of a related literary utterance to the same effect, "On Translating *Eugene Onegin*" (1954):

> O, Pushkin …
> I travelled down your secret stem,
> And reached the root, and fed upon it;
> Then, in a language newly learned,
> I grew another stalk and turned
> Your stanza patterned on a sonnet,
> Into my honest roadside prose –
> All thorn, but cousin to your rose.[77]

This Nabokov shows no reluctance to engage Pushkin directly by positioning his "I" against that of his favourite interlocutor. From the early 1950s onward, Nabokov the American Pushkinist will have no difficulty finding words to verbalize the subtlest aspects of Pushkinian singularity; in his commentary to *Eugene Onegin* he will have no trouble pointing out those instances where Pushkin relies on second-rate French sources, where his writing betrays his dependence on inferior models. This is but one aspect of his challenge to the "patriotic" Russian myth of Pushkinian singularity.

That such freedom of expression and interpretation was hard won is easy to surmise. My suppositions regarding the difficulties Nabokov overcame in his evolution from an ardent admirer of Pushkin at a loss for words to extoll Pushkin's virtues to one of Pushkin's most independent, articulate, and opinionated critics are in need of substantiation and expansion.

A short authorial digression in the unpublished poetic narrative "The Two" ("Dvoe"; 1919) succinctly summarizes an early point of departure in the evolution of Nabokov's attitude toward Pushkin. In "The Two" Nabokov confesses to keeping his volume of Pushkin in "sacrilegious" proximity to that of Paul Verlaine. Nabokov's readiness to couch his attitude toward Pushkin in markedly ecclesiastical terms is remarkable. That he would continue to employ such terminology in his attempts to formulate and advance a holistic interpretation of Pushkin's relevance in the twentieth century in general and Pushkin's relevance to the exilic predicament of his fellow Russian refugees in particular is noteworthy, as it marks a distinct stage in the development of Nabokov's attitude toward Pushkin. Few documents demonstrate this more effectively than Nabokov's 1931 Pushkin talk. In it Nabokov suggested a number of parallels between Pushkin the exiled and persecuted poet and the predicament of his fellow Russian émigrés. On this account Nabokov's conclusions were unequivocal: seemingly a scourge, banishment is a benevolent demon he dubs "a genius of exile." It proved to be a boon for Pushkin; it will be a blessing for those celebrating Pushkin's achievement abroad at a time of approaching upheavals.[78]

The 1931 Pushkin talk sought to console and encourage Nabokov's émigré listeners. What is remarkable is that throughout its length, Nabokov the professed individualist takes pains to abstain from speaking in the first person, as if to underscore that he came to speak to his community and on his community's behalf. And yet at a certain point in his talk, Nabokov comes close to using the first person when he tries to derive his vision of Pushkin's sense of sadness and despondency from Pushkin's own thoughts and emotions:

> And all the same the poet is triumphant. Let misfortune be ever at his heels, let slanderers scribble their calumnies and accusations, let his entire existence be savage and muddled like a delirious night in a filthy tavern at the side of a muddy road, let, as in a bad dream, countless checkpoints, quarantines prevent you from getting back to your happiness, let your last kopeck be lost at cards to a passing officer, let Benckendorff insult you with his meddling, and God wot with whom your pregnant wife is flirting, and life is such a burden that all you can do is to sigh "Ennui, ennui ..." and you long to go somewhere far away, and you get so envious when you see the Viazemskis off on a steamboat, and out there is the forbidden West, the theatres of Paris, the cast-iron railways of England, but what does it all matter – unanswerable slights retreat as soon as along with a village rain poetry starts dripping down.[79]

Few of Nabokov's listeners could appreciate that this "transmission" of Pushkin's inner monologue cited verbatim Pushkin's letter to his friend Prince Pëtr Viazemskii, dated 27 May 1826. Still fewer could understand that in selecting Pushkin's confessions to his friend, Nabokov censored the poet's self-expression. When in his exile to Mikhailovskoe Pushkin pined for "the forbidden West," along with such fruits of European civilization as "cast-iron roads," "steamboats," "English magazines," and "theatres," he also yearned to discover Parisian brothels.[80] Bound by the Russian tradition of poet-hero worship, Nabokov found himself unable to honour Pushkin's right to free speech, as it would not have fit the agenda of the solemn communal event at which he gave his speech. The force that prevented Nabokov from finding a way to celebrate Pushkin the complex human being in 1931 was the inertia of the Russian tradition of treating Pushkin as the national poet, the demigod, the proverbial sun deity of Russian culture. Speaking in 1931, Nabokov effectively reinforced a hundred-plus-year-old edifice of traditional Russian Pushkin worship. When in 1955 he rebelled against the "patriotic" Russian myth, he rebelled against his own former willingness to perpetuate it as well.

Toward the end of the 1931 talk, Nabokov comes tantalizingly close to breaking free of these self-imposed fetters:

> And once again comes back the thought of his perilous, murderous fate, of the fleetingness of his life, and one wants to surrender to an empty

> daydream: what would have happened, had he only ... What would have happened, had he only emerged unharmed from that duel, as from the one with Ryleev at Batovo or the one with Starov in Kishinëv? Can we imagine a gray-headed Pushkin, with gray sideburns, a Pushkin dressed in an eighteen-sixties frock coat, a restrained Pushkin, an elderly Pushkin, a decrepit Pushkin? What awaits him in his declining years – the morose shadows of the untalented Pisarevs and Chernyshevskis, or perhaps a wonderful friendship with Tolstoy, with Turgenev? But there is something impious, sacrilegious in such divination ... Pushkin's image is unthinkable without Pushkinian apprehensions and creations – and with what creations and apprehensions can we fill the remaining half-century of his possible life? He was in the noontide of his powers when he died, and his genius gave promise of much to come. But what he accomplished was sufficient. His silenced lyre had given rise to a resonant ceaseless ringing. A Pushkinian spirit permeates the lines of the poets who succeeded, but did not replace him – Lermontov and Tyutchev, Fet and Blok. Words, however, cannot define this Pushkinian spirit.[81]

What is so sacrilegious about this attempt to imagine Pushkin as an old man? Some answers to this question are more obvious than others. To do so would go against the tradition of celebrating Pushkin's tragic fate, to run the risk of trivializing it by showing him a mere mortal. To do so would be to envisage Pushkin's unwritten works, and how could one do such a thing without becoming Pushkin's interlocutor?

In this passage Nabokov already finds himself on the wrong side of sacrilege when he weaves a strain of personal family history into that of Pushkin's life and fate. Kondratii Ryleev's duel with Pushkin in Batovo – the estate that was to become the Nabokovs' country seat – is a speculative proposition.[82] Already here Nabokov is seen to be instilling Pushkin's fate with his own imagination. Even though he was reluctant to trust his natural instincts as a writer of fiction, he was to overcome that reluctance. In chapter 2 of *The Gift* Nabokov will return to this same situation, and it will result in a scintillating celebration of his fantasy, even under the mask of the invented nineteenth-century memoirist Suhoshchokov.[83] *The Gift* is a celebration of Nabokov's freedom to explore some of the most sensitive aspects of his attitude toward Pushkin.[84] It is a celebration of his freedom to envisage and imagine, a triumph of his fantasy and fiction. It is a further step away from the sterile tradition of Russian cultural sacerdotalism that customarily ascribed Pushkin supernatural powers but prevented one from establishing a closer, more immediate contact with the human being behind the myth. If *The Gift* was one spectacular result of this shift in Nabokov's attitudes, *Eugene Onegin* was another. Every bit as important as Nabokov's ability to overcome ritualized fears regarding what is and what is not appropriate as far as Pushkin is concerned was his ability conduct a dialogue with Pushkin, to contradict him.

Pnin offers one telling manifestation of this newly acquired freedom. On its surface this is a story of an unfortunate and persecuted man whose life is played out in full accordance with the Pushkinian formulation of "nature's indifference" to man's travails, drawn directly from Pushkin's "Brozhu li ia vdol' ulits shumnykh" (1829), translated here as "Whether I wander along noisy streets." The submerged but discernable significance of this novel's dénouement – Pnin's ability to elude his taunters – contradicts its famous Pushkinian leitmotif. It asserts nature's compassionate attitude toward the protagonist, who manages to emerge ruffled but triumphant from his clash with scoundrels and cheats, one of whom is his ostensible maker. In *Pnin*, fate – Pushkin's lifelong obsession – is repeatedly exposed as a superstition, whereas nature is presented as a fundamentally sympathetic entity. Here as elsewhere Pushkin's rationalist pessimism is counterbalanced with a sense of metaphysical certainty that is distinctly Nabokovian. In *Pnin* and especially in the *Onegin* opus, Nabokov challenges Pushkin in the personal idiom he succeeded in developing in his English-language works.

When assessed in their continuity, Nabokov's statements on Pushkin form an evolving discourse that increasingly asserts his personal views on a range of subjects against those of his interlocutor. Traditional worship gives way to a reconsideration of what may and may not be considered sacrilege with regard to Pushkin's memory, and a celebration of imaginative approach to Pushkin in *The Gift* gives rise to the formulation of a competing world view characteristic of Nabokov's subsequent works, a world view that eventually blossoms into the individual analytical perspective of the *Onegin* translation and commentary. An heir to an oppressively monologic tradition of the Russian poet-hero worship, Nabokov took time to develop an ability to introduce his "I" into imaginative and imaginary conversations with Pushkin. His English-language works proved to be best suited to provide him with a medium for an unfettered discourse on all things Pushkinian.

Being able to transition from Pushkin worshipper to Pushkin scholar, Nabokov was not able to subdue the artist within him as he strove to develop a novel individual appreciation of the Pushkin phenomenon.

His relationship with Pushkin was too personal, his emotional ties to the poet too close to be severed. Pushkin's spectre followed Nabokov for a good deal of his life, and he deliberately cultivated that connection. Born a century after Pushkin, Nabokov did not overlook other coincidences that seemed to connect him to the poet. Nabokov, who undertook to translate into English Pushkin's "Ia vas liubil" for the first time on the centenary of the poem's composition in 1929, may or may not have found out that his erstwhile fiancée Svetlana Siewert had married a member of the Andrault de Langeron family, as if to mirror the destiny of Anna Olenina, the addressee of Pushkin's poem. Into *Drugie berega*, however, he incorporates a reference to his hereditary connection with Pushkin via his father's cousin Ekaterina Danzas, "a grandniece of Colonel K.K. Danzas, Pushkin's second in his fatal duel,"[85] and even though in his *Onegin* commentary he parts with many features of his 1931 speech on Pushkin, he continues to insist that his Batovo estate was the site of the poet's duel with Ryleev.[86]

The *Onegin* commentary does abound in assertions of an intensely personal relationship with its subject, frequently expressed in a style too idiosyncratic for what ostensibly is a scholarly effort ("the literalist writes his own untranslatable poem," Michael Wood has quipped in the commentary's margins).[87] Indeed, as Michael Eskin has demonstrated, in many of the commentary's passages Nabokov resorts to speculative strategies that have a strong fictionalizing effect on his explications of the novel.[88] As far as Nabokov was concerned, however, this transformative subjectivity was one of the strengths of his *Onegin* oeuvre. He felt he had earned the right to assert his individual perspective on Pushkin. The invigorating effect his project has had on Pushkin studies makes itself felt decades after creating one of the biggest shockwaves ever sent throughout the world of translation and literary studies. For Nabokov, however, it became a celebration of his freedom to address his interlocutor as an equal.

This study opened with a reference to "On Translating Pushkin: Pounding the Clavichord," Nabokov's 1963 attack on Walter Arndt's rhyming version of *Eugene Onegin*. Easy as it is to sympathize with Arndt, Nabokov's position deserves to be examined in its context as well. As far as Nabokov was concerned, when he spoke in defence of "the helpless dead poet" he voiced his dissent from the prevailing general opinion regarding translation, one sanctified by the award of one half of the third annual Bollingen prize for the best translation of poetry in English to Arndt's industrious work in the literary, not literal, vein. Nabokov may have gone too far when he branded Arndt a "paraphrast," he may not have given him credit for demonstrating that it was possible to transpose the entirety of Pushkin's novel into English Onegin stanzas (something Babette Deutsch had already accomplished in 1936),[89] but the substantial part of his critical analysis makes it abundantly clear that Arndt's rendition upheld the status quo that permitted translation to replace its model. It is to this end that Nabokov chose to conclude his salvo with a list of all the academic dignitaries whose authority ensured the perpetuation of that status quo.

That in attacking Arndt Nabokov was disparaging a rival is indisputable. The Bollingen Foundation's endorsement of Arndt's translation, however, ensured that that rival was not as disadvantaged as it may seem to those who compare Nabokov's and Arndt's reputations today, when it is impossible to ignore the contrast between the global literary celebrity enjoyed by the former party and the limited professional acclaim earned by the latter. This impression, however, is deceptive. When Nabokov attacked Arndt in the *New York Review of Books*, he did not disparage him as a fellow writer. Against a widely held consensus represented and personified by Arndt, Nabokov pitted his individual notion of all things Pushkinian. Subjective as it may have been, his perspective on the substance of this argument was fortified by a superior knowledge of the phenomenon in question. His attack on the settled ideas concerning what translation can and cannot accomplish was guided not only by his sense of responsibility for the veracity of his methods and findings but also by his sense of informed loyalty to Pushkin's originality. Arndt's version conventionalized that phenomenon, and by stating this Nabokov raised awareness of the risks associated with following conventions when originality and individuality are at stake.

Was Nabokov's translation able to redeem the faults of Arndt's work? Or – to rephrase this question in terms of its immediate context – was Nabokov's "ideal of literalism" worthy of all the "sacrifice"? It was not "euphony" and "elegance" alone that he put on the altar of that ideal, after all, not even his reputation as an opponent of "knavery and tyranny." At stake was his cherished belief in art's ability to overcome material constraints. The fact that he chose not to insist on reproducing his "literal" rendition of Pushkin's verses as an interlinear text, or even *en regard*, as he initially hoped it would be done, shows that he too was open to compromise.[90] The published version of the *Onegin* opus put the translation before the original, while banishing Pushkin's text to the last section of the four-volume set, where it was reproduced photostatically in minuscule print. The realization fell short of the ideal behind it, obscuring the value of Nabokov's attempt to subjugate translation to its model. This, however, was but one aspect of the fallout from his elevation of literalism to the status of a dogma in the aftermath of a public debate concerning the fate of *Eugene Onegin* in English.

A closer examination of Nabokov's literalist legacy shows his implied position on the issue of translation to be more nuanced than his declarations and polemical statements. While *A Hero of Our Time* and *Eugene Onegin* follow the literalist dogma, *The Song of Igor's Campaign* breaks free from it. Even though Nikolai Karamzin's "Chto nasha zhizn'?" and Konstantin Batiushkov's "Ty znaesh', chto izrek" are mere epigrams, their presence in the *Eugene Onegin* commentary indicates that rhyme has other uses apart from "begriming" and "besliming" foreign works in inept imitations. It is regrettable that the fact that Nabokov's position proves to be more flexible in practice than his rhetoric suggests is lost on the majority of his critics and students.

The quintessence of Nabokov's stance on the issue of translation is captured by the following phrase from his response to Edmund Wilson's "The Strange Case of Pushkin and Nabokov": "I refuse to be guided and controlled by a communion of established views and academic traditions."[91] Was he prepared to be controlled by a single idea, even though that idea resulted from a laborious thinking process, even though he sacrificed to it a number of previous convictions? A search for a synthesis played out behind the facade of the literalist doctrine, a doctrine that had already proven not as uniform as the rhetoric in its defence implies.

Chapter Five

BEYOND *EUGENE ONEGIN* (1965–1977)

"Please take the Atlantic into consideration": Sybil Shade and the *Sunday Times* Translation Contests

On 4 April 1959, Vladimir Nabokov proved himself capable of surprising those with settled ideas about how he might behave or what he might do as far as the practical application of his own translating doctrines was concerned. After spotting in the 29 March 1959 issue of the *Sunday Times* a competition for the best translation of a verse fragment from Rémy Belleau's *La Bergerie* (Pastoral; 1565–72), he attempted to transpose this delicate miniature into English. The way he did it adds considerable intrigue to our understanding of his translation theory and practice in their development.

Why would Nabokov decide to enter that particular competition after ignoring many others organized by a newspaper he read regularly? He had at least two good reasons to be tempted by this task. First, the poem glorified the month of his birth; second, Belleau was an old friend. *Lolita* readers know that Humbert Humbert was well aware of one obscure work by that minor member of La Pléiade – in his diary he even toyed with the idea of citing it in the textbook he was allegedly compiling.[1]

That year's judges extracted a three-stanza fragment from a fifteen-sestet piece featured in Belleau's domestication of an Italian pastoral.[2] Not as explicit as the "blazon" to which Humbert Humbert was so partial, in its original form "Avril" sports a few erotic images nonetheless. The three sestets the *Sunday Times* Easter Competition organizers selected, however, would raise no eyebrows: they make up a short paean to the rejuvenating powers of spring. What was bound to exasperate those wishing to create this poem's literary translation were its form and vocabulary. The competition's rules, however, called for "poetical" versions.

Like its complete version, the curtailed "Avril" is a syllabic poem in which lines of variable length form sestets that open with couplets but close with quatrains featuring enclosing rhymes.[3] While the modern reader's eye may dwell on the obsolete spellings, it is the specific names of the various specimens of flora and fauna and their interplay that needed to be conveyed for a foreign-language translation to stand a competing chance. Such a version's odds would increase if it could capture the hint of melancholy in the second sestet, but to be a success, it would have to find a way to convey the intonation conjured by the poem's uneven lines.

Nabokov's entry offered all of the above and more. The self-proclaimed literalist had lost none of the flair that distinguishes the best of his pre-*Onegin* translation experiments.[4] Carefully applied archaisms mark the poem's vintage: in addition to the "thou" and "dost," the second sextet's first line terminates in "bland," used here in the late Middle English sense of "gentle in manner." The translation preserves "exile," that sestet's key image, and finds an ingenious solution to the problem of "messengers of Spring" ("du printempts les messagères") by turning them into its "forerunners." It is the translation's melody that carries the weight of its integrity: Nabokov's English replica of the French model preserves the interplay of longer and shorter lines while preserving the poem's strophic structure.

When Nabokov submitted his entry to the competition from the United States, he asked the judges to take the Atlantic into consideration, which they did. The authors of the anonymous verdict, however, damned his translation with faint praise, mentioning it among various "excellent versions" submitted to them.[5] Whereas Nabokov strove to remain as close to the model as possible, the judges favoured contenders' ability to combine frivolity with ingenuity and eagerly condoned "perfectly justifiable liberties." The first prize went to G.A. Langdon, who took multiple liberties with the poem's imagery to introduce "Afric shore" (from which the swallows return at Spring's beckoning), "Proserpine," and other embellishments not sanctioned by the original.

Nabokov's second entry into the *Sunday Times* translation contests would be his last, but in certain ways it was more remarkable than the first one, especially if we take into account the extraordinary circumstances under which it was executed. By 25 December 1962, when he entered his translation of one of Henri de Régnier's "odelettes," he had already been transformed into a resident of Montreux Palace and one of the most famous writers alive – it was that year's 25 April issue of *Newsweek* that had his portrait on its cover as "*Lolita* creator," against the background of Sue Lyon's profile. Not discouraged by the disappointing performance of his first competition bid, this time he decided to up the ante by entering the competition under a pen name, turning the entire affair into a far more interesting game.

When Nabokov sent his entry to the *Sunday Times*, the parenthetic attribution under this translation of Régnier's "Quelle doucer dans mes pensées" declared "translated by Sybil Shade." His attribution of "Passing of Youth" (as the competition organizers chose to call it) to one of the four central characters of *Pale Fire* was in line with the novel's plot – or rather amounted to a compact but not an insignificant extension of it.[6] The readers of canto 3 of John Shade's poem remember that translation was an outlet through which Sybil expressed her grief at the loss of her daughter to suicide: "You went on / Translating into French Marvell and Donne."[7] Charles Kinbote's note to these lines may be characterized by his trademark insensitivity, but it lifts the veil of mystery over these translations' significance for their maker: grieving Sybil translated John Donne's "Death be not proud" and Andrew Marvell's "The Nymph Complaining for the Death of Her Fawn."[8] Both translations are representative of Sybil's plight as a bereaved mother; both come under Kinbote's fire for their alleged inaccuracies. Kinbote's carping notwithstanding, the excerpts that he cites demonstrate that Sybil was a talented and sensitive practitioner who imbued her translations with personal significance without violating their integrity. Judging by these excerpts, Sybil's translations reflected Nabokov's own practice of selecting source texts that resonated with his thoughts and emotions while attempting to convey their significance with the fewest formal and semantic digressions. Sybil's – Nabokov's – translation of Régnier's "Odelette" ("Quelle doucer dans mes pensées") is one more translating experiment executed in this pre-literalist mode.

Régnier included this poem in his *Vestigia Flammæ*, a collection dedicated to the "remembrance of things past." Its title is a curtailed version of "Agnosco veteris vestigia flammae" – "I recognize the traces of the old fire" – a phrase with which Virgil's Dido confesses that in her feelings for Aeneas she recognizes the passion she felt toward her late husband.

Sybil Shade's translation of the poem offered two versions of the opening quatrain. The first stayed closer to the letter of its model, while the second resulted in what its translator designated a "prettier paraphrase" – as if by chance employing two words that Nabokov's literalist doctrine qualified as anathema. The first, complete, version of the translation opened with the following quatrain:

Within my thoughts what sweetness flows
On this soft morning, pure and bright,
Before those rocking barks with those
[1/4] Dead lanterns carrying no light.[9]

In addition to reproducing the original rhyme scheme, the more precise initial version preserves the enjambment connecting the quatrain's third and fourth lines. Sybil's postscript offered the "prettier paraphrase" of the same quatrain. Unincorporated into the body of the completed translation, it did away with the enjambment, but offered instead a variant featuring a richer orchestration:

What sweetness in my every thought
On this soft morning, pure and bright,
Before those rocking barks with nought
[2/4] In their extinguished lamps but night.[10]

Like many poems in *Vestigia Flammæ*, "Quelle douceur dans mes pensées" is a lament for vanished youth. Sybil's translation alters the poem's composition by refusing to follow its model's syntactic outline: while the original comprised two sentences – one encased in the first quatrain and two in the poem's penultimate and last quatrains – in her English version each quatrain carries a complete sentence. This shift permits the translator to end her English poem on a statement epigrammatic in its completeness:

And ceasing to be underway,
Worn by the surge's buffetings,
My heart, now sensible, will stay
[12] Wed with the old quay's iron rings.[11]

Sybil's translation of "Quelle douceur dans mes pensées" brings her character into a sharper focus. A superb translator from the English into French, she proves herself equally gifted at travelling in the opposite direction. As befits a work from the pen of John Shade's beloved wife, this translation is a verbal manifestation of Sybil's reticent elegance, impeccable taste, and attention to detail. Although it carries no implicit reference to her husband's violent death, this poem distils the feelings of a woman accepting solitude as the companion of her autumnal days. A widowed woman whose daughter has committed suicide, she chooses to wed her loneliness in the manner of the closing stanza.

Why would Nabokov want to enter the *Sunday Times* translation competition again? A sportsman to the marrow of his bones, he welcomed competition and was ever ready for a good fight. Those familiar with his career in translation, however, have a better purchase on the hidden reasons for this translation's coming into being at this particular moment in his career in letters.

While Nabokov greeted Rémy Belleau as an old friend, he had every reason to recognize in Henri de Régnier someone he had encountered many decades ago in Russia, a poet who helped him verbalize a theme that proved to be a paramount source of inspiration for *Pale Fire*. Nabokov's translation of Régnier's "L'Allusion à Narcisse" is among the earliest translated works preserved in his archives, and it is remarkable for the ways in which it presages the reflection motif that binds disparate parts of *Pale Fire* into a coherent unity. By attributing his translation of "Quelle douceur dans mes pensées" to Sybil Shade, Nabokov found a way to mark the occasion of his first verbalization of the reflection motif with the aid of Régnier's dialogic prompting.

Perhaps predictably, Nabokov's global literary fame, along with his obdurate pronouncements on translation, negatively affected Sybil Shade's chances of winning the 1963 competition. This time around the judges' justification made no mention of Vladimir Nabokov's name but took great care to ensure that he understood that they held his opinions on translation in low esteem. Lest Nabokov miss the implications of the first prize being awarded to Audrey Field's grotesquely inadequate version – Field's rendition of Régnier's concluding stanza featured Peter Pan, of all literary allusions – the anonymous judges' preamble opened with the following message:

> On the face of it the French poem … looked simple enough. There were no obscurities of sense or syntax, no concealed snags or ambiguities. But verse translation can seem deceptively easy until one gets to "the intolerable wrestle with words." All but the unblushing literalists among more than 750 contestants must have realized this by the end of the second line. Although there were no translations of outstanding merit – none that

> stood out as an English poem in its own right – everyone evidently went to it with will: the teenagers and octogenarians (among them the progenitor of "13 grandchildren none of whom speak French"), the high-flyers ("And peace inosculates my heart") and the busy housewife ("It was done while ironing"), the country vicars and the retired proconsuls.[12]

While I have not been able to ascertain if George Steiner had already assumed the responsibilities of organizing the *Sunday Times* translation competition – by 1968 he would – it is obvious that whoever wrote that preamble had a good sense of Nabokov's bellicose defence of literalism.[13] In addition to that, they knew their T.S. Eliot well enough to cite *Four Quartets* ("the intolerable wrestle with words"). The note reads as an attack on Nabokov, who would have been the only "unblushing literalist" among the 750 competition entrants, and who was meant to feel the sting of the barb that declared that no submission "stood out as an English poem in its own right." It is likely that the preamble's writer had read *Pale Fire* and appreciated the implications of Nabokov's attack on T.S. Eliot's *Four Quartets*, along with the place allotted in that novel to Sybil Shade. The wording of the preamble is an attempt to cut Nabokov down to size at a time when the writer was at the peak of his popularity and was getting ready to publish his *Onegin* opus.

Be that as it may, Nabokov's rhyming translations of Belleau's "Avril" and Régnier's "Quelle douceur dans mes pensées" amount to pieces of hard evidence testifying to his lack of desire to dismiss literary, poetical translation altogether. A search for "a synthetic solution" to the problem associated with his dogmatic stance on the issue was underway, and these two paraphrastic renditions of French poems marked the beginning of a difficult path toward it.

"A very special conjunction of stars in the firmament of the poem": The Literalist Relents

Had Nabokov's translation of Pushkin's "Pora, moi drug, pora! Pokoia serdtse prosit" (1834–6) appeared without his explanation of the translating methodology behind it, it would still have been a fascinating addition to everything he had said and done on the subject prior to 1 March 1965.[14] Fascinating and in no small degree puzzling: a short digression in his introduction to his English translation of *Despair* goes against much of his "literalist" rhetoric not only in "Problems of Translation: *Onegin* in English" (1955) and "The Servile Path" (1959),[15] but also in what was his most recent polemical piece, "On Translating Pushkin: Pounding the Clavichord" (1963). It was there where he condemned not only Walter Arndt's transposition of Pushkin's novel into "meretricious" English rhymes but also his own "lame paraphrases" of Pushkin and other Russian poets, since by "begriming and besliming" their models by rhyme, they "smacked" of "knavery and tyranny." "Problems of Translation: *Onegin* in English," along with other statements made in support of the "literalist" doctrine, had seemingly done away with the unquantifiable rhetoric that upheld the "poetical," "literary" mode in "The Art of Translation" (1941), that manifesto of "loving and tender sinning." As follows from the analysis of his translations of Rémy Belleau and Henri de Régnier – and especially from the implications of his presentation of Sybil Shade's translations of John Donne and Andrew Marvell in *Pale Fire* – the forceful literalist rhetoric cannot be taken to represent the totality of Nabokov's views on translation. Nabokov's preamble to his 1965 translation of Pushkin's "Pora, moi drug, pora! Pokoia serdtse prosit" reinfornces the validity of this conclusion.

On the surface of it, Nabokov provided this translation to assist his Anglophone readers in appreciating the portent of Hermann's invocation of the poem in *Despair*. The implications of his reasoning behind this poem's appearance in English, however, go above and beyond this applied task:

> The line and fragments of lines Hermann mutters in Chapter Four come from Pushkin's short poem addressed to his wife in the eighteen-thirties. I give it here in full, in my own translation, with the retention of measure and rhyme, a course that is seldom advisable – nay, admissible – except at a very special conjunction of stars in the firmament of the poem, as obtains here.[16]

While it may appear that Nabokov's literalist variants of Pushkin's originals override their literary antecedents, this melodious rhyming rendition reverses the course of this action with even greater certainty than that suggested by the Belleau and Régnier translations. The complete translation from the introduction to *Despair* revises the earlier variant of the poem's opening line from "'Tis time, my dear, 'tis time, for peace the heart is asking"[17] to "'Tis time, my dear, 'tis time. The heart demands repose,"[18] marking a situation where a subsequent *literary* version supplants an *earlier* literalist – ostensibly final – variant. The technical reason for this adjustment is transparent enough: it eliminates the issue that could arise from the presence of a feminine rhyming combination (cf. "is asking" and "repose") even though this line's model ends in a feminine rhyme. Along with the deletion of a decidedly unpoetic present continuous compound, this improvement clears the way to a rhyming English-language poem that comes to represent its source in a poetic guise. The mere presence of this translation, however, is not as significant as Nabokov's justification of the methodology he followed on this occasion.

The same translator who in 1955 expressed hope that "literal" translations "with no emasculation and no padding"[19] would one day supersede their "poetical" precursors once and for all deliberately violates his self-imposed strictures to follow a "seldom admissible" course of action. "A very special conjunction of stars in the firmament of the poem" absolves him of his blatant violation of his own doctrine, while reviving the rhetoric of "poetic genius" from the period of "loving and tender sinning." This translator's special relationship with the original places him above all the laws of translation he himself has formulated; his freedom is not to be curtailed – even by the laws of his own formulation.

The unambiguously prohibitive conclusions drawn at the end of "Problems of Translation: *Onegin* in English" were to be reiterated in the foreword to the finalized edition of the *Onegin* opus of 1975, where the question "Can ... any ... poem with a definite rhyme scheme be really translated?" would be answered "Of course ... no."[20] No match to such an expansive and forceful statement, the digression from Nabokov's introduction to *Despair* nonetheless amounts to a significant modification of his stance on the issue. As implied by the fact that he repeatedly took the "seldom admissible" course of action by rendering poetry by poetry, he returned to the practice of poetical, literary translation in a reversal of his earlier refusal to recognize in translation an art form. We recall that "The Art of Translation" elevated verbal artists in possession of "creative genius" above scholars and drudges alike, affording artists the freedom to transgress on their models' integrity as long as those transgressions were justified by a superior appreciation of their unique nature. The quintessence of the frankly speculative concept "loving and tender sinning," it amounts to the main implication of Nabokov's cryptic reference to "a very special conjunction of stars on the firmament of the poem." Apart from lifting the original poem skyward, this unabashedly poetic image tacitly consecrates its artist-translator's exceptional ability to reach that firmament.

"The proposition that all men are created equal": Nabokov Translates Abraham Lincoln

A commissioned job to render a piece of political rhetoric, a Russian translation of Abraham Lincoln's Gettysburg Address was no typical task by Nabokov's standards. But it was exactly what Roy P. Basler, Director of the Reference Department at the Library of Congress, invited him to consider as a form of "public service" on 5 April 1966. Nabokov accepted Basler's offer "with intense pleasure," confessed to having "always" admired the address as "a work of art," and expressed his hope that he could "turn it into reasonable Russian." He also observed that the translator's task is not made easy by Lincoln's "play" on "dedicate" (in "dedicated to the proposition that all men are created equal") and "other stylistic features of the speech." Nabokov's terms of engagement sent a clear message: this staunchly apolitical artist did accept Lincoln as an interlocutor, but elected to converse with him on *his* part of the field.

Nabokov's insistence on treating the Address as "a work of art" first and foremost did not mean that he was indifferent to its political import. Lincoln's definition of the United States' destiny as "a ... nation ... dedicated to the proposition that all men are created equal" may be interpreted as something Nabokov the individualist could see as a harbinger of potential dangers, against which he had wanted to inoculate readers of *Bend Sinister*. It should not be forgotten, however, that what may be loosely described as Nabokov's cult of individuality – his conviction that those in possession of creative genius are fated to be at odds with societies and their tendencies to equalize – presupposed the ability to create and innovate. For all their posturing, the Hermanns, Humberts, and Kinbotes are intellectually infertile, whereas John Shade – a mature Nabokovian epitome of fecund creative genius – is American to the marrow of his bones. Nabokov's insistence on treating the Gettysburg Address as a work of art was therefore not a projection of his individualist stance in and of itself. For him it was a way of setting the right conditions for a unique stylistic experiment. Its significance becomes apparent when we examine the aesthetic properties of his translation.[21]

What did Nabokov mean when he referred to the "other stylistic features of the speech" that posed difficulties for its Russian translator? The context and date of his "Rech', proiznesënnaia pri osviashchenii kladbishcha v Gettisburge" indicate that he had no current Russian idiom in which to place his translation. Since rendering it by means of a coarsely totalitarian Soviet political jargon was out of the question, he was faced with the task of conjuring a parallel linguistic dimension where egalitarian political discourse would be a norm. Nabokov was not being coy when he mentioned the difficulties associated with translating Lincoln's short speech. Translating a political statement of this nature into Russian in 1966 was no mean feat.

Son of a parliamentarian and grandson of a progressive statesman, Nabokov cast his stylistic net over the time when Russian civilization still nurtured the vision of a liberal path for itself. The type of discourse in which he resets Lincoln's eloquence balances archaism and innovation; at no point, however, does it bear any resemblance to the contemporaneous Russian – Soviet – political rhetoric.[22] Below I italicize the lexical items responsible for the creation of this stylistic effect:

> Now we are engaged in a great civil war …
> *Ныне* мы ведём великую гражданскую войну …
> It is altogether fitting and proper that we should do this.
> Такое действие нам вполне *подобает* и *приличествует*.
>
> It is for us the living, rather, to be dedicated here to the unfinished work which they who fought here have thus far so nobly advanced. It is rather for us to be here dedicated to the great task remaining before us – that from these honored dead we take increased devotion to that cause for which they gave the last full measure of devotion – that we here highly resolve that these dead shall not have died in vain – that this nation, under God, shall have a new birth of freedom – and that government of the people, by the people, for the people, shall not perish from the earth.
>
> Это нам, живым, скорее следует здесь посвятить себя незаконченному делу, которое сражавшиеся здесь двигали *доселе* столь доблестно. Это скорее нам следует посвятить себя великому труду, который ещё остаётся *пред* нами; *дабы* набраться от этих чтимых нами усопших *вящей* преданности тому делу, которому они принесли последнюю полную меру преданности; *дабы* нам здесь торжественно постановить, что смерть этих умерших не останется тщетной; что эта нация, с помощью Божьей, обретёт новое рождение свободы; и что правление народное, народом и для народа не сгинет с земли.[23]

The idiom into which Nabokov transfers Lincoln's words features a number of markedly archaic items, some of which are ecclesiastical in origin. This results in the creation of a text redolent of eulogies and encomia, yet remaining on the laic side of the equation due to its overwhelmingly neutral register. The archaisms *nyne, prilichestvuet, daby,* and *viashchii,* and the Slavonicism *pred* work together to ensure that while remaining neutral in its overall sound, this Russian version of Lincoln's speech broadcasts its connection with a non-Soviet tradition of verbalizing notions pertaining to equality, liberty, and justice.

Does our understanding of the stakes associated with this miniature stylistic experiment advance our notion of Nabokov's brand of dialogism? What kind of verbal vestige could it possibly have left on the compositions of a writer approaching his eighth decade? The answer to this question is in the experiment's context.

Nabokov's work on a Russian Gettysburg Address became a brief, if intense, distraction from the composition of *Ada, or Ardor*. In the parallel universe of Nabokov's invention where this novel is set, Russia finds itself in the western, not eastern, hemisphere of the planet "Antiterra." Known as "Amerossia," the country is governed by "Abraham Milton." In *Ada,* the lingua-stylistic experiment that had begun as Nabokov's version of Abraham Lincoln's Gettysburg Address acquired a fictional dimension universal in its scope. A fancy suggested by the difficulties associated with the need to generate a linguistic reality with precedents but no actual manifestation evoked a response to Lincoln's formula of his – and Nabokov's – nation's sense of destiny. In Nabokov's case, however, that sense could not be separated from an awareness of his emotional and intellectual lineage, which he projected into a parallel reality of his invention. Lincoln's role in shaping the dimensions and physics of that plane of being reveals itself not to have been as negligible as it might seem.

"When the true batch outboys the riot": Nabokov, Bulat Okudzhava, and the Soviet Reader

Nabokov's translation of Bulat Okudzhava's "Sentimental'nyi romans" is dated 2 February 1966.[24] Brian Boyd has shown that it at least in part came into being as an aftershock of Nabokov's verbal clash with Edmund Wilson on the pages of the *New York Review of Books* (where Wilson placed his "Strange Case of Pushkin and Nabokov," 15 July 1965) and the *Encounter* (which published "Nabokov's Reply," the polemical piece known as "Reply to My Critics," February 1966).[25] Today it is easy to overlook how Nabokov's substantiation of his literalist methodology as applied to *Eugene Onegin* and his competence as its annotator hid multiple dimensions. Yet apart from challenging Wilson's ability to be his judge in all matters Pushkinian, Nabokov felt the need to ward off the attacks of Wilson's supporters, who seized the opportunity to assail him. One such assailant was Robert Lowell, a winner of the National Book Award and a recipient of the Pulitzer Prize for Poetry. Lowell's creative output encompassed "imitations" of foreign poems whose originals he could not always appreciate, not knowing their language of composition. Nabokov's insistence on such a knowledge being a key qualification for any literary translator irritated Lowell. This irritation showed long before Nabokov published "On Adaptation" (1969), his most articulate deconstruction of Lowell's method.

Lowell's words in support of Wilson betray alarm at and discomfort with Nabokov's insistence on translators' unmediated access to their sources – but also a degree of tentativeness: "Edmund Wilson must be nine-tenths unanswerable and right in his criticism of Nabokov. The long arguments about Russian gerunds, the devious dictionary meanings of English and Russian words, etc., cannot conceal what is obvious, that Nabokov's *Onegin* is really, and perhaps only half intentionally, a spoof of his readers, rival translators, Pushkin, and Nabokov himself."[26] Lowell's support of Wilson is another early formulation of a popular interpretation of Nabokov's agenda in the *Onegin* opus. Far from being an independent arbiter, however, the author of *Imitations* had a stake in that argument.

Lowell's renditions of Osip Mandel'shtam's poems that appeared in 1963 and 1965 in the *Atlantic Monthly* and the *New York Review of Books* followed an approach diametrically opposed to everything Nabokov stood for in his insistence on possessing superior insight into the nuances of his models' language and context.[27] In terms of rigour, Lowell's technique was no match for Nabokov's considered methodology. Even though what Lowell composed were variations on themes suggested by Olga Andreyev Carlisle's English renditions of Mandel'shtam's poems, in his explanation of his methodology he vacillated between divergent, if not mutually exclusive, terms: "Our translations, while trying to be as faithful as possible to Mandelstamm's images and meter, are not literal. Rather, they are adaptations attempting to recapture Mandelstamm's tone and the atmosphere of his terrible last years."[28] Not differentiating between translation and imitation, committing himself to a "faithful" representation of the formal aspects of his models without being sufficiently equipped to shoulder such a task, Lowell saw "tone and atmosphere" as his main aims. In Nabokov the application of this approach could provoke nothing but dismay – and when it did, it compelled him to do something unprecedented.[29]

In a letter in the May 1966 issue of the *Encounter*, Nabokov refused to respond to Lowell's support of Wilson's censure of a literalist *Eugene Onegin*, citing Lowell's ignorance of Russian and urging him instead to stop "mutilating defenseless dead poets – Mandelshtam, Rimbaud, and others."[30] Privately, however, Nabokov was contemplating a way to make his dissatisfaction with Lowell's "imitations" known. After discarding the idea of creating a competing translation of a Pasternak poem Lowell had "imitated," he thought of turning to a different Soviet phenomenon, one he had discovered only recently. This sequence of events – and the polemical fervour that compelled Nabokov to action – gives us insight into Nabokov's relationship with contemporary Soviet culture, a closely guarded sphere of his intellectual interests.

The poet he chose to translate was Bulat Okudzhava (1924–97), the modest hero of unofficial "guitar poetry," a distinct and novel phenomenon associated with Nikita Khrushchëv's Thaw. Son of a purged Bolshevik, himself a World War II soldier, Okudzhava enjoyed a wide popularity among connoisseurs of nascent non-conformist Soviet culture. Older than such beacons of the Thaw generation as Bella Akhmadulina (1937–2010), Evgenii Evtushenko (1932–2017), and Andrei Voznesenskii (1933–2010), by 1966 Okudzhava had earned a distinct place in the culture of "the people of the sixties" (*shestidesiatniki*). The degree of Okudzhava's non-conformism was underscored by the fact that in addition to proliferating in homemade audio recordings, his poetry and prose were disseminated by such anti-Soviet émigré outlets as the Frankfurt-am-Main–based publishing house Posev. Even though it may not be possible to obtain all the details pertaining to Nabokov's discovery of Okudzhava and his brand of sung poetry, it is clear that after forming a good idea of this singer-songwriter's specificity, he developed genuine admiration for it. His keen interest in the Okudzhava phenomenon shatters the myth of a disdainful exiled elitist out of touch with his homeland.

Translation and translation polemics provided Nabokov with a pretext for broaching the idea of publicizing his version of a poem by a young Soviet poet through a major Western channel. To prepare his audience for their encounter with Okudzhava, he drafted a "Translator's Note" that was informative and deceptive in equal measure.

Opening with an overview of his views on translation, it proceeded to spell out Nabokov's dissatisfaction with Lowell's experiments:

> Recently I have been so distressed by a well-known American poet's impossible travesty of Mandelshtam's logic and magic that I cast around for some Russian poem that I could still save from the enthusiastic paraphrast who strangles another man's muse with his own muse's strong hair.[31]

By reusing the label "paraphrast," Nabokov ensured that his obloquy of Lowell harked back to that of Walter Arndt. The language of his invective, however, should not obscure something unexpected. In his preamble Nabokov made a startling admission – startling for those who are used to seeing his stance on literalism as something he was not willing to compromise. Echoing the sentiment expressed in his introduction to *Despair*, where he argued the existence of those exceptional situations where both the significance and the form of a poem composed in one language may be replicated in another due to "a very special conjunction of stars," he was prepared to argue that Okudzhava's "Sentimental'nyi romans" represented another such exception:

> Except in a very few cases, the form of the original poem in From, and especially its rhymes, cannot be retained in a literal Into translation. Those few cases are fascinating.[32]

Nabokov's description of the methodology behind his translation shows that he was willing to compromise a strict variant of literalism when confronting another "fascinating" exception to a general rule. In a development unprecedented in his post-1955 translation praxis, his "Translator's Note" qualifies the "scantiness" of rhymes found in his version as his "inaccuracy."[33] This shift in his position prepares the ground for another set of implications. To translate a poem means to adjust it in such a way that its transfer from its native linguistic and cultural setting to an alien one is guided by an overarching understanding of that poem's unique features. This semantic "no man's land" is where the translator's sense of propriety is tested, Nabokov implies: after accepting that compromise is unavoidable, it is the translator's responsibility to minimize its detrimental effects on the significance and formal features of the model.

> Could I render it in a form close to the original while preserving its literal meaning almost intact? I say "almost" because in my translation … I had

> to make several minute adjustments in order to preserve its throaty, guitar-like tonalities. It belongs to the popular Russian genre of sung poetry and is especially difficult to translate (which is why I chose it) because its impact upon the senses derives not from direct verbal originality but from an inspired combination of idiomatic clichés. The bilingual reader will note that I could not force myself to either use the name "Nadezhda" (unpronounceable in English) or turn it into the stiff, long-faced, long-aproned "Hope," hence my "Speranza" which reenacts dazzlingly the eloquent lilt of the original.[34]

If there was one area where Nabokov was not prepared for compromise, it was the translator's linguistic competence. Knowing Lowell to be a prominent poet in his native language, he chose not to revive his categorization of different types of translators in the manner of the nomenclatures produced during the period of "loving and tender sinning." Knowledge of what he calls "From" and "Into" languages, however, is something that any literary translator must possess:

> My version is faithful enough to prove … that a translator's adequate knowledge of both From and Into languages and a couple of sleepless nights can sometimes help to render not only the meaning, but also the music of a heartrending dit.[35]

Nabokov's preamble and the drafts of his translation of "Sentimental'nyi romans" show that he reserved for himself a considerable degree of freedom. Apart from renaming the addressee of Okudzhava's apostrophe "Speranza," he changed the poem's title to "Sentimental Ballad" and broke its iambic heptameters into tetrametric units in a clear indication of his appreciation of the fact that for Okudzhava's "guitar poetry," a poem's appearance is secondary to its aural constitution. His rendering of Okudzhava's markedly colloquial turn of speech "chtoby posledniaia granata menia prikonchit ne smogla" at the end of the poem's second stanza upholds his decision to shift its action to the world of old-fashioned chivalry: along with the title "Ballad," such a phrase as "coup de grace" ("to prevent the last grenade from giving me a coup de grace") re-enacts a romantic backdrop fitting for a variation on an Arthurian legend that Nabokov was fond of in his youth.

It is the poem's concluding stanza that should stop in their tracks those familiar with Nabokov's uncompromising anti-communism in general and his view of the Russian Civil War in particular. Okudzhava concluded his song on one of his most famous statements. Due to its popularity, it became the verbal quintessence of a special brand of Soviet romanticism that swept over the USSR after Khrushchëv had declared a return to the Leninist roots of the Soviet project:

> But if I suddenly some day
> Don't manage to protect myself,
> When the terrestrial globe is jolted,
> Whatever that new battle be,
> I'll always fall in the same war,
> The distant one, the Civil one,
> And commissars in dusty helmets
> Will bend in silence over me.[36]

After revisiting his multiple brushes with violent death on World War II battlefields, the poem's autobiographical protagonist longs to die in such a way that it would earn him the approval of the ghosts of the communist commissars. Okudzhava's depiction of the Bolshevik commissars wearing their characteristic helmets was fraught with personal significance and hinted at the toll Stalinist purges took on what he and his Soviet contemporaries considered the purest, most idealistic, and uncompromising generation of believers in the Soviet dogma. Okudzhava's father was one such Bolshevik, and it is his beyond-the-grave union with his executed father that the poem's last stanza suggests. Nabokov's ability to overcome his aversion to the political implications of Okudzhava's glorification of Bolshevism at its most violent is startling. The significance of his choice invites and rewards further scrutiny.

The cover letter with which Nabokov meant to convince William (Bill) Maxwell of the *New Yorker* to publish his take on Okudzhava's "Sentimental Ballad" implies that the "Translator's Note" was "the most important part of the performance" for Nabokov.[37] Taken at face value, this statement suggests that Okudzhava's poem was not as significant to him as another chance to engage the enemies of literalism. Was this, then, a replication of the *Onegin* experiment on the minute scale of a three-quatrain song? If yes, then the entire Okudzhava affair shows Nabokov as a manipulator ready to use his model to propagate his extremist views on translation while belittling those of his adversaries who dare to question the ethics of such procedures. The archival materials surrounding this translation – as well as the afterglow of Nabokov's encounter with

Okudzhava – make it clear that his interest in the young Soviet "guitar poet" preceded his desire to challenge his detractors.

Nabokov's marginalia in his copy of *Proza i poeziia* (Prose and Poetry; 1968) prove him a demanding, discerning, and committed reader of Okudzhava.[38] Unmoved by Okudzhava's experiments in the novelistic genre (*Bud' zdorov, shkoliar*), Nabokov read his poems with a pencil in hand, marking those he preferred. In a treatment equalling that which he reserved for the likes of Pushkin and Tiutchev, he singled out numerous texts that spoke to him in one way or another. They are "Lën'ka Korolëv," "Sentimental'nyi marsh" – the finalized version of the poem he translated using *Bud' zdorov, shkoliar. Stikhi* (Be Well, Schoolboy. Poems; 1964); "Ne ver' voine, mal'chishka" (Don't trust the war, boy); "V pokhod na chuzhuiu stranu" (On a raid to an alien country); "Ne pomniu zla, obid ne pomniu" (I don't keep memories of evil-doing, I don't hold grudges); "Goluboi chelovek" (Sky-blue man); "Devochka plachet" (A girl is weeping); "Svet v okne" (Light in a window); "Noch' proshchaetsia s letom" (The night is bidding the summer farewell); "Akh, kakie udivitel'nye nochi" (Ah, these nights are so amazing); "Sharmanka-sharlatanka" (The street organ, a quack enchantress); "Poslednii pirat" (The last pirate); "Eta zhenshchina" (This woman); "Chërnyi kot" (The black cat); "Beregite nas poetov" (Treasure us, poets); "Vesëlyi barabanshchik" (The cheery drummer); and "Detskii risunok" (A child's drawing). As songs, each one of these poems did not merely provide an aural leitmotif for the short-lived Krushchëv Thaw – together with similarly iconic statements from other "people of the sixties," they emblematized the renaissance of lyrical subjectivity in Soviet culture. The implications of Nabokov's partiality to Okudzhava and his phenomenon are unequivocal: in this singer-songwriter he discovered and greeted an interlocutor – a confrère – with whom he could conduct a dialogue across political divides.

"Sentimental'nyi romans" was not the only Okudzhava text Nabokov translated. His draft of an English-language version of "Chërnyi kot" ("In that yard there is a porchway") tantalizes with the possibility of his being privy to a popular interpretation, according to which this humorous take on a vicious tomcat's domination over an apartment-building corridor was in fact an Aesopian reference to Stalin's terror. This additional draft proves that Nabokov did not simply read and enjoy Okudzhava but went to great lengths to ascertain the reasons for his popularity with the Soviet reader. The after-effects of his dialogic engagement with Okudzhava were scintillating.

Ada's "Ursus" scene (2, 8) takes its protagonists Van, Ada, and Lucette to "the best Franco-Estotian restaurant in Manhattan Major." As their night out proceeds, they listen to a succession of "old" Russian songs and experience the "peculiar poignancy" of "heartwringing" "romances." While the majority of the songs referenced here came from Dmitri Nabokov's singing repertoire, one of them would seemingly have no place among compositions by the likes of Mikhail Glinka, Apollon Grigor'ev, and Ivan Turgenev. It is

> that obscurely corrupted soldier dit of singular genius
>
> *Nadezhda, I shall then be back*
> *When the true batch outboys the riot …*[39]

The rendition of the song's second line exemplifies the exuberant translingual wordplay for which *Ada* is famous. It puns on the Russian wording of the phrase *trubach' otboi sygraet*, which Nabokov had translated as "the bugler sounds retreat." Further into the scene Nabokov revisits "that soldier dit of singular genius" to solidify its place in his personal catalogue of the most piercing specimens of the Russian "romance" genre.[40]

The phrase "the bugler's sharp elbow" references Nabokov's rendition of the song's first quatrain: "The day the bugler sounds retreat, / When to his lips he'll bring the bugle, / And outward his sharp elbow turn."[41] Clever as this entire section is, what significance did it have for Nabokov? And, closer to this study's subject, what did it have to communicate – and to whom?

One of the few Nabokov translations of his contemporaries, the significance of his take on Bulat Okudzhava's "Sentimental'nyi romans" extends far beyond its immediate context of a convenient weapon in his war of words with his adversaries. It is a gesture full of meaning for our understanding of Nabokov's relationship with his new and growing audience, one comprising his Soviet readers. On one specific level, however, it is a greeting addressed to Okudzhava personally, a greeting that reached its intended recipient.[42] By singling Okudzhava out of an entire generation of new Soviet poets known to him, Nabokov signalled his preference for the least ostentatious member of that diverse group, a singer-songwriter who was revitalizing the tradition of Russian sung poetry to which Nabokov had been partial since his youth. Bestowed on "Sentimental'nyi romans," the praise unprecedented in the annals of Nabokov's stated literary preferences was also a gesture intended for Okudzhava's numerous Soviet admirers who at that time were discovering Nabokov. It is to them he extended his greeting across the seemingly insurmountable divide of that same, distant Civil War, omnipresent in all his interactions with his homeland.

"A poet's imagery is a sacred, unassailable thing": "On Adaptation"

According to Vivian Darkbloom, *Ada*'s opening, with its "*Anna Arkadievitch Karenina*" and "R.G. Stonelower," "ridicules" mistranslations of Russian classics and alludes to "transfigurations (Mr. G. Steiner's term, I believe) and betrayals to which great texts are subjected by pretentious and ignorant versionists."[43] The presence of this verbal vestige in *Ada* can hardly be called mysterious, yet delving deeper into Nabokov's reasons for integrating this reference to the translation wars of the 1960s proves profitable for our investigation of the dialogic foundations of his involvement with translation. Could it be that as he was prepared to enter his eighth decade, he was reinforcing these dialogic foundations by restating his commitment to literalism?

Published in the August 1966 issue of the *Encounter*, George Steiner's "To Traduce or Transfigure" identified Nabokov as the most prominent successor to an extended tradition of arguing that poetry cannot be translated into poetry. Following on the heels of the transatlantic debate between Nabokov and Wilson – Nabokov's "Reply to My Critics" appeared in the February issue of the same magazine,[44] only to be equipoised by Robert Lowell's letter in Wilson's support – Steiner's essay aimed to vindicate poetic translation by repudiating the literalist doctrine. To this end Steiner lauded Robert Lowell's "imitations" – especially those of Osip Mandel'shtam – as "criticism in the highest sense," capable of "making explicit … the genius of that it focuses on."[45]

Nabokov may be an heir to one line of thought that boasted Dante and Sir Richard Burton among its adherents, but Lowell stands on the shoulders of an equally illustrious tradition.[46] Steiner found the potential of poetical translation to carry poetry over temporal, linguistic, and political divides to be indispensable. Susceptible as it is to "failures" attributable "to the fact that the original cannot be rendered exhaustively," it will forever remain a reliable mechanism of cultural cross-fertilization. Pronounced "great" by a leading translation theorist, never did Lowell's "imitations" seem closer to becoming paragons.

In May 1966 Nabokov refused to respond to Lowell's allegation that his *Onegin* was "a half-intentional spoof," citing Lowell's inability "to tackle the special problems of translation" at issue in his polemic with Wilson.[47] In September 1969, however, he put together a short analytical riposte where he anatomized the results of Lowell's "imitation" of Osip Mandel'shtam's "Za gremuchuiu doblest' griadushchikh vekov" (1931, 1935) per Olga Andreyev Carlisle's *Poets on Street Corners* (1968). Entitled "On Adaptation," it appeared in the 4 December 1969 issue of the *New York Review of Books*. That out of all Carlisle's collaborators – among them were Barbara Guest, John Hollander, Stanley Kunitz, Denise Levertov, W.S. Merwin, John Updike, Theodore Weiss, and Richard Wilbur – Nabokov chose Lowell shows that his disagreement with the author of *Imitations* was a long-standing one. Although it may appear that by singling out Lowell, Nabokov was settling a score with a Wilson supporter who had openly challenged him, his aversion to Lowell's "imitations" predated Lowell's entry into the Nabokov-Wilson dispute.[48] There is no doubt, however, that Lowell's formulation of the tenets of the imitative technique in 1965 – along with his identification of the "true" reasons behind Nabokov's *Onegin* opus and Steiner's bestowal on him of Ezra Pound's crown of the leading contemporary "transfigurative" translator in "To Traduce or Transfigure" in 1966 – strengthened Nabokov's determination to challenge Lowell and the approach he personified.

Nabokov's essay demonstrated that be it an "imitation" or an "adaptation," Lowell's version of Mandel'shtam's poem, prepared with the aid of Carlisle's transposition, amounted to a fanciful variation on a theme provided by its model. Too fanciful, in fact, to reach its stated goal of "recapturing … Mandelstamm's tone and the atmosphere of his terrible last years." Against Lowell's "In the name of the higher tribes of the future," Nabokov contrasted his "For the sake of the resonant valor of ages to come." Stripped of much poetic artifice except that sanctioned by his understanding of the source, this unrhymed reproduction sought to prove that it brought its reader closer to Mandel'shtam's haunting images. Maintaining that "a poet's imagery is a sacred, unassailable thing,"[49] Nabokov showed that Lowell's inability to find exact or close parallels for Mandel'shtam's metaphors resembled an echo chamber where Lowell's poetic imagination deprived the reader of obtaining an informed idea of the text whose meaning and significance it purported to render.

Already in "The Art of Translation" (1941) – which in its turn had summarized his experiences as a Russian and French translator and translation critic – Nabokov discussed the risks associated with a strong poet's use of their "confrères'" texts as media for self-expression.[50] In addition to having the experience of having done precisely the same in his own early translating practice, Nabokov recognized in Lowell's "imitations" a realization of this very scenario.[51] Aggravated with Steiner's promotion of Lowell to the rank of trendsetters whose prominence was enabled by Pound's "enlargement" of the term "translation," Lowell's persistence in his ways was no mere challenge to Nabokov's taste.[52] It threatened the single most important principle of his understanding of translation, his insistence on the translators' unmediated access to their models.

It was to this end that Nabokov felt the need to restate the position he had formulated in 1941 – and alert his supporters and opponents alike to the risks associated with Steiner's legitimization – indeed canonization – of Lowell's approach. As he contemplated his polemical use of Okudzhava's "Sentimental'nyi romans" in 1965, he alluded to "the enthusiastic paraphrast who strangles another man's muse with his own muse's strong hair." As Steiner's approval of Lowell's "transfigurations" was making that nightmarish vision a reality, Nabokov had every reason to oppose "this kind of thing" becoming "an international fashion."[53] His legacy as translator and translation theorist being at stake, he was not prepared to cede his ground without a fight.

The author of "On Adaptation" was at the top of his form as a polemicist when he combined invective and irony to a devastating effect. The quality of Nabokov's reputation in the world of translation studies is such, however, that few would take at face value his invitation to Lowell to imagine what would happen if his "An unaccustomed ripeness in the wood" were to be subjected to his own "transfigurational" treatment.[54] And if we accept that Nabokov's rhetorical question "I wonder on whose side the victim would be?" is hypocritical and self-serving, what are we to make of his employment of Mandel'shtam's example as a weapon in his war of words with Lowell and those in his camp? After all, at the same time that Lowell was continuing to produce his "imitations" and "adaptations," Nabokov continued to publish "poetical" renditions of Belleau and Régnier, qualifying the "scant" rhyming in his version of Okudzhava's "Sentimental'nyi romans" as an "inaccuracy." Worse still, how are we to interpret his postscript "I fervently hope that this little essay managed to reach the poet's widow in Soviet Russia,"[55] now that we know that Nadezhda Mandel'shtam came to Lowell's defence, unleashing on Nabokov her eloquent fury?

The martyred poet's widow was the first to point out an apparent inconsistency in Nabokov's condemnation of Lowell's method. In doing so she took a stance on the issue virtually indistinguishable from Steiner's advocacy of the vitalizing power of what Dryden, following Ben Johnson's example, dubbed "imitation." In addition to that, her defence of Lowell invoked the notion of Parnassian kinship, not unlike that of the Nabokovian *confrèrie* that had paved the way to some of his most accomplished translations from the period of "loving and tender sinning":

> A poet's translation of foreign verses is always free. It is a kind of conversation, it is the best form of communication of those who are brothers speaking different languages ...
>
> It is an act of brotherhood of poets which has nothing to do *with literature.*
>
> [Nabokov] said "a poet's imagery is a sacred, unassailable thing." Lowell is a poet. His imagery must be considered as sacred though it is based on Mandelshtam's poem.[56]

Since Nabokov invokes the tenets of literalism more than once in "On Adaptation," this contrast between a frivolous variation and a close reproduction makes the essay another substantiation of the familiar doctrine. "Only this is translation," he insists unequivocally – and arrogantly in the eyes of so many. This surely eliminates all doubt that Nabokov's attack on Lowell settled a personal score and used Lowell, Mandel'shtam, and even Mandel'shtam's widow to deal a blow to Lowell's admirers Wilson, Steiner, and others who dared to speak against the literalist doctrine and its proponent. Instead of defending Mandel'shtam from "cruelty and deception," Nabokov proves himself to be a flippant *artiste* who can be seen praising Zhukovskii's and Baudelaire's adaptations of Schiller and Poe one day, translating poetry into poetry another, and destroying the reputations of the likes of Olga Andreyev Carlisle, Babette Deutsch, Sergei Krechetov, Ivan Tkhorzhevskii, Walter Arndt, Robert Lowell, and others when they threaten to steal his thunder in one way or another by doing much the same thing. Believable and convincing, this interpretation results from a misreading of a crucial passage from "On Adaptation" and misunderstanding of Nabokov's stance on translation.[57]

Considering "On Adaptation" in the context of Nabokov's consistent invocations of "exceptional circumstances" that permit translators to align their versions of their source texts with the constellations under which they were conceived throws into sharp relief a hitherto unnoticed feature of its rhetoric. It also points toward the direction Nabokov was going in his search for synthesis between paraphrastic and literalist modes of translation.

Summarizing his impressions from reading Carlisle's anthology in its entirety, Nabokov observes: "As to genius, nowhere in those paraphrases is the height of fancy made to fuse with the depth of erudition like a mountain orbed by its reflection in a lake – which at least would be of some consolation."[58] Less conspicuous and more cryptic, perhaps, than it could or should have been, "a mountain orbed by its reflection in a lake" is the image that unites all the post-1955 invocations of genius that reorient Nabokov's discourse on translation toward its literary, paraphrastic roots and away from his strict enforcement of the literalist doctrine. On this level, Nabokov's censure of Lowell's translation reveals its aesthetic dimension. Like all the "adaptations" included in Carlisle's *Poets on Street Corners*, Lowell's "In the name of the higher tribes of the future" falls short of becoming a "reflection" of the "mountain" that is Mandel'shtam's "Za gremuchuiu doblest' griadushchikh vekov." That does not mean that it was impossible in principle. The genius of the original remains unmatched by that of its reproduction, and what should have been a celebration of a brotherhood of poets turns out to be a case of mistaken identity, a re-enactment of an ancient comedic plot that travels from Plautus's *The Two Menaechmus* to Shakespeare's *Comedy of Errors*, but without a happy ending. What is it that goes wrong? Why did Nadezhda Mandel'shtam also feel compelled to admonish Nabokov for his lack of "kindness" toward Lowell?[59]

Counterintuitive as this may sound, Steiner's vindication of free translation – much like that of Nadezhda Mandel'shtam's defence of Lowell *and* Nabokov's denunciation of Lowell's adaptation – rested on the same premise. In each and every case it presupposed the translators' ability to initiate and maintain a meaningful conversation with their models. By demonstrating his receptivity to the idea that individual creative genius may reconstitute the delicate and magnificent effects of a foreign-language masterpiece, Nabokov was reiterating his lifelong insistence on the single most important requirement of his translation theory and practice.

At all junctures of his evolution as translator and translation theorist, Nabokov never parted with the conviction that translators must comprehend the language of their models' composition to be able to come into contact with the minds of their creators. Lowell's imitations and adaptations of texts he could not understand did not merely violate that essential principle, they threatened Nabokov's innate notion of translation as dialogue. All things considered, Nabokov's defence of translation from monoglossia was a defence of the generative power of dialogue from the solipsism inherent to monoglot consciousness.

"I come out alone upon the highroad": Leaving Lermontov and Pushkin Intact

The revised and finalized edition of the *Eugene Onegin* translation (1975) may not have fulfilled Nabokov's vision of having his version reproduced *en regard* or interlinearly, but if anything, it moved closer to that vision:

> In correcting my verse, I set myself a double task: in the first place, to achieve a closer line-by-line fit (entailing a rigorous coincidence of enjambments and the elimination of verse transposal), and in the second, to apply throughout, without a trace of halfheartedness and compromise, my method of "signal words" as represented in the Correlative Lexicon.[60]

In its finalized form the entire *Onegin* opus will forever remain the paradox epitomized in Anthony Burgess's bewildered, unintentionally bifurcated accolade: "a massive act of copulation with scholarship" on the one hand, and "the very perfection of scholarship" on the other.[61] All its limitations and idiosyncrasies notwithstanding, it is a monument to a translator's unmediated individual engagement with a source text and with the consciousness that engendered it. This work stands as a challenge to those who misinterpret translation's dependence on compromise as permission to compromise the sole prerequisite Nabokov was not prepared to abandon under any circumstances, no matter how well celestial bodies might align for two poetic texts, one of which owes its existence to the other. All said and done, this is the main thrust of Nabokov's preface to the revised edition that absorbed not only a decade's worth of debates on literalism but his entire life in translation:

> In an era of inept and ignorant imitations, whose piped-in background music has hypnotized innocent readers into fearing literality's salutary

jolts, some reviewers were upset by the humble fidelity of my version; the present improvements will exasperate them even more.[62]

A document entitled "Programme Notes" (1973) augments our understanding of Nabokov's final years.[63] Devised to accompany Dmitri Nabokov's audiocassette recording of an arrangement of Russian songs – with an admixture of Vasilii Solov'ëv-Sedoi and Mikhail Matusovskii's quintessentially Soviet number, "Podmoskovnye vechera" (1955) – the document contains two noteworthy additions to everything we know about Nabokov the translator. These texts are an equilinear, equimetric, and rhyming translation of Lermontov's "Vykhozhu odin ia na dorogu" (1841) and a partially rhyming rendition of Pushkin's "Noch'" ("Moi golos dlia tebia i laskovyi i tomnyi"; 1823).

In and of themselves these translations show that Nabokov – who by 1973 had become the face of the extreme literalist stance on translation – accepted that the choice of a given translation methodology may be subjugated to the purpose it aims to fulfil. Not content with providing commentaries to each song on the recording, as was the case with the musical settings of Apollon Grigor'ev's "Dve gitary" or Nestor Kukol'nik's "Somnenie" ("Uimites', volneniia strasti"), among others, he made an exception for the Lermontov and the Pushkin pieces and rendered them into English *in toto*. This choice was not dictated by his respect for the two poets: in the same document he left untranslated Aleksandr Borodin's setting of Pushkin's "Dlia beregov otchizny dal'noi."[64]

"I come out alone upon the highroad," Nabokov's take on "Vykhozhu odin ia na dorogu," revisits the practice of partial rhyming that ensured the success of his remarkable Russian renditions of Robert Schumann's and Franz Schubert's settings of the six *lieder* by Heinrich Heine in 1918 and proved helpful during the period of "loving and tender sinning." By retaining only the odd-line rhymes throughout the length of Lermontov's five-quatrain piece, Nabokov reserved for himself enough freedom to create a close approximation of his model's formal and semantic features. A rhyming rendition of Lermontov's trochaic pentameters – the poem is a classic example of a successful use of this relatively rare measure to an indelible effect[65] – provides a fitting closure to the extant selection of this poet's works in Nabokov's rhymed versions. As such it amounts to a return to the practices associated with the period of "loving and tender sinning," practices he denounced and disowned yet never abandoned.

A purposeful re-creation of the potent musicality of Lermontov's masterpiece, "I come out alone upon the highroad" is a verse translation that luxuriates in the possibilities open to the seemingly unforgiving medium of poetical translation. Nabokov's judicious application of partial rhyming and asymmetric redistribution of phrasal units within a close replication of his model's form proves that this adept of literalism remained a supreme master of *literary* translation well into his last decade.

The sole purpose of Nabokov's rendering of Lermontov's "Vykhozhu odin ia na dorogu" into equimetrical rhyming English verse was to create a translation that would fit its musical setting (presumed to have been composed by Elizaveta Shashina in 1861).[66] Apart from enriching his son's singing repertoire, Nabokov made an exception of this song and no other – not even the two pieces by Pushkin included in the same selection, one of which he translated. Despite his crude postscript to that translation,[67] the effort he invested in crafting a melodically rich rendition of the poem testifies to his personal involvement not only with the poem, but with the Russian *romans* based on it. This translation of not merely a poem, but a *song* engendered by that poem, testifies to Nabokov's lifelong partiality toward sung poetry. A frequent marker of middlebrow culture in his mature works, sung poetry reveals itself to be a reliably rich source of inspiration, from "Iz Geine" and the early English poem "The Russian Song" (1925), to "The Assistant Producer" (1943), to Okudzhava's "Sentimental'nyi romans" and Lermontov's "Vykhozhu odin ia na dorogu."

"Night" ("My voice that breathes for thee both tenderness and languor") is a version of Pushkin's "Noch'" ("Moi golos dlia tebia i laskovyi i tomnyi"). In a striking contrast with Lermontov's "I come out upon the highroad," while rendering Pushkin's text into an elevated idiom replete with "thees" and "thines," this version neglects to follow both the metre and the rhyming scheme of the original. To Pushkin's iambic hexameters Nabokov has variable iambs vacillating from four to six feet. The sense of the poem has been dutifully carried over into English, but the melody of its setting remained behind the language barrier.

No match for the *Onegin* opus in either magnitude or consequence, the two translations included in "Programme Notes" represent two poles of in Nabokov's practice of poetry translation in a proverbial nutshell. A literary rhyming translation dwells in the peaceful vicinity of a literal version. Neither of them, however, amounts to a paragon of exactitude, while personal preference – a whim, really – accounts for their creator's choice of the methodology employed therein. Hardly a counterweight to the uncompromising rhetoric of the introductory remarks to the revised and finalized *Eugene Onegin*, these two translated poems – along with the most irreverent postscript accompanying one of them – remind us that we are dealing with a man determined to reserve for himself the last laugh. It was he, after all, who in response to a question regarding his opinion of himself as a writer vis-à-vis his contemporaries chose to respond with the following rejoinder: "I often think there should exist a special typographical sign for a smile – some sort of concave mark, a supine round bracket."[68]

Responding to Nabokov's assault on his transposition of Pushkin's *Eugene Onegin* into rhyming English verse in 1964, Walter Arndt formulated the single most durable line of resistance to his opponent's criticism of translations he found inadequate:

> All prior invaders of the precinct of *Onegin* translation have found him coiled at the exit (see his article in *Partisan Review*, Fall, 1955) and have been dosed, jointly and severally, alive or posthumously, with much the same mixture of arrogance, cuteness, and occasional distortion. The living among them may again relish with a certain fascination the fine sparkle of pure venom behind the sacerdotal (albeit general and admirable) solicitude for textual integrity.[69]

When in 1967 Ronald Hingley observed that Nabokov's "works in general secrete about as much milk of human kindness as a cornered black mamba," he knowingly echoed Arndt's sentiment, and that Nabokov's demolition of Robert Lowell's "adaptation" of Osip Mandel'shtam's "Za gremuchuiu doblest' griadushchikh vekov" should have provoked a virtually identical response from his widow Nadezhda in 1969 speaks volumes. Time and again this same sentiment has been revived to refocus the observers' attention away from Nabokov's insistence on a direct, unmediated contact with the poets he translated to his less-than-charitable treatment of his translator colleagues. It must be admitted that even if one acknowledges the vindictiveness of some of his opponents, a share of the blame for this situation lands at Nabokov's feet.

No matter how prodigious his effort to subjugate his artistry to the applied, utilitarian task of replicating the verbal images of others in the foreign words of his choosing, Nabokov found it impossible to expel translation from the domain of his creative pursuits. An avowed enemy of sincerity in everything that concerned creativity, Nabokov the translator continued to engage in the game of masks that according to Christine Raguet-Bouvart characterizes his ever-fluid stance on the nature of this verbal transaction.[70] The determined literalist continued to engage in the paraphrastic translation of poetry into poetry at the same time as he argued against the advisability, indeed legitimacy, of such an approach. If, however, there could be an exit from the corner into which he "boxed himself," it would be found on the plane of self-irony and creativity.

Charles Kinbote's carping comments on Sybil Shade's superb literary translations from Donne and Marvell show that Nabokov never lost his ability to examine his stance on translation through the lens of self-irony. More to the point, his mockery of Kinbote's insensitivity toward the profound personal implications of these translations for Sybil shows that he appreciated the fact that translated texts acquire novel connotations, some of which have more to do with their translator's agendas than those conceived by their authors. Nabokov may have welcomed Charles Singleton's literal version of Dante's *Divine Comedy* as a respite from Robert Lowell's "adaptations" condoned by George Steiner,[71] but for those willing to look past the facade of the literalist rhetoric, he left enough breadcrumbs to discover that his vision of translation was more inclusive and flexible.

Conclusion

Do Mikhail Bakhtin's insights into the interactive underpinnings of verbal creativity amount to a "silver bullet" capable of piercing the carapace of Vladimir Nabokov's resistance to theorization and generalization? Not altogether redeeming our insufficient knowledge of artistic individuality's origins, they have proven helpful for my attempt to make sense of the most contentious and least studied aspect of Nabokov's literary legacy, his lifelong involvement with translation.

In answering Bakhtin's call to discover "the half-concealed life of the alien word in the new context of a given author," I have chosen to treat Nabokov's translations as "dialogic encounters." Predicated on Nabokov's individual polyglossia – in this respect Bakhtin's precondition for the emergence of novelistic "dialogic" discourse in the context of a national tradition correlates with Nabokov's individual evolution as novelist – this writer's uncommon dependence on translation reveals itself as a form of openness to the other. Intuitive, "elemental," at the outset of his career in letters, Nabokov's multilingual dialogic proclivities gave rise to his preoccupation with originality and replication, along with a host of issues associated with the ethics of interaction with one's predecessor, interlocutor, and indeed opponent. If one needs a vantage point from which to obtain an expansive overview of Nabokov's career in letters, translation offers as firm a foundation as any other. In doing so it obscures none of the contradictions and complexities associated with his polemical stances.

Multiple pieces of hard textual evidence surveyed and analysed on these pages – including those, or perhaps *especially* those that have never been discussed in terms of their "half-concealed" existence in Nabokov's original compositions – demonstrate that this writer did not merely "relax" in the company of his Parnassian confrères, but required that form of interaction for verbalizing the intuitions and convictions that shaped his philosophical and ethical outlook. No discussion of his notion of the otherworld is complete without taking into account the pivotal role played by his translations of Émile Verhaeren and Francesco Petrarca in his search for the words to express it. His stance on the issue of art's non-utilitarian nature is better understood when we become aware that its verbalization – "objectivization," as Bakhtin would call it – was a result of his agonistic and antagonistic encounter with Romain Rolland, an eloquent proponent of the opposite point of view. Nabokov may dismiss Rolland as a puffed-up nonentity and Stalinist stooge, but there is no unseeing how profitable was their encounter for the crystallization of Nabokov's aesthetics once its value for the future writer and thinker has been seen. The same can be said about each of his works in translation, so closely integrated are they into his literary pursuits and creative ambitions.

Nabokov's compositions teem with "verbal vestiges" of his dialogic encounters with others. Translation was not the only point of entry that admitted the words, images, and voices of others into his writing. Nabokov never translated Robert Browning, for example, yet no one can discount Browning's importance for such a sophisticated contemplation of a literary work's dependence on the other as *Pale Fire*. There are further examples of James Joyce, Franz Kafka, Marcel Proust, along with other interlocutors. Translation and translation alone, however, provides us with incontrovertible evidence of Nabokov's encounters with seemingly insignificant, frequently unexpected, but utterly indispensable sources of inspiration. Nabokov's denial of any knowledge of German has resulted in a major misunderstanding of his relationship with Heinrich Heine, while Jean Richepin's apparent absence from the list of his paragons does not diminish his significance for the formulation of Nabokov's belief in the superiority of individual creative consciousness to the sense of tribal identity based on place and tradition. No other aspect of this writer's activities highlights his early commitment to intellectual extraterritoriality better than translation.

Bakhtinian appreciation of literary discourse as an interactive, dialogic enterprise has guided my attempt to resolve a number of contradictions associated with Nabokov's insistence on the subjugation of translation to its model (the doctrine of literalism) on the one hand and his willful and outwardly inconsistent fulfilment of his own demands on the other. Silver bullet or not, Bakhtin's notion of dialogism – rather than its reductive iteration, "intertextuality" – permits us to make sense of Nabokov's outwardly combative and inflexible but inwardly fluid and accommodating approach to translation. What has been interpreted as a stale dogma at best and a manifestation of his narcissism at worst proves to have been a defence of translation as a direct, unmediated contact with the consciousness responsible for the formulation of a vision encapsulated in a given literary utterance. In this respect alone, Nabokov's notion of translation has shown itself to be profoundly dialogic. As such it was congruent with Bakhtinian understanding of literary discourse as a dialogic aesthetic activity, an understanding replete with implications for what is at stake in this form of communication. It is at this juncture that Nabokov's stance ceases to be at odds with more tolerant notions regarding translation, including those espoused by his opponent George Steiner. "To translate means to carry over from what has been silent to what is alive, from the distant to the near," Steiner stated before adding, "But also to carry back."[1] Conditioned as they were by his insistence on an open dialogue between minds, at no point during their evolution did Nabokov's views on translation contradict this aspect of Steiner's expansive and permissive premise. It was the threat of the tyranny of monologic solipsism – more palpable at the time when Nabokov spoke against it so forcefully than it appears today – that rendered his approach to translation so combative while inspiring his bellicose rhetoric on the issue. Treating it as his desire to impose on others his vision as the only valid article of faith is as much of a misunderstanding as a failure to account for the chronology and mutability of his views on translation.

Bakhtin's early philosophical treatise *Toward a Philosophy of the Act* (*K filosofii postupka*, ca. 1918–24) prefigures the formulation of his ideas concerning dialogue as a distinct feature of novelistic discourse in his accommodative sense of the term. What he terms here "aesthetic contemplation" (*esteticheskoe sozertsanie*) and "living/empathizing into" (*vzhivanie*) one's subject has uncanny parallels with Nabokov's understanding of translation as "travel" toward a "flowerhead" of an aesthetically significant literary phenomenon:

> An essential moment (though not the only one) in aesthetic contemplation is empathizing into an individual object of seeing – seeing it from inside in its own essence. This moment of empathizing is always followed

> by the moment of objectification, that is, a placing *outside* oneself of the individuality understood through empathizing, a separating it from oneself, a *return* into oneself. And only this returned-into-oneself consciousness gives form, from its own place, to the individuality grasped from inside, that is, shapes it aesthetically as a unitary, whole, and qualitatively distinctive individuality.[2]

It is difficult to find a more cogent summary of Nabokov's need for translation. It is only fitting that this formula should have appeared at a time when he was labouring to convert such and similar experiences into durable works of art. When he succeeded in doing so, the results of his "aesthetic contemplation" of the works of others proved to be among the best validations of the veracity of Bakhtin's insights.

Different in so many respects, Bakhtin and Nabokov prove to have been not all that dissimilar in their grasp of the mysteries of literary creativity and the stakes associated with it. Contemporaries and compatriots with first-hand experience of forced displacement, they both discerned in verbal art a form of communication that transformed readers capable of aesthetic appreciation into their interlocutors' co-creators. Both Bakhtin and Nabokov chose to persevere with their explications of their visions, each in his own domain. In and of itself this proves creativity's power to unite, its ability to withstand the onslaught of dogmas rooted in far less open forms of discourse.

It is enlightening to discover that Nabokov came to similar conclusions in the course of his scrutiny of Pushkin's allusiveness. Upon realizing that *Eugene Onegin* teems with verbal vestiges of its author's dialogic encounters with his peers, Nabokov took it upon himself to demonstrate the degree of Pushkin's dialogic integration into a larger continuum of European literature of his time. One senses that Nabokov did not have in mind Pushkin alone when he sought to assure his readers that his explorations of Pushkin's allusions do not aim at belittling a giant, but merely seek to provide an honest translator with a better understanding of the text:

> Some rude prying into Pushkin's workshop is inevitable, nor can one help being surprized at a great man's stealing from lesser men; but a knowledge of the period and place yields an obvious answer to those who would try to draw too strict a line between imitation and emulation. There is also Pushkin's sportive temperament to be reckoned with. To the parallelist as to the moralist he might retort in the manner of a famous epistle by his favorite André Chénier (I translate ten alexandrines, 97–102 and 137–140, into eleven pentameters, mostly unrhymed):

A bumptious judge, scanning my works, denounces
All of a sudden, with loud cries, a score
Of passages, from so and so translated:
He names their author, and on finding them,
Admires himself, pleased with his learning.
Why
Does he not come to me? To him I'll show
A thousand thefts of mine he may not know.
. . . .
Deeming himself most clever, the rash critic
Will give a slap to Vergil on my cheek,
And *this* (I stick to my own rule, you see)
Montaigne has said – remember? – before me.[3]

Pale Fire, the novel that engages the notions of artistic originality and the indispensability of dialogue with others, is but one example of Nabokov's contemplation of the ways in which literary creativity depends on interaction. Discoveries Nabokov made about the extent of Pushkin's integration into a network of "speech acts" reveal as much about his own oeuvre, his own transnational achievement.

It is my hope that this Bakhtin-inspired interpretative survey of Vladimir Nabokov's life in translation brings us closer to a deeper understanding of what is unique about him as an individual as well as those aspects of literary translation that render it so fascinating a representation of everything that makes direct interpersonal communication an elemental form of creativity accessible to everyone.

Notes

Introduction

1 *SO*, 106.
2 This was the reaction of Ellendea Teasley (Proffer), who challenged Nabokov's views on Dostoevskii when she met him in person in 1969 (see "'Nabokovy ne byli otrezany ot Rossii ...,'" 144–5).
3 *SO*, 52.
4 Remnick, "Translation Wars," 104–5.
5 Nabokov, "On Translating Pushkin: Pounding the Clavichord," 14.
6 It is common to misidentify Nabokov's adaptation of Lewis Carroll's *Alice's Adventures in Wonderland* (1923) as a work that preceded his two-year effort to Russianize Romain Rolland's *Colas Breugnon* (1922); see Beaujour, "*Nikolka Persik*," 558; and Baer, "Translation Theory and Cold War Politics," 180.
7 Boyd, *Vladimir Nabokov: The American Years*, 320–36.
8 Emerson, "Perevodimost'," 86.
9 Bellos, *Is That a Fish in Your Ear?*, 141–2.
10 See Nabokov, "On Translating Pushkin: Pounding the Clavichord" and "On Adaptation."
11 Robinson, *The Translator's Turn*, 60.
12 Alexandra Smith's "Vladimir Nabokov as Translator of Russian Poetry" is one such attempt. Like Remnick, however, Smith applies information derived from "The Art of Translation" to *Eugene Onegin*.
13 Robinson, *What Is Translation?*, 82.
14 Hingley, "An Aggressively Private Person," 14.
15 *L*, 314–15.
16 *LL*, 5.

17 Hofstadter, *Le Ton Beau de Marot*, 273.
18 Richard Rorty's "The Barber of Kasbeam: Nabokov on Cruelty" (in his *Contingency, Irony, and Solidarity*, 141–68), Nikolai Anastas'ev's *Fenomen Nabokova* (1992), Leland de la Durantaye's *Style Is Matter* (2007), and Dana Dragunoiu's *Vladimir Nabokov and the Poetics of Liberalism* (2011) are among the most thorough studies of Nabokov's ethics.
19 *SS*, 6:10.
20 See *Vladimir Nabokov, His Life, His Work, His World*, 124–5.
21 For a sensitive and informed exploration of the Bakhtin/Nabokov nexus, see Blackwell, "Dostoevskian Problems in Nabokov's Poetics."
22 *SO*, 183, 95.
23 *LRL*, 98.
24 Emerson, *The First Hundred Years of Mikhail Bakhtin*, 159.
25 *SO*, 69.
26 Tammi, *Problems of Nabokov's Poetics*, 4–5 and 99–101.
27 Couturier, *Nabokov ou La tyrannie de l'auteur*, 76–7.
28 See Linetskii, *"Anti-Bakhtin,"* 68.
29 See Boyd, "Words, Works and Worlds in Joyce and Nabokov," 46.
30 Naiman, review of *Delicate Markers*, by Gavriel Shapiro, 360.
31 John Burt Foster Jr's *Nabokov's Art of Memory and European Modernism* (1993) offers convincing proof that even more so than Dostoevskii's novels, Nabokov's prove receptive to interpretations fortified by Bakhtinian dialogism – even if they arrive in the stripped-down variant of intertextuality. Renate Lachmann's *Gedächtnis und Literatur: Intertextualität in der russischen Moderne* (1990) failed to produce similarly tangible results as it sought to present Nabokov's intertextuality as a generic feature of Russian modernism.
32 *SS*, 3:9–179.
33 Bakhtin was eager to include in his lectures on contemporary Russian literature not only the unambiguously Soviet writers whose works he damns with faint praise, but also Andrei Belyi and Aleksei Tolstoi – before their departure for Bolshevik Russia.
34 Nabokov may have been familiar with émigré reviews of Bakhtin's work on Dostoevskii (see Picon, "Bakhtin and Nabokov," 3n8); he read the works of Bakhtin's confidant and interlocutor Pavel Medvedev (see Shvabrin, "'Pechat' neprekhodiashchego,'" 215n24).
35 In his lectures on Belyi, Bakhtin stated that this writer's influence was "oppressively vast" (*SS*, 2:337–8).
36 As he focuses on the mysterious origins of the mind and imagination in the opening chapter of his autobiography, Nabokov invokes the

evolutionary "theory of recapitulation," touches on the "history" of his consciousness from its initial flashes to what he elliptically terms "the promise of fair Greece" (*SM*, 370, 372), implying that the growth of his artistic consciousness may be said to recapitulate the basic stages in the development of human civilization. Here as elsewhere Nabokov's personal vision of evolution bridges his notion of onto- and phylogenesis as it inadvertently echoes Bakhtin's ideas on literary evolution.

37 Aleksandr Dolinin has singled out Nabokov's adaptations of Romain Rolland's *Colas Breugnon* and Lewis Carroll's *Alice's Adventures in Wonderland* – along with the essay-cum-translation "Rupert Brooke" (all dating from the early twenties) – as a "creative laboratory" where he can be seen freeing himself from the cliché-ridden poetry and prose of his early youth (see Dolinin, *Istinnaia zhizn' pisatelia Sirina*, 30–2).

38 See Nabokov, *Nikolai Gogol*, 60.

39 *SO*, 64.

40 This feature of Nabokov's poetics corresponds to the ludic underpinnings of his art and world view and also to his competitiveness: it is far from accidental that he invites his readers to draw a parallel between the art of chess problem composition and literature in a deservedly famous section of *Speak, Memory*, chap. 14 (for a discussion of its relevance to our notion of Nabokov's relationship with his audience, see *NPFMAD*, 8–13).

41 For discussions of this inconsistency, see Kristeva, "Bakhtine, le mot, le dialogue et le roman," 440–1, and also Todorov, *Mikhail Bakhtin*, 64.

42 See *SS*, 3:532.

43 Todorov, *Mikhail Bakhtin*, 62.

44 Bakhtin, *Dialogic Imagination*, 279.

45 *SS*, 6:405–6.

46 Douglas Robinson discusses points of interrelationship between Bloom's six-phase "primal scene of instruction" as presented in *A Map of Misreading* and Bakhtin's "authoritative discourse" and "internal persuasive discourse" (Robinson, *Translator's Turn*, 112–14).

47 *SS*, 3:102.

48 Robinson, *Translator's Turn*, 105.

49 Kumar and Malshe, "Translation and Bakhtin's 'Metalinguistics,'" 115.

50 Witt, "Between the Lines," 152.

51 Maar, *Two Lolitas*, 57–8.

52 *Kristeva Reader*, 37; Kristeva, "Bakhtine, le mot, le dialogue et le roman," 440–1.

53 Pil'shchikov, "'Ante hoc, ergo propter hoc,'" 189.

54 Ibid.

55 Even a cursory check of the references provided by Kristeva in support of her statements concerning the Russian formalists' preoccupation with the notion of "linguistic dialogue" shows that her essay contains decidedly playful undertones: the works by Evgenii Budde and Lev Shcherba she cites in support of her statements have nothing to do with Russian formalism.

1 Before Sirin

1 See *PS*, 27.
2 Aleksandr Dolinin's dismissal of Nabokov's juvenilia encapsulates the prevailing attitude; see Dolinin, *Istinnaia zhizn' pisatelia Sirina*, 12, 29.
3 See MO, 167.
4 *SM*, 542.
5 *SM*, 363.
6 Boyd, *Vladimir Nabokov: The Russian Years*, 81, 543.
7 See Nabokov's letter to Sergei Potresov dated 28 September 1921 (Sergei Potresov Papers, The Bakhmeteff Archive of Russian and East European Culture. Butler Library, Columbia University, New York).
8 D. Barton Johnson has examined the lasting effect of Nabokov's childhood fascination with Mayne Reid in his "Vladimir Nabokov and Captain Mayne Reid" and also in "Nabokov's Golliwoggs."
9 *SM*, 525.
10 *SM*, 531.
11 *SM*, 532.
12 *SM*, 544.
13 For accessible reproductions of the translation published in the Tenishev School periodical *Iunaia mysl'* (Young Thought; 1916), see Grayson, "French Connection," 647–58; and *St*, 529–34.
14 Grayson, "French Connection," 614.
15 See *Des*, 9, 13, 15.
16 Davydov, *Despair*, 91.
17 As life refuses to dance to his tune and upsets his "perfect crime," Hermann is forced to add another, "asymmetrical" eleventh chapter to his narrative.
18 Brian Boyd has demonstrated that in *Pale Fire* Nabokov develops the mirror motif well past its initial "narcissistic" implications suggested by Charles Kinbote's solipsistic fixation on himself (see *NPFMAD*, 245).
19 Nabokov's manuscript lists the sonnet's number as 238 (CCXXXVIII); this was the number assigned to it in the majority of anthologies available at

that time (see, for example, Tomlinson, *The Sonnet*, 184–5). Modern editions list it as sonnet 279 (CCLXXIX) (Petrarca, *The Canzoniere*, 1:102–4).

20 Unwilling or unable to preserve Petrarch's rhyming scheme (abab/baba/cdc/dcd) while retaining a certain number of original lexical features, Nabokov follows the rhyming scheme traditionally associated with the Petrarchan sonnet (AbbABaaBDCCdFFd; capital letters denote feminine rhymes).

21 Dmitri Nabokov dismissed Ron Rosenbaum's attempt to find any connection between *The Original of Laura* and Petrarch (see Rosenbaum, *Dmitri's Choice*).

22 See *LL*, 240–1.

23 Difficult as it is to speculate as to what the finale of *The Original of Laura* may have been, we should not ignore such markers in Nabokov's hand as "Last §" and "Z" (see *TOoL*, 223).

24 *TOoL*, 226–7.

25 *SSRP*, 1:163–68; and *SVN*, 131–36.

26 *SSRP*, 113–39; and *SVN*, 500–22. "Solus Rex" and "Ultima Thule" are fragments of an unfinished novelistic endeavour that would find later realizations in *Bend Sinister* (1947) and *Pale Fire* (1962).

27 *SM*, 552.

28 Both Apukhtin and K.R., however, were to become prototypes for characters in *Pale Fire*.

29 Naiman, *Nabokov, Perversely*, 2.

30 Cf. Bouilhet, *Festons et astragales*, 34.

31 *SSRP*, 3:620–29; and *SVN*, 348–57.

32 See *SSRP*, 3:623; and *SVN*, 351.

33 Johnson, "Nabokov and Rupert Brooke," 187.

34 Verhaeren, *Poèmes*, 47.

35 Briusov, *Izbrannye sochineniia*, 2:239.

36 Nabokov's translation of the poem's first stanza makes it clear that he was familiar with the variant reproduced in the Mercure de France edition of 1917 (see Verhaeren, *Poèmes*), and not the variants opening with "(e)t par le traître écho des horizons plongeurs" or "(e)t par les yeux voilés des horizons songeurs" (cf. *Poèmes*, 1896, 51; and *Œuvres*, 2:45).

37 With the well-known exception of Chaikovskii's opera *Eugene Onegin*, Nabokov appreciated sung poetry, folk songs, and popular songs of his day. The cult of Gypsy singing permeated the atmosphere of Nabokov's early youth, at a time when the future writer was enamoured of Aleksandr Blok, who had a keen ear for it. In 1925 Nabokov wrote a madrigal to the famous singer Nadezhda Plevitskaia ("Plevitskoi"), who was later

revealed to have been a Soviet spy (see Nabokov's first English short story, "The Assistant Producer," 1943); in 1931 he demonstrated a knowledge of Aleksandr Vertinskii (see the reference to Boris Poplavskii's poems as "insufferable mixture of Severianin, Vertinskii and Pasternak" in Nabokov, "Boris Poplavskii. 'Flagi,'" 5). The reference to Bulat Okudzhava's "Sentimental'nyi romans" ("Kogda trubach' otboi sygraet ...," 1957) in *Ada* (chap. II.8) was prompted by Nabokov's admiration for the celebrated Soviet bard.

38 On Pierre Louÿs's place in Nabokov's oeuvre, see Johnson, "Nabokov's *Ada* and Pierre Louÿs' *Chansons de Bilitis*."

39 In the *Sistematicheskii katalog Biblioteki Vladimira Dmitrievicha Nabokova*, an 1898 Parisian edition of *Les Chansons de Bilitis* was catalogued under number 373 (see Johnson, "Nabokov's *Ada* and Pierre Louÿs' *Chansons de Bilitis*," 8).

40 *GP*, 108.

41 For a detailed analysis of Nabokov's adaptations of Louÿs's *Chansons*, see Shvabrin, "Vladimir Nabokov as Translator," 31–43.

42 Early references to Byron indicate that Nabokov was interested in both. Mention of Byron's lameness, effeminacy, and of his keeping a tame Russian bear while at Trinity College constitutes the commonplace of Nabokov's early Byronic topos (see "Kembridzh" [1921], *Smert'* [1923], and *Universitetskaia poema* [1926]). He uses a more sophisticated, multi-level – and only superficially Byronic – allusive construct in *Podvig / Glory* (see *P*, 144–5).

43 *SP*, 30.

44 *SM*, 568.

45 It is likely that Nabokov recognized in Byron's "Dream" the source of inspiration behind Mikhail Lermontov's early poem "Videnie" (1831).

46 See *VV*, 145–51, 153–73, and 201–5.

47 Album 19, 179 (VNA).

48 Byron, *Complete Poetical Works*, 3:468.

49 Ibid., 3:294.

50 The possibly unhealthy paleness of the heroine in the Russian version of the poem (cf. Nabokov's "ty bledna" for Byron's "thy looks are wan") only reinforces the impression that rather than being the fellow mourner of the English original, she is the very person whose passing is foretold in the first line of the translation.

51 For an accessible reproduction of these early poems, see *St*, 94, 95, 95, 96, and 97.

52 Byron, *Complete Poetical Works*, 3:305.

53 For the published version of the translation, see *GP*, 31; Nabokov's manuscript of the translation opens the "Carmina lucis" album, 1 (VNA); Elena Nabokova's transcript of the translation is available in Album 19, 7 (VNA).
54 Cf. Nabokov's version of "O skoro smert' prervet rastsvet chudesnyi tvoi!" (Oh! snatched away in beauty's bloom!).
55 See *Rul'* 257 (24 May 1923): 5–6.
56 According to Nabokov's introductory note, the action of *Smert'* takes place in the spring of 1806. Byron's *Hours of Idleness* appeared in 1807.
57 Byron, *Complete Poetical Works*, 1:177.
58 See especially "Lunnaia noch'" ("Poliany okropil kholodnyi svet luny …," 18.IX.18), "Storozhevye kiparisy" (25.XII.18), "Kiparisy" ("Sklonias' nad chasheiu prozrachnoi…," 22.III.19), "Krymskii polden'" ("Chereshni, osy – na lotkakh …," 6–24.XII.19), "Krym" ("Nazlo neistovym trevogam …," 30.VI.20), "Romans" ("I na bereg vesennii prishli my nazad …," 8.VI.20), all from *GP*; "Kak bylo by legko, kak pesenno, kak druzhno" (9.VII.21); and "Zhuk" ("V sady, gde po nocham luchitsia i drozhit …," published 1922). The last two poems were published but uncollected in Nabokov's lifetime.
59 *SM*, 568.
60 *SO*, 189.
61 Mirsky, *History of Russian Literature*, 132, 244.
62 Iakov Gordon's three-volume study *Geine v Rossii* (1973, 1979, 1983) offers a comprehensive survey of "Russian Heineana," which supplements Akhill Levinton's stupendous bibliography of the subject (1958). Katharine Hodgson's "Heine's Russian Doppelgänger" (2005) contains an insightful overview of the poet's Russian translations, while Iurii Tynianov's "Blok i Geine" (1921) lays the foundation for numerous explications of the two poets' affinity.
63 For a dedicated study of the Nabokov-Heine nexus, see Shvabrin, "Nabokov and Heine."
64 See Heine, *Historisch-kritische Gesamtausgabe der Werke*, I/1:151.
65 In Nabokov's own nomenclature, such a variation of an iambic line would be qualified as a "tilt" or a "tilted scud"; for a detailed discussion of this metrical phenomenon, see his "Notes on Prosody" (*EO*, 3:462–72).
66 See Schumann, *Dichterliebe*, 47.
67 Sams, *Songs of Robert Schumann*, 114.
68 Walsh, *Lieder of Schumann*, 106.
69 Sams, *Songs of Robert Schumann*, 107.
70 For a reconstruction of this text, see Shvabrin, "Nabokov and Heine," 379.

71 For a discussion of the problems associated with the transposition of poetic texts to music, see ibid., 374–6.

72 Nabokov's manuscript of the "Perevody iz Geine" cycle is preserved in the "Tsvetnye kameshki" album, 92–6 (VNA); for the first reproduction of the cycle and a number of accompanying archival documents, see ibid., 383–4.

73 These sentiments are on display in Blok's late essays "Krushenie gumanizma," and "Geine v Rossii. O russkikh perevodakh stikhotvorenii Geine" (both 1919; see Blok, *Sobranie sochinenii*, 6:93–115, 116–40).

74 Blok, *Nochnye chasy*, 51–68. Characteristically, the collection also featured "Rossiia" (Russia) and "Na zheleznoi doroge" (On the Railroad), which Nabokov was to translate into English in 1940s and '50s (see *VV*, 327, 329–31) in addition to the cycle "Ital'ianskie stikhi" (Italian Poems), which he was reading to his mother when they received the news of their husband and father's heroic but untimely death (see Boyd, *Vladmir Nabokov: The Russian Years*, 191–3).

75 Gasparov, *Izbrannye trudy*, 3:467.

76 *SO*, 572.

77 Blok's version of "Still ist die Nacht, es ruhen die Gassen" provides a more idiomatic Russian rendition of the poem while preserving the original rhyming structure intact. Annenskii's translation can be said to be closer to the original's lexis – thus he finds a Russian equivalent for Heine's "äffen" ("Was *äffst* du nach mein Liebesleid," l. 10) in "obez'ianit'" ("Blednyi tovarishch, zachem *obez'ianit'*," l. 9), a nuance lost in both Blok's and Nabokov's versions.

78 *SO*, 83.

79 This feature of the manuscript has permitted Chupin and Alladaye to talk about this motif's "omnipresence" in Nabokov's art (see their *Aux origines de "Laura,"* 304).

80 *TOoL*, 15.

81 See ibid., 31–3.

82 Chupin and Alladaye, *Aux origines de "Laura,"* 233–6.

83 Entries 487 and 485 in *Sistematicheskii katalog biblioteki Vladimira Dmitrievicha Nabokova*.

84 It was no accident that Maksim Gor'kii's early critics drew parallels between him and Richepin; see Ignatov, "Filosofiia bosiachestva [u Rishpena i g. Gor'kogo]."

85 Wedeck, "Last of the French Bohemian Poets," 482. Wedeck likewise points out Gor'kii's affinity with Richepin.

86 Richepin, *Les Blasphèmes*, 230–1.

87 Manuscript album "Carmina lucis," *Stikhi*, 56–7 (VNA).
88 Kipling, *Complete Verse*, 221.

2 Before Nabokov

1 Landor, *Imaginary Conversations and Poems*, 365.
2 Initially entitled "On Discovering a Butterfly" (early 1943; see Nabokov, *Selected Poems*, 132).
3 "Stikhi V.V. Nabokova," Album 4 (June 1919–Sept. 1919), 7 (VNA).
4 In both manuscripts and in the 1921 publication in *Rul'*, O'Sullivan appears as "Seimas." "The Sheep" and "Out of the Strong, Sweetness" originally appeared in O'Sullivan's debut collection of verse *The Twilight People* (pp. 2–3, 47; for the circumstances surrounding Nabokov's coming across these poems, see Boyd, *Vladimir Nabokov: The Russian Years*, 166).
5 Cf. *SSRP*, 1:641, and *St*, 367.
6 From Nabokov to his mother, to be copied and preserved in Album 19; from Nabokov to an editor at *Rul'*, where it was eventually published.
7 The English poem's opening reverses the order of appearance of the logical antecedent of the pronoun "they": "Slowly they pass / In the grey of the evening / Over the wet road, / A flock of sheep" (O'Sullivan, *The Twilight People*, 2).
8 *SM*, 423.
9 O'Sullivan, *The Twilight People*, 47.
10 Musset, *Poésies complètes*, 820–1n1.
11 "Stikhi V.V. Nabokova" (Album 4, June 1919–Sept. 1919), 18–19; and Album 19, 33, 35 (VNA).
12 Boyd, *Vladimir Nabokov: The Russian Years*, 176.
13 Beaujour, "Translation and Self-Translation," 714.
14 Ofrosimov, "Nikolka-Persik," 9.
15 "[Nabokov's] translation to a large extent purged [Rolland's novel] of its folk spirit" (Shor, "'*Kola Briun'on*,'" 225).
16 Liuksemburg, "Nabokov-perevodchik," 6.
17 As a young poet, Nabokov was singularly averse to ribaldry of any kind and purposefully downplayed sexual connotations of the works he translated (his treatment of Pierre Louÿs's "La Chevelure" is a particularly eloquent example of this anti-Rabelaisian tendency).
18 Known in the Anglophone world as *Rabelais and His World* (Hélène Iswolski's translation, 1968).
19 *SS*, 4/2:103.

20 *SS*, 4/2:107.
21 Zweig, *Romain Rolland*, 185.
22 *NP*, 13. Cf. "I had to put up with a lot of ill to navigate without shipwreck toward the port of marriage" (Rolland), and "I needed a lot of patience to steer her toward the coast of marriage without a wreck" (Nabokov).
23 Rolland, *Colas Breugnon*, 118.
24 See Quitard, *Dictionnaire*, 474.
25 Jacques de Berchem (ca. 1505–67) was among Rabelais's favourite composers (see *The Sixteenth-Century Chanson*, 27:91–3; and *New Grove Dictionary of Music and Musicians*, 3:304).
26 "Jehan de Lagny, mon bel amy, / Vous m'avez abusée, / Si ce n'eust este vostre amour, / Je fusse mariée. / Vous avez ouvert le guichet / La mouche y est entrée" (*Sixteenth-Century Chanson*, 27:91–3.
27 *NP*, 96.
28 MO, 167.
29 Rolland, *Colas Breugnon*, 118.
30 *NP*, 96.
31 Rolland, *Colas Breugnon*, 141.
32 *NP*, 115.
33 Shor, "'*Kola Briun'on*,'" 246–52.
34 Cf. *SSRP*, 4:383, and Rolland, *Colas Breugnon*, 117. The echo of Rolland's wordplay reached as far *Lolita*, where Humbert's companion Rita is described in the following manner: "In comparison to her, Valechka was a Schlegel, and Charlotte a Hegel" (*L*, 259). The novel's annotator Alfred Appel Jr qualifies this wordplay as "a nonsense rhyme" without taking into account its precedents in either *The Gift* or *Nikolka Persik*.
35 On this occasion the author of *Invitation to a Beheading* responded to his friend and critic Ofrosimov's old rebuke for choosing the Church Slavonic variant of the name "Martha" for such a mischievous heroine as Breugnon's daughter Martine: "And yet occasionally puzzlements occur: what for, for example, is this strained, stubborn Russification of the names Glasha and Martha (spelled with a 'Θ' to boot!)" (see Ofrosimov, "Nikolka-Persik," 9).
36 In *Strong Opinions*, to cite but one example, the author of *Colas Breugnon* concludes a list of "such formidable mediocrities as Galsworthy, Dreiser, a person called Tagore, another called Maxim Gorky, a third called Romain Rolland" (*SO*, 57).
37 For Rolland's role in the nomination of Ivan Bunin for the Nobel Prize, see Marčenko, *Russkie pisateli i Nobelevskaia premiia*, 213–20 and 223–6.
38 Rolland, *Quinze ans de combat*, 88.

39 Fisher, *Romain Rolland and the Politics of Intellectual Engagement*, xvii.
40 Rolland, *Colas Breugnon*, 154–5.
41 *NP*, 143.
42 *LL*, 374.
43 Dragunoiu, *Vladimir Nabokov and the Poetics of Liberalism*, 160. On this crucial issue Nabokov the literary scholar and writer and Nabokov the naturalist concur: "I discovered in nature the nonutilitarian delights that I sought in art. Both were a form of magic, both were a game of intricate enchantment and deception" (*SM*, 465).
44 *LL*, 374.
45 *L*, 16.
46 For a close reading of Nabokov's dialogic encounter with Keats, see Shvabrin, "Vladimir Nabokov's 'La Belle Dame Sans Merci.'"
47 See Blok, *Polnoe sobranie sochinenii*, 2:95.
48 In another telling departure from the original, in quatrain 7 her "elfin grot" will be transformed into "priiut mezhdu skazochnykh skal" (abode amid fairytale cliffs).
49 *NWL*, 87.
50 *SO*, 27.
51 See *PF*, 43, ll. 271–4.
52 Explicating the significance of Keats's "La Belle Dame Sans Merci" in *Lolita*, Alfred Appel Jr demonstrates it to be one of that novel lesser-known, yet paramount, dialogic points of reference (see *L*, 338–40, 400).
53 See Boyd, *Vladimir Nabokov: The Russian Years*, 182; and Johnson, "Vladimir Nabokov and Rupert Brooke," 183.
54 In *Problems of Nabokov's Poetics*, Pekka Tammi was the first to connect the reference to *potustoronnost'* in "Rupert Bruk" with Nabokov's widow's indication that it constituted her late husband's "most important theme."
55 Boyd, *Vladimir Nabokov: The Russian Years*, 182; see also Sisson, "Nabokov and Some Turn-of-the-Century English Writers," 528–36, 531; Johnson, "Vladimir Nabokov and Rupert Brooke," 187; and Dolinin, *Istinnaia zhizn' pisatelia Sirina*, 17.
56 Kemball, "Nabokov and Rupert Brooke," 36–7n3, 71–2.
57 Diment, "Uncollected Critical Writing," 734.
58 Nabokov dubs it "The Triple Dream" in an unacknowledged endorsement of Vladimir Solov'ëv's influential exegesis of the poem (see LM, 33–4; and *H*, v–vi).
59 RB, 214.
60 Ibid., 215.
61 See ibid., 229.

62 Nabokov was to translate Lermontov's "Angel" into English ca. 1944–6.
63 RB, 218.
64 Sergey Karpukhin has shown that Nabokov may not have been as well versed in the subtleties of Homeric allusions as Brooke was (see Karpukhin, "Vladimir Nabokov and the Classical Tradition," 85).
65 See RB, 231.
66 See ibid., 224.
67 Johnson, "Vladimir Nabokov and Rupert Brooke," 184–6.
68 Lehman, *Rupert Brooke*, 132.
69 Dated 29 January 1922, this translation was revised on 18 April 1924 but remained unpublished (VNA).
70 For accessible reproduction of these poems, see *St*, 72–3.
71 Boyd, *Vladimir Nabokov: The Russian Years*, 184.
72 Cf. Byron, *Complete Poetical Works*, 3:379.
73 Album 19, 187 (VNA).
74 "There be none of Beauty's daughters / With a magic like thee; / And like music on the waters / Is thy sweet voice to me" (see ll. 1–4 in Byron, *Complete Poetical Works*, 3:379).
75 Cf. ibid.
76 Album 19, 187 (VNA).
77 See Blackstone, *Byron*, 157.
78 Nabokov replicates the rhyme scheme of Byron's octave AbAbCCDD.
79 See last two lines of the closing quatrain of "V polnolun'e, v gostinoi pyl'noi i pyshnoi": "golubaia noch', i stranitsa iz Glinki / na roiale beleet davno" (see Nabokov [Sirin], *Grozd'*, 34–5).
80 See *SSRP*, 1:744–5. Nabokov's criticism of Krechetov's poetry echoes many pronouncements on the same subject made some twelve years earlier by Nikolai Gumilëv in his review of Krechetov's *Letuchii Gollandets* (see Gumilëv, *Polnoe sobranie sochinenii*, 7:42–3). In his ballad "Prokliatyi zamok" (1910), Krechetov broached the subject of a father-daughter affair.
81 The publication of Nabokov's translations from Yeats was announced in the Russian émigré press in advertisements for the almanac *Kubok* (1924).
82 Cf. Album 19, 23 (VNA), and Ronsard, *Œuvres complètes*, 1:400–1. Authoritative modern editions of Ronsard's poetry preserve the period spelling, which essentially is what one finds in Album 19.
83 See Boyd, *Vladimir Nabokov: The Russian Years*, 210.
84 Contemporary reproductions of Nabokov's version of Ronsard's "Quand vous seres bien vieille" uncritically rely on its initial publication in the *Rul'*, which rendered the sonnet's conclusion un-metrical and meaningless (see *St* 642–3 and Dolinin, *Kommentarii k romanu "Dar,"* 89). The correct reading

of ll. 13–14 is "Ne zhdite-zh mërtvykh dnei, tsenite den' zhivoi, / speshite rozy vziat' u zhiznennago maia" (see Album 19, 23–4, Album 8, 57 [VNA], and also Shvabrin, "Vladimir Nabokov as Translator," 213–14, and Vroon, "Akusticheskaia pamiat'," 449–50). The correct date of this translation's preparation is 16 May 1922.

85 Album 19, 23 (VNA); and Ronsard, *Œuvres complètes*, 1:400.

86 Album 8, 57 (VNA).

87 Since Yeats denied having anything to do with "Quand vous serez bien vieille," the editors of *The Collected Works of W.B. Yeats* reproduce it as an original piece, first published as a part of *The Rose* (1893). A. Norman Jeffares, however, reproduces the poem in the "Adaptations and Translations" section of his *Poems of W.B. Yeats: A New Selection* (1984).

88 Cf. *SSRP*, 4:216; and *G*, 29.

89 See *L*, 309. While Samuel Schuman is right to link *Lolita*'s concluding passage with the tenor of Shakespeare's sonnets (see his *Nabokov's Shakespeare*, 7–8), we cannot afford to overlook the fact that in Nabokov's world Shakespeare the sonneteer went hand in hand with Ronsard (see MO, 167), whose frivolous sonnets form another prominent dialogic vestige in that novel.

90 *L*, 315.

91 Nabokov's *Ania v Strane Chudes* was preceded by the anonymous (Ol'ga Timiriazeva – ?) *Sonia v tsarstve diva* (1879); Matil'da Granstrem, *Prikliucheniia Ani v mire chudes* (1908); Allegro (Poliksena Solov'ëva), *Prikliucheniia Alisy v strane chudes* (1909–10); Aleksanra Rozhdestvenskaia, *Prikliucheniia Alisy v strane chudes* (1910–11); anonymous (Mikhail Chekhov – ?), *Alisa v volshebnoi strane* (ca. 1913–14). Its publication in 1923 overlapped with that of D'Aktil (Anatolii Frenkel'), *Alisa v strane chudes*. Nina Demurova's "Alice Speaks Russian" features a detailed discussion of Russian translations of Carroll's tale.

92 See *SO*, 286.

93 See Boyd, *Vladimir Nabokov: The Russian Years*, 197, 557n4; and also *SL*, 520.

94 Karlinsky, "Anya in Wonderland," 312–14; Connolly, "*Ania v Strane Chudes*," 18–19.

95 This point is made in Connolly, "*Ania v Strane Chudes*"; Liuksemburg, "Nabokov-perevodchik," 10–12; and Demurova, "Vladimir Nabokov, Translator of Lewis Carroll's *Alice in Wonderland*."

96 This incongruity notwithstanding, Julia Trubikhina mentions *Nikolka Persik* only in passing, yet treats *Ania* as an example of Nabokov's "beginnings" (see Trubikhina, "The Translator's Doubts," 30–81).

97 Beaujour, "*Nikolka Persik*," 558.

98 Connolly "*Ania v Strane Chudes*," 24.

99 While Nina Demurova's works on the transformations of Carroll's *Alice* in Russian in general and on Nabokov's adaptation of *Alice's Adventures in Wonderland* in particular retain their value, Mariia Malikova's annotations to Nabokov's *Ania* provide specific information on that version of the tale (see *SSRP*, 2:772–6).

100 Even the game of croquet played by Carroll's English characters had already become a diversion popular with Russians by the time Nabokov's adaptation was published in Berlin – croquet figures prominently in the "Russian" chapter of *Pnin*.

101 In a few cases Nabokov uses stiff calques of the original English constructions that appear out of place in his Russian narrative. These phrases are "[e]to beret nekotoroe vremia" (for "that <generally> takes some time") and "napisano k nikomu" (for "it was written to somebody"); see also Demurova, "Vladimir Nabokov, Translator of Lewis Carroll's *Alice in Wonderland*," 190.

102 Carroll, *Annotated Alice*, 28 (emphasis added).

103 *ASC*, 8.

104 Parker, *Lewis Carroll in Russia*, 83.

105 Carroll, *Annotated Alice*, 56–7.

106 *ASC*, 30 (emphasis added).

107 Carrol, *Annotated Alice*, 43.

108 *ASC*, 19.

109 This definitely short-haired small dog acquires "chocolate (-colored) spots," "pink (cute little) belly" (*briushko*), and pointed ears.

110 Fox terriers appear four times in chapter 2 of *The Gift*, which is centred around the figure of Fyodor's father, whose mysterious disappearance presages other calamitous events in the protagonist's life.

111 *SM*, 487.

112 Ibid., 488.

113 Carroll, *Annotated Alice*, 85.

114 Demurova, "Vladimir Nabokov, Translator of Lewis Carroll's *Alice in Wonderland*," 191.

115 Connolly, "*Ania v Strane Chudes*," 24.

116 *SO*, 60–1.

117 *SO*, 81.

118 Self, "Dirty Old Man," 89.

119 Boyd, *Vladmir Nabokov: The Russian Years*, 201–2.

120 Edward FitzGerald called it "a wretched waste of power at a time of life when a man ought to be doing his best," while Thomas Carlyle, whose *French Revolution: A History* Nabokov found "admirable" (see *EO*, 3:343), pronounced it "very gorgeous, fervid, luxuriant, but indolent, somnolent, almost imbecile" (see Ricks, *Tennyson*, 180).

121 See, for example, *The Oxford Book of English Verse, 1250–1900*, 834.
122 Killham, *Tennyson and "The Princess,"* 218–20.
123 The poem opens and closes with quatrains; three couplet-like distichs make up its core.
124 Album 19, 183 (VNA).
125 "Now droops the milk-white peacock like a ghost, / And like a ghost she glimmers unto me" (Tennyson, *Poetry*, 196–7).
126 Album 19, 184–5 (VNA). In Album 19 a page break splits the quoted fragment into two parts.
127 Cf. "So fold thyself, my dearest, thou, and slip / Into my bosom and be lost in me," and "slozhis' i ty, liubimaia, i v serdtse / ko mne skol'zni – i rastvoris' vo mne."
128 It should not be forgotten that in its original context, the poem is recited by a female character overheard by a male protagonist.
129 *SM*, 558.
130 "... bon ou mauvais, inflexible ou fragile, / Humble ou fier, triste ou gai, mais toujours gémissant, / Cet homme, tel qu'il est, cet être fait d'argile, / Tu l'as vu, Lamartine, et son sang est ton sang" (Musset, *Poésies complètes*, 333).
131 "Il ne lui reste plus, s'il ne tend pas la main, / Que la faim pur ce soir et la mort pour demain" (Ibid., 331).
132 On the scarcity of polymetric structures in Nabokov's prosodic repertoire and on these two poems, see Smith, "Nabokov and the Russian Verse Form," 286.
133 See Grayson, "French Connection," 613–31.
134 Legouis and Cazamian, *History of English Literature*, 1070.
135 With Charles Lloyd (May 1798). Lamb subsequently revised the opening of the poem to exclude a reference to his mother's untimely death.
136 See Lamb, *The Letters of Charles Lamb*, 1:121.
137 See Courtney, *Young Charles Lamb*, 164.
138 Lamb, *The Complete Works and Letters of Charles Lamb*, 518.
139 Album 19, 189 (VNA).
140 Lamb, *The Complete Works and Letters of Charles Lamb*, 518.
141 Album 19, 189 (VNA).
142 XIX, *Le Premier livre des amours* (see Ronsard, *Œuvres complètes*, 1:34).
143 *Le Second livre d'amours*, Appendices (CXIV) (in Ronsard, *Œuvres complètes*, 1:287).
144 See "Tableaux de l'origine et du movement des pieces" (in Ronsard, *Œuvres complètes*, 1:1219, 1296).
145 Album 8, 56, 57, 58; Album 10, 106–7; and Album 19, 23–4, 25, 27 (VNA).
146 Cf. the commentary to the sonnet in the Pléiade edition of Ronsard's poems: "Ce sonnet constitue un nécessaire moment de doute, aussitôt

avant que ne s'affirme la puissance créatrice de Ronsard-Jupiter dans le sonnet XX" (Ronsard, *Œuvres complètes*, 1:1229).

147 Door, rather than a garden gate, as in modern Russian.

148 Nabokov has also managed to provide a parallel for Ronsard's interjection "ma foy" ("ma foi") with the mild Russian intensifier *ei-ei*.

149 Boyd, *Vladimir Nabokov: The Russian Years*, 183–4.

150 Ibid., 230.

151 Blackstone, *Byron*, 158.

152 All but one of the eighteen lines of the poem are tetrametric; the poem's concluding line represents an expressive curtailment of tetrameter to trimeter.

153 Khodasevich, *Sobranie sochinenii*, 2:394.

154 *Rul'* 1140 (3 September 1924), 2; Album 19, 31 (VNA).

155 Schuman, "Nabokov and Shakespeare," 512.

156 Boyd, *Vladimir Nabokov: The Russian Years*, 222.

157 *SP*, 12. "December, 1925," Nabokov's dating of the poem, is tentative (see Boyd, "Nabokov's Russian Poems," 22). Nabokov enclosed it with a 26 February 1924 letter to his mother (*St*, 587); it first appeared in print in *Zhar-Ptitsa* 12 (1924), 32.

158 For Samuel Schuman's interpretation of this poem in the context of Nabokov's evolving understanding of the Shakespeare phenomenon, see his *Nabokov's Shakespeare*, 23–6.

159 See Schuman, "Nabokov and Shakespeare," 517; and Schuman, *Nabokov's Shakespeare*.

160 Schuman, "Nabokov and Shakespeare," 517.

161 For a facsimile of the Thorpe's 1609 Quarto, see Booth, *Shakespeare's Sonnets*.

162 *Rul'* 2069 (18 September 1927): 7; Album 19, 189 (VNA).

163 The famous example of which occurs in sonnet 104: "For as you were when first your *eye I eyed*" (emphasis added).

164 *Rul'* 1140 (3 September 1924): 2; Album 19, 191 (VNA).

165 Further into his version, Nabokov decides to introduce the image of a pilgrimage not in the second quatrain, as Shakespeare has it, but at the end of the first one (cf. Shakespeare's "zealous pilgrimage," l. 6, and Nabokov's *palomnicheskii put'*, l. 4).

166 Stephen Booth contends that Shakespeare's "imaginary" signifies *imaginative* and *imagined, unreal* (see Booth, *Shakespeare's Sonnets*, 179).

167 For a detailed discussion of one such instance, see Shvabrin, "'... A Sob That Alters.'"

168 The year of the work's composition was presumably added by Véra Nabokov and was modified by a question mark placed beside it.

169 Ca. 1925 (VNA).
170 Tiutchev 1921, 63.
171 Ricks, *Tennyson*, 204.
172 Originally published in *Harper's Magazine* as "Lodgings in Trinity Lane" (January 1951).
173 The fragment brought the widowed Queen "great comfort" (see Tennyson, *Poetry*, 235n4).
174 On the significance of this rhyming scheme for Tennyson's poem see Ricks, *Tennyson*, 210.
175 Tennyson, *Poetry*, 243.
176 *Zveno* 173 (23 May 1926), 3.
177 Grayson, "French Connection," 624–5.
178 In "La Nuit de décembre," however, the Poet is confronted by "La Vision," which turns out to be an allegory of the Poet's solitude.
179 See Musset, *Poésies complètes*, 309.
180 Grayson, "French Connection," 624.
181 Musset, *Poésies complètes*, 307.
182 *Rul'* 2122 (20 November 1927): 3.
183 See Nabokov, "O Pushkine." "O Bloke," 210. Cf. Nabokov's translation of the Incantation of Euphrosyne (the so-called "Plach' Iaroslavny") from *The Song of Igor's Campaign*: "Why, lord [i.e., Great Wind], have you dispersed / my gladness all over the feather grass" (*SIC*, 64, ll. 707–8), which corresponds to the following utterance in the original: "Chemu, gospodine, moë veselie po kovyliiu razveia?"
184 *Rul'* 2122 (20 November 1927): 3.
185 Musset, *Poésies complètes*, 308.
186 Ibid., 306.
187 *Rul'* 2122 (20 November 1927): 3.
188 Grayson, "French Connection," 614.
189 *SO*, 225.
190 See ibid., 224.
191 *A*, 464.
192 Musset, *Poésies complètes*, 313.
193 Grayson, "French Connection," 650.
194 *Rul'* 2392 (7 October 7 1928): 2.
195 Dal', *Tolkovyi slovar'*, 1:462 (emphasis added).
196 *NP*, 225 (emphasis added).
197 As he imagines what a French translation of Pushkin might sound like to a French reader, Nabokov slips into PVV an unknowledged reference to "La Nuit de mai" ("et la Grèce, ma mère, où le miel est si doux").
198 "… *Ouvre ta robe, Déjanire* that I may mount *sur mon bûcher* …" (LA, 3:507).

199 See Dmitri Nabokov, "On Revisiting Father's Room," 134.
200 Nabokov, "Pis'ma V.V. Nabokova k G.P. Struve," 128.
201 Verlaine, *Œuvres poétiques complètes*, 72.
202 Album 15, 67 (VNA).
203 Ibid., 68.
204 Note Nabokov's transcription of "blessent" (from "blesser"), which omits the mute ending of the verb's conjugated form.
205 *SO*, 42–3.
206 Cf. Rimbaud, *Œuvres complètes*, 915, and Rimbaud, *L'œuvre intégrale manuscrite*, 3:237.
207 See Rimbaud, "Le Bateau ivre," 75–8.
208 See Rimbaud, *Œuvres complètes*, 915.
209 Cf. Rimbaud, *L'œuvre intégrale manuscrite*, 1:88, and Rimbaud, *Œuvres complètes*, 67, l. 27 (emphasis added).
210 Weinberg, "*Le Bateau ivre*," 175n4.
211 See Rimbaud, *Œuvres complètes*, 920.
212 *Rul'* 2451 (16 December 1928): 2 (emphasis added).
213 Vitkovskii, *Protiv entropii*, 2002.
214 Rimbaud, *Œuvres complètes*, 67.
215 See also Rimbaud, *Œuvres complètes*, 921n9, for Georges Izambard's persuasive attribution of the image to Aeschylus, and specifically to his *Prometheus Bound*.
216 *Rul'* 2451 (16 December 1928): 2.
217 See Rimbaud, *Œuvres complètes*, 916.
218 Ibid., 68.
219 *Rul'* 2451 (16 December 1928): 2.
220 Rimbaud, *Œuvres complètes*, 69.
221 Starkie, *Arthur Rimbaud*, 137.
222 *Rul'* 2451 (16 December 1928): 2.
223 Cf. Weinberg, "*Le Bateau ivre*," 190; Vitkovskii, *Protiv entropii*; Rimbaud, *Rimbaud Complete* (trans. Wyatt Mason), 88; Rimbaud, *Rimbaud: Complete Works* (trans. Wallace Fowlie), 134.
224 See Starkie, *Arthur Rimbaud*, 78–9; and Robb, *Rimbaud*, 76–80.
225 See Album 23, 33 (VNA).
226 See Boyd, *Vladimir Nabokov: The Russian Years*, 288–9.
227 In Albums 13 and 19, the translations marked and dated "Le Boulou," "early March 1929."
228 *Pushkin*, 3:58.
229 Nabokov's literal translation, *VV*, 131.
230 See Zholkovskii, *Izbrannye stat'i*, 46.
231 Album 13, 193; and Album 19, 154 (VNA).

232 TAT, 161.

233 Jean Paulhan's friend Supervielle published his poetry and prose in *La Nouvelle revue française*; a volume of Supervielle's complete verse in the "La Bibliothèque de la Pléiade" series appeared in 1996. Apart from translating Federico García Lorca and Lope de Vega into French, Supervielle translated Shakespeare (*Comme il vous plaira*, 1935; and *Le Songe d'une nuit d'été*, with his son Jean, 1956).

234 Cited in Cranmer, "Jules Supervielle," 193.

235 The cycle "Le Chaos et la creation" (*La Fable du monde*, 1938) represents this aspect of Supervielle's metaphysics particularly well (see Supervielle, *Œuvres poétiques complètes*, 351–62).

236 From Nabokov's account of his first visit to Supervielle: "We talked about literature. He promised to introduce me on Friday to [Jean] Paulhan, the editor of *La Nouvelle revue française*. He was very obliging. I'll go to him again on Tuesday morning, with *Luzhin*. He talked about his own work eagerly and loftily, but, overall, very attractively" (*LV*, 191).

237 *LV*, 195, 210.

238 Nabokov's letters to his wife reveal that Supervielle's vouching for him ensured the publication of his first substantial work in the French language (see *LV*, 252). The publication of the autobiographic novella in the April issue of *Mesures* paved the way for the placement of "Pouchkine, ou le vrai e t le vraisemblable" in Paulhan's *Nouvelle revue française*.

239 See *SM*, 607. Evident as it was in Poplavskii's surrealist poetics, Supervielle's impact on the "Prince of the Russian Montparnasse" came to light after the posthumous publication of Poplavskii's programmatic poem "Poet from Montevideo" ("For Jules Supervielle," 1924–35).

240 Scott, *Reading the Rhythm*, 215.

241 Supervielle, *Œuvres poétiques complètes*, 304.

242 Blair, "Jules Supervielle's Use of Imagery," 580.

243 Both poems were included in Supervielle's collection *Les Amis inconnus* (1934). Nabokov's Russian versions of the two poems are united under the same title, "Iz Zh. Siuperv'elia," but have no titles of their own, which can be taken as a sign of Nabokov's acquaintance with them prior to their acquiring titles. "L'Appel" first appeared as a part of a selection of Supervielle's poems published in the 1 October 1932 issue of *La Nouvelle revue française*; "Le Sillage" in the 15 February 1933 issue of *Europe* (see Supervielle, *Œuvres poétiques complètes*, 820, 828).

244 Initially entitled "Iz F.G.Ch." ("From F.G.Ch."), which in all likelihood means "From [the poetry of] Fyodor Godunov-Cherdyntsev," the future protagonist of *The Gift*, Nabokov's "L'Inconnue de la Seine" (1934) may

have been at least partially inspired by Supervielle's treatment of the theme of the unknown young victim of a suicide by drowning, whose plaster cast became a source of inspiration for so many of Supervielle's and Nabokov's contemporaries.

245 Johnson, "'L'Inconnue de la Seine' and Nabokov's Naiads," 237.

246 [Struve], "Vladimir Nabokoff Sirine," 142.

247 Both fragments appeared in *Rul'* 3010 (19 September 1930): 2.

248 *Rul'* 3039 (23 November 1930): 2.

249 See Shakespeare, *Hamlet*, 67.

250 In a letter to Edmund Wilson dated 9 February 1947, Nabokov voiced his concern regarding the authenticity of this fragment (see *NWL*, 212). To G.R. Hibbard, editor of *Hamlet* for the Oxford Shakespeare series, it seems "likely" that this fragment was intended as an "advertisement" for *Julius Caesar* (see Shakespeare, *Hamlet*, 355 n.i).

251 G.R. Hibbard is convinced that the "excision of these lines from F is a gain" (see Shakespeare, *Hamlet*, 366 n.xvi).

252 See *Rul'* 3010 (19 September 1930): 2.

253 See Schuman, "Nabokov and Shakespeare," 517n1. The first edition of this version of *Hamlet* was published by Oxford University Press in 1914.

254 See Shakespeare, *Hamlet*, 131.

255 Shakespeare, *Tragedy of Hamlet*.

256 In *Pnin* (completed 1955, published 1957) Nabokov has his simple-hearted hero lament the absence of such florid passages from the original: "whenever you were reduced to look up something in the English version, you never found this or that beautiful, noble, sonorous line that you remembered all your life from Kroneberg's text in Vengerov's splendid edition. Sad!" (*P*, 79). The line from Andrei Kroneberg's translation of *Hamlet* that Pnin is trying to remember comes from the same speech of the Queen that Nabokov discusses in "The Art of Translation" (act 4, scene 7).

257 TAT, 160.

258 *Rul'* 3010 (19 September 1930): 2.

259 Ibid., 2.

260 Shakespeare, *Tragedy of Hamlet*, 143.

261 Notes on various subjects, Box 2 (VNA).

262 VNA.

263 Pëtr Bartenev recounted this episode in the obituary for Dal': "За нѣсколько дней до своей кончины, Пушкинъ пришёлъ къ Далю и, указывая на свой только что сшитый сюртукъ, сказалъ: 'Эту выползину я теперь не скоро сброшу.' Выползиною называется кожа, которую мѣняютъ на себѣ

змѣи, и Пушкинъ хотѣлъ сказать, что этого сюртука надолго ему станетъ. Онъ дѣйствительно не снялъ этого сюртука, а его спороли съ него 27 Января 1837 года, чтобы облегчить смертельную муку отъ раны" (see B[artenev], "V.I. Dal'."). In chapter 1 of *The Gift* (1938) "vypolzina" designates the skin of a fruit ("в комнате у Яши держалась … жизнь, бананная выползина в тарелке" / "in Yasha's room life went on … the cast-off banana skin on a plate" [*SSRP*, 4:234/*G*, 48]). Yasha Chernyshevsky, the character who leaves behind this "vypolzina," has committed suicide, setting in motion a metaphorical likening of the transformation of a snake shaking off its old skin to the soul's transition after death.

264 For "lurking wrongdoing/malice" or "creeping misdeed" (cf. Shakespeare, *Hamlet*, 256; and Shakespeare, *Tragedy of Hamlet*, 144n158).

265 *BS*, 263. "Don't you think, sir, that this … and a forest of feathers on a hat, and a couple of [patterned] roses on incised boots, could, if fortune pushed me into it, earn me a stake in a theatrical guild, do you, sir?"

266 Shakespeare, *Tragedy of Hamlet*, 155.

267 See also Brian Boyd's exegesis of Nabokov's choice of *kamchatyi* to render Shakespeare's "Provincial" in the passage quoted above: "'patterned' … does scant justice to Ember's find for 'Provincial roses': a particular old style of silk pattern, and a play on remote Kamchatka province" (see *BS*, 690–1n263/8–12).

268 *BS*, 264.

269 Notes on various subjects, Box 2 (VNA).

270 See entry on *svivat'* in Dal', *Tolkovyi slovar'* 4, 148.

271 In his foreword to "Vechera na khutore bliz' Dikan'ki," Rudyi Pan'ko glosses *svitka* as "rod polukaftan'ia," which, together with Gogol's presentation of this article of clothing in the text of "Sorochinskaia iarmarka," makes it clear that Gogol had in mind a long shirt with sleeves (see Gogol, *Polnoe sobranie sochinenii*, 1:109).

272 See *Novye poety Frantsii*, [7].

273 See *SSRP*, 2:657–60.

274 See Verlaine, *Œuvres poétiques complètes*, 1148.

275 Ibid., 326.

276 See ibid., 1149; and Wright, "Verlaine's 'Art poétique,'" 268–9.

277 *Novye poety Frantsii*, 23.

278 Box 109, Folder 1 (GSP).

279 Verlaine, *Œuvres poétiques complètes*, 327.

280 Box 109, Folder 1 (GSP).

281 Nabokov, "Pis'ma V.V. Nabokova k G.P. Struve," 140.

282 Nabokov, *Nikolai Gogol*, 67.

283 Ibid., 68.
284 Goethe, *Sämtliche Werke*, 6.1:535.
285 *Poslednie novosti* 4285 (15 December 1932), 3.
286 *SVN*, 523.
287 Baudelaire, *Œuvres complètes* 1:74.
288 VNA.
289 David Rampton points out the incongruity of the essay's appearance in *La Nouvelle revue française*, "a journal whose pages in the 1930s creak and groan from all the heavy lifting done by fellow travelers and apologists for Stalin's Russia" (Rampton, "In Search of the Real Poet," 185).
290 *LV*, 295.
291 PVV, 373.
292 Ibid.
293 Monnier, "Un miroir pouchkinien," 21.
294 See PVV, 374.
295 Ibid.
296 The line in question is l. 11: "du temps, du jour que j'ai perdu," which renders "Mnoi utrachennago dnia" (see Monnier, "Un miroir pouchkinien," 21–2).
297 See *PLT*, 36. This is the full original context of this fragment: "Chto v nem? Zabytoe davno, / V volnen'iakh novykh i miatezhnykh, / Tvoei dushe ne dast ono / Vospominanii chistykh, nezhnykh" (Pushkin 1937, 195).
298 See also the ensuing discussion of his replacement of Tiutchev's "feathered creatures" with "thrush and oriole" ("Appeasement").
299 See PVV, 375; also Monnier, "Un miroir pouchkinien," 22–5.
300 PVV, 375.
301 See ibid., 375–6.
302 Ibid., 373
303 TAT, 161.
304 Ibid.

3 Before *Eugene Onegin*

1 Galya Diment finds little difference between the Rupert Brooke translations from the early 1920s and the rhymed versions of Pushkin, Lermontov, and Tiutchev made in the 1940s (see Diment, "Uncollected Critical Writing," 734).
2 *NWL*, 35.

3 *NWL*, 48. Nabokov's letter to Wilson dated 9 April 1941 lifts the veil on the nature of his collaboration with Wilson: Nabokov sought Wilson's criticism and suggestions, but made all the final decisions (see *NWL*, 48–9).
4 Wilson, "This dramatic poem by Pushkin…," 559. Wilson's preamble was reproduced in both *Three Russian Poets* and *PLT* minus this concluding claim, directed, as Galya Diment has inferred, at Avrahm Yarmolinsky's and Babette Deutsch's translations from Pushkin (see Diment, "*Three Russian Poets*," 709–10).
5 *VV*, 165.
6 Pushkin 1937, 796.
7 *VV*, 165.
8 If Nabokov's conclusion expands on the original, his setting of Salieri's soliloquy that closes the tragedy's first scene subtracts two lines from it.
9 Following its publication on the centenary of the poet's death, Nabokov used Modeste Hofmann's edition of Pushkin's collected works as his favourite source of Pushkin's texts. After purchasing it at a Christie's auction of Dmitri Nabokov's books in 2010, the Princeton University Department of Rare Books and Special Collections has made it available online as part of their Digital Library (see Pushkin 1937).
10 Fyodor recalls Salieri's envy for Mozart as he encounters his rival Koncheyev (see *SSRP*, 4:250).
11 *NWL*, 51.
12 Ibid., 52.
13 See Khodasevich, "Rusalka," 302–8.
14 Pushkin 1937, 784.
15 *VV*, 147.
16 Pushkin 1937, 785.
17 *VV*, 149.
18 *L*, 314.
19 Gifford, "Puškin's *Feast in Time of Plague* and Its Original," 38.
20 *E*, 34.
21 *G*, 65.
22 See Bailey, *Three Russian Lyric Major Folk Meters*.
23 *VV*, 177.
24 *EO*, 3:472. This gloss explains Nabokov's pen stroke in the margin of his Pushkin volume (see Pushkin 1937, 800).
25 *VV*, 173.
26 Apart from the 1941 essay published in the *New Republic* entitled "The Art of Translation" (TAT), we find Nabokov's letter to the editor in response to E.W. Nashe's correction of his misquotation from Charles Baudelaire's

"Invitation au voyage" (see "The Art of Translation." Letter to the editor) and such subsequent iterations of the 1941 essay as "Art of Translation" ("I thought I might say a few words about this pathetic business of translating") and "The Art of Translation" ("To begin – I want to say a few words about the art of translation").

27 *VV*, 8–9.

28 For a justification of this dating, see *VV*, 394–5.

29 "The Art of Translation" (II: "A Kind of V Movement") (see *VV*, 14–15).

30 Nabokov, *Selected Poems*, 148.

31 *SO*, 223.

32 See *New Directions in Prose and Poetry, 1941*.

33 See *SO*, 225.

34 For a facing reproduction of both Khodasevich's poem and Nabokov's translation of it, see *VV*, 340–3.

35 Bethea, *Khodasevich*, 181.

36 "V 'Ballade' … Khodasevich dostig … predelov poeticheskogo masterstva" (*SSRP*, 2:650).

37 For Gasparov's substantiation of this concept with the aid of Khodasevich's "Ballad," see his *Metr i smysl*, 149.

38 *VV*, 347

39 *NWL*, 126.

40 This follows from Nabokov's biographical cameos of the three poets found in both booklets. Thus, Tiutchev's "poetry … has quite exceptional qualities and reveals (in the thirties!) elements which characterize the fin de siècle renaissance of Russian poetry (also called decadence, also called symbolism – the student ought not to bother much about these terms)" (*VV*, 230).

41 This is what Nabokov accomplished when he prepared for his first Harvard course a booklet entitled "Translations from Russian Poetry by Vladimir Nabokov (1951–1952)," which, in addition to a more generous selection from Tiutchev, included poems by Nekrasov, Blok, and Khodasevich.

42 With the notable omission of Afanasii Fet, such ordering of Russia's great lyric poets first appeared in Nabokov's 1921 poem "Na smert' Aleksandra Bloka" (I. "Za tumanami plyli tumany," II. "Pushkin – raduga po vsei zemle"), where the spirits of Pushkin, Lermontov, Tiutchev, and Fet come out to welcome Blok's soul to paradise.

43 Nabokov's marginal notes in his personal copy of Pushkin's collected works document his engagement with this poem. Apart from establishing that "Ūpas" is "a Javanese tree of the mulberry family," he notes that in this context Pushkin's *smola* (sap) corresponds to the English word

"antiaris," defined in *Webster's Collegiate Dictionary* as "1. a poisonous gum or resin from the upas tree"; and "2. An arrow poison prepared from antiaris." The draft of this translation survives in the blank sections of the book's front matter (see Pushkin 1937, 177–8).

44 In his superb exegesis of the poem's source of inspiration, Richard F. Gustafson calls it "a lyrical cry of anguish about the ruler's injustice to the ruled and man's inhumanity to man, an epic celebration of the evil in nature, and a symbolic representation of the aggressive, even the sadistic tendencies hidden in the unconscious of every man" (Gustafson, "The Upas Tree," 109). For up-to-date studies of the poem's genesis and significance, see Berëzkina, "Stikhotvorenie Pushkina 'Anchar'"; also Dolinin's *Pushkin i Angliia*, 54–9.

45 For a survey of "Anchar's" earlier English translations, see Yarmolinsky, *Pushkin in English*.

46 *VV*, 15.

47 The metrical equivalence of this translation is complicated by Nabokov's liberal employment of enjambments unsanctioned by the original.

48 See *EO*, 2:192.

49 See *VV*, 14.

50 See Nabokov, "O Pushkine." "O Bloke," 204.

51 *EO*, 2:310–11.

52 Gershenzon, *Mudrost' Pushkina*, 49–54. Nabokov's misattribution of this interpretation to Burtsev is symptomatic. It is not at all likely that he would have forgotten Gershenzon's influential interpretation (later in this fragment of this commentary, he will refer to Pushkin's drafts that Gershenzon discusses at length as part of his defence of his interpretation of "Exegi monumentum").

53 Pushkin 1937, 276.

54 *VV*, 215.

55 This interpretation is corroborated by the recording of Nabokov's reading of the poem in Harvard College Library Poetry Room on 20 March 1952 (see *HM*, side 4, track 29).

56 See *EO*, 2:311; and *VV*, 216.

57 See Nabokov, *Selected Poems*, 132.

58 Ibid., 182.

59 See *PP*, 108, 109.

60 *VV*, 215.

61 *PLT*, 7–8.

62 "Not dearly do I value the loud rights," Nabokov's initial unpublished version of "Iz Pindemonte" ("Nedorogo tseniu ia gromkie prava"),

survives in the margins of his copy of Pushkin's collected works (see Pushkin 1937, 206).

63 Pushkin 1937, 206.

64 *VV*, 207.

65 Ibid., 105.

66 Pushkin 1937, 195.

67 *VV*, 135.

68 Priscilla Smith Heim, handwritten class notes from SLAVIC 152, 1951–2.

69 See LM, 31.

70 Ibid.

71 Ibid., 32–3.

72 Ibid., 34.

73 See LM, 34.

74 See RB 229.

75 LM, 32.

76 Lermontov, *Polnoe sobranie sochinenii*, 1:312.

77 *VV*, 297.

78 See LM, 34.

79 See *H*, vi.

80 In *The Eye* (1930), Smurov appropriates the poem when he fabricates the story of his military exploits: "I was bleeding to death, alone in a mountain gorge" (*E*, 49). This superficial indication of Smurov's mendacity becomes a prefiguration of his imagined ability to transcend the divide separating him from the world of the quick after his suicide.

81 LM, 35.

82 "The Angel," "The Sail," "The Rock," and "Imitation of Heine" first appeared in print in the *Russian Review* 5, no. 2 (Spring 1946): 50–1, while "Thanksgiving" was published in the *Atlantic* (November 1946), 108. If this order of appearance indicates the chronology of Nabokov's work on his translations, then "The Wish" and "Thanksgiving" were the last poems to be added to the finalized selection.

83 *NWL*, 182.

84 On Lermontov's contribution to the Russian adoption of Heinean accentual verse, see Ivanov, "Geine v Rossii," 432–4.

85 *VV*, 279.

86 The laudatory attestation of this poem in "The Lermontov Mirage" comes on the heels of *The Gift*, where "The Angel" figures as a required feature of any visualization of ethereal beings: "if there must be an angel, then with a huge chest cavity, and wings like a hybrid between a bird of paradise and a condor, and talons to carry the young soul away – not 'embraced' as Lermontov has it" (*G*, 192).

87 See *NWL*, 182.
88 *NWL*, 225–6.
89 See Nabokov, "Four Poems by Lermontov," 50.
90 *SVN*, 437.
91 *SVN*, 431.
92 *NWL*, 50.
93 Nabokov's notes for the public talk "The Art of Translation" (after 1941; VNA; no relation to the eponymous 1941 essay); partially preserved in *HM*.
94 See *NWL*, 123.
95 *VV*, 233.
96 Ibid., 235.
97 See ibid., 245
98 See ibid., 246.
99 *EO*, 2:328–9.
100 Cf. the King James Version, "This is my comfort in my affliction: for thy word hath quickened me," Psalm 119:50.
101 First published as a separate work in 1964, "Notes on Prosody" has been integral part of the *Eugene Onegin* four-volume set since its first publication later the same year (see *EO*, 3:448–541). For a superlative survey of "Notes on Prosody" and its place in the evolution of Nabokov's poetic practice and theory as well as in the study of Russian poetics, see Smith, "Nabokov and the Russian Verse Form," 271–5, and also Smith, "*Notes on Prosody*."
102 *EO*, 3:525.
103 For a detailed discussion of the origins of Nabokov's idiosyncratic notions regarding the evolution of Russian prosody, see Shvabrin, "'The Dreamy Stutter of Blok's Rhythms.'"
104 See Nabokov, "O Pushkine." "O Bloke," 212–13.
105 Robert Blattner's class notes taken in the SLAVIC 150 course indicate that Nabokov taught his students to see the admission of an extra syllable into the second line of "Posledniaia liubov'" as an "explosion" of the iambic rhythm.
106 Nabokov, *Invitation to a Beheading*, 193.
107 For a close study of how Nabokov's individual mythopoetics influences his cultural eschatology and vice versa, see Shvabrin, "'… A Sob That Alters.'"
108 *VV*, 257.
109 Scherr, "Yearning for a Last Love," 183, 189–90.
110 Ibid., 200.
111 Ibid., 189.

112 See Tiutchev 1921, 55.
113 See *VV*, 251.
114 See Tiutchev 1921, 55.
115 *LL*, 319, 350.
116 Eager as Nabokov was to impress on his students his famous identification of "the Man in the Brown Macintosh" as a creature's encounter with its creator (*LL*, 316–20), he urged them not to take that same character's re-appearance in chapter 12/episode 15 "seriously." His reluctance to dwell on the implications of the "Circe" episode in his classroom did not preclude him from furnishing *Pnin* with a mirror reflection of the Man in the Brown Macintosh's denunciation of Bloom as a "notorious fireraiser" (*LL*, 319). In *Pnin*, Nabokov has the title character denounce the author-like narrator Vladimir Vladimirovich N. as a "dreadful inventor" (*Pn*, 185).
117 *LL*, 352.
118 Joyce, *Ulysses*, 511.
119 Ibid., 502.
120 Ibid., 515–16, 517.
121 *LL*, 288.
122 Joyce's "stage directions" connect Virag's portrait (see *Ulysses*, 516) with *Hamlet*, where the Ghost mentions a glow-worm in a similar situation (act 1, scene 5). Brian Boyd has demonstrated that the Ghost's "glow-worm" constitutes an important pretext for Nabokov's *Pale Fire* (see *NPFMAD*, 177–9).
123 *VV*, 254.
124 Ibid.
125 Tiutchev 1921, 44.
126 *HM*, side 4, track 21.
127 Lane, "Tiutchev in English Translation," 158.
128 *VV*, 253.
129 Much to Nabokov's chagrin, it must be admitted (for his wrathful diatribe against these pictures, see *SL*, 84–5).
130 *EO*, 3:13.
131 Ibid., 33:14.
132 *VV*, 62.
133 Ibid., 205. In winter 1948, Nabokov informed his sister Elena that he had "just translated" the poem for his cousin (see *PS*, 52).
134 Michael Wachtel's commentary addresses the issue of Pushkin's fluid vision of this poem's overall emotional tonality to conclude that he "chose to reject" its "darker passages" (Wachtel, *Commentary to Pushkin's Lyric Poetry*, 329).

135 The Vengerov edition of Pushkin's collected works became a major step in the way the poet was presented and understood in Russia before 1917. Volume 4 of that six-volume set, published as part of the lavishly produced "Biblioteka velikikh pisatelei" series, contains a version of the poem that is closest to Nabokov's 1948 interpretation of it.
136 Nabokov's 1948 translation is informed by his acquaintance with Modeste Hofmann's "Posmertnye stikhotvoreniia Pushkina" 1922.
137 "Radio Talk for BBC. On April 3, 1954," 2 (VNA).
138 *VV*, 409.
139 *EO*, 3:145.
140 *VV*, 46–9.
141 *EO*, 2:380.
142 *VV*, 219.
143 Ibid., 226.
144 Ibid., 227.
145 Ibid., 225.
146 Nabokov's letters to his wife prove that Baratynskii's "Svoenravnoe prozvan'e" was indeed a part and parcel of their playful and affectionate private discourse (see *LV*, 151).
147 *PF*, 42.
148 *L*, 251 (emphasis added).
149 Nabokov, *Sobranie sochinenii amerkanskogo perioda*, 2:308 (emphasis added).
150 For a much subtler incorporation of Baratynskii's striking epithet into the texture of Nabokov's abandoned drafts of the second part of his last Russian novel *The Gift*, see Nabokov, "Dar. II chast'," 169.
151 We may expand the scope of Nabokov's linguistic acumen to no fewer six languages by including Latin. Sergei Karpukhin has discovered Nabokov's "imitation" of Catullus's "Vivamus, mea Lesbia, atque amemus" (Catullus 5) and found an indisputable "verbal vestige"of the writer's engagement with this text in *Bend Sinister* (see Karpukhin, "Vladimir Nabokov and the Russian Hexameter"). A passionate entreaty for love, "Zhit' budem, Lesbia, zhit' budem dlia ob'iatii," Nabokov's "imitation" is dated 14 February 1923. Catullus's poems to Lesbia are a frequent point of reference in *Lolita*.
152 *VV*, 266.
153 See *G*, 241.
154 Nabokov's copy of George Patrick's *Intermediate Russian Reader* with marginalia (VNA).
155 *VV*, 266.
156 For a study of the Keatsean verbal vestige in Nabokov's compositions, see Shvabrin, "Vladimir Nabokov's 'La Belle Dame Sans Merci,'" 116–22.

157 Notes to "The Art of Translation" talk (VNA and also *HM*).
158 See Tiutchev 1921, 195; and Nabokov, *Perepiska s Karpovichem*, 140.
159 *VV*, 263.
160 See *SM*, 382.
161 *VV*, 261.
162 See Tiutchev 1921, 71.
163 Nabokov, "Three Poems by Fet."
164 See *G*, 73, 200.
165 *VV*, 300, 301.
166 When Nabokov introduced his students to Fet, he saw fit to revert to the exalted idiom in which he lauded Russia's four great lyric poets – Pushkin, Lermontov, Tiutchev, and Fet – in "Na smert' A. Bloka" (I. "Za tumanami plyli tumany," II. "Pushkin – raduga po vsei zemle"), his commemorative piece of 1921 (see *Rul'* 225 [14 August 1921]: 2; and *Rul'* 256 [20 September 1921]: 4).
167 *SM*, 468–9.
168 *VV*, 304.
169 *Pn*, 136.
170 *VV*, 305.
171 See *PS*, 48.
172 "Logaoedic," a term that designates a poem composed in different metres recurring throughout its length, was not a part of Nabokov's elaborate individual prosodic nomenclature. Since he made no distinction between logaoedic and accentual verse, Nabokov saw no fundamental difference among the poems he identified as "pausative" by Tiutchev, Fet, and Blok.
173 *VV*, 417.
174 See *G*, 73.
175 Ibid., 65.
176 See *VV*, 307, and also *PP*, 125n.
177 To give his students an idea of Nekrasov's mastery of the "lyrical surge," Nabokov used the example of Robert Browning's "Prospice."
178 *G*, 251–2.
179 Notes to "The Art of Translation" talk (VNA, and also *HM*).
180 Cf. *SSRP*, 3:60, and *E*, 34
181 See *VV*, 317.
182 Ibid., 315.
183 See Rowe, *Nabokov's Spectral Dimension*, 62–6; also Barabtarlo, *Phantom of Fact*, 21–3.
184 *Pn*, 379.
185 See Bethea, "Nabokov and Blok," 374; Aleksandr Dolinin has argued that Nabokov's attitude toward Blok is best understood as a manifestation

of the Bloomian "anxiety of influence" (see Dolinin, *Istinnaia zhizn' pisatelia Sirina*, 355). For Vladimir Alexandrov's consideration of Blok's importance for the evolution of Nabokov's "mystically colored conception of love," see his *Nabokov's Otherworld*, 215–17.

186 Nabokov, "Cabbage Soup and Caviar," 93.

187 Nabokov, "O Pushkine." "O Bloke," 209–17.

188 *EO*, 3:539.

189 *VV*, 237.

190 Responding to Edmund Wilson's suggestion to include Jane Austen in his Cornell survey of novelistic masterpieces, he stated: "I … am prejudiced … against all women writers" (*NWL*, 268). Maxim Shrayer has contextualized this and other manifestations of Nabokov's attitude toward women writers in his *Nabokov: Temy i variatsii*, 240–50.

191 *NWL*, 20; and *SM*, 607.

192 *SL*, 41.

193 "The Art of Translation" ("To begin – I want to say a few words about the art of translation"), 2 (VNA).

194 Barabtarlo, *Phantom of Fact*, 109–10.

195 *Pn*, 180–1.

196 Scherr, "Settling Accounts with Russia's Silver Age," 37.

197 See TAT, 161.

198 Ibid., 162

199 Cf. Pushkin "did notice Mrs. Olenin's niece, Anna Kern (Cairn), née Poltoratski (1800–79), to whom at a second meeting (in the Pskovan countryside, July 1825) he was to dedicate the famous short poem beginning, 'I recollect a wondrous moment'" (*EO*, 2:30).

200 Pushkin 1937, 143.

201 Cf. TAT, 161; and *EO*, 3:210.

202 See *NWL*, 200.

203 Cf. *VV*, 12; and *HM*, side 3, track 18.

204 *VV*, 12.

205 *PS*, 18. It was no accident that when his sister asked him to share with her one of his translations, Nabokov sent her his versions of Tiutchev's "Silentium" and "Posledniaia liubov'" (see *PS*, 27–8 and 30).

4 *Eugene Onegin* in Its Element (1955–1965)

1 TAT, 161.

2 PT, 496.

3 The only invocation of "divine individual genius" throughout the essay concerns Pushkin.

4 PT, 504.
5 Ibid.
6 Ibid., 512.
7 See *The Translation Studies Reader*, 113.
8 See Nabokov, "On Translating Pushkin: Pounding the Clavichord," 16; also *SL*, 354.
9 *SL*, 251–2.
10 William Mills Todd III differs from Shaw's censure of the Nabokovs' (mis-) use of the simple past and past perfect tenses (see Todd, "*A Hero of Our Time*," 180 and 183n5).
11 See Shaw, review of Vladimir and Dmitri Nabokovs' and Eden and Cedar Pauls's translations of Lermontov's *Hero of Our Time* (both published 1958); and Boris Dralyuk's review of Natasha Randall's translation of the same novel (2009), 527.
12 LM, 36.
13 Ibid., 31.
14 Ibid., 36.
15 *H*, 18.
16 See ibid., xii.
17 LM, 37.
18 *H*, xiii.
19 Ibid.
20 Ibid., 47–8.
21 This confirms J. Douglas Clayton's observation that "Nabokov's literalist approach, which favors the semantic aspect, has its most useful application in the translation of artistic prose" (Clayton, "Theory and Practice of Poetic Translation in Pushkin and Nabokov," 93).
22 Nabokov's heightened awareness of the problems associated with the sources of his and his son's translation will boost this impression. It should not be forgotten that interest in the source text was alien to the translations made during the period of "tender and loving sinning," which owed so much to Nabokov's emotional and uncritical attachment to his favourite versions of his texts.
23 LM, 32.
24 *SM*, 586.
25 Cf.: "Why lord have you dispersed / my gladness all over the feather grass?" (*SIC*, 64).
26 *SIC*, 3.
27 Nabokov, "Pis'ma V.V. Nabokova k G. P. Struve," 134–6.

28 For Nabokov's summary and dismissal of Mazon's attack on the authenticity of the *Slovo* in Mazon's *Le Slovo d'Igor* (1940), see *SIC*, 8217n.
29 See *SL*, 46–7. Nabokov's letter summarized his evaluation of Guerney's translation in Nabokov, "Cabbage Soup and Caviar."
30 *NWL*, 236, 242–3, 254, 361, and 366; *SL*, 137 and 291–2; and *PS*, 76, 93 and 96.
31 Boyd, *Vladimir Nabokov: The American Years*, 136, 145, 215, and 311.
32 Diment, *Pniniad*, 37–9 and 41.
33 *NWL*, 361. Nabokov took immense pride in *The Song of Igor's Campaign*. It was in connection with this work that he told Wilson in March 1959, "Russia will never be able to repay all her debts to me" (*NWL*, 361), a claim he repeated to his sister soon thereafter (see *PS*, 96).
34 *SIC*, 17.
35 Ibid., 82n18.
36 *La Geste du Prince Igor'*, 38–78.
37 Ibid., 39–79.
38 See *SIC*, 87–8.
39 Ibid., 77.
40 Ibid., 101.
41 "The Discourse of Igor's Campaign," 2. See "The Discourse of Igor's Campaign," translated by Vladimir Nabokov (unpublished; Vladimir Vladimirovich Nabokov Papers, The Library of Congress, Washington, DC).
42 *SIC*, 33.
43 Priscilla Meyer has observed that the "translation of and commentary to [*The Song*] can become a key to the interpretation of *Pale Fire*" (Meyer, "Igor, Ossian, and Kinbote," 69).
44 See *SIC*, 82n17.
45 *EO*, 1:109.
46 Anderson, "Nabokov's Rewriting of Dryden's Laws of Translation," 36–9; Eskin, "'Literal Translation,'" 6–7 and 23–4.
47 *EO*, 1:viii–ix.
48 Ibid., 1:x.
49 Gerschenkron, "A Manufactured Monument?," 337.
50 *EO*, 4:[22].
51 Nabokov, "From Pushkin's *Eugene Onegin*," 38.
52 PT, 510–11.
53 *EO*, 1:110.
54 As noted earlier, his French translation of "Stikhi, sochinënnye noch'iu vo vremia bessonitsy" introduced "Lachesis" instead of Pushkin's *parca*, his

English version of "Chto v imene tebe moëm" allegorized "memory" as "Mnemosyne," and his English version of Tiutchev's "Uspokoenie" had "Thor" instead of *perun*.

55 Boyd, *Vladimir Nabokov: The American Years*, 320.

56 Shaw, "Translations of *Onegin*," 119.

57 Aleksandr Dolinin offers the most eloquent substantiation of this interpretation (see Dolinin, "*Eugene Onegin*," 124).

58 Boyd, *Vladimir Nabokov: The American Years*, 328. When the San Francisco-based Arion Press attempted to fulfill Nabokov's original vision in 2018, the resulting edition required a six-figure price tag (see *Eugene Onegin*).

59 Rosengrant, "Nabokov, *Onegin*, and the Theory of Translation," 20.

60 Boyd, *Vladimir Nabokov: The American Years*, 327.

61 *EO*, 1:162.

62 Michael Eskin's consideration of the theoretical implications of Nabokov's method and version convinces him that they "not only acquire belated actuality … but also prophetic significance" (see Eskin, "'Literal Translation,'" 20–1).

63 Gerschenkron, "A Manufactured Monument?," 337–8.

64 PT, 512.

65 *EO*, 1:viii.

66 Ibid., 1:338.

67 See *VV*, 203 and 409.

68 Douglas Hofstadter's "literary" translation of *Eugene Onegin* (1999) was a polemical response to Nabokov's insistence on the "mathematical" impossibility of rendering Pushkin's novel in rhymed English verse.

69 Shaw, "Translations of *Onegin*," 115–16. After Gerschenkron pointed out that "Nabokov does not like to give credit where credit is due" in 1965 ("A Manufactured Monument?," 345), Nabokov's treatment of his predecessors has been repeatedly cited as the commentary's defect.

70 Boyd, *Vladimir Nabokov: The American Years*, 346.

71 Ibid., 350–2.

72 Still more disturbing is the apprehension that Nabokov the literalist, who condemns the tyranny of "poetical" paraphrases over foreign-language literary works, may himself be mistreating Pushkin's work.

73 Wilson, "The Strange Case of Pushkin and Nabokov," 6.

74 Dolinin, "*Eugene Onegin*," 120, 124, 126–7.

75 Bozovic, *Nabokov's Canon*, 46.

76 PT, 501–2.

77 Nabokov, *Selected Poems*, 148.

78 Nabokov's 1931 talk marked the anniversary of Pushkin's death as Russian Berlin faced uncertainties associated with an increased polarization of German society and the ascent of fascism. For a discussion of the talk and its place in Nabokov's oeuvre, see Shvabrin, "'Pechat' neprekhodiashchego.'"
79 Nabokov, "O Pushkine." "O Bloke," 205–6.
80 "When I envisage London, cast-iron roads, steamboats, English magazines or Parisian brothels, my godforsaken Mikhailovskoe provokes in me ennui and rage" (see Pushkin, *Pis'ma*, 2:12).
81 Nabokov, "O Pushkine." "O Bloke," 206–7.
82 Iurii Lotman qualifies Nabokov's proposition as a "poetic hypothesis" (see his *Besedy o russkoi kul'ture*, 167).
83 It is here where Nabokov overcomes his initial resistance to his desire to envisage Pushkin as an old man.
84 In "Nabokov, Pushkin, Shakespeare: Genius, Generosity, and Gratitude in *The Gift* and *Pale Fire*," Brian Boyd discusses the motif of filial love that permeates Fyodor's attitude toward Pushkin in *The Gift* (see *Stalking Nabokov*, 203–13).
85 *SM*, 579.
86 See *EO*, 2:432–4.
87 Wood, *The Magician's Doubts*, 155.
88 Eskin, *Nabokovs version von Puškins "Evgenij Onegin,"* 117–24.
89 For a revised, edited, and finalized edition of Deutsch's translation, see Pushkin, *Eugene Onegin: A Novel in Verse.*
90 On 19 February 1955, Nabokov lamented Doubleday's refusal to publish "the thing and the Russian *en regard*" (see *NWL*, 322).
91 See *L*, 47; and *SO*, 266.

5 Beyond *Eugene Onegin* (1965–1977)

1 Alfred Appel Jr explicates this reference's erotic implications (*L*, 359n47/3).
2 Belleau, *Œuvres poétiques*, 1:201–3.
3 See *VV*, 384.
4 See ibid., 385.
5 "Literary Competitions: April in the South," *Sunday Times*, no. 7092 (19 April 1959), 30.
6 "For Holiday Thinkers: 'Passing of Youth,'" *Sunday Times*, no. 7284 (23 December 1962), 25.
7 *PF*, ll. 677–8, 476.

8 See ibid., 612–14.
9 *VV*, 389.
10 Ibid.
11 Ibid.
12 "Passing of Youth," *Sunday Times*, no. 7287 (13 January 1963), 12.
13 In 1968 Steiner judged the *Sunday Times* competition devoted to Baudelaire's "Je suis comme le roi d'un pays pluvieux" ("Spleen"; see Scott, *Translating Baudelaire*, 127).
14 For Nabokov's dating of this poem's composition, see his note in Pushkin 1937, 213, and *EO*, 3:214, where it is dated "about 1835."
15 For the Russian variants of "The Servile Path," see Nabokov, "Zametki perevodchika [1]"; and "Zametki perevodchika [2]."
16 *Des*, [xiv].
17 See *EO*, 3:253
18 *Des*, [xiv].
19 PT, 512.
20 See *EO*, 1:vii–ix.
21 Nabokov, ["On Democracy"] (1942), is the most succinct articulartion of Nabokov's views on this system of government.
22 Nabokov, "Vladimir Nabokov's Translation of The Gettysburg Address," 11–13.
23 Ibid.
24 Okudzhava included it in his second verse collection *Ostrova* (1959) under the title "Sentimental'nyi romans," renamed it "Sentimental'ny marsh" in *Vesëlyi barabanshchik* (1964), and settled on the second, deliberately oxymoronic version of the title. Okudzhava had little control over the preparation of the Natalia Tarasova–edited collection *Bud' zdorov, shkoliar: Stikhi* (1964).
25 See *SO*, 241–67; and Boyd, *Vladimir Nabokov: The American Years*, 507–8; for Wilson's counter-response to Nabokov, see his "Nabokov, Pushkin, Wilson."
26 Lowell, "Nabokov's Onegin," 91.
27 Lowell's practice of retelling the works of foreign poets was on full display in his *Imitations* (1961). T.S. Eliot warned Lowell against classifying such compositions as "translations" (see Hamilton, *Robert Lowell*, 289); Edmund Wilson praised Lowell's *Imitations* unreservedly (see Wachtel and Cravens, "Nadezhda Iakovlevna Mandel'shtam," 526n35).
28 Lowell, "Ossip Mandelstamm: Translation of Nine Poems," 17.
29 Nabokov hesitated before responding to Lowell in print (see *SL*, 385–8).
30 Nabokov, "Response to Robert Lowell," 91.

31 *VV*, 360.
32 Ibid.
33 Ibid.
34 Ibid.
35 Ibid., 361.
36 Ibid., 365.
37 See ibid., 359.
38 VNA.
39 *A*, 330
40 See ibid., 330, 331.
41 *VV*, 365.
42 Personal communication with Ol'ga Artsimovich-Okudzhava (12 January 2007).
43 *A*, 7, 469.
44 See Nabokov, "Nabokov's Reply"; and also "Reply to My Critics" (*SO*, 241–67).
45 Steiner, "To Traduce or Transfigure," 51–2.
46 Steiner's paean to Ezra Pound as Lowell's predecessor could not appeal to Nabokov, who refused to see past Pound's fascism.
47 Nabokov, "Response to Robert Lowell," 91.
48 Nabokov meant to challenge Lowell in his "Translator's Note" to his English version of Okudzhava's "Sentimental'nyi romans" (2 February 1966). In a letter to Gleb Struve dated 9 March 1969, he urged his old émigré ally and editor of Mandel'shtam's collected poems (1967) to take Lowell and Carlisle to task for their "revolting 'transfigurations' … of our … poor poets," while promising to make "a big noise" in good time (see Nabokov, "Pis'ma V.V. Nabokova k G.P. Struve," 37).
49 *SO*, 282.
50 See TAT, 161.
51 In "Reply to My Critics" Nabokov mentioned a reviewer who suggested that "a talented poet like Robert Lowell" should produce a version of *Eugene Onegin* "that really sings and soars," a vision Nabokov could only qualify as "infernal" (*SO*, 243).
52 Steiner, "To Traduce or Transfigure," 54. Nabokov was not alone in feeling compelled to sound the alarm on Steiner's elevation of Lowell to the status of a "great" poetic translator and Lowell's "readings" of Osip Mandel'shtam to the level of "criticism in the highest sense" (ibid., 52). In his response to Steiner's essay, Avrahm Yarmolinsky pointed out Lowell's "errors, sometimes real howlers" (see Yarmolinsky, "To Traduce or Transfigure," 90–1).

53 *SO*, 283.
54 See "A Lowell Sonnet" (*Time* 93/23, 6 June 1969, 120); subsequently included in Lowell, *Notebook 1967–68* as the penultimate poem in the cycle "Harriet, 1–4" (22).
55 *SO*, 355.
56 Wachtel and Cravens, "Nadezhda Iakovlevna Mandel'shtam," 529 (italics in the original).
57 See Utgof, "'Audiatur et altera pars.'"
58 *SO*, 293.
59 Upon seeing Nabokov's submission to the *New York Review of Books*, Nadezhda Mandel'shtam characterized his censure of Lowell's translation as "barking unworthy of a man of letters" and asked Robert Silvers to "tell Nabokov that I wish Nabokov to be kinder. Kindness is the best quality of men" (see Wachtel and Cravens, "Nadezhda Iakovlevna Mandel'shtam," 530).
60 *EO*, 1:xiii.
61 Burgess, "Pushkin and Kinbote," 74, 78.
62 *EO*, 1:xiii.
63 See *VV*, 366–80.
64 Ibid., 377.
65 Kiril Taranovsky put this poem at the centre of his study of the semantic auras associated with particular metres within given poetic tradition "O vzamootnoshenii stikhotvornogo ritma i tematiki" (see his *O poezii i poetike*, 372–403).
66 See *Pesni russkikh poetov*, 1:629.
67 See *VV*, 369.
68 *SO*, 133–4.
69 Arndt, "Goading the Pony," 16.
70 Raguet-Bouvart, "Les Masques du traducteur chez Vladimir Nabokov," 116.
71 See Boyd, *Vladimir Nabokov: The American Years*, 657.

Conclusion

1 Steiner, "To Traduce or Transfigure," 54.
2 See Bakhtin, *Toward a Philosophy of the Act*, 14; also *SS*, 18
3 Nabokov, "The Servile Path," 109. The lines Nabokov's translated came from Chénier's "Épitre sous ses ouvrages" ("Ami, chez nos Français ma Muse voudrait plaire"; see Chénier, *Œuvres complètes*, 159, 160).

Bibliography

By Vladimir Nabokov
(see Abbreviations for principal works)

"The Art of Translation." Letter to the editor. *New Republic* 105, no. 12 (1941): 375.

"Art of Translation." ("I thought I might say a few words about this pathetic business of translating"). Text of a public talk, after 1941 (VNA).

"The Art of Translation" ("To begin – I want to say a few words about the art of translation"). Text of a public talk, after 1941 (VNA).

"Boris Poplavskii 'Flagi.' Izd. 'Chisla'" [Review of Boris Poplavskii's *Flagi*]. *Rul'* 3128 (11 March 1931): 5.

"Cabbage Soup and Caviar." Rev. of *A Treasury of Russian Life and Humor,* ed. J. Cournos, and *A Treasury of Russian Literature,* ed. by B.G. Guerney. *The New Republic* 105, no. 12 (1944): 92–3.

"Dar. Chast II." Edited by Andrei Babikov. *Zvezda* 4 (2015): 157–75.

"Four Poems by Lermontov. "Translated from the Russian by Vladimir Nabokov. *Russian Review* 5, no. 2 (1946): 50–1.

"Four Poems by Tyutchev." Translated from the Russian by Vladimir Nabokov. *Russian Review* 4, no. 1 (1944): 45–6.

"From Pushkin's 'Eugene Onegin.'" *Russian Review* 4, no. 2 (1945): 38–9.

Grozd'. Berlin: Gamaiun, 1923. [December 1922; under pen name "V. Sirin"].

Invitation to a Beheading. New York, Vintage, 1989.

Mozart and Salieri. *New Republic* 104, no. 16 (1941): 559–65.

"Nabokov's Reply." *Encounter* 26, no. 2 (1966): 80–9 (see also *SO*, 241–67).

Nikolai Gogol. London: Editions Poetry, 1947.

"A Note on Vladislav Hodassevich." In *New Directions in Prose and Poetry, 1941,* 596, 597–600. Norfolk: New Directions, 1941.

"O Pushkine." "O Bloke." Edited by Stanislav Shvabrin. *Novyi zhurnal* 277 (2014): 189–217.

"On Adaptation." *New York Review of Books* 13, no. 10 (1969): 50–1.

["On Democracy."] *Wellesley Magazine*, April 1942, 212. Published as part of "What Faith Means to a Resisting People: Panel Arranged by the Emergency Service Committee." Dorothy Sells, Chairman, presiding," pp. 211–14.

"On Translating Pushkin: Pounding the Clavichord." With postscript to Walter Arndt's "Goading the Pony." *New York Review of Books* 11, no. 5 (1964): 14–16.

Perepiska s Mikhailom Karpovichem 1933–1959. Edited and annotated by A.A. Babikov. Moscow: Litfakt, 2018.

"Pis'ma V.V. Nabokova k G.P. Struve. 1925–1931." Annotated by E.B. Belodubrovskii and A.A. Dolinin. *Zvezda* 11 (2003): 115–50.

"Response to Robert Lowell." *Encounter* 26, no. 5 (1966): 91–2.

Selected Poems. Edited by Thomas Karshan. New York: Alfred A. Knopf, 2012.

Sobranie sochinennii amerkanskogo perioda. Edited by S.B. Il'in and A.K. Kononov. 5 vols. St Petersburg: Symposium, 1997.

"The Servile Path." In *On Translation*, 97–110.

"Three Poems by Fet." Translations. *Russian Review* 3, no. 1 (1943): 31–3.

Three Russian Poets. Norfolk: New Directons, 1944.

"Translation." Letter to the editors. *New York Review of Books* 5, no. 12 (1966): 30.

"Vladimir Nabokov's Translation of The Gettysburg Address." *Nabokovian* 24 (1990): 8–14.

By others

(see Abbreviations for Mikhail Bakhtin's and Brian Boyd's principal publications)

Akhmatova, A.A. *Sochineniia*. 2 vols. Moscow: Khudozhestvennaia literatura, 1986.

Alexandrov, Vladimir E. *Nabokov's Otherworld*. Princeton, NJ: Princeton University Press, 1991.

Anastas'ev, N.A. *Fenomen Nabokova*. Moscow: Sovetskii pisatel', 1992.

Anderson, Kristine. "Nabokov's Rewriting of Dryden's Laws of Translation." In *Translation Perspectives: Selected Papers, 1982–1983*, edited by Marilyn Gaddis Rose, 35–44. New York: SUNY-Binghamton, 1984.

Arndt, Walter. "Goading the Pony." *New York Review of Books* 11, no. 5 (1964): 16.

Baer, Brian James. "Translation Theory and Cold War Politics: Roman Jakobson and Vladimir Nabokov in 1950s America." In *Contexts, Subtexts and Pretexts: Literary Translation in Eastern Europe and Russia*, edited by Brian James Baer, 171–86. Amsterdam: John Benjamins, 2011.

Bailey, James. *Three Russian Folksong Meters*. Bloomington, IN: Slavica, 1993.

Bakhtin, Mikhail. *The Dialogic Imagination*. Edited by Michael Holquist. Translated by Michael Holquist and Caryl Emerson. Austin, TX: University of Texas Press, 1981.

– *Toward a Philosophy of the Act*. Translation and notes by Vadim Liapunov. Edited by Michael Holquist and Vadim Liapunov. Austin, TX: University of Texas Press, 1993.

Barabtarlo, Gennadi. *Phantom of Fact: A Guide to Nabokov's "Pnin."* Ann Arbor, MI: Ardis, 1989.

Barnstone, Willis. *The Poetics of Translation*. New Haven, CT: Yale University Press, 1993.

B[artenev], P[ëtr]. "V.I. Dal'." *Russkii arkhiv* 10 (1872): 2026.

Baudelaire, Charles. *Œuvres complètes*. Edited by Claude Pichois. 2 vols. Paris: Gallimard, 1975–6.

Bayley, John. "Nabokov's Pushkin." *Observer Weekend Review*, 29 November 1964, 26.

Beaujour, Elizabeth Klosty. *Alien Tongues: Bilingual Russian Writers of the "First" Emigration*. Ithaca, NY: Cornell University Press, 1989.

– "Bilingualism." In *Garland Companion to Vladimir Nabokov*, 37–43.

– "*Nikolka Persik*." In *Garland Companion to Vladimir Nabokov*, 556–61.

– "Translation and Self-Translation." In *Garland Companion to Vladimir Nabokov*, 714–24.

Belleau, Rémi. *Œuvres poétiques*. 2 vols. Paris: Alphonse Lemerre, 1878.

Bellos, David. *Is That a Fish in Your Ear? Translation and the Meaning of Everything*. New York: Faber and Faber, 2011.

Berëzkina, S.V. "Stikhotvorenie Pushkina 'Anchar.'" *Russkaia literatura* 4 (1997): 67–80.

Bethea, David M. *Khodasevich: His Life and Art*. Princeton, NJ: Princeton University Press, 1983.

– "Nabokov and Blok." In *Garland Companion to Vladimir Nabokov*, 347–82.

Blackstone, Bernard. *Byron: A Survey*. London: Longman, 1975.

Blackwell, Stephen H. "Dostoevskian Problems in Nabokov's Poetics." In *From Petersburg to Bloomington: Essays in Honor of Nina Perlina*, edited by John Bartle, Michael C. Finke, and Vadim Liapunov, 137–54. Bloomington, IN: Slavica, 2012.

Blair, Dorothy S. "Jules Supervielle's Use of Imagery." *Modern Language Review* 55, no. 4 (1960): 580–3.

Blok, A.A. *Nochnye chasy: Chetvërtyi sbornik stikhov (1908–1910)*. Moscow: Knigoizdatel'stvo "Musaget," 1911.

– *Polnoe sobranie sochinenii i pisem*. 20 vols. Moscow: Nauka, 1997.
– *Sobranie sochinenii*. 8 vols. Moscow: GIKhL, 1962.
Booth, Stephen. *Shakespeare's Sonnets*. New Haven, CT: Yale University Press, 1977.
Booth, Wayne C. *The Rhetoric of Fiction*. Chicago: University of Chicago Press, 1961.
Bouilhet, Louis. *Festons et astrageles. Melænis. Dernières chansons*. Paris: Alphonse Lemerre, 1880.
Boyd, Brian. *Nabokov's "Ada": The Place of Consciousness*. Ann Arbor, MI: Ardis, 1985. 2nd ed. Christchurch: Cybereditions, 2001.
– "Nabokov's Russian Poems: A Chronology." *Nabokovian* (Fall 1988): 13–28.
– *Stalking Nabokov: Selected Essays*. New York: Columbia University Press, 2011.
– *Vladimir Nabokov: The American Years*. Princeton, NJ: Princeton University Press, 1991.
– *Vladimir Nabokov: The Russian Years*. Princeton, NJ: Princeton University Press, 1990.
– "Words, Works and Worlds in Joyce and Nabokov, or Intertextuality, Intratextuality, Supratextuality, Infratextuality, Extratextuality and Autotextuality in Modernist and Prepostmodernist Narrative Discourse." In "Nabokov: At the Crossroads of Modernism and Postmodernism." Special issue, *Cycnos* 12, no. 2 (1995). http://revel.unice.fr/cycnos/index.html?id=1443.
Bozovic, Marijeta. *Nabokov's Canon: From "Onegin" to "Ada."* Evanston, IL: Northwestern University Press, 2016.
Briusov, V.Ia. *Izbrannye sochineniia*. 2 vols. Moscow: Khudozhestvennaia literatura, 1955.
Brooke, Rupert. *The Complete Poems*. London: Sidgwick & Jackson, 1977 (1942).
Brower, Reuben A., ed. *On Translation*. Cambridge, MA: Harvard University Press, 1959.
Burgess, Anthony. "Pushkin and Kinbote." *Encounter* 24, no. 5 (1965): 78.
Byron, George Gordon. *The Complete Poetical Works*. Edited by Jerome J. McGann. 6 vols. Oxford: Clarendon Press, 1980–91.
The Cambridge Companion to Vladimir Nabokov. Edited by Julian W. Connolly. Cambridge: Cambridge University Press, 2005.
Carlisle Andreyev, Olga. *Poets on Streetcorners: Portraits of Russian Poets*. New York: Random House, 1968.
Carroll, Lewis. *The Annotated Alice: "Alice's Adventures in Wonderland" and "Through the Looking Glass."* Edited by Martin Gardner. New York: World, 1972.
Chénier, André. *Œuvres complètes*. Edited and annotated by Gérard Walter. Paris: Gallimard, 1958.
Chulkov, G.I. "Tiutchev i Geine." *Iskusstvo* 1 (1923): 356–64.

Chupin, Yannicke, and René Alladaye. *Aux origines de "Laura": Le dernier manuscript de Vladimir Nabokov*. Paris: PUPS, 2011.

Clayton, Douglas J. "The Theory and Practice of Poetic Translation in Pushkin and Nabokov." *Canadian Slavonic Papers* 25, no. 1 (1983): 90–100.

Connolly, Julian W. *"Ania v Strane Chudes."* In *Garland Companion to Vladimir Nabokov*, 3–24.

Courtney, Winifred F. *Young Charles Lamb 1775–1802*. New York and London: New York University Press, 1982.

Couturier, Maurice. *Nabokov, ou La tyrannie de l'auteur*. Paris: Éditions du seuil, 1993.

– *Nabokov's Eros and the Poetics of Desire*. Basingstoke and New York: Palgrave Macmillan, 2014.

Cranmer, Jean R. "Jules Supervielle: Is Le Forçat Innocent?" *French Review* 55, no. 2 (1981): 193–200.

Dal', V.I. *Tolkovyi slovar' zhivago Velikorusskogo iazyka Vladimira Dalia*. 4 vols. St Petersburg and Moscow: Izdanie knigoprodavtsa-tipografa M.O. Vol'fa, 1880.

Davydov, Sergej. *"Despair."* In *Garland Companion to Vladimir Nabokov*, 88–101.

– *"Teksty-matrëshki" Vladimira Nabokova*. St Petersburg: Kirtsideli, 2004.

Demurova, Nina. "Alice Speaks Russian: The Russian Translations of *Alice's Adventures in Wonderland* and *Through the Looking-Glass*." *Harvard Library Bulletin* 5, no. 3 (1994–5): 11–29.

– "Vladimir Nabokov, Translator of Lewis Carroll's *Alice in Wonderland*." In *Nabokov at Cornell*, edited by Gavriel Shapiro, 182–91. Ithaca, NY: Cornell University Press, 2003.

Diment, Galya. *Pniniad: Vladimir Nabokov and Marc Szeftel*. Seattle: University of Washington Press, 1997.

– *"Three Russian Poets."* In *Garland Companion to Vladimir Nabokov*, 709–14.

– "Uncollected Critical Writing." In *Garland Companion to Vladimir Nabokov*, 733–40.

Dolinin, Aleksandr. *"Eugene Onegin."* In *Garland Companion to Vladimir Nabokov*, 117–30.

– *Istinnaia zhizn' pisatelia Sirina: Raboty o Nabokove*. St Petersburg: Akademicheskii proekt, 2004.

– *Kommentarii k romany Vladimira Nabokova "Dar."* Moscow: Novoe izdatel'stvo, 2019.

– *Pushkin i Angliia*. Moscow: Novoe literaturnoe obozrenie, 2007.

Dragunoiu, Dana. *Vladimir Nabokov and the Poetics of Liberalism*. Evanston, IL: Northwestern University Press, 2011.

Dralyuk, Boris. Review of *A Hero of Our Time*, translated by Natasha Randall. *Slavic and East European Journal* 54, no. 3 (2010): 527–9.

Durantaye, Leland de la. *Style Is Matter: The Moral Art of Vladimir Nabokov.* Ithaca, NY: Cornell University Press, 2007.

Emerson, Caryl. Editor's preface to *Problems of Dostoevsky's Poetics*, by Mikhail Bakhtin, xxiv–xliii. Edited and translated by Caryl Emerson. Introduction by Wayne C. Booth. Minneapolis: University of Minnesota Press, 1984.

– *The First Hundred Years of Mikhail Bakhtin*. Princeton, NJ: Princeton University Press, 1997.

– "Perevodimost'." *Slavic and East European Journal* 38, no. 1 (1994): 84–9.

Epstein, Mikhail. "Bakhtin and the Future of the Humanities." In *Critical Theory in Russia and the West*, edited by Alastair Ranfrew and Galin Tihanov, 173–94. London and New York: Routledge, 2010.

Eskin, Michael. "'Literal Translation': The Semiotic Significance of Nabokov's Conception of Poetic Translation." *Interdisciplinary Journal of Germanic Linguistics and Semiotic Analysis* 2, no. 1 (1997): 1–32.

– *Nabokovs Version von Puškins "Evgenij Onegin": Zwischen Version und Fiktion – eine übersetzungs- und fiktionstheoretische Untersuchung*. Munich: Wilhelm Fink, 1994.

Fisher, David James. *Romain Rolland and the Politics of Intellectual Engagement*. New Brunswick, NJ, and London: Transaction, 2004.

Foster, John Burt. *Nabokov's Art of Memory and European Modernism*. Princeton, NJ: Princeton University Press, 1993.

The Garland Companion to Vladimir Nabokov. Edited by Vladimir E. Alexandrov. New York: Garland, 1995.

Gasparov, Mikhail. *A History of European Versification*. Translated by G.S. Smith and Marina Tarlinskaja. Edited by G.S. Smith and Leofranc Holford-Strevens. Oxford: Clarendon Press, 1996.

– *Izbrannye trudy*. 3 vols. Moscow: Iazyki russkoi kul'tury, 1997.

– *Metr i smysl: Ob odnom iz mekhanizmov kul'turnoi pamiati*. Moscow: RGGU, 1999.

– *Sovremennyi russkii stikh: Metrika i ritmika*. Moscow: Nauka, 1974.

Gerschenkron, Alexander. "A Manufactured Monument?" *Modern Philology* 63, no. 4 (1996): 336–47.

Gershenzon, M.O. *Mudrost' Pushkina*. Moscow: Knigoizdatel'stvo pisatelei v Moskve, 1919.

La Geste du Prince Igor': Épopée russe du douzième siècle. Texte établi, traduit et commenté sous la direction d'Henri Grégoire, de Roman Jakobson et de Marc Szeftel, assistés de J.A. Joffe. New York, 1948. Distributed by Columbia University Press.

Gifford, Henry. "Puškin's *Feast in Time of Plague* and Its Original." *American Slavic and East European Review* 8, no. 1 (1949): 37–46.

Goethe, Johann Wolfgang, von. *Sämtliche Werke*. Edited by Karl Richter et al. 21 vols. Munich: Carl Hanser Verlag, 1985–98.

Gofman, M.L. "Posmertnye stikhotvoreniia Pushkina." In *Pushkin i ego sovremenniki: Materialy i issledovaniia*, 33–35 (1922): 392–400. Petersburg, Rossiiskaia Gosudarstvennaia Akademicheskaia Tipografiia, 1922.

Gogol, N.V. *Polnoe sobranie sochinenii*. Edited by N.L. Meshcheriakov et al. 14 vols. Moscow and Leningrad: Izdatel'stvo Akademii Nauk SSSR, 1937–52.

Gordon, Ia.G. *Geine v Rossii*. 3 vols. Dushanbe: Donish, 1973–83.

Grayson, Jane. "The French Connection: Nabokov and Alfred de Musset: Ideas and Practices of Translation." *Slavonic and East European Review* 73, no. 4 (October 1995): 613–58.

– "Vladimir Nabokov 1899–1977." In *Encyclopedia of Literary Translation into English*, edited by Olive Classe, 2:2987–90. London: Fitzroy Dearborn, 2000.

Gumilëv, N.S. *Polnoe sobranie sochinenii*. 10 vols. Moscow: Voskresenie, 1998.

Gustafson, Richard. "The Upas Tree: Pushkin and Erasmus Darwin." *PMLA* 75, no. 1 (1960): 101–9.

Hamilton, Ian. *Robert Lowell: A Biography*. New York: Random House, 1982.

Heine, Heinrich. *Historisch-kritische Gesamtausgabe der Werke*. Edited by Manfred Windfuhr. 16 vols. Hamburg: Hoffmann und Camper Verlag, 1975–97.

Hingley, Ronald. "An Aggressively Private Person." *New York Times Book Review*, 15 January 1967, 1, 14, 16.

Hodgson, Katharine. "Heine's Russian Doppelgänger: Nineteenth-Century Translations of His Poetry." *Modern Language Review* 100 (2005): 1054–72.

Hofstadter, Douglas R. *Le Ton Beau de Marot: In Praise of the Music of Language*. New York: Basic Books, 1997.

Holquist, Michael. *Dialogism: Bakhtin and His World*. London: Routledge, 1990.

"Hommage à Pouchkine 1837–1937." Edited by Zinaïda Schakhovskoy. Special issue, *Les Cahiers du Journal des Poètes* 28, no. 5 (1937).

Ignatov, Il'ia. "Filosofiia bosiachestva [u Rishpena i g. Gor'kogo]." In *Maksim Gor'kii: Pro et Contra*, 315–24. St Petersburg: PKhGI, 1997.

Ivanov, Viacheslav Vs. "Geine v Rossii." In *Poet s beregov Reina: Zhizn' i stradaniia Genrikha Geine*, by Lev Kopelev, 431–66. Moscow: Progress-Pleiada, 2003.

Johnson, D. Barton. "'L'Inconnue de la Seine' and Nabokov's Naiads." *Comparative Literature* 44, no. 3 (1992): 225–48.

– "Nabokov's *Ada* and Pierre Louÿs' *Chansons de Bilitis*: The Tree of Knowledge." Electronically circulated manuscript.

– "Nabokov's Golliwoggs: Lodi Reads English 1899–1909." https://www.libraries.psu.edu/nabokov/dbjgol.htm.

– "Vladimir Nabokov and Captain Mayne Reid." *Cycnos* 10, no. 9 (2008). http://revel.unice.fr/cycnos/index.html?id=1303.
– "Vladimir Nabokov and Rupert Brooke." In *Nabokov and His Fiction: New Perspectives,* edited by Julian W. Connolly, 177–96. Cambridge: Cambridge University Press, 1999.
Joyce, James. *Ulysses.* New York: Vintage, 1990.
Karlinsky, Simon. "Anya in Wonderland: Nabokov's Russified Lewis Carroll." In *Nabokov: Criticism, Reminiscences, Translations, and Tributes,* edited by Alfred Appel Jr and Charles Newman, 310–15. Evanston, IL: Northwestern University Press, 1970.
Karpukhin, Sergey A. "Vladimir Nabokov and the Classical Tradition." PhD diss., University of Wisconsin-Madison, 2015.
– "Vladimir Nabokov and the Russian Hexameter: Classical Imitations in His Early Poetry." *International Journal of the Classical Tradition* 1, no. 25 (2018): 1–23.
Keats, John. *The Poetical Works of John Keats.* World Classics series. London: Oxford University Press, 1948 [1901].
Kemball, Robin. "Nabokov and Rupert Brooke." In *Schweizerische Beiträge zum IX. Internationalen Slavistenkongress in Kiev, September 1983,* edited by Peter Brang, 35–73. New York: Peter Lang, 1983.
Khodasevich, V.F. "Rusalka: Predpolozheniia i fakty (Glava iz knigi 'Poeticheskoe khoziaistvo Pushkina')." *Sovremennye zapiski* 20 (1924): 302–54.
– *Sobranie sochinenii.* Edited by I.P. Andreeva, S.G. Bocharov, et al. 4 vols. Moscow: Soglasie, 1996.
Killham, John. *Tennyson and "The Princess": Reflections of an Age.* University of London: Athlone Press, 1958.
Kipling, Rudyard. *The Complete Verse.* London: Kyle Cathie, 1990.
Krechetov, Sergei. *Zheleznyi persten'.* Berlin: Mednyi vsadnik, [1922].
Kristeva, Julia. "Bakhtine, le mot, le dialogue et le roman." *Critique* 23, no. 239 (1967): 438–65.
The Kristeva Reader. Edited by Toril Moi. Oxford: Basil Blackwell, 1986.
Kumar, Amith P.V., and Milind Malshe. "Translation and Bakhtin's 'Metalinguistics.'" *Perspectives: Studies in Translatology* 12, no. 2 (2005): 115–21.
Lachmann, Renate. *Gedächtnis und Literatur: Intertextualität in der russischen Moderne.* Frankfurt am Main: Suhrkamp, 1990.
Lamb, Charles. *The Complete Works and Letters of Charles Lamb.* New York: Modern Library, 1935.
– *The Letters of Charles Lamb, to Which Are Added Those of His Sister Mary Lamb.* 3 vols. New York: AMS PRESS, 1968.

Landor, Walter Savage. *Imaginary Conversations and Poems: A Selection*. London: J.M. Dent, 1933.
Lane, R.C. "Tiutchev in English Translation: 1873–1974." *Journal of European Studies* 5, no. 1 (1975): 153–70.
Legouis, Émile, and Louis Cazamian. *A History of English Literature*. London: J.M. Dent and Sons, 1933.
Lehmann, John. *Rupert Brooke: His Life and His Legend*. London: Weidenfeld & Nicholson, 1980.
Lermontov, M.Iu. *Polnoe sobranie sochinenii*. 4 vols. Berlin: Slovo, 1921.
Levinton, A.G. *Genrikh Geine: Bibliografiia russkikh perevodov i kriticheskoi literatury na russkom iazyke*. Moscow: Vsesoiuznaia knizhnaia palata, 1958.
Linetskii, V. *"Anti-Bakhtin": Luchshaia kniga o Vladimire Nabokove*. St Petersburg: Tipografiia im. Kotliakova, 1994.
Liuksemburg, Aleksandr. "Nabokov-perevodchik." *Filologicheskii vestnik rostovskogo gosudarstvennogo universiteta* 3 (1999): 5–16.
Lotman, Yu.M. *Besedy o russkoi kul'ture*. St Petersburg: Iskusstvo, 1994.
Louÿs, Pierre. *Les Chansons de Bilitis: Roman lyrique*. Paris: Mercure de France, 1898.
Lowell, Robert. *Imitations*. New York: Farrar, Straus and Giroux, 1961.
– "Nabokov's *Onegin*." *Encounter* 26, no. 5 (1966): 91.
– *Notebook 1967–68: Poems*. New York: Farrar, Straus and Giroux, 1969.
– "Ossip Mandelstamm: Translation of Nine Poems." *New York Review of Books* 5, no. 10 (1965): 17.
Maar, Michael. *The Two Lolitas*. London: Verso, 2005.
Mandel'shtam, Osip. *Sobranie sochinenii*. 2 vols. Moscow: Khudozhestvennaia literatura, 1990.
Marčenko, Tat'jana. *Russkie pisateli i Nobelevskaia premiia (1901–1955)*. Cologne: Böhlau Verlag, 2007.
Markov, Vladimir. Review of *Poets on Street Corners*, by Olga Carlisle. *Slavic Review* 29, no. 1 (1970): 156–60.
Meyer, Priscilla. "Igor, Ossian, and Kinbote: Nabokov's Non-Fiction as Reference Library." *Slavic Review* 47, no. 1 (1988): 68–75.
Mirsky, D.S. *A History of Russian Literature*. Edited by Francis J. Whitfield. New York: Alfred A. Knopf, 1958.
Monnier, André. "Un miroir pouchkinien pour Nabokov." In *Vladimir Nabokov et l'émigration*. Edited by Nora Buhks. *Cahiers de l'émigration russe* 2 (1993): 19–25.
Morris, Paul D. *Vladimir Nabokov: Poetry and the Lyric Voice*. Toronto: University of Toronto Press, 2010.
Musset, Alfred de. *Poésies complètes*. Edited by Maurice Allem. Paris: Gallimard, 1957.

Nabokov, Dmitri. "On Revisiting Father's Room." In *Vladimir Nabokov, His Life, His Work, His World: A Tribute*, 126–36.

Nabokov, Nicolas. *The Return of Pushkin: An Elegy in Three Movements for High Voice and Symphony Orchestra*. Poem by A. Pushkin. Translated by Vladimir Nabokov. Bonn: Edition M.P. Belaieff, 1966.

Nabokov Upside Down. Edited by Brian Boyd and Marijeta Bozovic. Evanston, IL: Northwestern University Press, 2017.

Nabokov's "Invitation to a Beheading": A Critical Companion. Edited by Julian W. Connolly. Evanston, IL: Northwestern University Press, 1997.

"'Nabokovy ne byli otrezany ot Rossii ...': Beseda Stanislava Shvabrina s Ellendeiei Proffer." *Zvezda* 4 (2005): 143–50.

Naiman, Eric. *Nabokov, Perversely*. Ithaca, NY, and London: Cornell University Press, 2010.

– Review of *Delicate Markers: Subtexts in Vladimir Nabokov's "Invitation to a Beheading,"* by Gavriel Shapiro. *Slavic and East European Journal* 45, no. 2 (2001): 359–60.

New Directions in Prose and Poetry, 1941. Edited by James Laughlin. Norfolk: New Directions, 1941.

The New Grove Dictionary of Music and Musicians. Edited by Stanley Sadie et al. 29 vols. Oxford: Oxford University Press, 2001.

Novye poety Frantsii v perevodakh Iv. Tkhorzhevskago. Paris: "La Source," 1930.

Ofrosimov, Iu. "Nikolka-Persik." Review of *Nikolka Persik*, by Vl. Sirin. *Rul'* 602 (16 November 1922): 9.

Okudzhava, B.Sh. *Bud' zdorov, shkoliar: Stikhi*. Edited by Natalia Tarasova. Frankfurt-am-Main: Posev, 1964.

– *Stikhotvoreniia*. St Petersburg: Akademicheskii proekt, 2001.

On Translation. Edited by Reuben A. Brower. Cambridge, MA: Harvard University Press, 1959.

O'Sullivan, Seamus. *Poems*. Dublin: Maunsel, 1912.

– *The Twilight People*. Dublin: Whaley, 1905.

The Oxford Book of English Verse, 1250–1900. Edited by Arthur Quiller-Couch. Oxford: Clarendon Press, 1918.

Parker, Fan. *Lewis Carroll in Russia: Translations of* Alice in Wonderland, *1879–1989*. New York: Russian House, 1994.

Parker, Stephen Jan. "Nabokov in the Margins: The Montreux Books." *Journal of Modern Literature* 14, no. 1 (1987): 5–16.

– "Nabokov's Montreux Books: Part II." In "Nabokov: Autobiography, Biography and Fiction." Special issue, *Cycnos* 10, no. 1 (1993): 107–11. http://revel.unice.fr/cycnos/index.html?id=1307.

Patrick, George Z. *Intermediate Russian Reader*. New York: Pittman, 1945.

Pesni russkikh poetov. Edited by V.E. Gusev. 2 vols. Leningrad: Sovetskii pisatel', 1988.

Petrarca, Francesco. *The Canzoniere (Rerum Vulgarium Fragmenta)*. Translated by Frederic J. Jones. 2 vols. Leicester: Troubador, 2000.

Picon, Francisco Javier. "Bakhtin and Nabokov: The Dialogue That Never Was." PhD diss., Columbia University, 2016.

Pil'shchikov, Igor. "'Ante hoc, ergo propter hoc': Eshcho raz o kriteriiakh intertekstual'nosti, ili 'Sluchainye' i 'nesluchainye' sblizheniia (na materiale poezii pushkinskoi epokhi)." In *Sluchainost' i nepredkazuemost' v istorii kul'tury: Materialy vtorykh lotmanovskikh dnei v tallinnskom universitete (4–6 iunia 2010 g.)*, 188–207. Tallinn: Izdatel'stvo TLU, 2013.

Poets on Street Corners: Portraits of Fifteen Russian Poets by Olga Carlisle. New York: Random House, 1968.

Pushkin, A.S. [Complete Works.] Edited by S.A. Vengerov. 6 vols. Biblioteka velikikh pisatelei. St Petersburg: Brockhaus-Efron, 1907–15.

– *Eugene Onegin: A Novel in Verse*. Translated by Babette Deutsch. Edited, with a special introduction by Avrahm Yarmolinsky. Illustrated with lithographs by Fritz Eichenberg. Mineola, NY: Dover Publications, 1998 [1943].

– *Eugene Onegin: A Novel in Verse*. A novel versification by Douglas Hofstadter. New York: Basic Books, 1999.

– *Eugene Onegin: A Novel in Verse by Alexander Pushkin*. Translated from the Russian by Vladimir Nabokov. Introduction by Brian Boyd. The Russian in Cyrillic and transliteration prepared by Stanislav Shvabrin. San Francisco: Arion Press, 2018.

– *Pis'ma*. Edited by B.L. Modzalevskii. 2 vols. Moscow: Gosizdat, 1928.

Quitard, Pierre-Marie. *Dictionnaire étymologique, historique and anecdotique des proverbes*. Paris: P. Bertrand, 1842.

Raguet-Bouvart, Chrstine. "Les Masques du traducteur chez Vladmir Nabokov." *Annales du CRAA* 22 (1997): 115–27.

Rampton, David. "In Search of the Real Poet: Nabokov's Pushkin Essay Revisited." In *Nabokov Upside Down*, 185–96.

Régnier, Henri de. *Vestigia Flammæ*. Paris: Mercure de France, 1921.

Remnick, David. "The Translation Wars." *New Yorker* 81, no. 35 (2005): 98–109.

Richepin, Jean. *Les Blasphèmes*. Paris: Maurice Dreyfous, 1884.

Ricks, Christopher. *Tennyson*. London: Macmillan, 1989.

Rimbaud, Arthur. "Le Bateau ivre." *Le Manuscrit autographe* 12 (November–December 1927): 75–8.

– *L'œuvre intégrale manuscrite*. Edited by Claude Jeancolas. 3 vols. Paris: Textuel, 1996.

– *Œuvres complètes*. Edited by Antoine Adam. Paris: Gallimard, 1972.
– *Rimbaud Complete*. Translated by Wyatt Mason. New York: Modern Library, 2003.
– *Rimbaud: Complete Works, Selected Letters*. Translated by Wallace Fowlie. Chicago: University of Chicago Press, 2005.
Robb, Graham. *Rimbaud*. London: Picador, 2000.
Robinson, Douglas. *The Translator's Turn*. Baltimore: Johns Hopkins University Press, 1990.
– *What Is Translation? Centrifugal Theories, Critical Interventions*. Kent: Kent State University Press, 1997.
Rolland, Romain. *Colas Breugnon*. Paris: P. Ollendorff, 1919.
– *Quinze ans de combat (1919–1934)*. Paris: Éditions Rieder, 1935.
Ronsard, Pierre. *Œuvres complètes*. Edited by Jean Céard, Daniel Ménager, and Michel Simonin. 2 vols. Paris: Gallimard, 1993–4.
Rorty, Richard. *Contigency, Irony, and Solidarity*. Cambridge: Cambridge University Press, 1989.
Rosenbaum, Ron. "Dmitri's Choice." *Slate*, 16 January 2008. http://www.slate.com/articles/life/the_spectator/2008/01/dmitris_choice.html.
Rosengrant, Roy Judson. "Nabokov, *Onegin*, and the Theory of Translation." *Slavic and East European Journal* 38, no. 1 (1994): 13–27.
Rowe, W.W. *Nabokov's Spectral Dimension*. Ann Arbor, MI: Ardis, 1981.
Rutledge, David S. *Nabokov's Permanent Mystery: The Expression of Metaphysics in His Work*. Jefferson, NC: McFarland, 2011.
Sams, Eric. *The Songs of Robert Schumann*. London: Eulenburg Books, 1975 (1969).
Schakhovskoy, Zinaïda. "V.I. Pol' i 'angel'skie stikhi' Vl. Nabokova." In *Russkii Al'manakh*. Edited by Zinaida Shakhovskaia, Rene Gerra, and Evgenii Ternovskii, 231–5. Paris, 1981.
Scherr, Barry P. "Nabokov as Poet." In Connolly, *The Cambridge Companion to Vladimir Nabokov*, 103–18.
– "Poetry." In *Garland Companion to Vladimir Nabokov*, 608–25.
– *Russian Poetry: Meter, Rhythm, and Rhyme*. Berkeley: University of California Press, 1986.
– "Settling Accounts with Russia's Silver Age: Nabokov Writes Akhmatova." *Russian Review* 65 (2006): 35–52.
– "Yearning for a Last Love: Tjutčev's 'Poslednjaja ljubov' in English." *Russian Literature* 57, nos. 1–2 (2005): 183–204.
Schuman, Samuel. "Nabokov and Shakespeare: The Russian Works." In *Garland Companion to Vladimir Nabokov*, 512–17.
– *Nabokov's Shakespeare*. New York: Bloomsbury, 2014.

Schumann, Robert. *Dichterliebe: An Authoritative Score; Historical Background; Essays in Analysis; Views and Comments.* Edited by Arthur Komar. New York: W.W. Norton, 1971.

Scott, Clive. *Reading the Rhythm: The Poetics of French Free Verse 1910–1930.* Oxford: Clarendon Press, 1993.

– *Translating Baudelaire.* Exeter: University of Exeter Press, 2000.

Self, Will. "Dirty Old Man." Review of *The Annotated Alice: The Definitive Edition,* by Lewis Carroll, with an introduction by Martin Gardner. *New Statesman* 4518 (2000): 88–9.

Shakespeare, William. *Hamlet.* Edited by G.R. Hibbard. Oxford: Oxford University Press, 1987.

– *Shakespeare's Sonnets.* Edited by Stephen Booth. New Haven, CT: Yale University Press, 1977.

– *The Tragedy of Hamlet, Prince of Denmark.* Edited by Barbara A. Mowat and Paul Werstine. New Folger Library Shakespeare. New York: Washington Square Press, 1992.

Shaw, Thomas J. Review of *Eugene Onegin,* by Alexander Pushkin, translated by Vladimir Nabokov. *Slavic and East European Journal* 21, no. 2 (1977): 269–70.

– *A Hero of Our Time,* by Mihail Lermontov, Vladimir Nabokov, and Dmitri Nabokov; *A Hero of Our Own Times,* by Mikhail Yurevich Lermontov, Cedar Paul, and Eden Paul. *Slavic and East European Journal* 3, no. 2 (1959): 180–1.

– "Translations of 'Onegin.'" *Slavic and East European Journal* 24, no. 2 (1965): 111–27.

Shor, V.E. "'*Kola Briun'on*' na russkom iazyke." In *Masterstvo perevoda,* 219–66. Moscow: Sovetskii pisatel', 1970.

Shrayer, Maxim D. *Nabokov: Temy i variatsii.* St Petersburg: Akademicheskii proekt, 2000.

Shvabrin, Stanislav. "'And If My Private Universe Scans Right …': Semantics of Meter in Vladimir Nabokov's Poetry – and Worldview." In *Nabokov Upside Down,* 169–84.

– "'The Dreamy Stutter of Blok's Rhythms': On the Name and Nature of Nabokov's Notion of 'Pausative Verse.'" *Russian Literature* 66, no. 1 (2009): 99–130.

– "Nabokov and Heine." *Russian Literature* 74, no. 3–4 (2013): 363–461.

– "'Pechat' neprekhodiashchego': Nabokov-Sirin o Bloke, Pushkine – i o sebe." *Novyi zhurnal* 277 (2014): 189–217.

– "'…A Sob That Alters the Entire History of Russian Letters …': Cincinnatus's Plight, Tiutchev's 'Last Love,' and Nabokov's Metaphysics of Poetic Form." *Slavic and East European Journal* 58, no. 3 (2014): 437–64.

– "Vladimir Nabokov as Translator: The Multilingual Works of the Russian Period." PhD diss., UCLA, 2007.

– "Vladimir Nabokov's 'La Belle Dame Sans Merci': A Study in the Ethics and Effects of Literary Adaptation." *Comparative Literature* 65, no. 1 (2013): 101–22.

Sisson, Jonathan B. "Nabokov and Some Turn-of-the-Century English Writers." In *Garland Companion to Vladimir Nabokov*, 528–36.

Sistematicheskii katalog biblioteki Vladimira Dmitrievicha Nabokova. St Petersburg: Tovarishchestvo khudozhestvennoi pechati, 1904, 1911.

The Sixteenth-Century Chanson: Previously Unpublished Full Scores of Chansons from the Ateliers of LeRoy and Ballard, Moderne, and Waelrant and Laet. Selected and edited by Jane A. Bernstein. 30 vols. New York: Garland, 1987–95.

Smith, Alexandra. "Vladimir Nabokov as Translator of Russian Poetry." *Wiener Slawistischer Almanach* 51 (2003): 133–66.

Smith, Gerald S. "Nabokov and the Russian Verse Form." *Russian Literature Triquarterly* 24 (1991): 271–305.

– "*Notes on Prosody*." In *Garland Companion to Vladimir Nabokov*, 561–66.

Sobranie zapreshchënnykh stikhotvorenii A.S. Pushkina. Berlin: Izdanie I.P. Ladyzhnikova, [ca. 1920].

Solov'ëv, V.S. *Literaturnaia kritika*. Moscow: Sovremennik, 1990.

Starkie, Enid. *Arthur Rimbaud*. New York: New Directions, 1961.

Steiner, George. "To Traduce or Transfigure: On Modern Verse Translation." *Encounter* 27, no. 2 (1966): 48–54.

[Struve, Gleb]. "Vladimir Nabokoff Sirine, l'amoureux de la vie." *Le Mois* 6 (1931): 140–2.

Supervielle, Jules. *L'Enfant de la haute mer*. Paris: Gallimard, 1931.

– *Le Voleur d'enfants*. Paris: Gallimard, 1926.

– *Œuvres poétiques complètes*. Edited by Michel Collot et al. Paris: Gallimard, 1996.

Tammi, Pekka. *Problems of Nabokov's Poetics: A Narratological Analysis.* Helsinki: Suomalainen Tiedeakatemia, 1985.

Taranovskii, K.F. *O poezii i poetike*. Moscow: Iazyki russkoi kul'tury, 2000.

Tennyson, Alfred. *Poetry*. Edited by Robert W. Hill Jr. New York: W.W. Norton, 1999.

Todd, William Mills, III. "*A Hero of Our Time*." In *Garland Companion to Vladimir Nabokov*, 178–83.

Todorov, Tsvetan. *Mikhail Bakhtin: The Dialogical Principle*. Minneapolis: University of Minnesota Press, 1984.

Tomlinson, Charles. *The Sonnet: Its Origin, Structure, and Place in Poetry.* London, John Murray, 1874.
The Translation Studies Reader. Edited by Lawrence Venuti. New York and London: Routledge, 2004.
Trubikhina, Julia. "The Translator's Doubts: Vladimir Nabokov and the Ambiguity of Translation." PhD diss., New York University, 2005.
Tynianov, Iu.N. "Blok i Geine." In *Ob Aleksandre Bloke,* 237–64. Petersburg: Kartonnyi domik, 1921.
Utgof, G.M. "'Audiatur et altera pars': K probleme 'Nabokov i Louell.'" In *Kul'tura russkoi diaspory: Emigratsiia i mify,* edited by A. Danilevskii and S. Dotsenko, 219–38. Tallinn: Izdatel'stvo Tallinnskogo universiteta, 2012.
Venuti, Lawrence. *Rethinking Translation: Discourse, Subjectivity, Ideology.* London: Routledge, 1992.
– *The Translator's Invisibility.* London: Routledge, 1995.
Verhaeren, Émile. *Œuvres.* 9 vols. Geneva: Slatkine Reprints, 1977.
– *Poèmes.* Paris: Mercure de France, 1896.
– *Poèmes.* Paris: Mercure de France, 1917.
Verlaine, Paul. *Les Poètes maudits: Tristan Corbière, Arthur Rimbaud, Stéphane Mallarmé.* Paris: Léon Vanier, 1884.
– *Œuvres poétiques complètes.* Edited by Y.-G. Le Dantec and Jacques Borel. Paris: Gallimard, 1962.
Vitkovskii, Evgenii. *Protiv entropii.* 29 August 2007.
http://www.lib.ru/NEWPROZA/WITKOWSKIJ/s_entropia.txt.
Vladimir Nabokov, His Life, His Work, His World: A Tribute. Edited by Peter Quennell. London: Weidenfield and Nicolson, 1979.
Voloshin, Maksimilian. *Liki tvorchestva.* Leningrad: Nauka, 1988.
Vroon, Ronald. "Akusticheskaia pamiat' kak sverkhlichnostnyi tvorcheskii impul's (na materiale Nabokova, Brodskogo i dr.)." In *Pamiat' literaturnogo tvorchestva,* 448–56. Moscow: IMLI RAN, 2014.
Wachtel, Michael. *A Commentary to Pushkin's Lyric Poetry.* Madison: University of Wisconsin Press, 2011.
Wachtel, Michael, and Craig Cravens. "Nadezhda Iakovlevna Mandel'shtam: Letters to and about Robert Lowell." *Russian Review* 61 (2002): 517–30.
Walsh, Stephen. *The Lieder of Schumann.* London: Cassell, 1971.
Warnke, Frank J., and Alex Preminger. "Alexandrine." In *Princeton Encyclopedia of Poetry and Poetics,* edited by Alex Preminger et al., 11–12. Princeton, NJ: Princeton University Press, 1965.
Weaver, Warren. *Alice in Many Tongues: The Translations of "Alice in Wonderland."* Madison: University of Wisconsin Press, 1964.

Wedeck, Harry E. "The Last of the French Bohemian Poets." *Modern Language Journal* 31, no. 8 (1947): 482–5.

Weinberg, Bernard. "*Le Bateau ivre*, or The Limits of Symbolism." *PMLA* 72, no. 1 (1957): 165–93.

Wilson, Edmund. "Nabokov, Pushkin, Wilson." *Encounter* 26, no. 4 (1966): 92.

– "The Strange Case of Pushkin and Nabokov." *New York Review of Books* 4, no. 12 (1965): 3–6.

– "This Dramatic Poem by Pushkin…" [Preamble to Nabokov's translation of *Mozart and Salieri*]. *New Republic* 104, no. 16/1377 (21 April 1941): 559.

Witt, Susanna. "Between the Lines: Totalitarianism and Translation in the USSR." In *Contexts, Subtexts and Pretexts: Literary Translation in Eastern Europe and Russia*, edited by Brian James Baer, 151–68. Amsterdam: John Benjamins, 2011.

Wood, Michael. *The Magician's Doubts: Nabokov and the Risks of Fiction*. London: Chatto & Windus, 1994.

Wright, Alfred, Jr. "Verlaine's 'Art poétique' Re-Examined." *PMLA* 74, no. 3 (1959): 268–75.

Yarmolinsky, Avrahm. *Pushkin in English*. New York: New York Public Library, 1937.

– "To Traduce or Transfigure" [Response to George Steiner]. *Encounter* 27, no. 5 (1966): 90–1.

Yeats, William Butler. *The Collected Letters of W.B. Yeats*. Edited by John Kelly et al. 4 vols. Oxford: Clarendon Press, 1986–2005.

– *The Collected Works of W.B. Yeats*. Edited by Richard J. Finneran and George Mills Harper et al. 14 vols. New York: Macmillan, 1989–2008.

– *Poems of W.B. Yeats: A New Selection*. Edited by A. Norman Jeffares. New York: Macmillan, 1984.

Zholkovskii, A.K. *Izbrannye stat'i o russkoi poezii: Invarianty, struktury, strategii, interteksty*. Moscow: Rossiiskii gosudarstvennyi gumanitarnyi universitet, 2005.

Zweig, Stefan. *Romain Rolland: Der Mann und das Werk*. Frankfurt am Main: Rütten & Loening, 1923.

Index

www.ingramcontent.com/pod-product-compliance
Lightning Source LLC
La Vergne TN
LVHW090146080826
844660LV00013B/687/J

* 9 7 8 1 4 8 7 5 0 2 9 9 7 *